DEATH,
DISABILITY,
AND THE
SUPERHERO

D0887928

DEATH, DISABILITY, AND THE SUPERHERO

THE SILVER AGE AND BEYOND

JOSÉ ALANIZ

UNIVERSITY PRESS OF MISSISSIPPI
JACKSON

www.upress.state.ms.us

Designed by Peter D. Halverson

The University Press of Mississippi is a member of the Association of American
University Presses.

Copyright © 2014 by University Press of Mississippi
Manufactured in the United States of America

First printing 2014

∞

Library of Congress Cataloging-in-Publication Data

Alaniz, José.
  Death, Disability, and the Superhero : the Silver Age and Beyond / José Alaniz.
    pages cm
  Includes bibliographical references and index.
  ISBN 978-1-62846-117-6 (cloth : alk. paper) — ISBN 978-1-62846-118-3
  (ebook) 1. Comic books, strips, etc.—History and criticism. 2. Death in literature.
  3. People with disabilities in literature. 4. Body image in literature. 5. Graphic
  novels—History and criticism. I. Title.
    PN6710.A53 2014
    741.5'9—dc23   2014014241

British Library Cataloging-in-Publication Data available

To the memory of

Maximino Alaniz (1940–2012) and

Concepción Luévano Alaniz (1917–2013)

and to

Raquel Alaniz,

who bought me my first thousand comics

And superheroes come to feast

And taste the flesh

Not yet deceased . . .

—RICHARD O'BRIEN, 1973

CONTENTS

ACKNOWLEDGMENTS

Firstly, I would like to acknowledge the creators of the works examined in these pages; my interviewees for their time and insights; the editorship and staff at the University Press of Mississippi, especially Walter Biggins, Craig Gill, and Katie Keene; and the Smithsonian Institution (in particular the American Art Museum) for its support in summer 2012. Portions and obsolete chapter versions from this study have appeared in *The International Journal of Comic Art*, *Comics Forum*, and *The Ages of Superman: Essays on the Man of Steel in Changing Times*.

You could say I began mulling this topic, unconsciously, on the day I read my very first comics, *Marvel-Two-In-One*, vol. 1, #5 (Sept. 1974) and *The Defenders*, vol. 1, #15 (Sept. 1974), both drawn by Sal Buscema. The prominence of physically different bodies in these colorful stories—in stark contrast with their (to my unobservant eye) relative paucity as I grew up in the Rio Grande Valley of South Texas—planted a seed that would not bear fruit until much later, when as a graduate student, I started acquiring the interpretive and conceptual toolkit to address the paradox of fabulously powerful beings who are also "freaks." Along the way, many people have helped me—often without knowing it—with their insights, advice, emotional support, nerdy enthusiasm, and resistance to my readings. They all have my eternal gratitude. Of course, anything good in this study is owing to their influence; all the bad stems exclusively from me.

The list includes, chronologically, those with whom I first discussed, debated, and argued over comics all those years ago: Pedro Alaniz, Marcos Garza, Michael Reyna, Ramon Cantú, Luke Garza, Julian Castañeda, Sam Romero, Alan Vassberg, Luther Davidson, and Jerry Lyles. Later on came Armando Hinojosa, Frances Till, and Betty Harwell. In my "adult" phase, at UC Berkeley, Susan Schweik proved a model of what a Disability Studies scholar should be. And, though I would not pen a word of this book until after leaving that fine institution, the support and professional example of Eric Naiman, Francine Masiello, Mark Sandberg, Irina Paperno, and especially Linda Williams all proved crucial to making it what it is.

Of course, on any project devoted to comics, I cannot escape the gravitational pull of the usual suspects: Nicole Freim, Jason Tondro, Amy Kiste Nyberg, and the participants of the Comics and Comic Art area of the Popular Culture Association conference (where I first presented on this topic); as well as Gene Kannenberg, Craig Fischer, Bart Beaty, Ana Merino, Corey

Creekmur, Jeet Heer, Jay Dolmage, Joseph Darowski, Leonard Rifas, Jennifer Stuller, Roger Sabin, Paul Gravett, Richard Reynolds, David Lasky, Peter Coogan, Stanford Carpenter, Héctor Fernández-L'Hoeste, Ben Saunders, and other stalwarts at the International Comic Arts Forum, Comic Arts Conference and related venues over the years. And let me tell you, few things in life satisfy more than discussing: the finer points of Professor X's bald pate while strolling the streets of Madrid with Charles Hatfield; the jaunty flourishes of the cinematic Bane over pancakes in Hyattsville, Maryland, with Marc Singer; and whether Ben Grimm is a happy person with Scott Bukatman in New York City. Here I should also single out Charles—whose skull, I swear, is filled with Kirby Krackle—for his feedback on chapter 4, no less than for his tireless encouragement and friendship. Joseph "Rusty" Witek also deserves special mention for his detailed notes and warm support. I am lucky to live among such a fantastic community of scholars.

But once again, John Lent deserves the highest praise from me and many others involved in Comics Studies. More than anyone I've personally known, he taught me that this medium I love really matters—and we should tailor our comments thereto.

My colleagues at the University of Washington Department of Slavic Languages and Literature and the Department of Comparative Literature also have my thanks, along with those pursuing Disability Studies on our campus, especially Sara Goering, Dennis Lang, Joanne Woiak, and Sherrie Brown. And I never felt more validation for this project than from Diane Wiener, Rachael Zubal-Ruggieri, and all the staff of Syracuse University's wonderful "Fantastic! Heroic! Disabled?: Cripping the Comic-Con" event, for whose inaugural iteration I delivered the keynote address in April 2013.

Two very important people in my life, though, once more rise to the top of the list for their friendship and love, now counted in decades: Seth Graham (¡y familia!) and Tiziana Bertolini. Finally, my eternal thanks to Kristin for her love.

DEATH, DISABILITY, AND THE SUPERHERO

1

INTRODUCTION: "UNMASKED AT LAST!"
Death, Disability, and the Super-Body

As it oscillates between being a thing and my being, as it undergoes and yet disengages itself from reification, my body responds with a language that is as commonplace as it is startling. For the body is not only this organic mosaic of biological entities. It is also a cornucopia of highly charged symbols—fluids, scents, tissues, different surfaces, movements, feelings, cycles of changes constituting birth, growing old, sleeping and waking. Above all, it is with disease with its terrifying phantoms of despair and hope that my body becomes ripe as little else for encoding that which society holds to be real—only to impugn that reality. (Taussig: 86)

The French artist Gilles Barbier's installation *Nursing Home* (2002) features a sextet of wax figures: aged superheroes slumped over, gurneyed, or otherwise sprawled before a television set declaiming advertisements. A bald Mister Fantastic of the Fantastic Four sits at a table, staring dumbly into space, his flaccid limbs twisted and warped in impossible contortions. A shriveled Hulk, still in tattered purple pants, dozes in a wheelchair. White-haired Superman leans stoically on a walker.

Nursing Home comprised part—judging by press accounts, the most crowd-pleasing part—of the New York Whitney Museum of American Art's 2003 exhibition, "The American Effect: Global Perspectives on the United States, 1990–2003," which surveyed several international artists' responses to post-9/11 US hegemony.

The geriatric do-gooders proved a hit; while some, like Peter Schjeldahl in his *New Yorker* review, dismissed Barbier's work as "no-rate art" (82) derivative of Edward Keinholz, and faulted the entire exhibit for its "soft core" reproach of American cultural imperialism, most critics responded along the lines of Mark Stevens of *New York* magazine: "As a work of art, *Nursing Home* is essentially a one-liner—the punch line about America could hardly be more obvious—but it's also very funny." Similarly, Georgette Gouveia of New York's *Journal News* opined: "In one sense, it's an affectionate homage . . . to the comic-book hero as a staple of American creativity. In another sense, however, the installation can be viewed as a critique of our youth-obsessed culture, with its underlying fear of death."

Critically, Barbier's piece marks—in fact, banks on—the "viewer-friendly" appeal of superhero iconography as shorthand not only for American popular culture, but for American values and their global perception as velvet-gloved fascism as well. The fact that *Nursing Home* is the work of a foreigner drives home this point; many gallery visitors who have never read a *Fantastic Four* or *Captain America* comic book (and who in fact may not have access to such titles in their home countries) nonetheless immediately grasp Barbier's symbolism: "Superhero = America."[1]

The "super signifier" of the super-body thus reifies nation, death-denying vigor, and sexual potency. This makes *Nursing Home* a lacerating parody; Barbier reintroduces time, the one element inimical to myth, of whatever ideological stripe. He fuses the "flash" of fantastic superheroics and the can-do American optimism it incarnates with the deflating reality principle of the exhausted, decrepit, dying body. (Wonder Woman, Superman, and Captain America are all represented at something like the age they would be, given the actual number of years since their first appearance in the comics.) *Nursing Home* thereby equates the disabled bodies of the elderly heroes with the flawed, discredited, and obsolete American Dream.

Barbier's piece, of course, only enacts a reversal of conventional American pop iconography in a bid to overcome the high-low divide. Rather than turn the body "against" the icon, as Barbier does (and as a 2004 French public AIDS awareness campaign using emaciated superheroes also did),[2] much mainstream visual culture uses the superhero signifier to "enhance" the body to an imagined ideal—thereby displacing the disabled, dying or dead body. Indeed, no sooner had the "American Effect" exhibit closed and the ailing heroes of *Nursing Home* moved on than the Foundation for a Better Life unveiled a 2003 nationwide billboard campaign featuring Christopher Reeve. Star of the *Superman* movies of the 1970s and 1980s, Reeve suffered a paralyzing accident in 1995 and had since used his celebrity to advocate for spinal cord injury causes. Next to a head portrait of Reeve (which avoids showing his body below the neck), the billboard declares: "Super man/Strength/Pass It On."

The public service message advanced Reeve's image as a former Superman who publicly and insistently declared his intention to "beat" his quadriplegia and walk again—which he "did" through the magic of computer-generated effects in a notable 2000 Super Bowl ad for Nuveen Investments. The late Reeve's stance earned him the wrath of many in the disabled community, who deemed him a grandstanding celebrity misrepresenting the lived reality

Super man.

STRENGTH

Pass It On:

VALUES.COM THE FOUNDATION FOR A BETTER LIFE®

1.1 The Foundation for a Better Life's public service ad featuring Christopher Reeve, 2003.

of others in his situation (who had only a fraction of his resources).[3] Seen by millions on the American advertising industry's biggest day, the TV ad sparked a minor hysteria in some quarters over rumors that an able-bodied Reeve really had walked.[4] This, despite some rather obvious anatomical short-comings in the ad, as noted by a critical Charles A. Riley: "It featured a ludi-crously fake shot of a man walking with Reeve's head barely affixed digitally to his shoulders (the creators seemed to have forgotten the neck part, and the head was far too small for the proportions of the body)" (127). Such was the imagistic power of the super-body to tap into popular desires for a "cure."

No surprise, given its decades-long iconography (dismissed, disavowed, derogated, but casually embraced) of hyper-masculinized vigor.[5] As discussed throughout this book, the superhero makes an alluring figure both for the reimagining/representation of (national, sexual, psychosocial) selves and for a critique of the rhetorical/tropological modes that frame them. More par-ticularly, as shown by the works examined within these pages, the superhero serves as an entry point for interrogating the social construction of the (male) body, disability, death, illness, and "normality" in postwar American popular culture.[6] My reading hinges on an interpretation of the *super-body* as a site of elaborate, overdetermined signification. As a means of arriving at that reading, the next section briefly considers the history, ideological uses and popular perceptions of the superhero from its origins, through the Silver Age and beyond.

THE SUPERHERO

Since its inauguration in 1938's *Action Comics* #1, the superhero genre—as reflected all too graphically and for various purposes in Barbier's *Nursing Home*, the Nuveen ad, and their aftermath—has served as a disability and death-denying representational practice which privileges the healthy, hyper-powered, and immortal body over the diseased, debilitated and defunct body. The superhero, by the very logic of the narrative, through his very presence, enacts an erasure of the normal, mortal flesh in favor of a quasi-fascist physical ideal.

Canonical Golden Age heroes such as Superman (Jerry Siegel and Joe Shuster, 1938), Batman (Bob Kane and Bill Finger, 1939), Wonder Woman (William Moulton Marston, 1941), and Captain America (Joe Simon and Jack Kirby, 1941), no less than more obscure figures such as The Comet (Jack Cole, 1940), Stardust (Fletcher Hanks, 1940), The Flame (Will Eisner and Lou Fine, 1939), Phantom Lady (Eisner & Iger studio, 1941), and Dr. Mystic (Siegel and Shuster, 1936) all advance that corporeal archetype, flourishing fully equipped (white) bodies "ready for anything." Chief among its corporeal features: strength, control, unboundedness—an utter disavowal of fleshly fragility. As noted by Scott Bukatman, "The superhero body is a body in a permanent state of readiness *(this is a job for . . .)*. What's more, if random death now appears from nowhere, the superbody is more than merely resistant; it bears its own mysterious power" (Bukatman 2003: 53, italics in original).

Scholars like Bukatman have linked such weighted imagery to the comics' primary audience, adolescent boys, and in particular to their presumed power fantasies, need for substitute father figures, and will to domination.[7] Others emphasize the nationalistic aspects of superheroes as part of American "fakelore," traced to the heroic figures of the oral epics going back to the founding of the country, if not before. Similarly, some point to the superhero's evocation of nostalgia for an idealized past or personal childhood (the baggage such evocations often bear). The more psychoanalytical approaches mine superheroes for their often paradoxical messages about gender, denial, sexuality, fashion, modern anxieties, desire, and the split self. Still others see the superhero genre as a marginalized, much-maligned twentieth-century artistic and/ or literary form only recently subjected to critical and popular reassessment, with a concomitant admission to college syllabi.[8]

This list of the superhero's "uses"—which one could lengthen substantially—demonstrates the genre's appeal (popular, sociocultural, political), its flexible expediency for various ends. An inviting mode of representation, a "costume" easily appropriated and donned, the superhero in recent years has indeed received unprecedented (and long overdue) attention from scholars.

Books on the subject include the landmark *Superheroes: A Modern Mythology*, by Richard Reynolds (1992), built on earlier historical treatments such as *The Comic Book Heroes: From the Silver Age to the Present*, by Will Jacobs and Gerard Jones (1985); Arthur Asa Berger and M. Thomas Inge's attention to the cultural significance of the genre in the 1970s and 1980s, followed by such works as *The Many Lives of the Batman*, edited by Roberta A. Pearson and William Uricchio (1991); *How to Read Superhero Comics and Why*, by Geoff Klock (2003); *Superman on the Couch: What Superheroes Really Tell Us About Ourselves and Our Society*, by Danny Fingeroth (2004); *Superhero: The Secret Origin of a Genre*, by Peter Coogan (2006); *Batman and Philosophy: The Dark Knight of the Soul*, edited by Robert Arp and Mark D. White; *Grant Morrison: Combining the Worlds of Contemporary Comics*, by Marc Singer (2011); *Do the Gods Wear Capes?: Spirituality, Fantasy and Superheroes*, by Ben Saunders (2011); and *Hand of Fire: The Narrative Art of Jack Kirby*, by Charles Hatfield (2012).[9]

All these works, including the present study, owe a tremendous debt to the pioneering investigations of an earlier generation of scholars and popular historians which addressed superhero comics, at times in the face of institutional resistance, which includes Coulton Waugh, Roland Barthes, Umberto Eco, and Marshall McLuhan; the excursus which unfolds over the next few pages draws liberally and unavoidably on their insights.[10]

More recently, superheroes themselves have seen a steady expansion into literature, as evinced by novels such as Michael Chabon's *The Amazing Adventures of Kavalier and Clay* (2000); *Soon I Will Be Invincible*, by Arthur Grossman (2007); *Karma Girl*, by Jennifer Estep (2007), as well as works by Jonathan Lethem. In the 2000s, they also made major inroads into video games, television, film (*Smallville, Heroes, The Cape*, the *Spider-Man, Hulk, Iron Man, Fantastic Four*, and the *Batman* franchises, and even, arguably, *The Matrix* series), art (with Barbier being only one example) and American popular culture, of which they form a long-standing and indelible facet. We may remember the late twentieth/early twenty-first century, in fact, as the Age of the Multimedia Superhero, when—thanks largely to advances in special effects technology—the genre achieved near-ubiquity among the public, acclaim (or at least acceptance) from critics, and major box-office clout.

All this makes plain that superheroes—despite (or indeed because of) their seeming simplicity—serve as tantalizing palimpsests for thinking through many aspects of past and contemporary American life, while their seven-decade publishing record has produced a daunting accumulation of narratival complexity (not the least of which is their innumerable stylistic variations), especially for the most successful characters. As Bukatman puts it, "At first glance they are terribly crude—especially in their first decades of existence—but familiarity and developing history endow them with copious nuance" (2003: 184).

Launched by two Clevelanders barely out of their teens on the eve of World War II—and since made available for myriad ideological and cultural purposes (both utopian and dystopian)—the superhero genre represents (in its own parlance) a rich "mirror universe" of American society. Or, in the words of Douglas Wolk: "Superhero comics are, by their nature, larger than life, and what's useful and interesting about their characters is that they provide bold metaphors for discussing ideas or reifying abstractions into narrative fiction" (2007: 92).

Proceeding from Coogan's taxonomical treatment of the superhero[11] as resting primarily on four major pillars—mission, powers, (secret) identity and genre distinction (58)—and his deployment of a Wittgensteinian "family resemblances" or "constellation of conventions" model (40) to ground his definition (which privileges potentiality and an informed ecumenism over tiresome checklists for what does and does not "count" as a superhero),[12] let us examine the major features of the genre with an eye to how they inform the present study.

THE SUPERHERO, IDEOLOGY, AND MYTH

Firstly, Barbier's pointed critique of superheroes as stand-ins for America resonates with earlier treatments of these figures as quintessentially national symbols. Proceeding from the folklorist Joseph Campbell's Jungian-inflected reading of the hero myth across cultures (i.e., monomyth),[13] along with the historian Richard Slotkin's emphasis on "regenerative violence" and the national imaginary, Robert Jewett and John Shelton Lawrence argue for the ultimately religious roots of this most American of genres:

> Whereas the classical monomyth seemed to reflect rites of initiation, the American monomyth derives from tales of redemption that have arisen on American soil, combining elements of the selfless servant who impassively gives his life for others and the zealous crusader who destroys evil. The supersaviors in pop culture function as replacements for the Christ figure, whose credibility was eroded by scientific rationalism. (6)14

Super savior = Christ

They go on: "Powers that the culture had earlier reserved for God and his angelic beings are transferred to an Everyman, conveniently shielded by an alter
ego" (44), adding, "They cut Gordian knots, lift the siege of evil, and restore
the Edenic state of perfect faith and perfect peace. It is a millennial, religious
expectation—at least in origin—yet it is fulfilled by secular agents" (46).[15]

Jeffrey S. Lang and Patrick Trimble argue for a new twentieth-century
American monomyth in the guise of the superhero, who "does not represent
the American legal system, but a secularized version of New Testament justice. He personalizes the values of the Puritan work ethic in its most virtuous
form" (160). Similarly, for M. Thomas Inge, superheroes are the industrialized
version of heroic figures from the country's oral tradition transplanted to the
modern technologies of print, film, radio, and television:

> They have moved away, however, from the masculine worlds of the epic and
> frontier societies, where drinking and hunting prevail, to the urban society
> where the impact of industrialism has created the threats of crime, poverty,
> alienation and totalitarianism. Their conquests, courtships, adventures and
> travels remain central, however. (141–42)

Consumed by the youth of a youthful nation, superheroes function for Richard Reynolds as both nationalist ideology and fantasy space for displaced
anxieties of childhood and pre-adulthood: "Superman is an Oedipal myth for
the century which invented the liminal states of the teenager and adolescent,
when physical mastery of the world precedes social mastery. Superman is adolescence writ large" (66). For these scholars, then, the superhero is inelucta-
bly tied to a project of national mythology tinged (due to its association with
childhood) with a powerful nostalgia. As an ideological construct, it operates
through a potent deployment of affect for an idealized past (Gordon: 192).

The notion of a nostalgic relationship to the superhero implies ownership,
a protective posture towards one's personal and national past—something to
be safeguarded, whatever the cost. Here, we come to the nature of violence in
the genre as particularly reactive and reactionary, a sort of primary-color fascism. As noted by Reynolds, superheroes function as a "conservative" element,
defending the status quo from "progressive" forces, i.e., the criminals and supervillains who (try to) act as agents of change: "The hero is in this sense
passive: he is not called upon to act unless the status quo is threatened by the
villain's plans" (50–51). Heroes (who are also "Everymen") **defending law and
justice through unlawful means** (which brooks no appeal) thus produce a decidedly **American paradox**, according to Jewett and Lawrence: "The premise
of democratic equality is visible in that the superhuman powers have to be
projected onto ordinary citizens, yet their transformation into superheroes

renders them incapable of democratic citizenship" (46). Embodying the "displacement of sexual energy into aggression," notes Bukatman, superheroes seem "innately fascist at their core" (2003: 185).

It should come as no surprise, then, that critiques of the genre as "fascistic" vigilante fantasy have dogged it nearly since its inception. "In the hands of the Superman, private justice takes over," charged Gershon Legman in 1949. "Legal process is completely discounted and contemptuously bypassed. No trial is necessary, no stupid policeman [*sic*] hog the fun. Fists crashing into faces become the court of highest appeal" (quoted in Fischer: 334). Indeed, superheroes coercing confessions, brutalizing and beating information out of suspects, or otherwise physically dominating "normals" quickly became a staple of the genre. It was business as usual in the Golden Age.

In his first adventure, Superman destroys state property and forces his will not only upon wife-beaters, bullies, and corrupt lobbyists, but on a governor's manservant as well. In what solidified as a generic convention, he bounds high into the sky with suspects in tow, threatening to drop them unless they talk. (Superman's less savory Golden Age counterpart, the Comet, even delighted in dropping his foes to their deaths and melting them with eye-beams. While he also occasionally resorted to similarly lethal tactics, Superman has benefited from a "softening" of his image due to rebranding and hazy public familiarity with his earliest incarnation).[16]

An early Batman story, "The Case of the Honest Crook" (*Batman*, vol. 1, #5, Spring 1941, Kane/Finger), is revealing in this regard. After a grievous injury to his sidekick Robin, Batman explodes in a murderous rage, decimating a group of thugs with his bare hands. Not even bullet wounds can impede his Achilles-like wrath as he beats the mob leader Smiley Sikes to a pulp, before intoning, "Almost forgot my original reason for hunting you up in the first place. I want a written confession from you . . ." "Don't . . . don't hit me again!" cries Sikes. "I'll do anything . . . But don't hit me!" (Kawasaki 2005: 21, ellipses in original). At the police station where Batman delivers the criminal, confession in hand, even the policemen stare in wide-eyed astonishment at the masked figure after he leaves, saying, "Did—Did you see his face?" "Yeah! That's the first time I ever saw it like that! It—It was terrible . . . like a demon's!" (ibid.: 22).

In horrifying even the sanctioned representatives of law and order (which he willfully subverts for his own personal agenda), Batman here starkly demonstrates how physical dominance forms a key element of the superhero identity. The episode, in fact, seems to fulfill Susan Sontag's observation on fascistic aesthetics, that they "flow from (and justify a preoccupation with) situations of control, submissive behavior, extravagant effort, and the endurance of pain; they endorse two seemingly opposite states, egomania and servitude" (1983: 316).

Hence, the derogation of superheroes as sadistic mass-culture *übermenschen*, expressed in the psychiatrist Fredric Wertham's well-known concept of the "Superman complex"[17] and echoed more recently in Fischer's plaintively "syllogistic" question: "If superhero comics rely on lynch narratives, and comics can affect kids from disenfranchised backgrounds, does that mean that superhero comics can, under the right circumstances, function as fascist propaganda?" (334).[18] As ideological constructs aimed nominally at children, with an attendant implied pedagogical function (what were the 1954 congressional hearings about if not some version of "what are these books teaching our kids"?), superhero comics continue to prompt considerable handwringing among intellectuals, as illustrated by Chabon's novel *The Amazing Adventures of Kavalier and Clay*. A roman-à-clef about the Jewish-American men working in comics during the lead-up to World War II, Chabon's work—more eloquently than most—identifies a master/slave anxiety at the very heart of the genre:

> Joe Kavalier was not the only creator of comic books to perceive the mirror-image fascism inherent in his anti-fascist superman—Will Eisner, another Jew cartoonist, quite deliberately dressed his Allied hero Blackhawks in uniforms modeled on the elegant death's-head garb of the Waffen SS. But Joe was perhaps the first to feel the shame of glorifying, in the name of democracy and freedom, the vengeful brutality of a very strong man. For months he had been assuring himself, and listening to Sammy's assurances, that they were hastening, by their make-believe hammering at Haxoff or Hynkel or Hassler or Hitler, the intervention of the United States into the war in Europe. Now it occurred to Joe to wonder if all they had been doing, all along, was indulging their own worst impulses and assuring the creation of another generation of men who revered only strength and domination. (204)

Precisely such reverence for "strength and domination" does indeed underlie the superhero genre as a death- and disability-denying discursive practice, which (for the title characters, anyway) takes vigorous and potent bodies as a given—how else to muscle, batter and force one's way in the world? "They are answerable to no one but themselves," notes Jaime Hughes, "for they are above and beyond the worlds they choose to save" (547).

COSTUME AND IDENTITY

But such impressive physical capacities, while serving the needs of adolescent fantasy, fall short for the purposes of drama in serialized fiction. This, at least, seems to have been the calculation behind another critical aspect of the superhero explored in the present study, the dual identity trope (itself inherited from previous models, such as the pulps). How to be both myth and (usually) man? Umberto Eco, in his seminal 1962 essay "The Myth of Superman,"[19] isolates the paradox with characteristic perspicacity:

> The mythological character of comic strips finds himself in this singular situation: he must be an archetype, the totality of certain collective aspirations, and therefore he must necessarily become immobilized in an emblematic and fixed nature which renders him easily recognizable (this is what happens to Superman); but, since he is marketed in the sphere of a "romantic" production for a public that consumes "romances," he must be subjected to a development which is typical, as we have seen, of novelistic characters. (149)

Eco's larger argument about the "consumability" of time in the (commercial mainstream version of the) genre I address further on, in particular its implications for the depiction of death (or impossibility thereof) in mainstream superhero comics. For now let us note his description of the superhero stories as hybrid shotgun marriages between a classical "mythic" mode (e.g., Superman) and a modern "romantic" mode (e.g., Clark Kent/Kal-El) explains a great deal about their structure, conventions and often bizarre psychology—particularly in regard to sexual intimacy.

Indeed, an odd relational calculus—erotically potent but inaccessible super-body counterbalanced by a nebbish or emotionally immature alter ego—is present from the beginning, trapping the hero in a grotesque inhuman stasis. As Roger D. Abrahams notes, "They not only never marry, they never find the real heroic culmination in death. They are permanently stuck in the hero role" (quoted in Inge: 142). For Lang and Trimble, on the other hand, such peculiar compromises form the *sine qua non* of material that had to keep attracting readers month after month: "Sexual renunciation and serialization made it possible to move from adventure to adventure without need for normal human relationships" (162).

Nonetheless, the "secret identity" device, so crucial as the source of drama in these tales (as well as not a few ludicrous plot turns), opens a Pandora's box of dizzying ontological consequences for the ego-protagonist, who must perpetually shuttle back and forth between rival—in a sense warring—personalities, both of them authentic *and* illusory. All this, once more, bespeaks the fundamentally American nature of this genre, argues Christopher Murray. But as his Lacanian reading also maintains, the multiple identities theme reveals a disconcerting instability of ego that, taken to its logical conclusion, threatens to undo the very framework undergirding the superhero itself:

> Superman's civilian guise as Clark Kent, a rather pathetic and cowardly newspaper reporter, provides a good cover for his superheroic exploits, but it also indicates an essential duality in the character, a need to sublimate one identity and set of ideals to another self. This identity crisis mirrors themes of displacement in American culture, thereby commenting on the essential duality of American life, while also exploring the potential for self-invention offered by America. However, this duality somewhat undermines the myth of masculine control that pervades the superhero genre, as the secret identity theme usually involves a complicated love-plot, one in which desires are frustrated by the necessity for maintained secrecy. While this provides a dramatic impetus for the love plot, it also allows a sense of limitation and loss of power which complicates the identity of the superhero, building the superhero's failure and incompleteness into the framework of his or her identity. (189)

Murray's insight here strikes me as critical: stories fundamentally predicated on split-consciousnesses and proliferating selves—reflective of American paradoxes regarding freedom, racial/ethnic passing, assimilation, and "dual citizenship"[20]—render the genre a modern, open-ended psychodrama of masculine identity and the nation. William Savage, writing also on Superman, puts it most succinctly:

> Here was a seemingly human being who possessed a number of superhuman powers, a costumed hero with a secret identity, an alien from a dying planet who embraced American ideals and Judeo-Christian values—a kind of spectacular immigrant, as it were, come from afar to participate in the American dream. (5)[21]

More pessimistically, Berger does not see the secret identity as evocative of endless possibilities for reinvention made possible by the welcoming ethos of America—rather, like Murray, he detects an anxiety about the self's very viability:

The schizoid split within Superman symbolizes a basic split within the American psyche. Americans are split like Superman, alienated from their selves and bitter about the disparity between their dreams and their achievements, between the theory that they are in control of their own lives and the reality of their powerlessness and weakness. (157)[22]

Hence, Reynolds's reading of superheroes (many of whom are haunted by missing or dead parents) as man-children endlessly engaged in Oedipal dramas of deferral;[23] the fantasies of dominance veil a core castration angst. Such dread over *powerlessness* forms a central tenet of the present study; I return to it at several points in this book (most directly in chapter 3, on Daredevil, passing and identity politics). For now, we can say that superheroes, caught in the generic running wheel of constantly shifting selves, must perpetually don, uphold, and discard identities like the colorful costumes they favor; these costumes, in fact, metonymize those very transformations.

Indeed, scholars examining the costume in superhero comics—a primary generic marker in Coogan's and other taxonomies—have highlighted its dual status: "Two functions are woven together: the role of the costume as a narrative device (giving Iron Man the powers he needs to fight villains) and its role as a sign of identity (to wear the costume is to become Iron Man)" (Reynolds: 26–27).[24] The costume obscures as it reveals, broadcasts or if you will *assumes* the preferred public identity.[25]

The costume as alchemical element of transfiguration—which both "hides" Clark Kent while retaining his traces – gives license for Superman not only to do what he does but, crucially, *be what he is.* Not surprisingly, this leads Chabon and other scholars to liken the costume to a form of transvestism ("superdrag") for the expression/assumption of otherwise impermissible selves; Bukatman sees in the superhero much of the dandy, a role allowing a level of exuberant performativity which most white heterosexual males have historically had to keep "in the closet." Drag facilitates the breaking of such boundaries—ethnic, gender, sartorial—to embrace flamboyant identities else reserved for ethnic/sexual others (e.g., gays, pimps). No wonder, as Bukatman pithily puts it, "superheroes don't wear costumes in order to fight crime, they fight crime in order to wear the costumes" (2003: 216).[26]

More than this. As Reynolds argues, the super-costume, obligatory generic marker of the new identity (to the exclusion of a partially jettisoned "ordinary" alter ego), itself bears much of the superbody's "power," attesting to its fetishistic essence:

Superman's prowess in defeating Butch Matson [a bully] is only the earliest of many examples of the sudden virility and sex-appeal gained when a character changes "into costume." What if the costume were more than just a sign of the inner change from wimp to Superman? What if the costume itself were the sexual fetish and the source of sexual power? (32)[27]

In other words, when it comes to the costumes and the bodies, who's wearing whom? And what does such a mercurial basis for identity mean in the context of iconic figures that heroicize a national past and tap quasi-fascist fantasies to salve adolescent male anxieties—fantasies of heath, of vigor, of violent mastery, sexual potency, and sadomasochistic triumphalism? Fantasies that routinely scrub evidence of disability, mortality, or any sort of bodily "defect" from sight?

THE SUPER-BODY

Long the object of doctors, anthropologists, and the social sciences, in the last thirty years the body has been "rediscovered" by the humanities. Emerging from the critical insights of modern philosophy and history (Henri Lefebvre, Friedrich Nietzsche, Michel Foucault, Mikhail Bakhtin); phenomenology (including Edmund Husserl and Maurice Merleau-Ponty, especially the latter's *Phenomenology of Perception*); sociology (Erving Goffman, Bryan Turner); feminism (Simone de Beauvoir, Julia Kristeva, Luce Irigaray, Hélène Cixous, Judith Butler and in particular Elizabeth Grosz' "corporeal feminism");[28] and more recently, as explored in this book, Disability Studies and Death and Dying Studies, body theory restores the corpus to the center of attention—as both nature and social construct—seeking to complicate a long-standing hierarchy of Platonic-Cartesian metaphysics in which ethereal minds direct and mechanical bodies obey.[29]

A line of argument of particular relevance to this study, advanced by, among others, Gilles Deleuze, Felix Guattari, and Butler, sees the body (like the subject) as structured through discourse and—to a disquieting degree—as primarily constituted by it. Popularized by Foucault, the concept of an eighteenth-century "medical gaze" sees the body as produced, beckoned out of non-existence, by the schooled observations of clinicians. As David Armstrong describes the matter:

The fact that the body became legible does not imply that some invariate biological reality was finally revealed to medical enquiry. The body was only legible in that there existed in the new clinical techniques a language by which it could be read. The anatomical atlas directs attention to certain structures, certain similarities, certain systems, and not others and in so doing forms a set of rules for reading the body and for making it intelligible. In this sense the reality of the body is only established by the observing eye that reads it. The atlas enables the student, when faced with the amorphous undifferentiated mass of the body, to see certain things and ignore others. In effect, what the student sees is not the atlas as a representation of the body but the body as a representation of the atlas. (2)

In other words, as noted by the Disability Studies scholar Lennard Davis, "The body is never a single physical thing so much as a series of attitudes to it" (2002: 22). Similarly, Elaine Scarry, in her landmark work *The Body in Pain*, describes the material reality of the body as fundamentally resistant to (linguistic) representation, with pain (i.e., the Lacanian Real) reducing the subject's discourse to inarticulacy, a process likened to the unmaking of the world itself. This leaves us a portrait of the body as, in essence, the things we can say about it. While a corrective to the humanities' traditional elision of "body issues," the subjection of the physical to the discursive rouses an anxiety perhaps best expressed by Diana Taylor:

How do we hold onto the significance of the "real" body even as it slips into the symbolic realm through representational practices? . . . It's hard to even imagine a body prior to the social construction that produces subjectivity. Assuming there is a "real" body before or somehow distinguishable from the cultural construction of it, how can we begin to think of it? (147)[30]

Absent a "pure" or so to speak "real-iable" representational strategy for the body, it serves as palimpsest, as medium of political contention, as breathing symbol of disparate ideological colorings. In narrative, the body is text—though (as argued by Peter Brooks and others), all texts bear something of the body.

Gail Weiss, through a Husserlian approach to the "narrative horizon" of the reading experience, argues convincingly that "the body is . . . the omnipresent horizon for all the narratives human beings tell (about it). As such, it grounds our quest for narrative coherence" (70). She offers Kafka's "The Metamorphosis" as an especially compelling instance of how texts anchor themselves in an embodied materiality of reading—even when the point of view and narrative world depicted challenge conventional categories of apprehending reality: "Kafka is exemplary in showing how the body serves as the quintessential narrative horizon that drives the quest for narrative intelligibility and, at the same time, thwarts it" (ibid.).

I would add that the story of the sick, deformed, abject, and dying Gregor—who disrupts the Samsa household's social order to the point that he/it must be systematically banished and destroyed—serves as a potent allegory of the inadmissibility (even obscenity) of certain classes of bodies from the stage of the normal, one which casts the reader in that very derogated "embodied" role. As in many disability narratives, Gregor is a riposte to, in the words of Rosemarie Garland-Thomson, the "abstract, self-possessed, autonomous individual" (1997: 40), a part here played by the hero's healthy sister Grete. As we will see, the narratives of the Silver Age and beyond which we will examine share something of this representational strategy. For now, I want to stress the somatic aspects of narrative: how, as Weiss and others argue, the body is embedded in the text; how, largely subconsciously, this fact structures the reading experience.

Of course, body theory takes on additional shades when dealing with fantastic narratives such as those in superhero comics. First and foremost, the protean super-body signifies "power": a unified, self-contained corpus/text, its meaning as clear and legible as the rippling muscles so often shrink-wrapped in bright primary colors, enacting an expansion of the narrative horizon beyond the human. As Bukatman has noted, these works represent a "significant somatization of modernist and postmodernist social concerns" (49). He goes on:

> Superhero comics present body narratives, bodily fantasies, that incorporate (incarnate) aggrandizement and anxiety, mastery, and trauma. Comics narrate the body in stories and envision the body in drawings. The body is obsessively centered upon. It is contained and delineated; it becomes irresistible force and immovable object. The body is enlarged and diminished, turned invisible or made of stone, blown to atoms or reshaped at will. . . . The superhero body is everything—a *corporeal*, rather than a *cognitive*, mapping of the subject into a cultural system. (2003: 49, italics in original)

Baroque, absurd, and overdetermined, the super-body has its origins in fantasies of physical mastery typical of male adolescents (comics' primary demographic since the 1960s), which, as mentioned, intersect with American national, ideological, and sexual myths. As Gerard Jones puts it:

> Superheroes were a latent-phase dream, embodying sex but invulnerable to it. They distilled that moment of swelling, big-kid pride in the new power and agility of the body, that last moment before the body begins to make its own scary demands and the world turns the mechanisms of shame against it. (232)

The implications of the superhero's provenance in the bodies and psyches of preteen boys at the dawn of World War II extend to all corners of the genre: it accounts for these figures' invulnerability and utter resistance to death;[31] the commonly encountered sexual awkwardness of the alter ego discussed above; the older, "father-figure" appearance of many villains (especially pronounced in the *Spider-Man* series); and the often inept, overly eroticized depiction of female heroines, to the present day.[32]

In short, the superhero body incarnates the anxieties and desires of the age (in the sense of the reader's chronological age and the epoch in which he/she is reading). Bukatman isolates the figure's vexed and multivarious nature, its usage for disparate ends, better than most:

> Superheroes negotiate dichotomous roles: the child (the orphaned Bruce Wayne) and the Father (Batman), the servant of law (crime fighter) and the autonomous outsider (vigilante) are condensed into a single, titanic figure. Displacement and condensation are the real superpowers. Thus have superheroes been reduced to a standard set of psychoanalytic and sociological maneuvers. No wonder they were neurotic by the 1960s. (2003: 185)

The last point, on the genre's "neurosis" by its third decade of life, concisely and elegantly diagnoses the situation at the dawn of the Silver Age. As seen in the work of Stan Lee, Jack Kirby, Steve Ditko, and others, in this era much of the genre's latent content, what since its inception it had universally repressed about bodies and minds, came spectacularly to the fore.

THE SILVER AGE

This study examines the Silver Age of DC and especially Marvel,[33] for its increasingly complex depiction of disability and death—indeed for its full-scale introduction of such adult subject matter into the genre in unprecedented ways. This came about for several reasons, chief among them the cultural realities of postwar America, the economic incentive to innovate, and the genre's own evolution into a sort of meta-narratival introspective mode. As argued by Charles Hatfield:

> Silver Age superhero comics differed from their Golden Age forebears in that they exhibited self-consciousness about the genre—that is, a historical memory and reflexive self-awareness, an understanding that superhero comics constitute a discreet genre with an experienced audience and with conventions that are at once generative and restrictive. . . . By 1960 . . . the

superhero was an established if dated element of pop culture, no longer ascendant but instantly recognizable and open to a variety of ironic reinterpretations. (2009: 18)

In addition, superheroes participated in the nervous questioning of authority characteristic of the early Cold War; as Bradford W. Wright notes in *Comic Book Nation*, these stories functioned among other things as cautionary tales about the "fragility of civilization in the atomic age" (203).

Inaugurated in 1956, largely through the efforts of DC editor Julius Schwartz, the Silver Age brought the first appearance of the Earth-1 Flash (the alternate version of a Golden Age character), the formal establishment of series continuity, a "multiverse" narrative structure and greater psychological depth, as well as a winking metafictive playfulness to superheroes, which had languished since the end of World War II, ceding market share to other genres. These new elements were cemented and developed much further in the Marvel series beginning early the next decade, with the first issue of Marvel's *Fantastic Four* (1961). Lee and Kirby's admixture of irony, tragedy, and alienation in that series—about heroes whose powers separate them from society and complicate their interpersonal dynamics—would become the industry standard. It matched the strengths of the genre with the new zeitgeist, as noted by Wright: "Marvel's introduction of ambiguity into the vocabulary of the comic book superhero fused the disorientation of adolescence and the anxieties of the Cold War into a compelling narrative formula" (215). Like soap operas, to which they are often compared, these stories focused much more on issue-after-issue character development than action and violence— though there was also plenty of that. As Will Jacobs and Gerard Jones, in the first major history of the Silver Age, described it: "In [Lee and Kirby's] work, plot, pace and mystery were shunted into the background while their brawling, bickering heroes took center stage, soaking the pages in pathos, anger and romantic melodrama" (52).[34]

Wright highlights the appeal of the new, wounded, more "real" Marvel superheroes to the burgeoning youth culture (which preferred them to the older, stodgier DC superheroes) as a critical factor in their success, noting that "Marvel presented its cautionary tales not through moral platitudes but in the form of alienated anti-heroes" (203), which fit with the times. Jacobs and Jones point to Ben Grimm/the Thing of the Fantastic Four (to whom we return at length in chapter 4), as the example *par excellence* of the new Marvel hero:

Until 1961, no comic writer would have suggested that acquiring strange powers might drive a wedge between a man and his society, bringing him more misery than contentment. But Ben Grimm, who would call himself only the Thing, had paid for his powers with an unalterably monstrous appearance; his enormous strength could not console him for the loss of his humanity. Resenting the world as strongly as he felt bound to protect it, he had to struggle as fiercely against his own bitterness and self-pity as against any villain. This was a turning point in comic book characterization. (50)

Indeed, more than just two decades separated the affable, invulnerable, quasi-Aryan Superman from the grotesque, petulant, unstable Thing (though they were both the creations of working class Jewish-Americans); as explored in this book, the complicated realities of East-West confrontation; the rise of feminism; the "men's crisis"; the rattling of prewar certainties in all spheres of American life; a young generation's need for heroes that gave vent to its anxieties (not just aspirations); as well as new possibilities for the political/artistic representation of marginalized groups, made the disabled and dying figure a potent symbol for this transformative era. (Most strikingly, disability—rather than remaining largely invisible and marginalized as it had for decades in the genre—is foregrounded and incorporated into the identities of several Marvel Silver Age characters, as I highlight in the next chapter.)

Nonetheless, for all their novel wallowing in postwar angst, the Silver Age superheroes retained their fundamental character as uplifting models for young people; these were still stories that by the final turn of the page affirmed basic social values. As Hatfield concludes: "Marvel, despite its trademark ironies and Lee's self-mocking editorial banter, also trafficked in an earnest humanism; if its stories challenged, they ultimately recuperated the genre's basic moral didacticism" (2009: 18). For his part, Douglas Wolk characterizes the Silver Age as "the era when troubled and flawed characters could nonetheless be relied on to do right in a crisis, when there was always a vein of lightheartedness in their stories, even at their darkest" (2007: 109).

CRISIS OF INFINITE MASCULINITIES

Of the historical and sociocultural factors which led to the strong contrast between the Silver Age heroes and their Golden Age predecessors, particularly in the depiction of corporeal complexity and spiritual malaise, one seems of critical importance: the changing role of men in the postwar era, and especially during the Cold War. Sociologists, historians, and feminist critics' interventions into Men's Studies have yielded a rather grim picture for males growing up in the mid-twentieth century, as well as for their fathers returning from overseas. The switch from a war footing to a service economy; the humiliating early failures of the space race; the constant looming threat of nuclear devastation; and the inaccessibility of customary "male" outlets for rage in an increasingly "feminized" society of bland mass consumerism, all redounded to men's unease, deflation, and even (metaphorical) impotence. A full-blown "crisis of masculinity" seized the nation in the 1950s, as bemoaned and ballyhooed by writers such as Arthur Schlesinger, Philip Wylie, Norman Mailer, and others who "lamented the decline of manliness and how the lack of virility was undermining the American ability to stand up to the communists" (Costello: 55).[35]

Michael Kimmel, writing in *Manhood in America: A Cultural History*, calls this national distemper "the masculine mystique," comparable in some respects to Betty Friedan's "feminine mystique" concept of the same era.[36] A "Goldilocks dilemma" of unpalatable identity choices beset the "stronger" sex at a historic cultural axis: "In the 1950s American men strained against two negative poles—the overconformist, a faceless, self-less nonentity, and the unpredictable, unreliable nonconformist" (236)—in other words, between the father and the son in *Rebel Without a Cause* (1955).

Over time things only worsened, from the perspective of the traditional American male. The rise of the youth culture and women's movement; the stalemate in Korea; the reverses in Vietnam; and the civil-rights marches, all extracted a heavy toll on the prewar image of straight white men. That old totem fell under greater and greater strain into the 1960s and 1970s, as other social groups and minorities asserted their claim for full inclusion into what had always served as WASP male preserves of privilege:

Together feminism, black liberation, and gay liberation provided a frontal assault on the traditional way that men had defined their manhood—against an other who was excluded from full humanity by being excluded from those places where men were real men. It was as if the screen against which American men had for generations projected their manhood had suddenly grown dark, and men were left to sort out the meaning of masculinity all by themselves. (Kimmell: 280)[37]

Kaja Silverman explains the masculine unease described by Kimmell in psychoanalytic (specifically Lacanian) language, which grounds male subjectivity on the disavowal of its own lack. Said disavowals are buttressed by nationalistic/ideological structures. In this process, culture's "dominant fictions" play a crucial role—thus their dismantling triggers profound masculine anxiety:

Not only does a loss of belief in the dominant fiction generally lead to loss of belief in male adequacy, but the spectacle of male castration may very well result in a destructive questioning of the dominant fiction. Male subjectivity is a kind of stress point, the juncture at which social crisis and turmoil frequently find most dramatic expression. (114)[38]

Starting in the early 1970s the comics industry responded to the countercultural "turmoil" with series and characters that privileged topicality and "relevance," a strategy I treat in some detail in chapter 6. For now, I want to stress that such policies progressively introduced what were once considered "abject" bodies—racial, sexual, and physical others, including the dying and disabled—into the visual field of comics.

To return to the beginning of this (still unfolding) process, the "masculinity crisis" that preceded the Silver Age: Susan Faludi, in *Stiffed: The Betrayal of the American Man*, offers a compelling metonym of the cultural trends that in the end *torpedoed* traditional manhood:

In truth, despite all their wartime heroics, the fathers abandoned their sons, however inadvertently, in an image-based, commercial-ruled world that they had largely created in their postwar haste to embrace the good life.... Symbolically speaking, what the fathers really passed on to their sons was not the GI ethic but the GI Joe "action figure," a twelve-inch shrunken-man doll whose main feature was his ability to accessorize. (36)

Gender anxieties of this sort were virtually unheard of in the Golden Age, a time of emergence from economic depression and entrance into war, with no such imagined threat to "dominant fiction" constructs of masculinity; hence, its heroes are not problematized in that fashion. Conversely, the early Silver Age superheroes served, in effect, as elaborate funhouse reflections of Faludi's "GI Joe lack": from tacit acknowledgement of the compromised male state, the stories moved to fantastic (ir)resolutions—to only-ever-partial erasures and denials of same.[39]

UNMASKED AT LAST

Just how dark and generically destabilizing, as well as (semi-) recuperative Silver Age narratives could get, is attested to by a 1970 Spider-Man story, "Unmasked at Last!" (*Amazing Spider-Man*, vol. 1, #87, Aug. 1970, Lee/Romita)—crucially, an illness scenario. The plot involves Spider-Man's panicked alter ego, Peter Parker, deliriously concluding he has lost his superpowers when overcome by dizziness, fever, and weakness. The physical symptoms—ultimately revealed as a simple flu—lead to a full-blown identity crisis: "It means that . . . *Spider-Man* has taken his *final swing!*" Peter proclaims (6, ellipses, emphasis in original).

Unsteady on his feet, the web-swinger almost misses his landing on a ledge (3), suffers blurry vision (2), and several times falls and loses his balance (6). More radically, he briefly turns to crime, thoughtlessly breaking open a jewelry store safe to retrieve some pearls as a gift for his girlfriend, Gwen. (Realizing his confusion, he replaces the pearls in shame – but leaves the safe badly damaged.) Enacting a fundamental conflict between infirmity and superheroics—as if one nullifies the other—Peter comes to fear not just a loss of vigor but of life: "Maybe I'm—actually—*dying!*" (13, emphasis in original). He even speculates that the radioactive blood which endows him with powers has turned fatally toxic.

Page six presents Peter's downfall: the hero laid low, barefaced, on his knees and sweating, weakly clutching the mask of his super-identity, as "powerlines" ironically emanate from his debilitated form. "I always *wondered* . . . if and when I'd ever *give up* my secret identity!" he moans. "But now . . . *fate* has made that decision *for* me!" (6, ellipses, emphasis in original). Within three pages, Peter takes the final step in his self-demolition, committing a sort of genre suicide. Before an astonished party of his friends, he holds up his mask and utters: "I . . . *had* to tell you . . . Can't keep it a *secret* anymore . . . Spider-Man is *finished!* His career is *ended* . . . forever! *I'm* . . . the only one . . . who could *know* that! Because . . . *I'm Spider-Man!*" (9, emphasis, ellipses in original).

"Unmasked At Last!" is an apocalyptic text. Though by story's end Peter recuperates and recruits the Prowler in a scheme to fool his friends into discounting his earlier confession, and though the temporary "unmasking" trope dates back to the Golden Age, very rarely has the superhero's ruination and defeat appeared so total, so pathetic. Notice, too, that no supervillain is involved; it is the inverse of a heroic death in battle. Spider-Man's annihilation is engineered by an invisible enemy—a plain virus—paired with Peter's hysteria in the face of frailty. (His elderly Aunt May has often handled her illnesses with more spine!) The tale carries an inescapable gender component: the hero is, in effect, *unmanned*. The slightest hint of enfeeblement signals anathema to his super-self.[40]

Death markers abound in the twenty-page story, from Harry Osborn's dismissive platitude that Peter would be "late for his own *funeral!*" (7, emphasis in original) to the sunset that accompanies the hero's doldrums, before he hits on a plan to salvage his identity (figured by dawn) (15). Moreover, the crisis of a psyche struggling with its own mortality and loss of bodily function echoes

1.2 Peter Parker, beset by illness, renounces his Spider-Man identity in "Unmasked at Last!" (*Amazing Spider-Man*, vol. 1, #87, Aug. 1970).

postwar thanatographies such as John Gunther's 1949 *Death Be Not Proud*, on the death of his son by cancer. Finally, and most salient of all, Peter's journey closely recapitulates the theories of psychologist Elisabeth Kübler-Ross, whose landmark *On Death and Dying* (1969) had introduced the five stages of grief model (anger, denial, bargaining, depression and isolation, and acceptance) the year before *Amazing Spider-Man* #87's publication. The book, which launched a public discussion on death in America, was subject to much reappropriation in the popular culture, as seen by such manifestations as "Unmasked at Last!"

Lee/Romita's work echoes a conversation then in vogue in the culture, refracting it through an allegorical generic lens. Its conclusion: death, disability, and superheroics do not mix. Other stories from the Silver Age and beyond which we will examine, ranging from the late 1950s to the early 1990s, reiterate, distort, flout, and complicate that fatal dichotomy, epitomizing Wolk's assertion that superheroes—whether in mass cultural formats like Spider-Man comics or fine art manifestations such as Barbier's *Nursing Home*—"provide bold metaphors for discussing ideas or reifying abstractions into narrative fiction" (92).[41]

ORGANIZATION OF THE BOOK

I have divided this study into two major parts. The first portion addresses the theory and representation of disability in the superhero genre, with chapters devoted to characters both familiar (Daredevil, Thor, Iron Man, the X-Men, Doom Patrol) and more obscure (She-Thing, Human Fly, the Shroud, Rot Lop Fan). The second part deals with death and superheroes, once more partly through case studies of the well-known (Superman, Spider-Man, Hulk) and the less so (Captain Marvel, Strikeforce: Morituri). I look to the body of the superhero in the Silver Age and beyond (roughly 1961–93) through the lens of Disability Studies and Death and Dying Studies, to uncover its operating denials of bodily difference and impairment.

In this way the study sheds light on the structuring principle of the super-body, and thus of the superhero genre itself—what Douglas Wolk calls "the public and private shame of American comics" (2007: 100): that it comes about (and for most of its history has existed) through an always-erased though always-implied disabled/dying/dead body.

2

SUPERCRIP
Disability, Visuality, and the Silver Age Superhero

In fact, the able body is the true image of the Other. It is a prop for the ego, a myth we all accept for the sake of enjoyment, for we all learn early on, as Lacan explains, to see the clumsiness and ineptitude of the body in the mirror as a picture of health—at least for a little while. (Siebers 2008: 60)

Disability Studies coincides with, in part emerged from, and to some extent has had to contend with the recent wave of scholarly interest in representations of the body and "embodiedness" to which I've already alluded. From such early tracts as Leslie Fiedler's *Freaks: Myths and Images of the Secret Self* (1978) to its more recent intersections—and frictions—with feminist, racial, psychoanalytic (especially Lacanian) cultural studies, death and dying debates, and identity politics, disability as an area of scholarly inquiry had to emerge from beneath the shadows of other, "stronger," more established categories for defining the body.[1]

This new and heightening *visibility* of the disabled has come about, within and without the academy, as a result of political change in the culture, chiefly disability rights activism since the 1970s leading to landmark legislation that culminated in the 1990 Americans with Disabilities Act (ADA). There also arose a widespread recognition in the humanities of a long-ignored or *"invisible"* facet of the human experience: "Disability, always an actively repressed *memento mori* for the fate of the normal body, [is gaining] a new, non-medicalized, and positive legitimacy both as an academic discipline and as an area of political struggle" (Davis 1997A: 1). As Simi Linton, who uses a wheelchair, wrote in *Claiming Disability*:

> A host of factors have typically screened us from public view. We have been hidden—whether in the institutions that have confined us, the attics and basements that sheltered our family's shame, the "special" schools and

classrooms designed to solve the problems we are thought to represent . . . The public has gotten so used to these screens that as we are now emerging, upping the ante on the demands for a truly inclusive society, we disrupt the social order. (3)

Much of the theoretical work on disability in the humanities of the last twenty years or so derives from feminist theorizations of the body and physical difference. Scholars such as Elizabeth Grozs, Marsha Saxton, Rosemarie Garland-Thomson, Tom Shakespeare, Linton, and others foregrounded physical disabilities (as opposed to "unseen" ones such as cognitive impairment or deafness) in their agitation for disability rights, access to jobs, and socioeconomic capital. Indeed, disability-rights activism since the 1970s favored spectacular attention-grabbing media events, such as the occupation of the San Francisco Health Education and Welfare offices in 1977 and the notorious "crawl-up" the steps of Capitol Hill by members of ADAPT in 1990.[2] The point of such actions was to make oneself hyper-visible, impossible to ignore. As Garland-Thomson, one of the earliest to apply a Visual Studies model to disability, succinctly phrased the matter: "To be recognized, one needs literally to be seen" (2009: 194).

Such an emphasis has had a profound effect on the development of the field, including the present study; visuality became the predominant discursive frame for examining, arguing or critiquing disability as a cultural construct. As Garland-Thomson put it: "The visual—whether it is looking toward or away—is the major mode that defines disability in modernity" (2001: 340). Echoing that language, Lennard Davis writes in a Lacanian vein that "disability . . . is a disruption of the visual, auditory, or perceptual field as it relates to the power of the gaze. As such, the disruption, the rebellion of the visual, must be regulated, rationalized, contained" (1997B: 55). Susan Schweik, in her history of America's nineteenth- and twentieth-century "Ugly Laws" sees the scrubbing away of the disruptive, offending "dys-appearing body"[3] and its "deformances" (90) as emblematic of how the disabled have been dealt with in modernity (as opposed to the tolerance for freak shows and disfigured street beggars of previous eras). She concludes: "Modernity, we might say, was controlled appearance" (86, emphasis in original).

However policed, the prominent visibility of the disabled has a long pedigree; only that visibility has been defined and (mis-)valued from without. In her important 2001 essay "Seeing the Disabled: Visual Rhetorics of Disability in Popular Photography," Garland-Thomson goes so far as to note: "The history of disabled people in the Western world is in part the history of being on display, of being visually conspicuous while being politically and socially erased" (348).[4]

Like Davis, Garland-Thomson advances the stare as emblematic of the power relations between able-bodied and disabled, much as the gaze functions in other contexts. She writes:

Gazing—which has been highly theorized as the dominant visual relation in patriarchy between male spectators and the female objects of their gazes—differs from staring in that it usually encompasses the whole of the body. Staring at disability, in contrast, intensely telescopes looking toward the physical signifier for disability. Starers gawk with abandon at the prosthetic hook, the empty sleeve, the scarred flesh, the unfocused eye, the twitching limb, but seldom do they broaden looking to envelop the whole body of the person with a disability. . . .

Staring is the social relationship that constitutes disability identity and gives meaning to impairment by marking it as aberrant. Even if disability is not apparent, the threat of its erupting in some visual form is perpetually present. Disability is always ready to disclose itself, to emerge as some visually recognizable stigmata, however subtle, that will disrupt social order by its presence. (2001: 347)

Striking in this passage (besides the phantasmatic, quasi-religious imagery) is Garland-Thomson's evocation of disability as inescapably—if at times only potentially—imbricated with the visual; the plainly legible physical markers of physical difference, such as hooks, prostheses, scarred flesh, a wheelchair, constitute the disability's "surface" manifestation. On the heels of an era when the disabled were re-emerging from an enforced relegation to the shadows, image came to predominate as *the* mode for understanding and advancing what disability "is." "We are here, stop the stares," such a stance declares, "but look upon us, see us for what we are, stop ignoring us as human beings."[5]

Similarly, disability theory and scholarship has sought, in the terms of David T. Mitchell and Sharon Snyder, to highlight and reverse the historical marginalization of disabled bodies amid a long-standing and "perpetual circulation of their images" (2000: 6). In short, the disabled have since antiquity been portrayed by others as pitiful, inspiring, mysterious, grotesque, or evil, but exceedingly rarely as ordinary human beings with an incidental physical or cognitive difference. Disability—what Mitchell and Snyder call "the master trope of human disqualification" (ibid.: 3)—has instead served a structuring function: to define by counter-example the category of the "proper" or "normal" body.

Through comparison to an "average" man (an 1842 invention of Belgian statistician Adolphe Quetelet), Western medicine, the state and culture marginalized physical difference as defective, deviant, tragic, and economically unproductive; in a Weberian vein, Garland-Thomson argues that modern postindustrial civilization, with its emphasis on work and utility as moral virtues, as well as on predictability and sameness, has no place for the radical otherness of physical/cognitive difference (2009: 30). Or as Mitchell and Snyder explain:

> The body is up against an abstraction with which it cannot compete because the norm is an idealized quantitative and qualitative measure that is divorced from (rather than derived from) the observation of bodies, which are inherently variable. This false model of an ideal body also fails to consider the contingencies of bodies functioning within specific social and historical contexts. It is, in other words, a body divorced of time and space—a thoroughly artificial affair. (2000: 7)[6]

The latter observation, of course, bears more than passing similarity to common descriptions of the superhero body, as previously discussed. It too is a corpus constructed through the elimination of undesirable traits. For instance, in his examination of the "secret identity" trope, Michael Chabon notes that it conceals "all that we *lacked*, and *all that we were not*, before the [radioactive] spider bit us" (2008: 22, my emphasis). While as noted in chapter 1, Scott Bukatman describes Superman as someone with a "body that retains no marks, on which history cannot be inscribed" (2003: 197).

In their critique of such eugenicist ideologies (what Leslie Fiedler called "the tyranny of the normal"), Disability Studies scholars have highlighted the contingent and constructed nature of the "average" body; Garland-Thomson proposed the neologism "normate" precisely for that purpose, to uncover the "veiled subject position" of "the figure outlined by the array of deviant others whose marked bodies shore up the normate's boundaries" (1997: 8).[7] Another strategy has emphasized the socially invented character of disability itself, how bodies are shaped by circumstance and culture at least as much as by "nature." Such a view poses a distinction between impairment (denoting the physical fact of bodily/cognitive difference, such as a missing limb) and disability (the sociocultural context that determines how the impairment is interpreted). As Davis writes, wheelchair users "have impairments that limit mobility, but are not disabled unless they are in environments without ramps, lifts and automatic doors" (2002: 12).[8]

The relation of built—usually urban—surroundings to various physical types thus formed a focus of critique and commentary, as exemplified by Tobin Siebers: "When a disabled body moves into any space, it discloses the social body implied by that space. There is a one-to-one correspondence between the dimensions of the built environment and its preferred social body—the body invited inside as opposed to those bodies not issued an invitation" (2008: 85). Through such arguments (which as noted often centered on the visual), disability activists and scholars since the 1970s have attacked the medical and eugenicist constructions of the disability experience, in favor of a civil-rights, egalitarian, inclusive social model.[9] The barriers they have sought to bring down are both physical (stairs, curbs) and social (preconceptions, the medical model).

Finally, there does exist another aspect to US debates about the disability experience relevant to our discussion of superheroes, which we might bluntly call its "anti-American" cast. As Garland-Thomson describes it in *Extraordinary Bodies:*

> Freighted with anxieties about loss of control and autonomy that the American ideal repudiates, "the disabled" become a threatening presence, seemingly compromised by the particularities and limitations of their own bodies. Shaped by a narrative of somatic inadequacy and represented as a spectacle of erratic singularity, the disabled figure delineates the corresponding abstract cultural figure of the self-governing, standardized individual emerging from a society informed by consumerism and mechanization. Cast as one of society's ultimate "not me" figures, the disabled other absorbs disavowed elements of this cultural self, becoming an icon of all human vulnerability and enabling the "American Ideal" to appear as master of both destiny and self. At once familiarly human but definitively other, the disabled figure in cultural discourse assures the rest of the citizenry of who they are while arousing their suspicions about who they could become. (1997: 41)

As depicted here, the disabled body represents both a threat to, as well as a vital element in, the construction of patriotic self-esteem—though the latter function can only adhere if the "offending" otherness of physical difference remains safely occluded or removed from the scene (like the gold in Fort Knox, its defining function requires safeguarding). Once in evidence—in plain sight—disability's moral panic proves a quick corrosive agent to the cheery "can-do" attitude of stereotypically healthy American selves. As the late paraplegic anthropologist Robert Murphy assessed, "We are subverters of an American ideal, just as the poor are betrayers of the American dream" (116–17).

Disability's Kryptonite-like effect on US optimism logically appertains to that most American of figures, the superhero (with apocalyptic consequences, as demonstrated by Peter Parker/Spider-Man's travails in "Unmasked at

Last!"). Leave it to a phylogenetically buoyant American culture, then, to meet that threat with a sort of compromise—between the "disheartening" reality of bodily impairment and the unbounded possibilities for human potential so much a part of US identity.

THE SUPERCRIP

The superhero's illusory promise of bodily integrity and transcendence made it an alluring effigy for disability discourse, serving equally well as a subject of celebration—and burning. In fact, of the many ideological disjuncts that continue to divide much of the disabled community both within itself and from the wider, "abled" culture, the figure of the "supercrip" remains the most fraught. The term, which came into popular use around the time of the passage of the ADA in 1990, denotes a type of disabled person more likely to appear in the mainstream mass media (itself part of the problem). As Joseph Shapiro writes in his seminal history, *No Pity*, the supercrip is the "inspirational disabled person . . . our most glorified disabled role models, lavishly lauded in the press and on television . . . [a] model deeply moving to most nondisabled Americans and widely regarded as oppressive by most disabled ones" (16).

The supercrip represents the antithesis to that other despised master image of disability in mainstream culture: the sentimentalized, pathetic poster child wheeled out for telethons and tearjerkers. The supercrip *defies* pity. Whether manifesting in the person of Mark Wellman, a paraplegic park ranger who climbed granite peaks in Yosemite National Park; Terry Fox, a one-legged cancer survivor who ran across Canada on his prosthetic limb; Sarah Reinertsen, an amputee athlete who competed in the TV series *The Amazing Race,* and titled her 2009 memoir *In a Single Bound: Losing My Leg, Finding Myself, and Training for Life*; or the many awe-inspiring participants of the Paralympics, the stereotype of the supercrip, in the eyes of its critics, represents a sort of overachieving, overdetermined self-enfreakment that distracts from the lived daily reality of most disabled people. "The power of the Supercrip is a false power," writes Beth Haller:

> People with disabilities are put on pedestals because of their inspirational quality in doing ordinary things, which is actually a patronizing way to laud people, imbued with charity. Presenting someone as inspirational is just another way of pitying them for the "tragedy of fate" . . . Society holds few expectations for people with disabilities—so anything they do becomes

"amazing." Any disabled person who does any basic task of living becomes "inspirational." And any disabled person who does more than daily living, such as competing as a professional golfer or playing pro baseball with one arm, becomes a Supercrip.

Laura Remson Mitchell, who has lived with muscular dystrophy since 1978, highlights the harm posed: "All too often, such stories leave the impression that only some kind of superhero could possibly live a meaningful life with MS, or with any serious disabling condition. That is a very destructive message—and it's simply not true!"[10]

The supercrip's appeal is nonetheless real and powerful. To an ableist media-saturated society, it moves, soothes, and stirs, reaffirming the indomitability of American bodies—with good pictures into the bargain. To the disabled who assume its mantle, in one fell swoop they can escape the confining strictures of the "tragic, pathetic crip" role and don a new super-identity—passing not as normal, but as *supranormal*. To the extent that the superhero signifier also expresses a particularly nationalistic message, the assumption of such an identity intimately associates the new persona with national values, with "truth, justice and the American way," reassuring disabled and non-disabled alike that we really are "one people . . . indivisible," united by our can-do spirit.

But as the term suggests, through its derivation from Superman and the superhero comics genre, "supercrip" implies an exaggerated, absurdly hyper-realist overreaching, an ego-driven overcompensation for lack, all the more dangerous for its misrepresentation of an entire community. And just as fictional figures like Superman partly act as our contemporary myths or "fake-lore," so does the supercrip function as a modern, secularized version of the "wondrous," the oldest category in Garland-Thomson's taxonomy of Western culture's "visual rhetorics of disability."

As she notes, "the wondrous capitalizes on physical differences to elicit amazement and admiration" (2001: 341) in the form of the monsters, dwarves, freaks, and oracles of the premodern world. Since the marginalization and disappearance of the dime museum and freak show in the twentieth century, the allure of physical difference as spectacle gravitated to other, "safer" channels, either in modern televised freak shows like the Maury Povich, Howard Stern, or Jerry Springer talk shows (all of which featured disabled and disfigured guests), the annual Jerry Lewis MDA telethons, or, safest of all for mainstream sensibilities, the inspirational, feel-good feats of the supercrip. But as with its premodern manifestations, the contemporary "wondrous" figure pays a heavy price—namely, its humanity—for all the prominence and acceptance. In going from one extreme of marginality to the other, what the supercrip leaps over ("in a single bound," so to speak) is not tall buildings but "normality," which lies presumably somewhere in the broad middle, as inaccessible as ever.

Thus, the superhero figure constitutes an enticing but highly problematic icon of transformation: "normate" (or, as we shall see, disabled) body into superhuman; "amazing" body, though one predicated on a eugenicist cult of perfectibility; and pitiful identity into a new "super-persona" that defies pity—but which also, like the supercrip, denies lived reality. It seems both the essence of American optimism, and its outright parody.[11] We should bear in mind the supercrip stereotype as a figure obsessively, indeed maniacally, over-compensating for a perceived physical difference or lack, since, as we shall see, this aspect ties in quite neatly with the genre specificities and narratival concerns of so much Silver Age superhero literature.

THE DISABLED BODY IN LITERATURE AND ART

Such paradoxical disabled figures as the supercrip, the deformed villain or the Tiny Tim-like pathetic sufferer have not escaped the notice of literary scholars; indeed, disability, often in the guise of "overheated symbolic imagery," has appeared as a "pervasive tool of artistic characterization" in literature going as far back as Homer, argue Mitchell and Snyder (2000: 16). The difference today, as with the renewed interest in representation of racial and sexual minorities, is in the political stakes involved, which bear directly on meaning: "Disability is a product of an interaction between culture, author, text and audience . . . that create and re-create the disabled body as a potent product of literary investment" (ibid.: 27). Such a product, of course, comes freighted with the suppositions and outright prejudices borne by disabled people in society, something particularly true of accounts written by non-disabled authors. This is why, as argued by Ato Quayson, we must rigorously interrogate texts that claim to represent the disabled experience: "Because disability in the real world already incites interpretation, literary representations of disability are not merely reflecting disability; they are refractions of that reality, with varying emphases of both an aesthetic and ethical kind" (36).

Indeed, Leslie Fiedler, the first major critic to give sustained attention to literary discourses of disability as far back as the 1970s, saw a great advantage in this expressional mode as it pertains to ethics. For precisely in art and literature do otherwise proscribed notions such as the transgressive sentiments provoked by the disabled find free utterance. The "safe space" of the text allows for a play of ideas critical to the development of a moral response to the "problem" of disability in the world. As he wrote in the essay "Pity and Fear: Images of the Disabled in Literature and the Popular Arts," the literary mode releas[es] much in us that we customarily repress, thus making us aware of, more at home with, certain dark responses to certain of our fellows—attitudes we tend consciously to despise, even to deny . . . Mythic song and story provide us with a way of acting out, vicariously and thus harmlessly, attitudes that our avowed principles (whether based in politics, morality, religion or psychology itself) tell us are socially undesirable, sinful or pathological. (1996: 35)

Similarly, Garland-Thomson's discussion of artistic portraits of disabled and disfigured subjects emphasizes their "safe space" aspects, investing them, like Fiedler, with a political power to effect social transformation, one aesthetic interaction at a time: "These portraits enable visual pilgrimages of deliberate contemplation that might be scuttled in a face-to-face encounter on the street. The invitation to look that a portrait offers precludes our skittish staring and instead allows us to look deep into these unfamiliar faces made strangely familiar" (2009: 84). Siebers also contends that disability as an aesthetic value "participates in a system of knowledge that provides materials for and increases critical consciousness about the way that some bodies make other bodies feel" (2010: 20). In so many words, the right to explore unfamiliar realities granted by words and pictures about the disabled also authorizes new notions, attitudes and interactions with them in the "real" world.

At the same time, literary/artistic portraits always come with baggage. Hence, the other obvious fact about the representation of the disabled in art and literature through the ages: they have consistently been subjected to prevailing preconceptions of aberrance and "worthwhile" lives—in brief, bigotry. Mitchell and Snyder, pointedly, mince no words on this matter: "the literary efforts to illuminate the dark recesses of disability produce a form of discursive subjugation" which prompts the move to encapsulate an exotic corporeal difference within "a regime of tolerable deviance" (2000: 6–7). They call such textual strategies towards disabled bodies "narrative prosthesis," and posit the task of the modern critic *"to make the prosthesis show, to flaunt its imperfect supplementation as an illusion"* (ibid.: 8, emphasis in original). The most direct means of accomplishing this involves mining the archive of discourses (including literature, film and comics) to, as they put it, demonstrate the kaleidoscopic historical responses to disability, in order to "denaturalize" the ideological beliefs of today (ibid.: 44). The present study, with relish, takes up precisely this challenge.

OUT OF SIGHT

As noted, much of the advancement of and resistance to disability rights has revolved around the *visuality* of the disabled body and its representation in various media: the greater culture's psychic urge to police disability's visible reminder of the body's contingency and fragility (on the one hand) versus its avowed intentionality to individual agency and public openness (on the other). This has not meant easy struggle or steady progress; paradoxically, the disabled still too often attract unwanted stares, yet remain underrepresented in the workplace, university hall and social arena.[12] As pointed out by W. J. T. Mitchell, images and their absence both carry power to effect change:

> Hypervisibility, and the invisibility that derives from it, are certainly crucial to the experience of disability. Such stereotypes as cripple, gimp, retard, freak, or monster can lock people inside of images that have their own perverse life and logic, condemning individuals to repeat certain ritual behaviors and narratives, or struggle against them as a condition of daily existence. (394)

In the task of "rereading" or "recuperating" established cultural expressions about disability in a progressive light, then, the issue of hyper- vs. invisibility often comes insistently to the fore—perhaps no more dramatically than when we put superhero comics under the Disability Studies microscope. For what better exemplifies the willfully ableist, physique-driven aesthetic of the wider social structure than the all-powerful, disability-denying superhero? Upon what, indeed, can we base the genre's entire logic and *modus operandi*, if not its fantastic, quasi-eugenicist apotheosis of the perfected body?

This study confronts such questions by seeking to demonstrate that the superhero as commonly received, and certainly in its Silver Age incarnation, would not, cannot exist without the underlying rationale of a disabled, structuring Other—crucially, an Other that must literally and routinely be made to *vanish from sight*. In bringing this disabled Other out of its invisibility and back into "view," we will delve further into the peculiar role visuality plays in the curious *fort-da* game[13] which is the "narrative prosthesis" representational strategy for the disabled body in superhero comics of the era under discussion.

For indeed, like the supercrip, the Marvel Silver Age (ushered in by the landmark work of Stan Lee, Jack Kirby, Steve Ditko, and others at Marvel Comics in the early 1960s) puts "overcompensation" for lack literally at the

2.1 The lame Don Blake transforms into the physically idealized Thor (*The Avengers*, vol. 1, #1, Sept. 1963).

center of the action—only for the word "overcompensation" to describe this phenomenon, we may substitute the established genre term "superpowers." This description, of course, would more or less apply to superheroes of the Golden Age as well—the weak Clark Kent "disappears" when he becomes Superman, Billy Batson vaporizes to make room for Captain Marvel.

The Silver Age's innovation: to keep bringing the alter ego—*who is often disabled*—back from the shadows into the light, and moreover to make this back-and-forth circulation a central tenet of the dramatic action, character motivation, and readerly identification. In case after case, a superpower "overcompensates" for a perceived physical defect, difference, or outright disability. Almost universally, the superpower will *erase* the disability, banishing it to the realm of the unseen, replacing it with raw power and heroic acts of derring-do in a hyper-masculine frame. But the persistent return of the disabled alter ego, and moreover the highlighting of his body's "incompatibility" with the surrounding environment, comes to form a predominant aspect of the heroic self. As we know, such moves comprised part of the Silver Age strategy to stimulate sympathy, enhance psychological depth and raise the dramatic stakes.

As explained by Will Jacobs and Gerard Jones:

By 1963 Lee had finally found the formula to ensure that all his heroes possessed the originality he sought. The key to the formula lay in the idea of a flawed hero. Two of his earlier co-creations, the Thing and the Hulk, were monstrously disfigured; now Lee and his collaborators moved on to develop heroes who were more subtly impaired, either by common handicaps or spiritual unease.

This served a twofold purpose: first, it set Marvel comics thoroughly apart from those of the competition, populated as they were by flawless heroes; and second, it opened the doors to melodrama, which Marvel's fans valued as highly as adventure. (88)[14]

Paul Levitz makes a similar historical argument for the Silver Age reflecting changes in early 1960s US culture, just then beginning to recognize a wider range of humanity in more sophisticated ways, including the disabled. As he told me:

You're at the point where the massive homogenization and bowdlerization of comics is just beginning to fade. And this is maybe one of the earlier manifestations of that. We haven't gotten to ethnicity yet, we're about to get to ethnicity, we haven't gotten to religion yet, but we're beginning to step out [in this direction]. At the point that you're having all this happen, you're moving away from what the field has been going through for 25 years, in which . . . there's no individuation on many, many levels of humanity. The characters have no ethnicity, they have no religion, they have no personal identity on many different levels. They represent the broadest form of stereotype of whatever they might be. The change in terms of disability is sort of a subset of that process, that moment of evolution where we're beginning to say, "In fact, these are people of different life experiences, with different elements going on." (2011)

In fact, examples drawn from the origin stories of several Silver Age characters (from Marvel as well as DC) reveal a landscape rife with marked, disabled bodies linked to the fabulous, unproblematic super-body of convention, with each "haunting" the other.

Thor (*Journey into Mystery*, vol. I, #83, Aug. 1962, Lee/Kirby): lame Dr. Donald Blake stumbles upon the ancient mystic hammer Mjolnir, which when struck upon the ground transforms him into the Norse god of thunder, Thor—minus Blake's limp. The series' odd identity issue—why should a lame doctor, whom Bradford Wright describes as "frail" (213), routinely transform into a majestic long-haired deity?—was finally addressed in "The Answer at Last!" (*The Mighty Thor*, vol. 1, #159, Dec. 1968, Lee/Kirby): Thor's father and ruler of the Norse gods, Odin, *invented* Blake when he exiled his braggart son to Earth, to teach him humility through overcoming: "Though thou art supreme in thy *power*, and thy *pride* . . ." Odin pronounces, "thou must know *weakness* . . . Thou must feel *pain! . . .* [On Earth] shalt thou learn that none can be truly strong unless they be truly humble!" (18, some ellipses and emphasis in original). The tale concludes with Blake realizing: "Even my injured *leg* had an Odinian *purpose* . . . to teach me that any *handicap* can be endured . . . and *overcome!*" (20, ellipses and emphasis in original). The series' double identity trope is resolved, with the alter ego's disability made a necessary psychological component of the superhero's motivation. In the final three panels, Blake stamps his cane on the floor and Thor triumphantly replaces him, as the closing caption all but bellows: "So be it!" (20).

Iron Man (*Tales of Suspense*, vol. 1, #39, Mar. 1963, Lee/Larry Lieber/Don Heck): millionaire industrialist Tony Stark is wounded by a Communist booby trap in South Vietnam, which sends shrapnel on a slow fatal path to his heart. The renegade Red physicist Yin Sen helps him to fashion a body of metal to keep his heart pumping. In order to stay alive, Stark must regularly don the armor and become Iron Man. From the series' inception, Lee stresses on the "tragic" aspects of his protagonist's disability. For example, the opening three pages of "The Uncanny Unicorn!" (*Tales of Suspense*, vol. 1, #56, Aug. 1964, Lee/Heck) find Stark, in his Iron Man armor, demolishing his lab, afflicted over his reliance on technology to sustain his life. Over several panels of property destruction, the following monologue unfurls:

> I'm *sick* of being Iron Man! Sick of having to wear an electronic chest plate 24 hours a day! Sick of living on borrowed time . . . never knowing which moment will be my last!
>
> Inside my iron armor, I'm one of the strongest beings to walk the earth! My transistor-powered strength is capable of almost any task!
>
> The name of I*ron Man* makes strong men tremble!
>
> But what *good* does it do me?? I can never relax . . . Never be without my chest plate . . . never lead a normal life!! (1–2, ellipses and emphasis in original)

The tirade ends with Stark sitting among the rubble and ruined equipment, head in hands:

> *Nobody* can help me! Nobody can repair my damaged heart! Nobody can guarantee how much longer it will keep beating! Nobody can ever know the torment felt by Iron Man!
>
> No! I must continue to live in a shadow world . . . spending half my days as the Golden *Avenger*, and the other as *Anthony Stark*, the envy of a million men . . . but one of the unhappiest humans alive!! (3, ellipses and emphasis in original)

Iron Man/Stark's romantic travails also related to his compromised physical state, which interfered with consummating his love for Pepper Potts.

2.2 Tony Stark/Iron Man afflicted over his reliance on technology to sustain his life (*Tales of Suspense*, vol. 1, #56, Aug. 1964).

(Other would-be couples in the Marvel and DC universes found themselves in the same predicament: Ben Grimm/Alicia Masters; Matt Murdock/Karen Page; Don Blake/Jane Foster; Larry Trainor/Rita Farr; even, early on, Professor X/Jean Grey.)

Doctor Strange (*Strange Tales*, vol. 1, #115, Dec. 1963, Lee/Ditko): Stephen Strange, an arrogant but brilliant surgeon, suffers extensive nerve damage in his hands as a result of a car accident, which ruins his career. In despair, he seeks out "The Ancient One" in India, and this sage takes him on as a student.

Strange eventually becomes Dr. Strange, Master of the Mystic Arts—with no trace of his previous impairment. **Daredevil** (*Daredevil*, vol. 1, #1, Apr. 1964, Lee/Bill Everett): teenager Matt Murdock rescues a blind man from a runaway truck, but a "radioactive canister" falls from the truck onto Murdock's head, robbing him of his sight. Later, Murdock discovers that though blind, his remaining senses operate at superhuman levels, and he has gained a "radar sense." After the gangland murder of his father, intense physical training and a law degree, he takes on the mantle of Daredevil to fight crime. **X-Men** (*X-Men*, vol. I, #1, Sept. 1963, Lee/ Kirby): mutants, born with physical differences, fight to save the world that persecutes them, led by the mysterious wheelchair-using Professor X.[15] **Doom Patrol** (*My Greatest Adventure*, vol. I, #80, Jun. 1963, Arnold Drake/Bruno Premiani): the "world's strangest heroes" band together to protect a world that alienates them, under the leadership of the mysterious wheelchair-using Chief (Niles Caulder).[16]

If disability is (temporarily, imperfectly) wished away by an overcompensating superpower in the case of Thor, Iron Man, and the like, then a second category involves the imposition of disability on an abled person, as in the case of Bruce Banner turning into the **Hulk** (*The Incredible Hulk*, vol. I, #1, May 1962, Lee/Kirby) or Ben Grimm transforming into the **Thing** (*Fantastic Four* #1). In these cases, the superpower itself is both the disability *and* its compensation—another way in which Marvel introduced highly fraught dramatic tension into the superhero genre. In fact, the Silver Age characters by Lee, Kirby, Ditko, Drake, and others problematize their socially determined bodies' relationship with their overcompensating superpowers in ways never seen in Golden Age literature. (Wonder Woman, Batman, Captain America, Green Lantern, The Sub-Mariner, and The Flash are not "disabled" in the aforementioned sense, and only Superman, with his aversion to Kryptonite, can be described as perhaps suffering from an environmental sensitivity.)

The Silver Age introduced disability as a major and consistent component of superhero comics. More than that, this era made it a vital building block of the narrative itself. The present study lays particular stress on the Marvel Silver Age, because it was in the work Lee, Kirby, et al. that we see the earliest examples of disability as repressed, reimagined, obsessed over, even celebrated—sometimes all at once—in a profound rebuke of the customary repression/disavowal model of Golden Age superheroes (and much other prewar literature). Disability fluctuates, growing visible, then invisible, then visible again, becoming both ever-present and haunting. Such a problematizing of physical life added a new wrinkle to the genre's double/secret identity trope: the characters now interact with their shifting bodies as bodies, with all the complications involved. The early Marvel heroes, particularly the disproportionate number with disabled secret identities, are enfleshed as never before in this genre; because they are more complexly portrayed in their psychologies and how they relate to their own physical "flaws," they seem more human.[17]

A SUPERHERO DISABILITY TIMELINE: 1950S–1980S

Let us now consider in greater detail some examples of the Silver and Bronze Age "superhero/supercrip" paradigm that demonstrate the centrality and visuality of disability (and its containment) to characterization and plot in mainstream superhero comics, thereby tracing a pattern over time of increasing inclusion of the disabled experience. As argued, such changing—and ever more progressive—representations of disability in the superhero genre (of both major and supporting characters) reflected in part greater sensitivity to US disability rights activism and demands in the pre-ADA era. To better quantify and situate the depictions, I will use Ato Quayson's typology of disability representation from *Aesthetic Nervousness,* comprised of nine (often overlapping) categories. My sample, while unavoidably selective, is representative both of the disabled's evolving depiction in mainstream superhero narratives, as well as of trends in the culture that led to ever-greater recognition of disability; the sample refracts the disabled's growing visibility and profile in American society over the closing decades of the twentieth century.

"The Girl in Superman's Past" (*Superman,* vol. I, #129, May 1959, Bill Finger/ Wayne Boring). In this "flashback" story, college student Clark Kent suspects his wheelchair-using girlfriend Lori Lemaris of spying for a foreign power, only to discover she is an Atlantean mermaid who uses the wheelchair as a cover for her real identity (and to hide her fish tail). The story bears many of the hallmarks of sentimentalized depictions of disabled people in the era before activist agitation (what Quayson calls "disability as moral test"), foregrounding pathos, overcoming, and the "courage" of living with impairment. As Lemaris explains, "You see, I cannot walk! It is a problem, but I decided not to let it prevent me from leaving my native country to enter your college!" A smitten Kent thinks, "She's a paralysis victim! But this courageous girl hasn't let it stop her from getting an education!" (Gold and Greenberger: 140).

The story, like "Unmasked at Last!" of ten years later, constructs an incompatibility between disability and superheroics—one cancels the other out. Upon deciding to marry this "girl of rare beauty and courage," Kent chooses to reveal his secret identity to Lori and give up a crime-fighting career for love (ibid.: 143).[18] When she refuses, a heartbroken Kent says, "But—if it's because of your legs, that doesn't matter to me! After all, I'm *Superman!* I'll search

2.3 Heroes struggle with various physical impairments in "The Case of the Disabled Justice League!" (*Justice League of America*, vol. 1, #36, June 1965).

the universe for a cure that can make you walk again!" (ibid.: 144, emphasis in original). As seen in this dialogue, Kent's stance towards Lori's condition reflects the medical model of disability; she is sick and in need of a "cure." The restoration of normalcy, the filling of a lack, becomes the hero's fixation and quest.

In "The Girl in Superman's Past," Lori's disability and gender, and the vague Cold War threat embodied by her foreign nationality, add up to a Siren-like menace: her seductive powers can sap the male hero's drive and make him compromise his credo. Moreover, disability here is likened to a supernatural, folkloric state, with centuries of mermaid legends fueling the image of Lori as inhuman (though ironically Kent, an extraterrestrial, is the real alien). This makes it a good example of Quayson's "disability as interface with otherness" category. At the same time, Lemaris's depiction has its progressive aspects: in refusing Kent, she acts as her own woman; she bravely rescues victims of a dam disaster, alongside Superman; and, most importantly, she convinces Kent (along with the reader) that she is not "disabled" at all—merely possessed of a physical difference that actually confers advantages under certain conditions (the ocean), and which with proper accommodations (the saltwater tank she keeps in her bedroom) allows her to function perfectly well on land. The story's overall tone, however, proceeds from its construction of the disabled body as mysterious, gendered, other, and by turns pitiable and "inspiring."

"The Case of the Disabled Justice League!" (*Justice League of America*, vol. I, #36, Jun. 1965, Gardner Fox/Mike Sekowsky). Members of the Justice League of America decide to stage a mock battle with Batman disguised as a monster, for the benefit of disabled children in a hospital ward, who, as their doctor describes it, have "lost the will to fight their afflictions!" (Kawasaki 2007: 497). During the show, the supervillain Brainstorm (for some reason, accompanied by his non-superpowered brother) intervenes, using his meta-abilities to render each of the JLA disabled in some fashion: Green Arrow loses his arms; Superman his vision; Flash has his legs fused together; Hawkman develops asthma; Green Lantern begins to stutter "m-m-mentally as w-well as ph-physically" (ibid.: 500) so that he can't control his power ring. Though at first flummoxed by their physical changes, the team rallies to defeat the villain and inspire the "handicapped patients" to overcome their disabilities. As Hawkman insists, "It'll give us an opportunity to turn this into a valuable object-lesson to those handicapped youngsters watching us . . . Each of us has a handicap to match theirs! When we overcome ours—it will encourage them to overcome their own disabilities!" (ibid.: 502).[19]

Bizarrely, so determined are the heroes to prove themselves individually to the kids, they refuse to cooperate—even though the entire point of the

Justice League is presumably to work together! Hawkman demands, "We must *overcome* our individual handicaps by ourselves!" (ibid.: 503, emphasis in original). Eventually, through adjustments to their fighting styles and use of powers (e.g., Green Arrow fires missiles using his feet and mouth), the team vanquishes Brainstorm (and his brother). The delighted children pledge not to "gripe anymore" and become "even better than we would have been without [their disabilities]." Breaking the "fourth wall," the heroes remind the reader of famous historical figures who surmounted their "afflictions," including Franklin Delano Roosevelt, John Milton, Beethoven, and Pete Gray, one-armed outfielder for the St. Louis Browns. The story closes with a paean to tolerance, a pact written by Flash on a scroll unfurled over portraits of more famous disabled personages (e.g., Helen Keller). The pact swears:

1. That we shall meet those among us who are physically handicapped, as fully our equals . . .
2. That we shall control our feeling of pity, as *they* would want it controlled, and treat them as they want to be treated: not as people apart, but as people normal and intelligent, and desirous of making their own way in life as a result of their own efforts. (ibid.: 519, ellipses and emphasis in original)

"The Case of the Disabled Justice League" makes plain the profoundly paradoxical, didactic, well-intended, and offensive treatment of disability in the early Silver Age, before the characterological innovations mentioned previously had taken hold. Despite the progressive language in its "pact," it is very much a throwback to an earlier era[20] in its infantilization of the disabled, obsessive focus on "overcoming" (the word appears three times on one page, 503), and cheerful acclamations to American individualism and the "can-do" spirit. It posits "no griping" as an antidote to "affliction." (We see disability here not as a social problem to be addressed through legislative or collective action, but rather as a personal matter—of one's own "attitude.")

And while Fox and Sekowsky routinely used similarly absurd situations in their plots (such as the JLA fighting its own clothes), the "real world" issue of disability here makes such an approach exceedingly distasteful. The depiction of Green Lantern's condition seems especially crude, premised on the false notion of stuttering as somehow a failure of the will (through which Green Lanterns control their power rings). Preposterously, GL even stammers in his thought balloons, musing, "S-sure am g-glad my *m-m-muscles* d-don't s-s-stutter!" (ibid.: 506, emphasis in original). The story, like others in Quayson's "moral test" category, ultimately achieves the opposite of its stated aims: in presenting the disabled as helpless children who need heroes to fight for them (they are reduced to watching the battle on a screen in their hospital ward),

2.4 Lessons learned in the conclusion to "The Case of the Disabled Justice League!" (*Justice League of America*, vol. I, #36, June 1965).

the authors shower them with ill-concealed contempt, making their opening lines ring especially hollow: "How much braver they have to be, to confront the world about them without sight – or hearing – or the lack of an arm or leg!" (ibid.: 495). Worse, and despite its good intentions, it makes of disability little more than a spectacle—a gimmick (something that applies equally well to the children as to the "disabled" heroes).

"The Origin of Metamorpho" (*The Brave and the Bold*, vol. I, #57, Jan. 1965, Bob Haney/Ramona Fradon). In this DC series, Rex Mason, daredevil and "wonderful, crazy, reckless, marvelous . . . hunk of man" (Greenberger: 9, ellipses in original), runs afoul of his employer, the tycoon Simon Stagg, who sends him on a mission to Egypt to retrieve the mystical Orb of Ra. Betrayed by his partner, Mason is exposed to an ancient meteorite's radiation, which transforms him into a being capable of willing himself into any element. But the energy also renders his body freakish, a patchwork of multicolored, scaly flesh. Though in many respects a broad parody of superhero narratives drawn in a "cartoony" style, this Metamorpho tale reflects some of the Silver Age's innovations in regard to character psychology and "body issues."

As with Lori Lemaris, we still see an emphasis on disability as sickness: Mason demands Stagg restore him to normal, saying, "We're going to find a cure for this somehow . . . sometime!" (ibid.: 22, ellipsis in original). Similarly, romance becomes dauntingly difficult for Mason as a result of his new condition; as he tells his lover Sapphire, "But, honey . . . You can't tie your life to a freak—a walking chemistry set!" (ibid.: 24, ellipsis in original). However, as with the blind Alicia Masters's devotion to Ben Grimm in the concurrent competitor Marvel series *Fantastic Four*, Sapphire surprises Mason by not rejecting him, saying, "Oh, Rex, don't you see? You can *use* these great powers you have—for *good*—until the day we find a cure!" He replies, "I—I never thought of that, baby! You're right . . . I've got to make the best of it! And I will—if you stick by me, sweetheart!" (ibid.: 25, emphasis and ellipsis in original).

Strikingly, "The Origin of Metamorpho" demonstrates how the paradigm of the "tragically deformed" superhero had taken hold by the mid-1960s. With figures such as Grimm, several of the X-Men, and Cliff Steele of Doom Patrol having set the pattern earlier, Metamorpho's authors are free to lightly satirize the (always male) monster/hero. Both Sapphire and Mason in fact get past their initial trauma over the change remarkably fast: she goes from fainting in horror at her fiancée's altered form to pledging her steadfast love within four pages; he goes from despising his new body to sunny optimism about his powers within two panels. This puts Metamorpho's origin in Quayson's "disability as epiphany" category, for how it—parodically—reveals to Mason his true potential as a hero.[21]

"Brother, Take My Hand!" (*Daredevil*, vol. I, #47, Dec. 1968, Lee/Gene Colan). The blind lawyer Matt Murdock helps a blind Vietnam veteran, Willie Lincoln, beat a false bribery charge, while Murdock's alter ego defends him from the mob. While somewhat maudlin in its depiction of the African-American vet, the story brings a fresh, more mature perspective on the plight of disabled people, the injured of America's ongoing Southeast Asia conflict, and racial minorities. Lincoln's depression and isolation is alleviated by Murdock's encouragement that he can indeed reintegrate into society. Lee and Colan set up many parallels between their protagonist and Lincoln; the composition of the cover suggests the vet, with his cane and dark glasses, "transforms" into the superhero. Disability creates a sort of community, shared identity or brotherhood, as underscored by the title. The story ends with Lincoln pondering whether he should return to the police force, his previous civilian job. The innovations and social realism of "Brother, Take My Hand!" land it in Quayson's "moral test," "interface with otherness," and "normality" categories.

"A Vow from the Grave!" (*Detective Comics*, vol. I, #410, Apr. 1971, Denny O'Neil/Neal Adams). In pursuit, through a forbidding forest, of the fugitive murderer Kano Wiggins, Batman encounters a family of "human oddities": acromegalic Goliath, skinny man Charley Bones, fat lady Maud, and mute Flippy, who crawls on the ground due to his flipper-like limbs. While in many ways a standard "good vs. evil" scenario, O'Neil and Adams's story exemplifies their forays into socially conscious subject matter in the early 1970s, an attempt "to advance the creative and commercial potential of comic books" (Wright: 227).[22] The approach colors not only their depiction of the "freakish" characters, but page design as well.

On their initial meeting, the carnival sideshow family is frightened of Batman after he has "whipped Goliath"; Maud cowers: "Is that a *man*—or some kinda *bird? Whatever* it is—it *scares* me!" (Levitz 1978: 4, emphasis in original). The superhero appears as himself, a brand of "freak." The panel shape—shorter and "stubbed" with a caption that stands out from the border into white space—mirrors the ambiguity of the bodies on display. The next page's design carries this conceit even further: Adam's oddly disjointed panels seem to clash with each other; the dominant panel leaves a "tail" of empty space that reproduces the shape of Flippy's body (ibid.: 5). This and other "oddities" of Adam's page compositions and storytelling signal a link between disability, representation, and "deviance," what Quayson terms "disability as articulation of disjuncture between thematic and narrative vectors" (41). Furthermore, through Flippy's mostly "tragic" appearance—though he does supply Batman with a critical clue to crack the case—the tale betrays aspects of the "disability as moral test" model: when Goliath says of Flippy, "Nature short-changed the tyke worse'n the rest of us—He can't talk . . . an' he's not too bright in the head!" (Levitz 1978: 7, ellipsis in original), the child looks on with a piteous expression.[23]

All the same, "A Vow from the Grave!" represents a fascinating transitional moment in the superhero genre's depiction of disability. The "monsters" prove more psychologically complex; they act out of good (Bones, Flippy, Maud) and evil (Goliath). Flippy's condition alludes to the 1960s thalidomide disaster, which resulted in similar congenital deformities for thousands of babies worldwide; his body's origins are social, not "supernatural." The story functions as a sort of genre amalgam as well, combining superheroic action with EC horror-type atmosphere (though none of the humor). Finally, the normate-bodied murderer Kano stands revealed, due to his unrepentant evil and sadism, as the most inhuman of figures. The criminal scoffs, "*Hah!*—The

2.5 Baroque page/panel design leaves a "tail" of empty space that parallels the shape of Flippy's body in "A Vow From the Grave!" (*Detective Comics*, vol. I, #410, Apr. 1971).

great *Batman* goin' soft for a bunch of scruffy *freaks!*" But the dark knight replies, looking at the "freak" family: "Courage—and *love*—come in strange shapes . . . But you wouldn't understand that, Kano – you just wouldn't understand!" (ibid.: 15, emphasis and ellipsis in original). The story incorporates elements of so many of Quayson's categories – disability "as moral test," "as interface with otherness," "as disjuncture of thematic/narrative vectors," even, in its conclusion, "as normality"—as to constitute a hybrid; "disability" is no longer "easy" to label. "A Vow from the Grave!" conveys that, like the carnival sideshows which the "freak family" inhabit in the national collective unconscious, the dismissal of the disabled as merely monstrous or pitiful is an anachronism.

"Cyborg" (*Tales of the New Teen Titans*, vol. I, #1, Jun. 1982, Marv Wolfman/ George Pérez). The first in a miniseries devoted to the origin stories of *New*

Teen Titans members (and capitalizing on that series' success), "Cyborg" re-counts the biography of Victor Stone, whose scientist parents' research into other dimensions releases a burning slime creature which kills Stone's mother and horribly disfigures him. Stone's father, a weapons research scientist, re-builds his son into a cyborg warrior. Bearing many resemblances to the origin of *Doom Patrol's* Cliff Steele/Robotman (examined in chapter 5), Cyborg's tale evinces a new emphasis on the psychological labor of "overcoming" massive injury, as well as a graphic depiction of trauma, recovery and adjustment to new physical realities. No less significantly, Cyborg, a major new African-American character, introduced race into the discussion of disability in the genre (explored further in chapter 4). The foregoing places the story, follow-ing Quayson, in the categories of disability as "inarticulate and enigmatic tragic insight" and as "normality"—unprecedentedly so for this genre.

"The Price" (*Daredevil*, vol. 1, #223, Oct. 1985, O'Neil/Jim Shooter/Dave Maz-zuchelli). This remarkable stand-alone story demonstrates the ways *Daredevil* presented the most progressive image of disability in superhero comics to that point. Daredevil's alter ego, Matt Murdock, a highly successful lawyer who happens to be blind, has long accepted his physical difference with equa-nimity and grace, to the point that he deems it vital to his sense of self. Invert-ing conventional symbolism, he even fashions a blind man's walking stick (the ultimate signifier of weakness) into a weapon, his "billy club."

A poignant chapter in the *Secret Wars II* multi-title crossover series, "The Price" recounts how, through the genre's typically ludicrous and convoluted set of circumstances, the omnipotent alien Beyonder restores Murdock's sight. For a day, he and love interest Glorianna tour his native New York City, which Murdock has not actually seen since his adolescence. Though overwhelmed by the visual beauty of the world opened up to him, Murdock nonetheless resolves to give up this gift of vision out of duty to his "profound sense of jus-tice." He says, grimly, "There's no place for anything that compromises it—or *might* compromise it" (20, emphasis in original). Murdock renounces sight because of its threat to his integrity and identity, founded on his disability, which the supercrip would try to somehow "transcend." Murdock refuses the gift of vision even as the Beyonder relinquishes his hold over him. Puzzled, the omnipotent being utters, "Why should you suffer such *incompleteness?*" (21, my emphasis). Murdock answers, "Take it back. Or I'll *sue*" (ibid., empha-sis in original).

"The Price's" devastatingly conveyed moral is that Murdock is *not* in any way "incomplete." The supercrip mentality is turned on its head: the hero re-claims his personhood precisely by *not* seeking to overcome a widely per-ceived lack, but by "staying true" to his sense of self with all its "imperfections."

2.6 A sighted Matt Murdock/Daredevil demands the Beyonder restore his blindness (*Daredevil*, vol. 1, #223, Oct. 1985).

(This, of course, is an unusual fable in a genre long dominated by "overcompensating superpowers" conventions, which leads to some paradoxes: even as Murdock loses his sight again, he retains his radar, hypersenses and superior fighting skills.) We have entered the realm of disability as identity politics, away from an assimilationist model of culture to more of an ethnic pride paradigm—precisely the model pursued by American disability rights activists in their march to the 1990 legislative triumph of the ADA. O'Neil, Shooter, and Mazzucchelli's parable also raises questions relevant to debates on "fixing" the disabled, for example those in the deaf community regarding cochlear implants (which some have resisted as a eugenicist affront to deaf culture).[24] Like no superhero story before it, "The Price" fits into Quayson's categories of "interface with otherness (race, class, social identity)" and "normality."

"In Blackest Night" (*Green Lantern Annual*, vol. 1, #3, May 1987, Alan Moore/ Bill Willingham). A perversely clever short story featuring the supporting character Katma Tui of the Green Lantern Corps, "In Blackest Night" allegorizes two pillars of disability theory: the social model and accommodation. Seeking to recruit a new Green Lantern in a lightless void called the Obsidian Deeps, Tui befriends the native silicone life form, Rot Lop Fan, and offers him membership in the Corps. But there is one big problem. To her shock, Tui discovers that, living in an abyss, Fan has no eyes, and the concepts of light and color hold no meaning for his species. Consequently, the translator function of Tui's power ring utterly fails to convey the phrase "the Green Lantern Corps" into Fan's language, rendering it "the (untranslatable) Corps" (3). Similarly, it turns the Green Lantern oath, with lines such as "brightest day" and "escape my sight," into an opaque mass of "(untranslatable)." "Mmm," responds a bemused Fan to Tui's futile efforts. "Perhaps it *loses* something" (4, emphasis in original).

Tui solves the dilemma through an inspired act of cultural translation: she tells Fan to imagine himself not as a Green Lantern but as an "F-Sharp Bell," part of a galactic peace-keeping corps that uses "power bells" to manipulate sound waves into energy patterns for defense. To periodically recharge the bell, Tui explains that Fan must use a sort of "tuning fork" (actually a GL power battery) and recite the modified oath: "In loudest din or hush profound/my ears catch evil's slightest sound/Let those who toll out evil's knell/Beware my power: the F-Sharp Bell!" (6).[25]

Moore and Willingham's story elegantly and brilliantly illustrates how environments *construct* what we call "disability," which, as Tobin Siebers puts it, "is technically invisible until it becomes visible under the pressure of social convention" (2010: 129). Or, as he writes elsewhere, "Constructions are built with social bodies in mind, and when a different body appears, the lack of fit reveals the ideology of ability controlling the space. The presence of a wheel-chair at the Polk County courthouse exposes a set of social facts about the building" (2008: 124). "In Blackest Night" also points the way to a social/environmental solution to the "problem" of disability: adjustment and accommodation (an approach codified in the ADA, however imperfectly implemented).[26] More boldly, Moore's script challenges the ableist presumptions in Tui's language—and the reader's, which as Brueggeman, et al., argue "is laden with metaphors of ability." They offer such examples as "sight equaling insight"; "turning deaf ears" and "coming up with 'lame ideas'" (2001: 369).[27] An important part of disability activism and scholarship, she adds, echoing Mitchell and Snyder, is one of "making the invisible visible and of examining how language both reflects and supports notions of Other" (371).

That is precisely what "In Blackest Night" does, through its fantastic science-fiction setting and by (humorously) drawing attention to the perception-shaping power of words. Filled with puns and sly linguistic turns, the story pivots on Tui's realization that "ring" (noun), source of a Green Lantern's power, can also be interpreted as "ring" (verb)—something which dawns on her when Fan uses the phrase "ring of truth" (4).[28] Other language games abound: the tale opens with Tui—in a willfully mysterious mood—announcing to her overseers, the Guardians, a kind of riddle: that she succeeded in recruiting a protector for the Obsidian Deeps, but he is not a Green Lantern. The recounting of her adventure serves as explanation of that odd utterance. Moreover, Fan's aural-centric speech is filled with reworkings of familiar ocularcentric clichés, e.g., "By the *Primal Chime!* Will you listen to *that!*" (5, emphasis in original). Moore even parodies and inverts the conventional "commiserating" discourse often aimed at the disabled: after touching her face, Fan says to Tui, "Such a terrible pity that you should bear this tactile deformity. Your *voice* sounds so kind . . ." (3, ellipsis and emphasis in the original). Tui, after all, is the alien life form on Fan's lightless planet, with an "inadequate" body: "I cannot say what it was like," she tells the Guardians, ". . . I saw no more than a searchlight's width of it at any given time" (2, ellipsis in original).

Thus, the story prompts a rethinking of assumptions critical to disability theory: about spaces and bodies (what they are, what they do); about what kind of life is worth living; about the "invisible," ideologized nature of discourse. All the same, Moore and Willingham reproduce some ableist presumptions themselves: Fan has vestigial eyes (disability as lack or defect); he seems oddly unable to perceive others unless they speak (the disabled as helpless); while Tui's "solution" carries a whiff of colonialism: her inspired act of translation is also a trick at Fan's expense—she even chooses not to tell him of the power ring/bell's vulnerability to the color yellow, which would seem some crucial information to omit, even in a dark cosmos (6). Nonetheless, we

2.7 Katma Tui inducts the blind Rot Lop Fan into the Green Lantern Corps as the "F-Sharp Bell": "In Blackest Night" (*Green Lantern Annual*, vol. 1, #3, May 1987).

have clearly come a long way since "The Case of the Disabled Justice League." Corporeal/cognitive difference here functions not as something to be pitied or overcome; rather, the reorganization of environments (social, physical, mental) is vital to unlocking the hidden potential always already there. These features place the story most securely in Quayson's "disability as normality" category.

"Lost Love" (*Superman*, vol. 2, #12, Dec. 1987, John Byrne). An episode in the post-*Crisis on Infinite Earths* reconfiguration of DC continuity,[29] this story refashions and updates the Superman/Lori Lemaris plot of 1959. Both homage and amendment, "Lost Love" reproduces much of the language of the original, but also enhances the tragic mood: we learn at the beginning of the story that Lemaris has already died.[30] The tale also serves as a document of progress in the representation of the disabled since its predecessor: evidence of accommodation and access three years before the ADA—such as the wheelchair ramp attached to Lori's trailer home—are prominent; though their love is still doomed, Kent and Lemaris are able to openly date, even kiss, and their romance becomes "the talk of the school" (10); partly because Byrne resets the story to a time before Kent assumes the identity of Superman, there no longer exists an incompatibility between superheroics and disability, so in this version Kent does not offer to give up crime-fighting for Lori's sake.

Most critically, the original's emphasis on disability as sickness has nearly vanished—it appears only to be rebuffed. While Clark still thinks of Lori as a "brave girl" (6), his offer to find a cure literally dies on his lips: "Is it because of your *paralysis?*" he says. "You know that doesn't affect the way I feel about you. But . . . I could search the whole world . . ." (emphasis and ellipsis in original, 11). Lori's response to this is to coldly ask to be taken home. On the other hand, the question of pitying the disabled remains a conspicuous facet, touched on when Lori explains why they can never be together: "It was more *pity* than love that drew you to me, Clark. You saw what you thought was a brave, crippled girl fighting to overcome her handicap. The image touched your heart, and you mistook it for love . . . as did I" (emphasis and ellipsis in original, 19).

So, while the changes are more than superficial, the tone more serious, "Lost Love" retains the central message of "The Girl in Superman's Past": romance between the disabled and able-bodied is foredoomed and impossible. Byrne underscores this by having Lori fall in love instead with one of her own kind, the merman surgeon Ronal (who, ironically, cures her of paralysis). Such mixed messages make the story a combination of various Quayson categories: disability "as moral test," as the interface with otherness," "as enigmatic tragic insight," "as normality." Such complexity coming at the end of this (admittedly selective) timeline indicates, if nothing else, that the representation of the disabled in mainstream superhero comics had, by the late 1980s, undergone some fundamental changes, while also clinging to vestiges of a problematic past.

In the nearly three decades that divide "The Girl in Superman's Past" and "Lost Love," America's disabled went through a remarkable shift in both media and political representation. They became more "visible," on their own terms. Despite cultural backlashes against such change, dismissive ridicule of the perceived excesses of "political correctness," and characterizations of disability as "the straw that breaks the camel's back of identity politics" (Mitchell and Snyder 2000: 35), the trend went in the direction of greater rights, access and autonomy for the "shadow population." The year of breakthrough was 1990, when the legal reality of the ADA cemented gains borne of an entire generation's struggle.

As a consequence of all this, the appearance of disability in mainstream superhero comics of the Silver and Bronze ages—the time period covered in this book—went from mostly single-note exercises in "moral test" sentimentality to (in the best cases) much more complex portraits of individuals. Though traces of older approaches remained, writers and readers could less easily take disability for granted as a marker of pity or "courage"; testament to this was, if nothing else, the sheer variety of personality and outlook embodied by disabled Bronze Age characters such as Box and Puck from *Alpha Flight*; the Avengers' Hawkeye (who suffers hearing loss in battle);[31] Cloak of *Cloak and Dagger*; the *Teen Titans'* Jericho and Cyborg; 3-D Man; Human Fly; the Shroud; Stick from *Daredevil*; She-Thing; Tom Thumb of *Squadron Supreme*; and others, up to and including arguably the most complex of all, Oracle, aka Barbara Gordon. (To say nothing of revisionist heroes such as the amputee Oliver in Frank Miller's *The Dark Knight Returns* [1986]; the mentally ill Rorschach in Alan Moore/Dave Gibbons' *Watchmen* [1986]; and Grant Morrison, et al.'s, revamped *Doom Patrol* [late 1980s/early 1990s].) The old models no longer held firm sway; it was a new, post-feminist, post-masculine-crisis, post-pity moment.

In sum: at the dawn of the Silver Age, the superhero's often-disabled alter ego came to incarnate the phallus-wilting tensions of postwar America, only to be magically exorcised, replaced with the usual invulnerability and potency. But the dramatic thrust of Silver Age stories demanded that the "problem" routinely reappear (like an uninvited house guest in a wheelchair), becoming central to the storyline. "Borderline cases" (the Hulk, the Thing) went even further, foregrounding the "problem" of excess, uncontrolled bodies, acting as generic destabilizing forces, as challenges to the comfortably fantastic prowess of the "reconstituted" white male (as examined in chapter 4).

Logically enough, it is left to the supervillain, another sort of vital, structuring Other to the genre itself, to bring the ultimate "destabilizing force" to bear—and his threat operates most devastatingly through the "deviant" visuality of his body.

DISABILITY AND THE SILVER AGE SUPERVILLAIN

In turning to the supervillain, one might expect a fairly straightforward, streamlined, or simplified task of reading in relation to that of the disability-denying superhero. After all, virtually all supervillains of the Silver Age and after, even more so than their heroic counterparts, come off as blatant caricatures: cackling, hand-rubbing megalomaniacs uniformly bent on world domination, often misshapen in some way, motivated exclusively by power-lust and/or greed. As foils, they play a vital oppositional role in the genre, often acting as "engines of diachronic continuity" (Reynolds: 50) to the heroes' "status quo" inclinations.[32] Peter Coogan sees them as inversions of the superhero, with their own "selfish, anti-social" mission (77) tied to a "personal defect" (79) which spawns a "superiority complex" (83).

Moreover, supervillains—following the Gothic tradition of revealing the inner deformity of the soul through the disfigurement or spectacular otherness of the body—simplistically reify the ableist reader's unconscious anxieties and prejudices regarding difference (racial, gender-related, nationalist, class-based, or physical).[33] As Paul Longmore characterizes it:

> Physical handicaps are made the emblems of evil. . . . Giving disabilities to villainous characters reflects and reinforces, albeit in exaggerated fashion, three common prejudices against handicapped people: disability is a punishment for evil; disabled people are embittered by their "fate"; disabled people resent the nondisabled and would, if they could, destroy them. In historic and contemporary social fact, it is, of course, nondisabled people who have at times endeavored to destroy people with disabilities. As with popular portrayals of other minorities, the unacknowledged hostile fantasies of the stigmatizers are transferred to the stigmatized. (2003: 133–34)

Several scholars have characterized the villain as bearer of aspects (moral, ideological, corporeal) which the hero disavows.[34] Such a status grants the villain tremendous freedom but also condemns him to isolation and inhumanity.[35] This transgressive outsider status corresponds to a significant degree with that of disabled people, long considered "historical scapegoats" (Mitchell/Snyder 2000: 20). Such thinking has naturalized the notion of deformed and disabled figures as villains, what Quayson terms "disability as bearer of moral deficit/evil" (42). In sum: "villainous" disabled characters often cited by disability scholars, such as Ahab, Captain Hook, Dr. No, and Dr. Strangelove, seem possessed of traits straight out of the ableist's worst nightmare: malformed, malevolent, mighty.

Golden Age supervillains—such as Batman's enemies, the Joker, Two-Face, and Penguin—typically manifest the "deformed malefactor" type, while the Marvel Silver Age's first supervillain, the Mole Man, makes society's contempt for the misshapen the originary motivation for his evil plans to rule Earth. In "The Fantastic Four!" (*Fantastic Four*, vol. 1, #1, 1961), Mole Man—only subsequently was his true name, Harvey Rupert Elder, revealed—recounts his story: shunned by his peers, who mock his stunted, large-nosed appearance, he flees society in search of the earth's center, where a fall causes him to lose most of his vision but where he eventually gains control of an army of monsters with which to terrorize the surface world.

Kirby's layout on the page illustrating the villain's biography underscores, through contrasting portraits and panel size, the isolation and loathing he suffers. At top left, the Mole Man's tiny head begins his sorry tale of an outcast, while immediately below three small horizontal panels show different "normal" people's cruel reactions to him, as they stare directly at the reader: "What? *Me* go out with *you?*" a woman says. "Don't make me laugh!"; "I *know* you're qualified, but you can't work here!" scoffs a suited gentleman. "You'd scare our other employees away!"; "Hey, is that your face, or are you wearin' a mask? Haw haw!" jokes a caddish-looking fellow (22, emphasis in original). The direct address puts the reader in the villain's place, to witness firsthand the public's "bad staring" at the physically different, which as Garland-Thomson (referencing Susan Sontag) notes, "fails to make the leap from a place of discomfort, shock or fear toward empathetic identification" (2009: 187).

The next four panels depict Mole Man (in medium and long shot) traversing desolate regions of the earth on his quest, while in the last panel—when he has found the earth's center after his fall and blinding—his face appears in close-up, with impressionistic shadows, against a red background of "power lines." "I was *stranded* here . . ." he concludes, "like a human mole!!" (ibid., ellipsis and emphasis in original). The large, close-up portrait (the most intimate picture yet of Mole Man's face) stands in opposition to, and in a sense supersedes, the many smaller, diverse images of him and the normals elsewhere on

2.8 The origin of the Mole Man (*Fantastic Four*, vol. 1, #1, Nov. 1961).

the page; it seems to announce that he has found his true, unified identity and purpose at last—a purpose beyond the petty, hurtful prejudice of those who scorned him.

The effect is one of transformation, from the tiny upper-left head shot of Mole Man in the same visual space as the normals (though due to his visor and cowl still standing apart from them) to the dominant large close-up portrait of his new, blind, triumphant self at bottom right. The page functions as a visual chronicle of abreaction to trauma; moreover, the water, cave, and tunnel imagery identify it as a scene of rebirth—the impressionistic shadows on Mole Man's final rendering make him, among other things, resemble a neonate. The deformed supervillain: conceived, born of, shaped by "normate" derision, with no place among humanity.[36] Kirby's layouts convey, not without sympathy, the villain's compelled outsider position. As Reed says in the story's closing panel, after the Mole Man has presumably perished, "There was no place for him in our world" (25).[37]

Other Silver Age villains undergo similar transformations from disabled alter ego to grotesque fiend, such as Curt Connors turning into the Lizard (first appearance *Spider-Man*, vol. 1, #6, Nov. 1963) and Kirk Langstrom becoming Man-Bat (*Detective Comics*, vol. I, #400, Jun. 1970)—in both cases, it is the experiments these scientists perform to cure their impairments (Connors wants to restore an arm lost in war, Langstrom wants to keep from going deaf) that lead to the creation of their evil identities.[38] The Brain (*Doom Patrol*, vol. I, #86, May 1964) represents an extreme case of this type: a lab accident reduces the unnamed scientist to a brain floating in a nutrient bath, wreaking vengeance on the world entirely through technology and second parties—a malevolent near-total amputee/quadriplegic (as further examined in chapter 5).

In short, disabled supervillains in the Silver Age evince some of the innovations in psychological complexity observed in the heroes, and in some cases share in the dramatic pathos of figures like Ben Grimm or the Hulk. But they of course go much further in their bitter reactions to the injustices they suffer, while the needs of the genre for antagonists and moral nemeses imposes strict limits on sympathy for their plight.[39]

THE FACE OF DOOM

Garland-Thomson identifies the disabled villain as a distortion of American values, a sort of hyper-individualist gone amok, both morally and physically. Melville's Captain Ahab, whom she calls "perhaps the quintessential disabled figure in American literature" (1997: 44), conjures in the reader both a sublime admiration and terror through his superhuman obsession and Nietszchean will to power. At the same time, his amputated limb flouts notions of autonomy and physical perfection central to US identity, as previously discussed. The captain thus constitutes a monstrous contradiction:

> Ahab is, perhaps above all else, different from other men. At once compelling and repelling, he represents both the prospective freedom of nonconformity and the terrible threat of antinomianism. The outer mark of his difference is his ivory leg, and the inner manifestation is his monomaniacal fury. . . . [But h]is disabled body testifies to the self's physical vulnerability, the ominous knowledge that the ideology of individualism suppresses. (1997: 45)

Such attributes appertain to the foreign-born Silver Age tyrant Doctor Doom, arch-enemy of the Fantastic Four, whose bodily deformity seems of a piece with his anti-American threat—and, I will argue, incarnates a "gender threat" as well. In his "origin story" (*Fantastic Four Annual*, vol. I, #2, Sept. 1964, Lee/Kirby), Doom first appears as an angelic Gypsy boy in the Central European country of Latveria. When his father, a renowned healer, is killed by the reigning monarch, young Victor Von Doom swears that "all mankind shall pay" for the murder of his parents. The boy soon learns that his slain mother was a great witch, and embarks on learning the family trade, despite the misgivings of his kinsman Boris (Watson: 5).

Victor grows into a handsome swindler with the "features of a demi-god and the cunning of a demon!" (ibid.), wreaking vengeance on all Latveria by selling people bogus "trick" merchandise. He also displays a tremendous talent for creating duplicate selves, in the form of ultra-realistic androids. He eventually winds up at State University in America, where the arrogant Doom coldly rebuffs a bright freshman, Reed Richards, and his offer to room together. To his misfortune, Doom also rejects Reed's advice that he recheck some miscalculations on a secret science project involving "matter transmutation and dimension warps"—the machine blows up, disfiguring the once-handsome foreigner and getting him expelled.[40]

Devastated by his deformity, Doom vows to hide his visage from the world, and joins a mysterious order of monks in the Tibetan mountains. He ultimately takes over the sect and has them fashion an imposing suit of armor for him, with a dread iron mask to forever conceal his ravaged face. So anxious is Doom to don the facial covering that he orders it seared, still hot from the forge, onto his bare flesh. From that moment, Doom declares himself reborn as the scourge of a world that hated and vilified him, pledging to take over first his home country of Latveria and then dominate all mankind.[41]

Dr. Doom falls in with the standard literary representation of the "monstrous" disabled, whose physical differences, Longmore notes, "typically involve disfigurement of the face and head and gross deformity of the body . . . [expressing] disfigurement of personality and deformity of soul. Once again, disability may be represented as the cause of evildoing, punishment for it, or both" (2003: 135). All this in spite of the possibility that Doom's original "disfigurement" in the experiment gone wrong may not have been so severe after all. "Some have speculated," writes Tom Brevoort in the introduction to *The Villainy of Doctor Doom*,

> that, if you were to peel away that cold metal and take a gander at the features underneath, you'd see only the slightest scar marring an otherwise handsome visage—but that tiny imperfection is all it took to drive Doom to a life of villainy and hatred. (Watson: iii)

Yet even if this were the case, the hyper-narcissistic Doom still subsequently chooses to destroy his slightly damaged face with the burning mask rather than tolerate a "tiny imperfection," thereby reinscribing ableist prejudices of the body's perfectibility.[42] That Doom never gives up those prejudices is reflected in his maniacal obsession with restoring his "perfect" face—but always in some exterior imago. In the 1978 "Overthrow of Doom" storyline by Marv Wolfman/Keith Pollard and others, he fashions a statue of himself that will "set the new standards for masculine beauty throughout the globe" (*Fantastic Four*, vol. 1, #85: 16); clones himself a "son," emphasizing his beauty (*Fantastic Four*, vol. 1, #199: 30); and uses another (unscarred) statue of himself to control the world through mesmerism (*Fantastic Four*, vol. 1, #200: 37).

Despite such schemes, Doom clings just as obsessively to the safety of his mask, even *sleeping* in it (*Astonishing Tales*, #4, Feb. 1971: 5, 7). He often cites his disfigurement as the source of all his failures and misfortunes in life (e.g., *Fantastic Four*, #200: 22, 43; *Fantastic Four*, #199: 23), even comparing it to the Thing's ugliness (*Fantastic Four*, #198: 15).

How to resolve these fraught views of Doom's face/mask—by Doom himself? How can Doom despise the very features that have driven him not only to madness, but, on several occasions, to the brink of world domination? Has he indeed followed in the footsteps of tragic literary deformities like Frankenstein's monster, Quasimodo, Polyphemus? We can answer through a reading of a climactic chapter in Doom's history, as well as the techniques used to portray Doom's face since Kirby's time; for what lies behind Doom's mask has resonances for several Silver Age supervillains.

First of all, we can say that ambiguity remains over the exact nature of Doom's initial injury in his college lab explosion because—in one of the great

2.9 Kirby depicts Doom without showing his disfigured face (*Fantastic Four*, vol. I, #85, Apr. 1969).

2.10 Doom first dons his mask—searing his face (*Fantastic Four Annual*, vol. I, #2, Sept. 1964).

"in-jokes" of superhero comics—his face has almost never been depicted post-blast.[43] For example, in "Within This Tortured Land" (*Fantastic Four*, vol. I, #85, Apr. 1969, Lee/Kirby), when Doom poses for a portrait, Kirby draws him holding a mirror over his face (17). But much earlier, in the origin story, we can already observe Kirby progressively obscuring Doom's face with various props as the fateful moment of the accident approaches. By the page before the explosion, Doom's face, as visual element, has clearly transcended the mere storyline and entered another signifying realm (Watson: 9, 10, 11). The first time Doom "turns" to the reader after the accident, in fact, he is wearing his new mask, declaring, "From this moment on, there *is* no Victor Von Doom! He has vanished . . . But in his place there shall be another . . . Dr. Doom!" (ibid.: 11, ellipses in original). What is it that remains forever off-frame or concealed by Doom's imposing mask? What is the face of Doom?

As pointed out by art and drama historians, the word "person" derives from the ancient Greek "persona," which described the masks actors donned during classical dramatic performances. "*Persona*, 'the mask,' is related to personality, the self or ego we reveal to the world," writes George Ulrich. "Masks have the ability to conceal, change, or transform the 'person' behind the image into something or someone else other than who we are."

In the case of Doom, the iron mask concealing his "ravaged" features—which no Silver Age reader had ever seen—works to hide another iconic emblem of classical myth: the gaze of the medusa. Disability scholar Lennard Davis has likened the act of seeing the disabled to the dread and fascination of the horrid Gorgon, whose countenance petrified its victims:

The "normal" person sees the disabled person and is turned to stone, in some sense, by the visual interaction. In this moment, the normal person suddenly feels self-conscious, rigid, unable to look. The visual field becomes problematic, dangerous, treacherous. The disability becomes a power derived from its otherness, its monstrosity, in the eyes of the "normal" person. (1997B: 55)

Something similar to this seems to happen on the few occasions when Doom slips his guard and allows others to see him without his mask, as when Sue Richards, the Invisible Woman, catches a glimpse of his face—and is stupefied (*Fantastic Four*, vol. 1, #236, Nov. 1981: 35). Yet, like the basilisk, Doom seems the most susceptible of all to the horrid spectacle of his own destroyed visage. Davis further relates the act of gazing upon the radical otherness of the disabled body to a regressive episode, a return to the Lacanian mirror stage, in which the child initially experiences the body as fragmentary, with discreet and uncoordinated organs and limbs. Only by taking on an "armor" (read: "identity") and entering the Symbolic Order does he manage to contain that threat of fragmentation.

But the different, disabled corpus inverts that process, forming

a direct imago of the repressed fragmented body. The disabled body causes a kind of hallucination of the mirror phase gone wrong. The subject looks at the disabled body and has a moment of cognitive dissonance, or . . . cognitive resonance with the earlier state of fragmentation. . . . Rather than seeing the object of desire, as controlled by the Other, the subject sees the true self of the fragmented body. (1997B: 60)

This description lends itself to a productive interpretation of a climactic scene in "When Titans Clash!" the culmination of the epic "Overthrow of Doom" arc by Wolfman and Pollard (*Fantastic Four*, #200, Nov. 1978). In the story, an infuriated Doom sees his various schemes to make a perfect, unscarred clone of himself who will "inherit" the throne of Latveria; to telepathically dominate the United Nations (and hence the world) through a specially equipped statue of himself (again, without the scarred face); and last but not least, to destroy the hated Fantastic Four, all fail. In a final, bare-knuckle, no-holds-barred showdown with Reed Richards (aka Mr. Fantastic), Doom is stripped of his mask, and stands helpless before a million reflections of his obliterated face staring back at him from his massive crystal Solartron, the iridescent power source for his many weapons (44). His self-image at such odds with the "fragmented" bodily reality, there is no room for misrecognition; the sight drives him insane – his Medusa's gaze thrown back at him.

Furthermore, Doom's mask itself, concealing and impersonating the disabled supervillain's "monstrous" identity, forms a multi-pronged threat to the

2.11 Susan Richards/Invisible Woman glimpses Doom's ravaged visage (*Fantastic Four*, vol. 1, #236, Nov. 1981).

male subject. Rhonda Berenstein, writing on classic horror cinema, emphasizes the transgender aspects of the "monster" and its appeal to "cross-over" spectators, a viewing practice she calls "spectatorship-as-drag." Working from Judith Butler's concept of the performativity of gender, Berenstein argues that the monster in classic horror film comes to represent a "sexually ambiguous" other, a moment of bisexual rupture in the "safe space" of the cinema. As she writes:

> Spectatorship-in-drag . . . transposes horror's sex and gender ambiguities to the spectating domain. Part of horror's and drag's draw for spectators is opening a space for an attraction to figures that revel in sex and gender fragmentation, and posit something more than the conventional sex-role and gender options available to men and women in American patriarchy. (261)[44]

The monstrous Dr. Doom carries precisely that trace of sexual vagueness (cowl, monk's dress, reproduction by cloning, dandy-like preoccupation with his body, a good "maternal" leader to the nation of Latveria), while his iron mask contains nothing less than the face of the Medusa, the classical symbol of the castrating female gaze (taken up as an empowering trope by feminist critics such as Hélène Cixous).

In conclusion, if the Silver Age superhero represents a (superficially) hypermasculine, ableist compensation for male physical disability and lack at a time of masculine anxiety (the Cold War), then the supervillain—its foil and structuring Other—must represent the return of that repressed,

2.12 The unmasked Doom is driven insane by innumerable reflections of his face (*Fantastic Four*, vol. 1, #200, Nov. 1978).

2.13 Byrne's portrait of Doom, with scarred flesh visible (*Fantastic Four*, vol. 1, #247, Oct. 1982).

body-disrupting, feminizing force. Moreover, this dread figure embodies not just castration anxiety (through an all-but undepicted, polyvalent signifier of sexual difference), but the threat of the Mirror Stage's fragmented, unresolved self—in other words, the unmasking of lack in all senses.

The masked, deformed Silver Age supervillain, Dr. Doom perhaps most suggestively of all, embodies exactly these dangers to the male subject. Doom's mask, as drawn by John Byrne, shows the malevolent, contingent nature of that mask: the penetrating eyes, with traces of scarred flesh just visible, barely held back by the iron faceplate, which presses up against the so-called "unhealing wound" (see, for example, *Fantastic Four*, vol. 1, #247: 22). Too powerful and overdetermined a signifier, the double threat of castration and physical disability can never be shown, only hinted at, disavowed, deflected, literally marginalized by placing it ever and only just "off-frame."

Many Silver Age supervillains in the Marvel universe in essence repeat the pattern of Dr. Doom vis-à-vis their masks—which become their personae. For one thing, so many of them sport masks, and almost never remove them: Psycho-Man, Diablo, Annihilus, Ultron (an android whose face looks like a mask), the Celestials, Galactus. The more powerful the figure, in fact, the less likely he will be to show his face beneath the mask. In some cases, like that of the Destroyer, removing the mask is impossible without risking *annihilation*. The Red Skull, in a literalization of the metaphor, actually adopts his mask *as* his face, when he falls victim to his own "Dust of Death."[45]

In short, the villains—like the heroes—of Marvel's Silver Age insistently have something to hide: physical disability, feminizing threat of castration, the subversion of the gender order itself. And through every means at his disposal—overcompensating superpowers, fantastic resolutions, searing iron masks to hold back Medusa's gaze—hide in plain sight is precisely what the villainous supercrip does.

As we turn, in the next several chapters, to detailed case studies of disability and its "overcompensation" in superhero comics of the Silver Age and beyond, let us recall that disability has never stood for any one thing. Rather, as should be made clear in the pages that follow, it is as complex and diverse as any aspect of human experience.

3

"WHAT CAN WE EVER HAVE TO FEAR FROM A BLIND MAN?!!"
Disability, *Daredevil*, and Passing

Now look at Daredevil. Talk about split personalities! He thinks he's three different people—Daredevil, Matt Murdock, and Mike Murdock. Sure, a super-hero needs a secret identity, but not two of them! Worst of all, Matt doesn't know which one he wants to be. He wants to be all three! If J. Jonah Jameson picks on anyone for being neurotic, it should be Daredevil. I think he's flipped! What with debonair Matt, idiotic Mike, and fanatic Daredevil, who can tell? (Paul DeSimone, *Let's Level With Daredevil* Letters Page, *Daredevil*, #32, Sept. 1967.)

The first Marvel Silver Age series devoted to a prominent "disabled super-hero," *Daredevil* (created by writer Stan Lee and artists Jack Kirby and Bill Everett in 1964) tells the story of Matt Murdock, who as a boy is struck by a radioactive canister which both blinds him and enhances his remaining senses to superhuman levels, compensating for his lost vision with a fantastic "radar sense." After the death of his father at the hands of the mob, Murdock devotes himself to fighting crime in his public identity as a successful trial lawyer and in his secret identity of Daredevil, hero of Hell's Kitchen.

In many ways, the Daredevil series proved a landmark for the depiction of disability in a notoriously ableist genre that celebrates idealized, hypermasculine bodies as a matter of course. Murdock's impairment does not stand in the way of having a brilliant career and earning the respect of his community as the most admired half of the Nelson & Murdock law firm, while his alter ego Daredevil, rather than hide the "weakness" of his disability as other superheroes so often do (e.g., Tony Stark/Iron Man, Don Blake/Thor), openly displays and transforms his blind man's markers: his mask has no eyeholes; he adapts his cane into a weapon (a billy club for smiting or launching cables for swinging across the air); and adopts a derisive childhood nickname coined by bullies as his *nom de guerre*. Daredevil's radar sense—an alternative means of interacting with the world—is superior to normal human vision: with it he

3.1 Matt Murdock creates his Daredevil costume, crafting a blind man's cane into a weapon, his "billy club" (*Daredevil,* vol. 1, #1, Apr. 1964).

can sense around corners, fight in the dark, and maintain a 360-degree field of perception at all times.

In short, Murdock/Daredevil succeeds not in spite of but because of his disability/superpowers; rather than vulnerabilities to be hidden away, they form a crucial part of his identity.[1] This amounts to quite a progressive representation of disability for the mid-1960s, the era of March of Dimes charity appeals, the Jerry Lewis MDA Telethon, and other media depictions which deployed sentimentality and a "pity model" to solicit funds for the "unfortunate." This was also a period in which the so-called "medical model" of disability held sway, when doctors largely determined the identity, opportunities, and fates of the disabled, seen as cases first, human beings second. Moreover, the infamous "ugly laws" were still in place in many municipalities, which compelled the blind to, among other things, cover their "deformed" eyes and avoid unsightliness as they signaled their impairment, at the risk of fines and jail time (Schweik: 45, 73 and passim). In such a climate, a series about a successful blind lawyer who doubled as a superhero in theory made for quite an empowering message, a precursor to our post-ADA age and its identity politics and civil rights-based social model of disability.

In other ways, however, *Daredevil* falls well short of what Lennard Davis calls a "dismodernist" stance, which advances a positive vision of personal identity linked to bodily difference (see chapter 5). First and foremost, in time-honored superhero tradition, Murdock feels the need to act weak and ineffective (especially around his love interest, the secretary Karen Page) so as to maintain his secret crime-fighting career as Daredevil. This leads to much romantic pining and frustration on both their parts (analogous to that experienced by the lame Dr. Don Blake and nurse Jane Foster in the concurrent Stan Lee/Jack Kirby series *The Mighty Thor*). While a cliché of the genre (as seen through a comparison with Clark Kent's performance of "cowardliness" before Lois Lane in *Action Comics*, #1, 1938, which was the debut of Superman), Murdock's persistent displays of defenselessness, contrasted with Daredevil's superheroic feats, hardly challenge entrenched stereotypes of the disabled. Furthermore, the series' frequent use (especially in its first fifty issues) of what even the most generous, broad-minded fans saw as the silliest plots and supervillains (the Matador, Leap-Frog, Stilt-Man, Masked Marauder, the Jester), as well as its ludicrous depiction of the American legal system (in one issue, Murdock lectures on how extraterrestrials would influence the law),[2] made for hard-to-ignore distractions from its more serious themes. Thus, *Daredevil* both affirmed and undermined a positive vision of disability.

Such unfortunate paradoxes and mixed messages attained critical mass in the much-maligned mid-1960s "Mike Murdock" storyline of issues 25 through 41. Long derided by fans and critics, this sixteen-month run by Stan Lee and

3.2 The ultra-obnoxious invented twin brother, Mike Murdock (*Daredevil,* vol. 1, #26, Mar. 1967).

Gene Colan represents for many a nadir in Silver Age superhero silliness in general, and writer Lee's ineptitude in particular. Some have attributed the profound wrongheadedness of this subpar premise to Lee's overcommitment as Marvel impresario and writer of several ongoing titles at the time; as evidence of the shortcomings of the Marvel Method Lee pioneered; as a flawed strategy to fill pages despite the hero's lack of appealing powers and/or villains; and as proof of the fundamental untenability of the indifferently selling, second-tier title *Daredevil* itself.[3]

Matt Murdock, confronted with proof of his secret identity as Daredevil by his coworkers Foggy Nelson and Karen Page, concocts an identical twin brother on the spot, "Mike Murdock," who he tells them is actually Daredevil

(*Daredevil,* vol. 1, #25, Feb. 1967: 6). Though at first they don't believe him (Nelson and Murdock after all were close roommates in college, and this is the first Matt has ever mentioned a brother), some deft wardrobe-switching, obnoxious acting, and "playboy hipster" mannerisms by Matt soon convince the rather gullible pair of the ruse. For the next sixteen issues, the irritatingly flirtatious and arrogant "Mike Murdock" would vie for Karen's affections in ways the nebbish Matt would never dare; annoy Foggy with his braggadocio and James Cagney impressions; and don the mask of Daredevil.

As mentioned, the Mike Murdock story arc—even accounting for the generic expectations of superhero comics—strains the bounds of credibility and taste; as one blogger (Jared M.) put it, "a daytime soap opera would reject this fake twin for being 'too ridiculous.'" Yet its central theme, the (mis-)management of multiple identities, sheds a fascinating light on key aspects of both the superhero and the disabled figure in postwar America, in particular how they both often confront stigma, demasculation, and the dread of powerlessness; and deploy strategies of passing, in particular what Tobin Siebers has called "disability as masquerade." Here, I briefly examine some of the chief theorizations these questions have provoked among sociologists and Disabilities Studies scholars, for what I hope will lead to a reassessment of this much-derided storyline.

SPOILED (SECRET) IDENTITIES

The sociologist Erving Goffman, just before the publication of *Daredevil's* first issue, produced the most penetrating study of the role played by stigma in identity formation in American life. His 1963 book, *Stigma: Notes on the Management of Spoiled Identity,* remains the touchstone for Disability Studies in the social sciences for its advancement of stigma theory—the socially shaped process of marking specific categories of people as "deviant" from an established norm—and the various strategies employed by the stigmatized to manage what he terms "spoiled identities." In the chillingly clinical language that is his trademark, Goffman writes:

> By definition, of course, we believe the person with a stigma is not quite human. On this assumption we exercise varieties of discrimination, through which we effectively, if often unthinkingly, reduce his life chances. We construct a stigma-theory, an ideology to explain his inferiority and account for the danger he represents, sometimes rationalizing an animosity based on other differences, such as those of social class. We use specific stigma terms such as cripple, bastard, moron in our daily discourse as a source

of metaphor and imagery, typically without giving thought to the original meaning. We tend to impute a wide range of imperfections on the basis of the original one, and at the same time to impute some desirable but undesired attributes, often of a supernatural cast, such as "sixth sense," or "understanding." (5)

Goffman's work provided a working model, a sort of handbook, for the myriad ways in which the position of an able-bodied, privileged subject defines itself through the abjection, abnegation, and dehumanization of physical difference, including that of disability.[4] Assessing Goffman's contribution to the field, Disability Studies scholar Rosemarie Garland-Thomson notes that stigma theory

> resituates the "problem" of disability from the body of the disabled person to the social framing of that body.... [it] reminds us that the problems we confront are not disability, ethnicity, race, class, homosexuality, or gender; they are instead the inequalities, negative attitudes, misrepresentations, and institutional practices that result from the process of stigmatization. (1997: 32)

Or, as Lennard Davis puts it in what has become a tenet of disability theory: "It isn't necessarily bad to be disabled, but it is bad to be discriminated against, unemployed, poor, blocked by bad laws, architecture, and communication" (2002: 5).

Among the coping mechanisms employed by stigmatized, marginalized disabled people, passing seems the most relevant to the case of Daredevil/ Matt Murdock and the logic of the superhero genre itself; building on the work of Goffman and others, a large body of literature has emerged in Disability Studies investigating the advantages and pitfalls of passing as a strategy for survival and mainstream acceptance. Among the advantages: control of one's impression or image within the social world, escape from Goffman's "spoiled identities" pigeonholing, and economic opportunity. Among the pitfalls: the risk of inauthenticity, what Garland-Thomson likens to "self-betrayal" (1997: 13).

First associated by sociologists with the phenomenon of light-skinned black people posing as white or "Southern European" to avoid prejudice (so-called "racial passing"), the concept has been extended to instances of boundary-transgression of many sorts: living as the opposite sex; altering one's speech to cover up a stutter; closeted gays; and those with "invisible" disabilities who for whatever reason choose not to reveal their status.[5]

3.3 A recurrent series motif: the superpowered Murdock passes as blind (*Daredevil*, vol. 1, #29, Jun. 1967).

With their secret identity subplots, superhero stories have also long been described as "passing narratives," by, among others, Jules Feiffer (13); Danny Fingeroth (2007: 46); Scott Bukatman (2003: 72); and Jason Bainbridge (71). Passing—the act of successfully presenting oneself as something one is not— is what Daredevil does; his blindness is not known to the various villains he fights and civilians he rescues. Matt Murdock, in turn, engages in the particular form of passing which Tobin Siebers calls "disability as masquerade": he plays up his weakness, exaggerating his "spoiled identity" (in Goffman's terms) as a blind man, so as to deflect suspicion of his superhuman status.

This formed a repeated motif of the series: in *Daredevil*, vol. 1, #29 (Jun. 1967), Murdock senses his law partner Foggy Nelson bound and gagged on the floor of their offices—yet pretends not to notice him until he hears his moans and "stumbles" over him. A typically hyperbolistic thought balloon tells us how Murdock feels: "I have to play the role of a *blind man* . . . no matter how much I want to go into *action!*" (ibid.: 8, emphasis in original). Later in the scene, a freed Foggy gives Murdock a note left by the criminals; Murdock reads it with his super-sensitive fingers, yet gives the impression that it is inaccessible to someone without sight, and tosses it to Foggy (ibid.: 9).

In *Daredevil*, vol. 1, #47 (Dec. 1968), we're reminded that Murdock is even perfectly capable of *fighting* without his costume—but only in the dark. He does this not only to preserve his civilian identity, but to reaffirm cultural expectations about the defenselessness of blind people. As Siebers describes it, disability as masquerade "represents an alternative method of managing social stigma through disguise, one relying not on the imitation of a dominant social role but on the assumption of an identity marked as stigmatized, marginal, or inferior" (2008: 102) so as to achieve a desired anonymity, marginality and in a sense, tranquility within ableist culture. As Siebers concludes: "The masquerade shows that disability exists at the same time that it, as masquerade, does not" (ibid.: 103). All this underscores what Davis terms the fundamental instability of the category of disability itself; its ontology depends on who is looking (or as it happens, who is "radar-sensing").

"ONE-MAN REPERTORY THEATER"

With the introduction of the fake "Mike Murdock" personality, a further complication arises. Now Murdock is passing as a charismatic superhero beloved of all New York; as a defenseless blind lawyer; *and* as a wisecracking sighted man who dresses like a pimp. (In fact, the Mike figure functions as a grotesque hybrid of the Daredevil/Matt identities; he looks like the latter, but acts and flaunts the flamboyant fashion sense of the former.) This leads to Murdock's torturous split-personality confusion; proliferating identities; compulsive drive to performance; and ludicrous plot turns that have earned this storyline decades of fanboy scorn. *Daredevil* stands revealed as even more invested than the typical superhero title in the logic of passing; there is never a time when Murdock is *not* passing as something or someone, raising doubts about his mental health. (Particularly disturbing are the scenes in which he works out in his private residence, in his Daredevil costume without the mask, but still wearing his blind man's dark shades—another grotesque hybrid.)

The stigma of disability and its consequent coping strategy, passing, precipitates in Daredevil/Murdock a disturbing schizophrenic psychodrama[6] in which obsessive-compulsive villains like Mr. Hyde and the Cobra (because their motivations remain dully consistent and obvious throughout) seem by far the most sane. It leads to scenes like the one in which a euphoric Daredevil, on his way to finally propose marriage to Karen Page, can proclaim: "But, I *still* haven't figured out . . . do I propose to her as *Matt* Murdock . . . or should I pop the question to her as *Mike*? If only I *myself* knew which one of us is the *real* me!! But what's the difference . . . as long as she says *yes!!*" (*Daredevil*, vol. 1, #29, May 1967: 6, ellipses and emphasis in original).

3.4 Matt transforms into "Mike"
(*Daredevil*, vol. 1, #26, Mar. 1967).

The "fake twin" storyline represents an extreme case, but even a cursory glance through the Daredevil series in its Stan Lee/Gene Colan phase of the mid-1960s reveals that the blind Murdock's playacting formed the central plot device, repeated in endless variations. Role-playing deceit is Murdock's most oft-deployed weapon, as effective as his billy club; he seems driven to be anyone but himself—whoever that might be—pointing to the fundamentally performative character of both disability and the superhero genre.

In the opening scene of "Stilt-Man Strikes Again!" (*Daredevil*, vol. 1, #26, Mar. 1967), over the space of a page made up of five panels, Daredevil transforms first into Matt, then into Mike. Calling himself a "one-man repertory theater," Murdock in his running commentary makes numerous references to the dramatic arts: Alec Guinness, method acting, and Stanislavsky. Moreover, Lee's dialogue and Colan's art emphasize the physical and personality changes Murdock effects: tousled hair, "more colorful" glasses, cocksure smirk (3). On the next page, the metamorphosis is complete: "Mike" assumes an absurd pose, his feathered hat and dandified outfit insuring the reader will not confuse him with his "strait-laced," "Ivy-league" alter ego. As the more mentally grounded Karen and Foggy enter the room, Mike remains physically separate from them, in a dark void that figures the resounding hollowness of his identity; he is all surface, all props, all performance (4).

A still more dramatic, improbable Matt/Mike/Daredevil transformation occurs in the middle of a fight sequence in "Mike Murdock Must Die!" (*Daredevil*, vol. 1, #27, Apr. 1967). Over six panels, Matt manages to escape his bonds,

3.5 Matt (passing as Mike) changes into Daredevil in mid-battle (*Daredevil*, vol. 1, #27, Apr. 1967).

leaps out of a helicopter, catches its undercarriage with his leg, doffs his civilian clothing and swings over through the craft's other door as Daredevil, his feet landing on the villainous Masked Marauder's chin; to emphasize the change, the panels shift from square to rectangular as DD makes his grand entrance (15–16). Foggy, Karen, and the Marauder (all of whom think they know our hero's true identity) are witness to an act of double-masquerade: Matt passing as Mike passing as Daredevil. He even wisely informs Karen, "And you needn't worry about *Matty boy!* I *caught* him and lowered 'im to a rooftop with my *cable!*" (16, emphasis in original). The scene makes plain both Murdock's elaborate management and mercurial fluidity of his identity. To underscore the split-psyche shenanigans, Colan depicts Daredevil's visage confronting the reader, half in light, half in shadow, intersected by the panel border (16, panel 3).

But perhaps the "Mike Murdock" storyline's most vertiginous (and for some most laughable) episode of identity-juggling takes place in one of the most-mocked stories in the entire run: "—If There Should Be a Thunder God!" (*Daredevil*, vol. 1, #30, Jul. 1967). In order to lure two Thor villains, Murdock visits a costume shop and dresses up as the Norse god himself. Oddly, he wears his Daredevil costume under the Thor costume, and the "Mike" persona's "cool" dark glasses beneath both masks. When he visits his friends, Foggy states what seems to him the obvious: "*Mike Murdock*—in the identity of *Daredevil*—disguised as *Thor*—in order to trap two *other* loons! How can *anyone* tell who's *who* around here anymore??!" (ibid.: 8, emphasis in original). Of course, it's even weirder than that: Matt passing as Mike passing as Daredevil passing as Thor.

Yet this surreal identity quadrafecta makes sense in light of postwar American attitudes to disability: the four stages illustrate a progression from the despised, stigmatized disabled body (Matt) to the white heteronormative body (Mike) to the superheroic body (Daredevil) to the transcendently Aryan physical ideal of the super-superheroic body (Thor, one of the most physically and cosmically endowed characters in the Marvel universe, a literal god figure). Each stage/identity is more desirable (from a white, heterosexual, able-bodied male perspective), as well as more illusory and unattainable.

Murdock's choice of disguise has additional significance: despite being a complete mismatch for Daredevil in terms of powers, Thor also has a disabled alter ego—the lame doctor Donald Blake. All the same, the early Silver Age *Daredevil* and *The Mighty Thor* were very different titles in how they dealt with disability. As mentioned in chapter 2, Thor represents the much more common strategy of banishing the impaired secret identity from the field of vision, to be replaced by the fantasist ideal hypermasculine superhero. Blake taps his walking stick on the ground, and vanishes—only then does Thor

3.6 Proliferating identities: Matt passing as Mike passing as Daredevil passing as Thor (*Daredevil*, vol. 1, #30, Jul. 1967).

appear. Blake and Thor by definition cannot coexist; each succeeds the other in a binary economy of opposing body types.[7]

Daredevil, as we have seen, operates along a completely different visual and psychological scheme, not binary but hybrid. Murdock never vanishes from sight once he dons the horns; on the contrary, what we see is Murdock *passing as a superhero* (just as he passes for a helpless blind lawyer in civilian life) at the same time as he *is* a superhero – after all, everyone assumes he can see. (Daredevil and Murdock are one in ways most other heroes are not; recall that even the name "Daredevil" is a childhood taunt which Murdock suffered.) The layering of identities acts as a palimpsest, revealing Murdock's compulsive simultaneous performance of multiple personalities—like the bizarre quadruplication in this story—as emblematic of the essential instability of the postmodern psyche (or as Davis would put it, the dismodern psyche). This made Daredevil unique among early Marvel Silver Age titles; if the god-figure Thor functions as the desirable mirror image we misrecognize as us, Murdock/Daredevil is a house of mirrors, reflecting a fractal infinity of possible selves, each one distorted, de-idealized, and deformed.

In "—If There Should Be a Thunder God!" we see a visual correlate to the identity-overlapping to which Murdock is so prone. In his portraits of the ersatz Thor, Colan mostly avoids drawing the eyes—since our hero is supposedly wearing his dark glasses underneath the mask, but also in observation of the taboo (even in the case of disguise!) against depicting a blind man's pupils.[8] Instead, "Thor" often squints, looks cross-eyed, or has his eyes in shadow. This, coupled with decidedly un-Asgardian utterances such as "Say it isn't *so*, pussycat!" (7, emphasis in original) make for yet another grotesque hybrid.

3.7 Binary vs. hybrid: Thor's gale-force winds strip the impostor's costume to shreds (*Daredevil*, vol. 1, #30, Jul. 1967).

Murdock himself mocks the ludicrous strain of having to maintain four separate personalities: "Boy! My *biggest* problem'll be keeping all these *identities* straight!" (ibid., emphasis in original).

All this proves insufferable to the real, no-nonsense Thor, who arrives, realizes the deception, and in a rage conjures up gale-force winds to strip the pseudo-thunder god's costume right off. The episode allegorizes the confrontation between binary and hybrid modes of disability representation in superhero narratives—with the binary "triumphant." Murdock's scraps of the Thor costume flailing in the wind, the Daredevil costume emerging from underneath, visually mark the fragmented, core instability of the hybrid (13). Thor, who wants to discover the impostor's "true identity," of course never does; this is impossible for a figure who takes on and discards multiple identities with a fetishist's zeal. Those supernatural winds can only scratch the surface.

But perhaps the most impressive, vertigo-inducing act of passing committed during the "fake twin" storyline occurs in "Unmasked" (*Daredevil*, #29, Jun. 1967). In a bid to trick the kidnappers of Karen Page, Murdock undertakes what he calls "the *greatest performance* of my *life . . . !*" (*Daredevil*, vol. 1, #29: 10, emphasis in original). The role: "*himself.*" He bursts in on the crooks in his Daredevil costume, wielding a gun and waving a hand uncertainly in front of him—as if he cannot see. The criminals quickly apprehend him and

3.8 Murdock passes as "himself" in "Unmasked!" (*Daredevil*, vol. 1, #29, Jun. 1967).

remove the mask: it's Murdock, complete with his blind man's glasses, "pretending" to be Daredevil to draw attention away from his "brother" Mike, the "real" Daredevil. "I thought . . . if I could *impersonate* him . . . get you to shoot *me* first," he says, " . . . then you'd think he was *finished* . . . and you wouldn't be *expecting* him!" (12, ellipses and emphasis in original). Everyone (except the reader) falls for the deception; they have no idea our hero has outright revealed his deepest secret to the world, that Matt Murdock *is* Daredevil. But the truth is too absurd, too laughable, even when a version of it is put on full display: "If *he's* Daredevil," says the mob boss, "*I'm* Peter Pan!" He concludes, "Leave Murdock where he is! Ain't nothin' a *blind* man can do to stop us!" (ibid., emphasis in original). This posture, of course, seals their doom.

This last point underlies much of what I have been discussing in these passing narratives, something emphasized by Goffman and developed further in the line of queer theory inaugurated by Eve Kosofsky Sedgwick's *Epistemology of the Closet*: the passers and their audiences are collaborators in the social construction of the masquerade. The passer, an expert manipulator, plays precisely to the prejudices of the greater culture; Murdock is a minstrel, acting in "blind-face" for the consumption of a crowd that sees—that must see—a debased spectacle tailor-made to its expectations. As Siebers poignantly notes: "Passers are skillful interpreters of human society. They recognize that in most societies there exists no common experience or understanding of disability on which to base their identity. For where a common acceptance of disability exists, passing is unnecessary" (2008: 118).

"Blind Man's Bluff!" (*Daredevil*, vol. 1, #31, Aug. 1967), a climactic episode in a three-part saga, brings together all these themes—the collaborative nature of successful passing; how it both feeds on and reinforces collective prejudices; and the real costs to life, limb, and mental health of the passer. Daredevil, in a battle with the villains Mr. Hyde and the Cobra, falls victim to one of Hyde's chemical potions, which deadens his hypersenses and radar, leaving him truly blind (*Daredevil*, #30: 20). This accomplished, the villains are so confident in their victory they don't even bother to kill Daredevil as they had planned; after all, as Hyde proclaims, "What can we ever have to fear from a *blind man?!!*" (*Daredevil*, #31: 10, emphasis in original).

For several pages, Lee and Colan depict a completely helpless Daredevil stumbling through the city, looking for his apartment, feigning sight for crowds of concerned and curious onlookers. "Are you *okay,* fella?" one of them asks. "Anything we can *do?* Should we call the *cops?*" (4, emphasis in original). Daredevil reassures them he's fine, simply recovering from a "shellacking"—but he keeps inadvertently dropping clues to his condition. His anxiety builds as the superhero façade cracks further and further. The gawking crowd literally starts to tear him apart, as a star-struck woman reaches out to strip a piece of his mask off, nearly exposing his face! The tear in his costume visually marks the ongoing breakdown of his now out-of-control public identity: a truly disabled superhero is a contradiction in terms—it starts to disintegrate on contact with the world. "If only I could *admit* that I can't see!" Murdock muses, melodramatically. "But it would mean my life! It would be *open-season on Daredevil* thruout [*sic*] the entire underworld!" (5, emphasis in original).

Eventually, Daredevil resolves to continue his battle with the villains on New York's rooftops. Seeking to convince Hyde and the Cobra that his vision has returned so he can save the civilians below from being crushed by Hyde's boulder, our hero hatches a desperate plan: with the help of Foggy, he shoots his billy club's cable from one building to another, and proceeds to unsteadily walk the tightrope held by his partner across the chasm between skyscrapers. "I've *got* to make Cobra and Hyde absolutely *convinced* that I'm the same old *Daredevil!*" he determines (16, emphasis in original).

Over three pages, the blind man, his body a trembling mass of tension and uncertainty, awkwardly negotiates the cable, questioning every step like it might be his last. Colan illustrates the suspense and strain with power lines as Daredevil stumbles, loses his footing and starts to fall (17). Only dumb luck and his acrobat's skill save our hero from a twenty-story plunge to death.

3.9 Daredevil's death-defying stunt fools the villains in "Blind Man's Bluff!" (*Daredevil*, vol. 1, #31, Aug. 1967).

Yet, as in a miracle, Daredevil's plan works brilliantly: the crowds and the villains all construe his clumsy, near-disastrous performance as self-assured "clowning around," a confused Hyde and Cobra retreat. No one witnesses Foggy's help, so Daredevil's last-ditch gambit comes off as confident bravado by a fun-loving man's man, acting alone.

The scene functions as a textbook example of how the passer and his rubes work together to pull off a credible illusion of the invented identity. Daredevil is a superhero. Therefore, anything he does, even his staggered wanderings through New York, even his graceless teeter-tottering on the rope which almost kills him, is interpreted by onlookers in heroic terms. In Daniel G. Renfrow's words, "The mark of passing successfully is the lack of a mark of passing" (489). The audience plays a critical role in smoothing over the performance and erasing inconsistent "marks."

Once settled, the superheroic impression is, indeed, impervious to contradictory evidence or appeal. Later, when the Cobra and Hyde catch wind of Daredevil's deception and kidnap him, Foggy rushes to the police. But when he tells them their hero is blind, they scoff. As one sergeant explains, "I *saw* him on that *tight-rope* a few hours ago . . . hammin' it up for the crowd like an *acrobat*! I even saw the act he put on when he pretended to lose his *balance* a couple of times! I'd sure like to see a *blind man* handle himself like

3.10 The police sergeant's fond reminiscence of Daredevil's wire-walking (*Daredevil*, vol. 1, #32, Sept. 1967).

that!" (*Daredevil*, vol. 1, #32, Sept. 1967: 4, ellipses and emphasis in original). A large panel shows the police sergeant, his head propped on his hand, dreamily recalling Daredevil's derring-do. Colan's double-portrait of our hero indeed seems far steadier, more self-possessed, in the sergeant's version. The logic is the exact inverse, and just as impenetrable, as that of Hyde and the mob boss who had previously "unmasked" Daredevil: by definition a blind man is not a threat, and a superhero cannot be blind. Everybody knows that.

CONCLUSION: THE TIGHTROPE OF MANHOOD

As Tobin Siebers reminds us, passing for the disabled is a sword that cuts two ways:

> On the one hand, to free themselves from curiosity, prejudice, economic disadvantage and violence, disabled people develop sophisticated tactics designed to help them blend into society, but these tactics may also exact a heavy toll on individuals both mentally and physically, leading to psychological crises and secondary health problems. (2008: 117)

And yet the allure of real power—not only over themselves and their self-image, but more immediately over the management of others' impressions of them—holds very strong appeal, as it does for all passers living in a society that as a matter of course treats them as less than fully human.

Understandable, then, that the feeling of power comes from knowledge of the intricate mechanisms of a culture that seeks to keep them at arm's length. As Tanya Titchkovksy notes, "[passing for the blind] means knowing . . . the minutest details of how everyday existence is oriented to the expectations that sight is an ever-present feature of that existence; it means knowing the customs, habits and signs of seeing people" (70). She adds that most sociological studies of passers—characterized almost uniformly as conniving—focus on the "devious" interactional techniques employed to manage their "spoiled" identities (ibid.). Daredevil functions as just such a handbook—albeit a surreal and preposterous one—for passing and its limits, for how (and how far one might go) to gain acceptance.

In the Mike Murdock storyline, the strategy of passing leads to an outlandish parade of confused identities verging on a psychotic break: a (radar-enhanced) blind man pretending to be non-blind who is now actually blind, pretending to be (non-radar-enhanced) non-blind! No wonder the long-suffering Karen Page was driven to despair.

Yet this story arc serves not only as precursor to future explorations of Matt Murdock's mental instability, a consistent theme of this title over its decades-long run. The secretly blind Daredevil "clownishly" courting death on his tightrope tells us something else about manhood and its crisis in Cold War America of the 1960s. For just as the disabled passer engages in an elaborate masquerade, so does his opposite, the heteronormative white male, exposed here as a sort of meat puppet, constrained just as tightly, and compelled just as brutally, to perform.

As Michael Kimmel described it, by the mid-1960s the various blows buffeting the traditional image of the self-made American man—the switch to a service economy, the rise of feminism, the Vietnam War, the Soviet threat—had drastically narrowed his accustomed field of action. "The 'masculine mystique,'" as Kimmel called it, "—that impossible synthesis of sober responsible breadwinner, imperviously stoic master of his fate, and swashbuckling hero—was finally exposed as a fraud" (262).

Yet, in what some have called a species of "gender schizophrenia" (ibid.: 212), our hero had to keep up the façade, go on laughing, walking the tightrope, hold himself up somehow over the abyss. For how much longer would his audience, like Daredevil's, help him pass?

4

BORDERLINE CASES
Gender, Race, and the "Disabled" Superhero

Because superhero comics have evolved their own conventions for representing the dilemmas of a divided self, they have the potential to become perfect vehicles for exploring minority group identity; similarly, from the perspective of the comics, minority groups may be ideal subjects for these same reasons. Superhero comics can literally personify the otherwise abstract ontological divides of minority identity, assigning each self its own visual identifier, its own body, and then charting the effects as these bodies house and are housed by the same mind. (Singer: 116)

We have thus far mostly observed instances of the disabled body as the shadow figure of the superhero genre: a physically "defective" alter ego vanishes from sight, instantly replaced by an idealized (usually white, male) physique—an act which whisks away any inkling of weakness, sickness, or compromised masculinity. I have related such sleight-of-*corpus* to postwar American anxieties over the changing place of men in the economy and culture; the early Silver Age's impulse to pathos and melodrama; and the genre's gradual inclusion of ethnic/physical others. I have labeled the requital for the disabled body's lack of "superpowers"—the genre's answer to the emasculating threat of disability, embodied by such alter egos as the heart-sickened Tony Stark, the lame Donald Blake, the blind Matt Murdock—a representational tactic which recalls Mitchell and Snyder's "falsely superhuman portrait of the overcompensating crip" (2000: 23) or supercrip.

This chapter turns to a separate category that emerges definitively in the early Marvel Silver Age—and indeed, did much to define it: the "borderline" case, in which the deformity or disability, far from hidden, presents as the superpower itself. By its visible nature, these figures' bodily difference flouts the "erasure" strategies so far discussed, often leading to a fraught destabilization of superheroic conventions. Through an examination of such Silver and Bronze Age characters as Ben Grimm/Thing, Sharon Ventura/She-Thing, and Victor Stone/Cyborg, we will see how the "borderline" case (whose superpower *correlates* to his/her disabled body) straddles (and, at times, crosses) the line between "good guys" and "bad guys"; such instability owes to "out of control" disabilities which stubbornly remain "in plain sight."[1] Furthermore, I will argue, the borderline case represents the clearest example in the genre of disability's engagement with other forms of physical difference along racial, ethnic and gender axes, what Rosemarie Garland-Thomson calls "the intersectional alliances among femininity, coloredness and monstrosity" (2005: 1565).

Relying on the stigma theory of Erving Goffman, Garland-Thomson holds that a feminist-inflected Disability Studies explores such intersections by "resituat[ing] the 'problem' of disability from the body of the disabled person to the social framing of that body," so that "the problems we confront are not disability, ethnicity, race, class, homosexuality or gender; they are instead the inequalities, negative attitudes, misrepresentations, and institutional practices that result from the process of stigmatization" (1997: 32). Such thinking dovetails with the pioneering cultural criticism of, among others, Cornel West, whereby a new cultural politics of difference "trash the monolithic and homogeneous in the name of diversity, multiplicity and heterogeneity" (West: 203–204). In his own writing on such intersectionalities of otherness, Tobin Siebers emphasizes how disability compels a critical rethinking of identity politics itself "beyond communities of interest based on race, nation, class, gender and sex," concluding, "it is crucial both ethically and theoretically to give a place to disability in the field of minority studies" (2008: 72).[2]

With his disability that refuses to "vanish from sight," how does the "minoritized," racially, sexually, and physically othered superhero function in a "economy of visual difference" (Garland-Thomson 1997: 8) that tends to read deformity, abnormality, and visible impairment as grotesque and adversarial—if not outright villainesque?[3]

"I LIVE IN A WORLD TOO SMALL FOR ME!"

Stan Lee/Jack Kirby's the Thing, of the Marvel super-team the Fantastic Four (1961), inaugurates the borderline case (if not the Silver Age itself), representing the most consistently problematic of these figures, since from the series' inception his frequent "bodily instability" and poor self-image continuously disrupt the team's family dynamics. Like his teammates, Ben Grimm is exposed to cosmic rays while piloting a spacecraft in Earth orbit. After a crash landing, the quartet discovers—initially to their horror—that the radiation has endowed them with incredible abilities: Reed Richards becomes the rubber-bodied Mr. Fantastic; Sue Storm the Invisible Girl; Johnny Storm the flaming

Human Torch; while Grimm transforms into a super-strong, misshapen orange rock creature immediately dubbed the Thing. (Note how his sobriquet sharply contrasts with the others', by foregrounding his "inhumanity.")

Prone to appalling rages, profoundly embittered by his turn of fate, the Grimm of the series' first year often lashes out against a world that hates, fears and alienates him[4]—so much so that by the second issue's story, "The Fantastic Four Meet the Skrulls From Outer Space!" (*Fantastic Four*, vol. 1, #2, Jan. 1962), Sue wonders, in an alarmed whisper, "How much more of this can we take! Sooner or later, the Thing will run amok and none of us will be able to stop him!" (Sedlmeier 2011: 32).

Scholars of the Silver Age single out the creation of the Thing as a turning point in the genre and a decisive break with the sunnier Golden Age. As Matthew J. Costello argues, "The hideously disfigured Ben Grimm was, in numerous ways, a detonator who would set off a constellation of changes—changes that would expand and complexify the notion of comic book heroes fundamentally and forever" (29). Bradford Wright calls Grimm "the most compelling and original" of the series' characters, noting that "despite his monstrous appearance and awesome power, the Thing's tragic flaws [*sic!*] ironically made him one of the most 'human' characters ever created" (205). Lee and Kirby had produced a hero whose repulsive body, self-loathing, and animosity led him to despise the world as much as he felt bound to defend it.

As Lee himself described his "favorite character":

> The Thing was perhaps the first hero who not only wasn't handsome, he was downright grotesque. . . . The Thing served, and still serves, two great purposes in the strip. One, as a normal man who had become a monstrous freak, he provided a sense of pathos. Fate had dealt him a tragic hand when the superpowers were handed out. Two, he also provided the strip with a constant opportunity for humor because of his bad attitude. (Lee/Mair: 117).[5]

Such "humor" becomes apparent from the moment of Grimm's very first appearance, on the third page of *Fantastic Four* #1. We find him at a haberdashery, where a nebbish clerk insists the shop carries nothing "big enough to fit a man *your* size!" (emphasis in original). Disguised in a large raincoat, hat, and dark glasses, Grimm mutters, "Bah! Everywhere it is the same! I live in a world too small for me!" (Sedlmeier 2011: 3). Richards's Fantastic Four flare then summons the Thing into action; he doffs his civilian costume ("What a relief to get rid of those tight rags!"), and—as the bald clerk faints in shock—Grimm smashes through a doorway, bursting out onto the pavement in a spray of debris. "Why must they build doorways so *narrow?*" he growls, while a passerby exclaims, "Holy smoke!! A—A—*monster!*" (ibid.: 4, emphasis in original).

4.1 Ben Grimm/the Thing makes his debut (*Fantastic Four*, vol. 1, #1, Nov. 1961).

The appearance of this terrifying orange creature throws the entire block into chaos; to escape some policemen who open fire, Grimm rips apart a manhole cover (along with a large chunk of the street) and drops down to the sewer. After floating in the water for a panel, he decides to re-emerge—though he sees no manhole. "Bah!" he grumbles. "I cannot delay! I'll *make* an opening!" He again tears through the street, shards flying, just in time for a car's front end to crumple against him on impact (ibid., emphasis in original).

Echoing Lee's description, Charles Hatfield not unfairly labels Grimm's antics in this introductory scene "ironic humor" (2012: 117); at the same time, every line of dialogue, piece of *mise-en-scène*, and action depicts an object out of scale with its physical and social environment, and the inevitable destruction such disjuncts cause. Grimm does not "fit in," as person or body; this alone leads to pandemonium. The markers of modern urbanity (streets, doors) explode, their fragments often hurling forward to the reader.[6] Kirby renders the pavement and unfortunate car in particular as if made of paper, easily ripped or warped by Grimm's powerful hands.

The scene underscores a tenet of Disability Studies discussed in chapter 2, as expressed by Siebers:

> The social body is the standard—presupposed but invisible—until a non-standard body makes an appearance. Then the standard becomes immediately apparent, as the inflexible structures of furniture, rooms, and streets reveal their intolerance for anyone unlike the people for whom they were built. (2008: 85)

The Thing, as absolute outsider, exposes the presumptions (social no less than architectural) of a city built to scale for the able-bodied. His inadvertent rampage—comical because he is only trying to make his way across town, like any New Yorker—illustrates the barriers (of all sorts) unthinkingly placed in the way of unconventional physiques in "democratic" modernity.[7]

Note also how Grimm's "outsider" status leads Lee and Kirby to introduce him in ways that contrast sharply with his teammates' first appearances: Sue is having tea with a "society friend," while her equally blond and blue-eyed brother Johnny and his pal are tinkering with a car—activities in keeping with their gender, race, and class allegiances. Even Richards—who appears before the others, on page one, as a "mysterious figure" signaling with a flare for his team to assemble—still clearly seems to be an average-looking human being. Only after the reader has seen these three in "normal" human activities do their strange powers manifest.

Not so for Grimm: apart from the clumsy raincoat disguise, he has no visibly human aspect to his identity. He is shopping alone, not engaged in pleasant socializing but dealing with the tedious (if vital) task of "fitting in" as best he can. While Richards and the Storms fully control their powers and can return to normal at any time, Grimm is always at best ambiguous and, once revealed, *all monster*—at that point there is no "unseeing" that fact.

Such a reading is underscored by the first close-up of Grimm's face in panel 6 (Sedlmeier 2011: 4), shown as he is traversing the sewer: an abject body repudiated by the surface dwellers. Yet this first close-up also demonstrates part of what makes Grimm such an alluring figure: we can clearly see here his only human physical feature, his blue eyes. In keeping with the Kristevan abject, he both attracts and reviles. As Elizabeth Grosz writes, "The freak is ... not an object of *simple* admiration or pity, but is a being who is considered simultaneously and compulsively fascinating and repulsive, enticing and sickening" (56, emphasis in original).

No, he is not all monster after all. Indeed, the Thing's inauspicious public debut scene bears many resemblances to the villainous Mole Man's origin story, discussed in chapter 2: both men inspire fear and disgust, but also sympathy. As with their literary forebears (such as Frankenstein's monster or Quasimodo) the world's ill treatment leads to a profound alienation and desire for revenge. As a borderline case, however, Grimm never definitively crosses that threshold; he wavers on it throughout the series' first two decades—paying ample dramatic dividends. As Hatfield puts it: "The possibility that the Thing's anger might turn him against his teammates was often reused as a plot tease. Related plot mechanisms were the guilt that the Fantastic Four's leader, Reed, felt for 'causing' Ben's condition and, on the other hand, the possibility that Ben might be forever cured, that is, made 'a man' again" (2012: 117).

The series returned almost obsessively to these themes during and after Lee/Kirby's 102-issue run, bespeaking the dramatic stakes evoked by the volatile borderline figure; arguably the most consistently recurring threat to the Fantastic Four's stability throughout the Silver Age was the Thing himself. "The Brutal Betrayal of Ben Grimm" (*Fantastic Four*, vol. 1, #41, Aug. 1965), makes for a particularly chilling example.

At the story's opening a despondent Grimm, having just reverted to the Thing after a brief period of "normalcy," beweeps his outcast state. Wandering a lonesome back alley, he once more rehearses his plight: as the only member of the team who cannot "switch off" his physical difference after exposure to cosmic rays, Grimm suffers from public stares and general horror at his grotesque appearance, a situation made all the more poignant by his teammates' easy off-duty "humanity": Sue and Reed are soon to be married, Johnny has his "chicks and sports cars." "But me," Grimm bemoans, "I'm a walking *monster* again . . . and I'll probably *stay* this way . . . forever!" (Abernathy: 2, ellipsis and emphasis in original).[8]

4.2 The ending of "The Brutal Betrayal of Ben Grimm" (*Fantastic Four*, vol. 1, #41, Aug. 1965).

Grimm's torment over his body image in fact leads to the break-up of the team, and (along with some goading and hypnosis by the insidious Wizard) to the Thing joining forces with their villainous analogues, the Frightful Four. At issue's end, with his former teammates immobilized, Grimm initiates this discomfiting exchange:

> GRIMM: *You* did this to me, Richards!! *You* turned me into something so ugly that they can only call me . . . a *Thing!*
> RICHARDS: *Ben!* You don't know what you're *saying!* You've got to snap out of it . . . for *all* our sakes!!
> G: *Shuddup,* Richards! I ain't *listening* to ya! I'm gonna change *you* now, hear? I'll do to *you* what you did to *me!* An' *nothin'* can stop me!
>   Then, when *you're* finished, I'll git the *rest* of the Fantastic Four . . . like I shoulda done a long time ago!!" (ibid.: 20, emphasis, ellipses and unconventional spelling in original)

In this, one of the series' bleakest cliffhangers, Grimm's deep-seated hostility not only spills over into territory normally reserved for villains—it taps into entrenched stereotypes of disabled people's lives as "inevitably leading toward bitterness and anger that ma[kes] them objects of suspicion" (Mitchell/Snyder 2000: 19). Grimm's betrayals, in keeping with superhero convention, are often explained away as hypnosis, the effect of suggestion or radiation—but his routine defections point to another causative factor: his "understandable" receptiveness to abandoning (if not destroying) the team due to his disruptive physical difference. The disabled's lot makes them envy and hate the able-bodied, and, like the vengeful protagonists in Tod Browning's *Freaks* (1932), secretly wish they could make all the normates "one of us"—or so the logic goes. Grimm's harrowing, nihilistic monologue confirms the stigmatizer's fears about the stigmatized. Thus, Grimm turns against the team with impressive regularity, his outer ugliness made to mirror his inner state—a veritable "creature-hero."[9]

The mind-altering Mad Thinker, villain of "By Ben Betrayed!" (*Fantastic Four*, vol. 1, #69, Dec. 1967), even says as much: "I've finally made the bludgeoning *Thing* as truly *evil*—as unconquerably *dangerous* as he *looks!*" (2, emphasis in original). Once again, through minor "chemical" brainwashing, Grimm is manipulated into attacking the team; once again, he doesn't need much prodding, as his deep-rooted resentments fuel his vengeance: "[Richard's] the one who turned me into—the *Thing*—the one who made me a *monster!!* An' he's gotta *pay* fer it—with his *life!*" (13, emphasis and unconventional spelling in original). Rampaging through the city, Grimm draws the attention of the military, which sends fighter jets to strafe him – a scene reminiscent not only of monster movies but of several issues of the Hulk (another important Lee/Kirby "creature-hero"). As expressed by a fireman tamping down the resultant fires, the public's reaction to the "unreasoning destructive monster" is as fear-laden as it is dehumanizing: "He's gotta be *stopped*—for good—like a *mad dog!*" (20, emphasis in original).

A later story, produced by the next generation of Marvel creators, retains the "disloyal Thing" trope, making the association with the Hulk even more explicit—by positing Grimm and the "jade giant" as equal partners against the world. In "Titans Two!" (*Fantastic Four*, vol. 1, #167, Feb. 1976, Thomas/Pérez), Grimm objects to the treatment of the captured Hulk and, mentally affected by the latter's gamma radiation, vents his frustrations on the team, the US military and any who come to oppose the strange duo.

When Richards tries to talk him out of his traitorous rage, Grimm replies, "Save yer *breath,* Reed-sweetie! You *human* types been *exploitin'* me long *enuff.* From here on in, you can change your name to—the *Fantastic Three!*" (7, emphasis and unconventional spelling in original). The art parallels the normate/monster divide: George Pérez often pairs the Thing and Hulk as visual analogues of each other. The opening splash page places them in the foreground, posed identically and so closely that Hulk's chest practically presses against Grimm's back, as together they confront the more human-looking figures in the background. Later, the two break through a wall in tandem (6) and smash a pair of air force jets by swinging them at each other in mirror-image.

Over the course of the story, however, as the army attacks them and they make their last stand on St. Louis' Gateway Arch, Hulk and the Thing's differences (mental, emotional, visual) come increasingly to the fore. Ultimately, Grimm "comes to his senses" and turns on the Hulk, who is attacking "my *buddy*" Richards (27, emphasis in original). Significantly, in the middle of

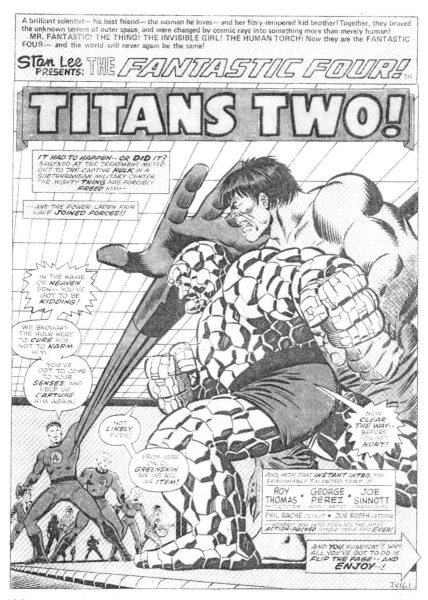

4.3 Grimm once more betrays the team, this time siding with the Hulk (*Fantastic Four*, vol. 1, #167, Feb. 1976).

battling his green former accomplice, Grimm suddenly transforms back to human—an unexpected effect of the gamma rays. The monster/normate dichotomy established since page one is thus cemented; Grimm has crossed back across that divide and rejoins his Homo sapiens cohorts. Sealing that "ontological" chasm is an image of the Hulk, atop the arch, abandoned by his erstwhile partner. "*So!* they have done it *again*. Just like they *always* do. Whenever Hulk finds a *friend*—they take him *away*—And Hulk is *alone* again!" (31, emphasis in original).

In the borderline case we see most clearly enacted the brutal economy of the supercrip, who is first and foremost a deviant—before "admiring" his feats, however noble, society must necessarily label him a freak.[10] Grimm's status as the most physically powerful member of the group, no less than his distinguished war record and experience as a pilot, are all trumped by the unignorable fact of his outward form. This impinges on his personal life, leading him to question even the devotion of his girlfriend, the blind Alicia Masters.[11]

Moreover, Grimm's recurrent sowing of chaos links him to a long history of seeing the disabled as narcissists obsessed with their own traumas, unable to relate to others and foisting unreasonable demands on society—making them deserve the public's "just" retribution.[12] So, in running amok and flouting team loyalties, Grimm—even his civilian name marks him as dour and glowering, to say nothing of the name's connection to fairy tale trolls—internalizes, acts out normate culture's view of him as evil ("Well, maybe they're right! Maybe I *am* a monster!").

The Thing's marginalization by a society that fears him returns us to the question of disability's intersectionality with other forms of difference, in particular the ethnic sort. As hinted throughout Kirby's run, and established definitively in 2002, Benjamin J. Grimm is a Jew.[13] What links can we draw between the foregoing and the history of anti-Semitism, in particular to long-held attitudes about the abject Jewish body?[14] The Thing, it seems, not only resembles the Golem in his exterior form—he *is* the Golem: a man-made monster that defends the ghetto but oversteps its bounds, goes out of control and must be subdued.[15]

The Thing, dubbed "Jack Kirby's greatest creation" by his longtime inker Joe Sinnot (Alexander: 29), proved so tremendously influential to the genre as to in essence reinvent it. The age of the antihero had begun. I submit that the figure's resonance with readers, on the cusp of the countercultural swells of the 1960s, owes largely to its gathering together and subtly critiquing American prejudices over different sorts of emergent otherness (ethnic, racial, corporeal, religious). But it was left to another Marvel character, in the 1980s, to explore even more fully the fraught paradoxes of the borderline case—in the process challenging nothing less than the gender order.

"IT'S DIFFERENT FOR WOMEN!"

Sharon Ventura came to prominence in "The Thing and the Thunderiders" (*The Thing*, vol. 1, #27, Sept. 1985, Carlin/Wilson). Billed as a love interest for Grimm, who had temporarily left the Fantastic Four, the statuesque redhead would eventually undergo a procedure to confer super-strength and compete in the Unlimited Class Wrestling Federation. Unbeknownst to Ventura, the man who bankrolled the procedure, the Power Broker, was a supervillain. Breaking free from his influence with Grimm's help, she eventually donned a skintight red, yellow and blue outfit and took up the nom de guerre Ms. Marvel.[16]

She and Grimm had various adventures together, though romance proved difficult, as Ventura carried the scars of psychological abuse from her deceased father. Matters worsened when, while battling the Power Broker with Captain America, Ventura was captured and subjected to (sexual?) torture by the villain's lackies. She developed a full-blown hatred and mistrust of men, as well as body-image disorder, making her uncomfortable in "over-eroticized" situations.[17] Nonetheless, she maintained a friendship with Grimm, whose misshapen form she found less threateningly "manly." When Reed and Sue Richards went into semiretirement in 1987, Grimm returned full-time to the Fantastic Four, assuming its leadership, and (despite some misgivings about her mental stability) asked Ventura to join the team.[18]

The foregoing only serves as prologue, though, for a surprising twist introduced by scriptwriter Steve Englehart at the end of "Things to Come!" (*Fantastic Four*, vol. 1, #310, Jan. 1988, Englehart/Pollard). Having defeated the supervillain Fasaud, Grimm and Ventura find themselves plunging to earth in a powerless space shuttle craft. Though they survive their crash-landing, Grimm discovers—in a horrific recurrence of the original accident which created the Fantastic Four—that due to cosmic ray bombardment in orbit he has mutated further, into a bulkier, stronger, spiky version of the Thing. The closing splash reveals Ventura's fate: she too has mutated, into a grotesque "she-thing" (23).

The very next issue's opening splash details Ventura's reaction to her new body: from a low angle we see the reshaped heroine, her costume in tatters, plummeting from a cliff. She screams the story's title, "I Want to Die!" (*Fantastic Four*, vol. 1, #311, Feb. 1988, Englehart/Pollard: 1). Her expression and form recall Edvard Munch's *The Scream* (1893), modern art's *locus classicus* of alienation and terror. Ventura's suicidal leap, however, proves ineffectual; her body is as resilient as it is "ugly." In another reiteration of the Fantastic Four's origin, she breaks a tree in half (as Grimm had done, in his own first display of super-strength).[19] But here she uses the weapon not to threaten her comrades, but to stab herself—again, to no avail. Later, Ventura once more courts suicide by trying to slice her throat against a jagged outcropping and engaging a Wakandan android, repeating, "I want to die" and "Kill me!" (ibid.: 3, 14).

The vexed issues of suicide, depression, and the "right to die" have preoccupied the disabled community since the 1970s; the case of Elizabeth Bouvia, a woman with cerebral palsy who in 1983 petitioned a California Superior Court for permission to end her life through starvation, proved a particular flashpoint. The community's response to that case, which unfolded just prior to the Ventura/"She Thing" storyline, has come to typify its efforts to combat what many disabled activists consider the casual genocide aimed at their number.

Bouvia, of Riverside, California, had experienced several reversals in her personal life, including a divorce, miscarriage, a family member's death, expulsion from graduate school, and inadequate personal care, all conditions conducive to depression. Rather than take such factors into account, however, the court, her hospital, and even the American Civil Liberties Union emphasized her physical condition as the sole reason for Bouvia's "understandable" urge to self-slaughter. In the words of a judge in 1986, "She, as the patient, lying helplessly in bed, unable to care for herself, may consider her existence meaningless" (quoted in Asch: 311).

The question of how to dispose of one's own life lies at the intersection of autonomy, free will, and societal preconceptions about "worthwhile" lives. In the case of the disabled, who live in ableist societies with eugenicist histories and a climate of medical paternalism, such a question hits especially close to home. The community—many of whom lived fruitfully and independently with conditions identical to Bouvia's—mobilized. These activists, Adrienne Asch notes,

> agree that people with disabilities deserve to have their views respected. However, they argue that such end-of-life decisions arise because people with disabilities have experienced constant discrimination, denials of information about life possibilities, inability to obtain legally available services and supports, and often abandonment by family and friends. They assert that despair and depression about life prospects cause people to give up on life, just as depression and despair cause people without disabilities to end life for all sorts of reasons. (312)

"If Bouvia were to be educated in a more welcoming institution," Asch goes on, obtain more personal assistance to increase her access to community life, rebuild or create personal loving relationships, and accept disability as a part of her identity rather than reject it and the community of disabled people available to support her and fight with her for dignity, perhaps she might regain a sense of hope and desire to live. (ibid.)

Or, as Mary Johnson writing in *The Disability Rag* put it more bluntly: "When society gave disabled the right to live with dignity, then, and only then, might we might [sic] talk about the right to die! Society had no business talking about a disabled person's right to die before it had given them a right to live!"(1997).[20]

Bouvia's petition to end her life was eventually denied, in part due to disabled community activism and the media attention it brought to the case. But as recounted by Joseph Shapiro in his seminal history of the disability rights movement, *No Pity*, this was no isolated incident. Larry McAfee, who became a quadriplegic after a 1985 motorcycle accident, in 1989 won a Georgia court's permission to switch off the ventilator that kept him alive, citing monotony, despair, and lack of prospects. Like Ventura, McAfee often said repeatedly, "I want to die." His family agreed with the decision. As Shapiro details, however, McAfee's poor quality of life could be traced to how Georgia apportions assistance to the disabled; among other things, it would pay for nursing home care (often indifferent) but not for home care and services which in other states allow the client greater decision-making, access to work, assistive technologies, and a fuller life. Moreover, the McAfee case exposed an all too common ableist prejudice in deciding such end-of-life questions:

> [A] judge saw a man with a translucent plastic coil connecting a hole in his throat to a machine and eagerly ruled this a life not worth living. . . . A nondisabled man who asked the state to help him take his life would get suicide-prevention counseling, but McAfee had not been considered rash or even depressed. Instead, a judge had praised him as sensible and brave. It was a bitter insult to the millions of other people with disabilities who were living successfully on their own—including those so severely disabled that they used respirators daily. (Shapiro: 260)

For many, the McAfee and Bouvia cases incarnated fears of "a disabled life devalued" (274) to the extent that the state actively aided and abetted the suicidal impulses of depressed people whom the system had failed. Shapiro grimly described the unwritten rule: "disabled people had a duty to die rather than be a burden to their families and society" (ibid.: 270).

4.4 Sharon Ventura reacts to her transformation into She-Thing (*Fantastic Four*, vol. 1, #311, Feb. 1988).

McAfee ultimately changed his mind about committing suicide, and died of pneumonia in 1995, at age thirty-nine. But David Rivlin, another quadriplegic from Michigan who also successfully argued to end his life, went through with his decision. Eighteen years after the 1971 surfing accident that broke his neck, Rivlin, at age thirty-eight, received a dose of morphine and valium from a hospice doctor. After he'd lost consciousness, the respirator was switched off. Rivlin died within thirty minutes (Dougherty/Tessler).

Disability scholars and activists such as Paul Longmore see poor counseling, inadequate services, and quasi-eugenicist biases—not end-of-life "autonomy"—as largely to blame for people like Rivlin choosing to die. He writes, "Elizabeth Bouvia in California, Larry McAfee in Georgia, and Kenneth Bergstedt in Nevada were all denied appropriate psychological diagnosis and counseling. Bouvia and McAfee were deprived of adequate financial support for independent living. The only real aid the system offered any of them or Rivlin was assistance in ending their lives" (1991: 616).

In the wake of such cases, groups such as Not Dead Yet (formed in 1996) organized to vigorously contend that in a culture and medical system still scornful of the disabled, and where many disabled people themselves internalize such prejudice,[21] there can be no truly impartial end-of-life decision-making. (The group actively rallies against so-called physician-assisted suicide, and drew much media attention during the 2004 Terry Schiavo case.)[22]

Discourses such as those from the Bouvia, McAfee, and Rivlin cases, generated just before, during, and after the She-Thing storyline in the *Fantastic Four*, clearly played a role in framing the issue of Ventura's suicidal response to her new bodily state (as well as the way readers consumed it). Her utter revulsion and urge to self-annihilation attests to ableist assumptions underlying the concepts of both the "normal" and the superhero in 1980s America—whereas Grimm's reaction serves as a subtle critique of the illusory self-reliant "will to autonomy" which forms such a pillar of ableism itself. "Look at the way ya *jumped off the cliff* and *survived!*" Grimm tells her. "If ya wanna have a body fer *getting' things done, this kind's* the kind ta *have!* . . . *Livin'* ain't no different fer *anybody*—and livin's what it's *all about!*" (*Fantastic Four*, #311: 3, emphasis and unconventional spelling in original).[23]

Not that Ventura, shocked at her mutation, is ready to accept such counsel just then. She soon enters a catatonic state, so mentally divorced from her surroundings that a giant jungle snake slithers over her without registering (a rather ineffective piece of comic business) (ibid.: 10). But as we shall see, the character's arc of development charts precisely such a journey towards eventual acceptance—and away from death.[24]

But only eventual. Ventura's immediate, suicidal response to her transformation by cosmic rays into a female version of the Thing, as noted, evokes critical issues pertaining to gender, disability, sexuality, body image, and morality. At the time of the character's debut, She-Thing challenged conventional notions of beauty and femininity, in the process destabilizing the team—and proved a deeply divisive figure for fans and even for Marvel's editorship. Englehart, in fact, told me he considered She-Thing the most polarizing character he ever created, and a major factor in his removal from the series (2012).[25]

Ventura's response to her new corporeal reality is indeed strikingly gendered. She justifies her suicidal drives by calling herself a monster; as tears flow, she imagines her human self (pictured in a thought-balloonish nimbus), saying, "I was *screwed up* before, but that was only in my *mind*—I could still lose myself in my *body*—but now even *that's* gone away!" Her verdict on the new physique: "It's *ugly!* It's *ugly* and *lumpy* and *orange* and *I hate it!*" When Grimm tries to calm her down, pointing out the advantages of her new, stronger body, she replies, "It's *different* for women!" (*Fantastic Four*, #311: 3, emphasis in original).

It *is* different for women: from her very origin, She-Thing (despite awesome super-strength and membership in the world's premiere super-team, and unlike previous male "creature-heroes") suffers from severe body dismorphia which plunges her into a gender crisis. Many fans (presumably young men) responded only with scoffs and scorn, seeing everything about her, even her name, as some sort of monstrous joke unworthy of Marvel's flagship title.[26] The story itself plays up this tension. At one point, Grimm tries to lighten the mood: "Hey, ya don't mind if I keep calling ya *Shary*, or *Ms. Marvel*, do ya? I mean, *She-Thing* just don't *cut* it—an' the *Thingette*, now . . . they'll laugh us outta *town* if we try *that!*" (ibid.: 10, emphasis and unconventional spelling in original). Such ridicule outlived even the character's heyday; as one misogynist blogger put it in 2007, "[She-Thing] is as attractive as her name implies. She's the type of woman who makes your testicles crawl into your abdomen and hide. . . . It's the Thing with breasts, man! Yeesh!" (Aquilone).

Such queasy, defensive responses from male readers underscore the ways She-Thing visually reifies the age-old association of monstrosity with femininity, which Garland-Thomson traces to Aristotle's dictum that "the female is, as it were, a deformed/mutilated male" (1997: 20). More than this, the abject disabled woman erodes gender binaries, occupying an intragender position best apprehended as "a product of a conceptual triangulation. She is a cultural third term, defined by the original pair of the masculine figure and the feminine figure, but also imagined as the antithesis of the normal woman" (ibid.: 29).

Conventionally applied to the representation and cultural denigration of women in wheelchairs, with visible deformations, amputations or physical impairments (e.g., the late lawyer Harriet McBryde-Johnson),[27] such a feminist disability analytical mode casts into relief the gender politics involved in

4.5 Ventura and Grimm discuss their mutations (*Fantastic Four*, vol. 1, #311, Feb. 1988).

the "borderline" transformation of the superheroine: "If the male gaze makes the normative female a sexual spectacle, then the stare[28] sculpts the disabled subject into a grotesque spectacle" (ibid.: 26). Along similar lines, Mairian Corker in her discussion of women and disability argues that "reading 'the monstrous body' as a cultural text avoids consideration of whether it has or can have intrinsic value, because, in this account, value is always socially constructed and, I would argue, 'easily' (though not necessarily simply) read" (46). In other words, hegemonic female beauty norms compel the male reader to recoil from the "ugly" disabled female, towards a dehumanizing "asexual object[ification]" (Hahn: 30), prompting expressions of disgust and mockery.

Thus, while in its time Grimm's transformation elicited sympathy and pathos, She-Thing's continues to inspire ridicule, fear, misogynist dismissals of the character as a "concrete version of Janet Reno" (Aquilone)—and worse.[29] The "borderline" superheroine is doubly othered, scarred, a disquieting gender chimera—the inverse of Scott Bukatman's super-body which "retains no marks, on which history cannot be inscribed" (2003: 197). Far from unmarked, She-Thing becomes "pure body, unredeemed by mind or spirit" (Garland-Thomson 2004A: 78), a paradoxical monster embodying a sexual threat to the phallus.[30] Such a state, not coincidentally, closely aligns her with Lennard Davis's "gaze of the medusa" model of gender confusion applied to the

4.6 She-Hulk/Jennifer Walters uses feminine wiles to defeat Dragon Man (*Fantastic Four*, vol. 1, #321, Dec. 1988).

villain Doctor Doom in chapter 2. For their part, women, "the primal freaks in Western history" (ibid.: 78), whose identity popular imagination grounds in appearance and sexual appeal, suffer a profound schizoid breakdown in the wake of the "borderline" transformation.

I find it illuminating to compare Ventura to another "disabled" female superheroine who—despite some surface similarities to She-Thing—escapes this quandary. She-Hulk (aka Jennifer Walters), a derivative spin-off character created by Stan Lee for trademark reasons,[31] shares the green skin, super-strength, and (at first) surly temperament of her better-known cousin, the Hulk. Yet her more human appearance and deshabillé habits led to a gradual hyper-sexualization, so that by the time she encountered Ventura/She-Thing in "After the Fall" (*Fantastic Four*, vol. 1, #321, Dec. 1988, Englehart/Lim) the story's resolution pivots on her erotic appeal to the sexually underdeveloped Dragon Man. The scantily clad She-Hulk (artist Ron Lim depicts her throughout the issue in a skimpy tank top and bikini bottoms) fends off the monster's attack by doing little more than posing provocatively. "I'm gonna come right *over* there—and give you—a big wet kiss!" she coos (27, emphasis in original).

As made plain by the story, She-Hulk operates along a quasi-ethnic, assimilationist model, which as Cornel West argues, "elide[s] the differences (in history and culture)" between the races (210). She maintains and foregrounds her sex appeal through eroticized different-but-not-too-different green skin; her "racialized" female super-body remains desirable to the reader, to the extent that she disempowers Dragon Man precisely through her seductive, feminine to-be-looked-at-ness.[32]

More germane to our discussion, the denouement of "After the Fall" functions as a study in contrasts—in more ways than one. Unlike the "grotesque" She-Thing/Ventura, She-Hulk/Walters revels in her newfound body's heteronormative sexual allure, constantly reaffirmed: after a cowed Dragon Man flies off, a bearded passerby openly gawks at her, prompting Ventura to hiss, "Excuse us—you're *drooling* all over your shirt!" (*Fantastic Four*, #321: 29, emphasis in original).[33] More critically, the story's conclusion seals another change: Ventura has come to accept her new body, on her own terms. As she tells Walters, "I was really *messed up* when I joined the FF! Hated *men*—hated *myself*—! . . . My life was a *disaster* when I was cute! I'm not saying there's anything *wrong* with being tall and well-built, but *this* is much better for me!" (20–21, emphasis in original). Later, she adds, "But *really*, add all the *hassles* together and it's *still* a pretty small *price* to pay for everything I've *gained!*" (29, emphasis in original).[34]

What Ventura has gained through her abject "intragender" positionality is emancipation from what Garland-Thomson calls the gender-inflected "disability system," which "functions to preserve and validate such privileged

4.7 Grimm and Ventura consummate their relationship, referencing Rodin's *The Kiss* (*Fantastic Four*, vol. 1, #317, Aug. 1988).

designations as beautiful, healthy, normal, fit, competent, intelligent—all of which provide cultural capital to those who can claim such status, who can reside within these subject positions" (2004A: 77).

With emancipation comes the opening up of new possibilities for challenging assumptions over women's appearance and, more radically, the gender order itself. Ventura comes not only to accept her new "intragender" status but to see it as advantageous—for dealing with her misandry, for personal growth, and even for becoming a person capable of giving and accepting love. Though she initially continues to resist Grimm's advances after her change, by "Last

Kiss" (*Fantastic Four*, vol. 1, #317, Aug. 1988, Englehart/Pollard) Ventura's con-
fidence and self-esteem have grown to the point that she herself initiates their
first tryst; as if to "authorize" their romance, the couple's pose as they embrace
(11) resembles that of the lovers in Rodin's *The Kiss* (1882), with "power lines"
and twinkling "stars" as accents to the scene.[35]

This unconventional, liberatory model of sexuality (between two rock crea-
tures) recalls Elizabeth Grosz's discussion of hermaphroditism—its potent
reminder that sex exists along a gender and anatomical continuum whose
more unorthodox manifestations have traditionally been labeled "freakish"
by ableist culture (60). Tobin Siebers echoes that point, noting that "a crucial
consideration for people with disabilities is not to judge their sexuality by
comparison to normative sexuality but to think expansively and experimen-
tally about what defines sexual experience for them" (2008: 151).[36]

Memoirs by women with disabilities affirms that stance, as seen in the
work of Nancy Mairs, a woman with multiple sclerosis. Like Ventura, Mairs
initially struggled with the bodily changes brought on by her condition, particularly with how they posed a threat to traditional notions of being "pretty"
and "womanly." But as expressed in her 1990 essay "Carnal Acts," Mairs comes
to embrace and celebrate her new way of being a woman:

> To be silent is to comply with the standard of feminine grace. But my crip-
> pled body already violates all notions of feminine grace. What more have
> I got to lose? I've gone beyond shame . . . I've "found" my voice, then, just
> where it ought to have been, in the body-warmed breath escaping my lungs
> and throat. Forced by the exigencies of physical disease to embrace my self
> in the flesh, I couldn't write bodiless prose. The voice is the creature of the
> body that produces it. I speak as a crippled woman. (60)

In her reading of Mairs's work, Madonne Miner highlights its feminist potential, with a "brave new world" breathlessness which one feels it merits:

> As MS pushes Mairs further away from model womanhood, she happily
> chucks such models and begins to delight in the liberatory possibilities of
> stepping out of bounds, of pushing the envelope. Rather than mourning
> losses, Mairs glories in new opportunities. Rather than looking backward,
> she looks forward. Ironically, Mairs' disability stories suggest that her dis-
> ease frees her from a subordinate gender position. (286)

Similarly, Ventura's acceptance, even exultation, of her "borderline" condition—woman, heroine, monster—a condition she asserts by taking Grimm
as her lover, effectuates an empowering, redefining model of disability,

femininity, and sex.[37] She-Thing comes out—like Grimm in his first appearance, smashing the doorway to smithereens in the process. How much more complex (and interesting) than a She-Hulk-style assimilationist paradigm which simply reinscribes habitual gender norms and sexual oppression![38]

Ventura went so far beyond the gender system that many readers recoiled, yet still found love on her own terms, "at the margins." That this exacerbated the discord between Marvel's editorship and the writer, so that within months Englehart felt compelled to remove his name from the series credits, is testament to the radically decentering message of the She-Thing storyline.

Of course, in a corporate, serialized, melodrama-heavy, mainstream format, Ventura's resolution could not last. By "Only Death Be My Salvation!" (*Fantastic Four*, vol. 1, #379, Aug. 1993, Defalco/Ryan), the depressive "grotesque" She-Thing would return, to wreak havoc with her will to self-destruction, reestablishing with a vengeance what Mitchell and Snyder call "the critical connection between disability and femininity as monstrous deviance" (2000: 39). As the title bears out, Ventura's suicidal impulses return full force after Doctor Doom mutates her further, into an overly muscled "misshapen *monstrosity* separated from humanity by an infinite and agonizing gulf!" (Defalco/Ryan: 15, emphasis in original). To underscore the point, the caption just quoted accompanies an image of two normate heterosexual lovers walking arm-in-arm in sunlight, with the freakish She-Thing gazing at them from a dark alley. Her once-empowering "intragender" status is thus reduced to that of embittered, envious, malformed brute.

Driven to a frenzy, her old insecurities and alienation revived, she once more enacts the role of "malignant disabled avenger" (Mitchell/Snyder 2001: 25), terrorizing New York on the road to self-annihilation. (In case the message wasn't clear enough, the issue's cover features the mutated Ventura holding a car aloft and snarling, in "blood-curdling" letters: *"I don't need your pity—I am a monster!"*) Her dialogue within the actual story is no less disheartening and paper-thin: "*What's the use of even trying anymore?!*" she howls at Richards's attempts to "cure" her (6); "I have *nothing!* My life is already *over!* Doom ended it when he stole my *humanity!*" and "I want you to remember me the way I was! Not like *this!*" (22); "I . . . I *can't* live like this! I have no choice! I know what must be done—*!*" (18, all emphases in original). A more generous reading of this episode would hold that scriptwriter Defalco does not flinch from depicting the real struggles and reverses of living with deformity—though the two-dimensional exposition argues otherwise. In short, the disability/feminist-positive vision of the Englehart run is dismantled in one fell swoop.

In the end, Ventura leaps onto a subway station's electric third rail in a bid to end her torment (a clumsy allusion to Tolstoy's *Anna Karenina*); like before, she fails in her goal, though a misapprehending Grimm is set on a course

4.8 In "Only Death Be My Salvation!" (*Fantastic Four*, vol. 1, #379), Ventura further mutates into a "monstrous" form—once more destabilizing the team.

to avenge her "death" (28). Thus, the demoralizing return to a "disability/femi-ninity as monstrosity" paradigm robs Ventura of all agency; she is now again simply a plot point in Grimm's more central narrative arc. The unfolding of the She-Thing storyline in the period covered illustrates the perils and lim-its of discussing such subject matter in a mainstream context. It reminds us that speaking of disability within a "gendered discursive field" (Miner: 285) determined by ableist, phallocentric culture often involves—to use an ableist metaphor—taking one step forward and two steps back.

"SICKNESS DOESN'T KNOW COLOR, MAN"

Akin to Grimm and Ventura, the final case examined in this chapter, DC's Af-rican-American superhero Cyborg (aka Victor Stone), exemplifies the pitfalls as well as dividends for representing the "borderline" qua racialized super-subject. As one of the New Teen Titans, Stone's surly demeanor and misgiv-ings about the traumatic origin of his powers (in an accident that took the life of his mother) at times complicate his interaction with other group members in ways similar to what we've observed in the Fantastic Four. Unlike Grimm and Ventura, however, he does not routinely turn against his teammates. This is because, as I will argue, Cyborg's origin story (recounted in 1982) ultimately serves as a parable of assimilation, political moderation, and resistance to the "disfiguring" effects of racism—and only secondarily as a narrative about disability.

We may attribute such a stance to a structural feature of racialized depic-tions in mainstream superhero comics since the Silver Age. As highlighted by Adilifu Nama and other scholars, black superheroes more than other minori-ty representations have perforce found themselves cast as "metaphors for race relations in America," cultural ciphers for, among other things, the "shifting politics of black racial formation." They "symbolize American racial morality and ethics" and "overtly represent or implicitly signify social discourse and ac-cepted wisdom concerning notions of racial reciprocity, racial equality, racial forgiveness, and, ultimately, racial justice" (4).[39]

As elaborated by Marc Singer, these circumstances sprang in part from a historically problematic system of visual typology which made superhero comics "fertile ground for stereotyped depictions of race." And while "the superhero genre's own conventions can invite a more nuanced depiction of minority identity" (2002: 107),[40] minority characters often run the risk of be-ing absorbed into a "generic ideology of the superhero" which as discussed in my introduction often works to preserve the status quo. Therefore, Singer maintains, "any examination of race in superhero comics must consider these

4.9 Victor Stone confronts his father after the accident that disfigured his body (*Tales of the New Teen Titans*, vol. I, #1, Jun. 1982).

innate tensions, as the handling of race is forever caught between the genre's most radical impulses and its most conservative ones" (ibid.: 110).[41]

Cyborg/Stone's[42] origin story, "Cyborg" (*Tales of the New Teen Titans*, vol. I, #1, Jun. 1982, Wolfman/Pérez), seems to be a tailor-made illustration of the pitfalls Singer's thesis describes. Raised as a lonely prodigy by scientist parents working for both the military and S.T.A.R. Labs, the young Stone latches on to Ron Evers, an Artful Dodger-like juvenile delinquent who instructs him in such vices as smoking, petty theft, and gang violence. Stone's rift with his parents, especially his father Silas, widens as he grows into an athletically gifted young man partly swayed by Evers's racially charged diatribes against "the Man." One day, Stone visits the lab to discover an accident has released an extra-dimensional life form with a corrosive exterior which kills his mother and liquefies half of Stone's body. After disposing of the threat, Elias saves his son's life by grafting hi-tech military armor to Stone's skin, transforming him into a man-machine.

As with Ventura (and the McAfee and other cases of traumatic injury cited earlier), Stone initially reacts to his transformation into a "freak" with intense horror and suicidal urges.[43] Filled with anger and hatred at his father, he screams, "*Why couldn't you let me die!?!?*" (Wolfman/Pérez: 17).[44] Stone spends the next several months in painful physical therapy, learning to live with/ in his new prostheticized body. Eventually he breaks with Silas, renting an apartment in Hell's Kitchen and battling depression. His loss of "normality,"

4.10 Stone undergoes months of physical therapy (*Tales of the New Teen Titans*, vol. I, #1, Jun. 1982).

abandonment by his girlfriend Marcy, and rejection by his old football coach, as well as the stares of passersby in public—"I felt their eyes boring into me. Fear. *Hate*. It hurt so much. But never so much as when kids ran away from me. I was a *monster*. A blasted *Frankenstein*" (ibid.: 19)—make him open to Evers's incitements to revenge: "It was the *man* that did you in. The man does us *all* in, bro" (ibid.: 20, all emphases in original). Stone appears to agree to help Evers with his latest salvo in an ongoing race war: to blow up the United Nations building. But in the end, Stone decides to stop Evers's black-power terrorist cell; standing against them atop the UN building in sharp relief against the moon, Cyborg resembles a knight in shining armor.

What is fairly clear from this synopsis is that "Cyborg," in some ways a standard "overcoming" story (see chapter 6) whose narrative prosthesis involves a diabolical foil (Evers) tempting the hero to succumb to his bitterness and anger, ultimately subsumes disability under its preferred tropes of post-humanist sci-fi and racial tolerance. Pérez in fact often melds the two themes through his close-up split-face portraits of Stone (half-black man, half-robot).

Yet the "post-human" approach to disability, popularized by feminist Donna Haraway's "A Cyborg Manifesto" (1985), has sustained heavy critique by disability scholars who deride its fetishization of technology over the real experiences of disabled people. As noted by Tobin Siebers:

> Haraway is so preoccupied with power and ability that she forgets what disability is. Prostheses always increase the cyborg's abilities; they are a source only of new powers, never of problems. The cyborg is always more than human—and never risks to be seen as subhuman. To put it simply, the cyborg is not disabled. (2008: 63)[45]

The story likewise stacks the deck in its depiction of 1970s racial politics, which borders on the reactionary. Stone's flirtation with alternative black culture—he "talks jive" and hangs a "Black Power" poster in his bedroom (9)—is blamed on family dysfunction, the angry posturings of a confused young man.[46] Wolfman's script further reduces the structural injustices of white privilege and inner city violence primarily[47] to the deluded fantasies of the extremist race warrior Evers (whose name ironically recalls the Mississippi civil-rights activist Medgar Evers, slain by a white supremacist in 1963). In short, those who resist white hegemony are con men, criminals, and terrorists. In opposing them, Stone casts himself as a heroic figure.

Cyborg seems to be a conscious attempt to move past the blaxploitation-era black superhero typified by Luke Cage and Black Lightning, who were "often characterized in their origins, costumes, street language, and anti-establishment attitudes as more overtly macho than their white-bread counterparts"

(Brown: 178). Stone (blessedly) has none of their "Sweet Christmas!"-style affectations. In fact, through all his clashes with his high-achieving technocrat parents, as he rejects their plans for his future, even as he takes up the fight against crime, the issue of race recedes into a broad liberal vision of presumed equality.[48] While this is laudable in some respects, such a move mostly elides the social forces that produce someone like Evers. Dismissed as a caricature, he nonetheless, more than any other character in "Cyborg," embodies what Jeffrey Brown calls the "black male paradox": "emasculated, but at the same time feared . . . grounded in a long tradition of subjugation and resistance" (170).

Instead, as depicted, Evers is simply mendacity and evil personified—a man who through his own racism has "scarred [him]self beyond reason" (24). As Stone berates him:

> You're *bad news*, Ron. You always *were*. Always blamin' someone *else*, too. When we were kids, you blamed the *adults*. When we got older, every problem in the world was caused by the *whites*. *Sickness* doesn't know *color*, man. And you've been twisted *sick* right from the start! (23, emphasis in original)

Not race, then, and not disability, but racism is the true disfiguring force: its trauma likened to nothing less than terrorism. Stone's successful rite of passage, the acceptance of his new corporeal state, comes about at last through definitively rejecting the extremism represented by Evers—who, like Satan, falls (presumably to his death, from the roof of the UN building)—by staying grounded in his own ethical identity.

Having recounted his origin story to his teammates while on a Grand Canyon retreat, Stone hardly seems triumphant; life is no picnic for a half-mechanized man. As with Ventura and Grimm, Stone's misgivings about his "borderline" condition—years after his accident he still refers to himself as a "galvanized *freak*" (Wolfman/Pérez: 3, emphasis in original)—point with unusual candor to his continuing struggles to adjust. Though driven to near-despair, Cyborg demonstrates through his story the essence of his heroism: to find the personal wherewithal to change, what Sharon Packer has termed "post-traumatic strength disorder" (238).[49] This explains why "Cyborg" opens with the tag line: "From the fiery depths of tragedy comes the birth of a new hero!" (1). Of course, we cannot forget that for the borderline figure, the serialized format (and effectively endless continuity) of mainstream superhero comics means there is always the danger of, at some point, slipping back to despair, embitterment, and outright villainy.

CONCLUSION

In her essay "Infinite Representational Crisis: Race, Gender, the Superhero," Rebecca Wanzo notes that the reinvention of superhero identity brought about during the Silver Age has been "particularly challenging for women, African-Americans and other minorities" (22). The disabled "borderline" journeys of Ben Grimm/the Thing, Sharon Ventura/She-Thing/Ms. Marvel and Victor Stone/Cyborg—among the most vexed iterations of the superhero archetype in this period—bear out that thesis, through their "different cultural elaborations of women's and men's bodies, bodies of color and white bodies, as these cultural elaborations intersect in narratives of illness and disability" (Miner: 285).

These are not "easy," unproblematic narratives of covering up and over-coming a perceived lack, but rather cases in which the superpower, in a sense, *is* the problem (a "problematic embodiment," in Garland-Thomson's words) and no "covering-up" (ideological, psychological, sartorial) is forthcoming. Any resolution, therefore, has to start with the acceptance of the embodied "problem" itself, and ultimately, with its celebration along novel bodily norms.

These stories thus represent a new hybrid model of disability politics, transgender triumphalism, and racial tolerance, of the sort increasingly seen in mainstream American culture since the 1960s. They demonstrate most vividly and problematically the conflation often observed between different human categories—gender, race, disability—along the shifting, unstable border that divides superhero from supervillain.

5

DISMODERNISM AND "THE WORLD'S STRANGEST HEROES"

One of the oddest near-synchronies in superhero comics history, DC's Doom Patrol (in the series *My Greatest Adventure*) and Marvel's *X-Men* premiered within three months of each other, with respective cover dates of June and September 1963. The overlaps did not end there.

Both super-teams consisted of societal outcasts led by a strong patriarchal figure in a wheelchair, who all live together in alternate communities hidden from the world, and fight to defend the public that alienates them. Both had members who feel cursed by their powers and struggle with their "freak" status. Both faced an opposing group of "freaks" with a name that starts "the Brotherhood of Evil." Even their cover tag lines mirrored each other: "the world's strangest heroes!" (Doom Patrol); "the strangest superheroes of all!" (X-Men).

Such coincidences have fueled decades-old fan debates over *X-Men* scribe (and Marvel editor) Stan Lee's supposed "plagiarism" of DC editor Murray Boltinoff and writer Arnold Drake's ideas—though the tight timeline argues against it.[1] Furthermore, the Doom Patrol itself represented a direct response to Marvel's genre-reinventing success of the early Silver Age. As explained by Will Jacobs and Gerard Jones: "The Doom Patrol, with its heroes cut off from society and doubting the worth of their own powers, was the first DC comic to incorporate some of the ideas being pioneered by Marvel. It also brought an air of darkness and mystery into the usually sunny world of DC heroes" (100).

Whatever their initial convergences, the two series saw starkly different fates. A modest-selling title[2] which Marvel cast into the limbo of reprint status with vol. 1, #66 (Mar. 1970), *X-Men* became the company's most successful superhero series with its 1975 revamping under writer Chris Claremont and artists Dave Cockrum and John Byrne.[3] The cerebral, paraplegic Professor Charles Xavier, director of Xavier's School for Gifted Youngsters in upstate New York, uses the institution as a front for his X-Men, a group of teen mutants born with superpowers[4] who conduct an endless secret war against Magneto, his Brotherhood of Evil Mutants and other menaces bent on dominating Homo sapiens to the will of "Homo superior." Fans came to read the series as a mirror for US race relations and identity politics, with mutants as the beleaguered minority struggling for inclusion in a world predisposed to fear them.

Danny Fingeroth calls *X-Men* "the most direct metaphor for tolerance, racial and otherwise, ever to grace the pages of a comic book" (2007: 113); Douglas Wolk dubs the stories "allegories about difference and identity politics" (95);[5] while Charles Hatfield points out the series' key innovation of the early 1960s:

> Instead of defending the status quo . . . the X-men redefined the world by their very presence. Instead of defending against random "crime," the X-Men battled other mutants, for humanity's sake. Unlike the superhero comics that came before it, then, *The X-Men* started from a premise that was not conservative but potentially transformative. (2012: 137)

Scott Bukatman, for his part, has centered on how the series' dizzying corporeal heterogeneity reflects post-Cold War anxieties over fleshly mutability: "The mutant body is explicitly traumatic, armored against the world outside yet racked and torn apart by complex forces within. The mutant body is oxymoronic: rigidly protected but dangerously unstable" (2003: 51). Indeed, the X-Men stories abound in such paradoxes and compromises: Cyclops is terrified of losing control of his eye blasts; Beast agonizes over his deformity; Rogue's power always threatens to hurt those around her; Wolverine/Logan fears losing his humanity in one of his berserker rages; Nightcrawler/Kurt Wagner, like the Fantastic Four's Thing, is persecuted for his freakish appearance; Phoenix/Jean Grey trembles at the prospect of becoming Dark Phoenix and destroying the Universe—all as they routinely save the world. The formula proved enduring and profitable well past the Silver and Bronze ages.[6]

Doom Patrol, on the other hand, started strong for DC (earning the team's name on the title after only six issues), but fizzled over the course of its five-year run. It suffered an ignominious if legendary cancellation with vol. 1, #121 (Sept.-Oct. 1968), when—as discussed in chapter 7—Drake and Boltinoff killed the entire original team in an explosion, for "real." Revived in subsequent decades with new rosters, the Doom Patrol retained a "cult" status, particularly under the helm of writer Grant Morrison in the late 1980s and 1990s,[7] but not strong sales. Nonetheless, the original run by Drake and artist Bruno Premiani remains notable for its bizarre amalgam of absurdism, tragedy, and Pop Art verve.

The mysterious, choleric Chief (later identified as Dr. Niles Caulder), who uses a wheelchair, brings together three "misfits": Robotman/Cliff Steele, victim of an auto-racing accident whose brain has been transferred to a grotesque robot body; Elasti-Girl/Rita Farr, a film actress who after breathing supernatural fumes can substantially alter her body size; and Negative Man/ Larry Trainor, an air force pilot whose disfiguring radiation exposure in a sub-orbital flight grants him the ability to summon a powerful "negative" entity from inside his body for up to sixty seconds at a time. The Chief offers them a new life with a purpose: to defend humanity against all threats while inspiring it to become more tolerant of people with physical differences.[8] Over the next sixty issues, the group—often raucous and squabbling among themselves—confronts a gallery of über-preposterous villains: the elderly General Immortus; the Brotherhood of Evil led by the disembodied Brain; the category-defying Animal-Vegetable-Mineral Man.

Fifty years after their debuts, the verdict is clear: critically and in fan discourses DC produced the more sophisticated series, at least in the 1960s. Where the Lee/Kirby run of *X-Men* often proved repetitive, stiff, and rudderless—as Hatfield noted, "the series cast about uncertainly for subplots, hooks, and distinctive characterizations" (2012: 131)[9]—with concepts that would not definitively bear fruit until a later era, *Doom Patrol* from its first issue expertly tapped the genre's potential for surreal hilarity and camp, while staying grounded (thanks in no small part to Premiani's realistic art style) in psychologically complex, self-conscious figures who somehow rose above all the weirdness, earning a readerly sympathy that made their sudden deaths at the end of the series all the more shocking. Like no title before it—and few since—*Doom Patrol* raised ironic superhero tragicomedy to new heights, with astonishing consistency throughout its run. More often than not, its creators out-Marveled Marvel.

The foregoing helps explain why the two series, from their inceptions, differed markedly in another key respect: their treatment of disability. Let us take the representation of Caulder, Xavier, and their wheelchairs as illustrative.

WHEELCHAIRS

A long-standing and persistent "association of disability with malevolence" (Longmore 2003: 131) in art has produced such villainous/tragic ogres as Shakespeare's humpbacked Richard III, Melville's amputee Captain Ahab, and Shelley's Frankenstein's monster. More recent depictions like Peter Sellers's darkly humorous turn as Dr. Strangelove, an evil genius in a wheelchair

5.1 Captain America battles Cadavus (*Captain America*, vol. 1, #104, Aug. 1968).

from Stanley Kubrick's Cold War satire *Dr. Strangelove, or How I Learned to Stop Worrying and Love the Bomb* (1964), manifested the type in postwar US cinema. For many disability scholars this character in particular has come to represent modern ableist anxieties (undergirding oppression and exclusion) about those who use wheelchairs as a type of threatening "disabled cyborg" (Raphael), enacting disability "as the mark of constitutive lack" which leads to "the moral panic that has historically obtained in social encounters between disabled and nondisabled people and that often gets refracted within literary discourse to become normalized and unquestioned" (Quayson: 33–34).

No less than other media, Silver Age superhero comics partook of such stereotypical shorthand as well. In "Slave of the Skull!" (*Captain America*, vol. 1, #104, Aug. 1968, Lee/Kirby), the star-spangled avenger takes on a bevy of villains assembled by his arch-nemesis, the Red Skull. Among them: Cadavus, "monarch of the murder chair," a dwarfish elderly man in an enormous fur collar who commands a wheeled mini-arsenal that doubles as his conveyance. "*What?*" scoffs Cap upon laying eyes on him. "I'm expected to pit my skill against an aged *invalid?!!*" (12, emphasis in original). Tellingly, the cackling Cadavus trains his chair's "jet blasts" on the Captain's legs—a literalization of ableist nightmares regarding the secret revenge fantasies harbored by the mobility impaired, to wit: "disabled people resent the nondisabled and would, if they could, destroy them" (Longmore 2003: 131)—or make them "one of us." To banish such fears, Cap crushes the "murder chair"; a now-helpless Cadavus is humiliatingly borne away on the wrestler Krushki's back (19).

Another frequently appearing Captain America supervillain, the Lee/Kirby creation M.O.D.O.K. (Mental Organism Designated Only for Killing),[10] cements the cyborg qualities of the "wheelchair-user" menace: M.O.D.O.K. essentially functions as an oversized head capable of locomotion only through the assistance of his heavily armed "hover chair." Such "othering" depictions confirm the contrast often struck between physically weak, "intellectual" foes and strong, virile heroes in the Silver Age; as noted by Mike Conroy: "Inevitably, [M.O.D.O.K.] returned to plague Captain America, whose physical perfection he so resented" (253). Similarly, the Green Lantern adversary Hector Hammond (created by John Broome and Gil Kane)[11] is rendered immobile and mute by extreme head growth brought on by meteorite radiation; through mental control and hyper-intelligence he—it should come as no surprise—relishes in stealing the happy thoughts and memories of the able-bodied.

But what happens when the immobilized figure is a hero?

The origin stories to both the X-Men and Doom Patrol first make the reader aware of their leaders' paraplegia through a dramatic reveal. In the opening panel of "X-Men" (X-Men, vol. 1, #1, Sept. 1963: 1), we glimpse a seated Xavier through a French window; the second panel switches to an interior view of the professor on an armchair recliner, a blanket covering his lap. The artwork and both panels' captions emphasize his remoteness and insularity while presaging his paralysis: "a strange silent man sits motionless, brooding . . . alone with his indescribable thoughts . . .", "Then, while he remains completely motionless . . ." (ibid., ellipses in original).

Xavier's use of a wheelchair is made plain (albeit rather clumsily) some seven pages later, in a long horizontal panel in which he introduces Jean Grey to her new teammates. Until that oddly downplayed reveal (considering how much else is going on in terms of establishing the setting), the professor could simply be a seated able-bodied human (with telepathy). Furthermore, the enlightened Grey makes no comment on Xavier's true state after the clarification; he explains two pages later, "Due to a childhood accident, I myself must remain in this chair . . ." (11). The treatment of Xavier's wheelchair in these scenes evinces a remarkably progressive, "normalizing" impulse, with the students (and presumably the reader) simply accepting the professor's physical difference along with his superpowers. The mood of "normality" is underscored by the fact that Jean's arrival and induction take place in daytime, in Xavier's study: everything is clear, visible, transparent, even mundane—at least as mundane as superheroics ever get.

5.2 Charles Xavier's staid "reveal" as a wheelchair-user (*X-Men*, vol. 1, #1, Sept. 1963).

Contrast this staid domestic affair with Caulder's reveal in the Doom Patrol origin. From the first panel, Drake and Premiani construct a noirish, sensationalistic atmosphere, all shadows and carnival-barker calls to voyeurism. Over a splash that shows Caulder from the chest up, illuminated by a spotlight, with three murky silhouettes in the background, a caption declares: "You are about to experience one of the strangest meetings ever convened—a joining of the four most unusual people on earth! Sit quietly in the shadows of this clandestine conference and observe it well!" (*My Greatest Adventure*, vol. 1, #80, Jun. 1963: 1).

As Caulder berates his guests in what looks like a dark cellar full of scientific equipment, telling them they should join him despite their disabilities and stop "feeling sorry" for themselves, the tension rises; they like neither him nor his words. Then, in the story's fifth panel, he proves his point—by pushing back from his desk. "A *wheelchair!*" Farr shrieks (2, emphasis in original). "You see," a stern Chief explains, "I too, have a handicap! But I conquered it with my *brain* by mastering every field of knowledge! In these rooms, I go on my own adventures ... *adventures with my mind!*" (ibid., emphasis and ellipsis in original).

The confrontational "clandestine conference," with its melodramatic surprise revelation, partakes of what Ato Quayson describes as the *unheimlich* "epiphanic use" of disability in literature:

> The suddenness and unanticipated emergence of the impairment with the multifarious metaphors that are attached to it become the means to accentuate the unusualness of the entire event. The disclosure of the impairment acts much like a discursive punctuation mark, providing a vehicle for the intensification of ethical contradictions made sharply evident at that point in the text. (44)

5.3 Niles "The Chief" Caulder's much more dramatic, noirish "reveal" (*My Greatest Adventure*, vol. 1, #80, Jun. 1963).

Indeed, as this opening scene demonstrates, *Doom Patrol* far more often than *X-Men* invokes the "epiphanic"—some might label them "freakish"— qualities of the wheelchair-as-disability marker, while it paradoxically depicts Caulder as a powerful, post-human figure in his own right, more along the lines of villains such as Cadavus. Xavier's (frequently overturned) wheelchair, meanwhile, consistently appears as a signifier of weakness, passivity, and dependence, as we shall see.

In fact, upon casual scrutiny the notable differences between Caulder and Xavier's representations quickly mount. While both men suffer paralysis as a result of heroic action (Caulder in an elaborate bid to outsmart General Immortus; Xavier in battle against the villain Lucifer), the X-Men's leader is cerebral, emotionally removed, vaguely androgynous—a dome-pated "egghead" emblematic of Kirby's "critical and anti-intellectual" rendering of scientists, according to Hatfield (2012: 268fn).[12] Stern, hyper-intelligent and even inhuman, Xavier gives orders but stays above the fray; in vol. 1, #7, he designates Summers as his deputy so as to attend to other, non-interpersonal matters. Furthermore, perhaps owing in part to the largely invisible nature of his mental powers, with the concomitant impulse to show his physical incapacity, Xavier often appears helpless without his chair, sprawled on the ground after being thrown from it or else borne away to safety in the arms of his students.

Such examples abound throughout Lee/Kirby's 1963–66 *X-Men* run. The cackling Vanisher calls Xavier "A helpless human . . . alone and defenseless" (vol. 1, #2, Nov. 1963: 20); the Blob calls him *"helpless!"* (vol. 1, #3, Jan. 1964: 22); the professor also speaks of himself in such terms not infrequently, as when, deprived of his chair, he agonizes, "My *X-Men* are prisoners of the gigantic *sentinels,* within that deadly fortress . . . while I lie helplessly outside—unable to help them—hardly able to defend *myself!*" (vol. 1, #16, Jan. 1966: 2); infantilizing imagery is typified by an episode in which the students gingerly put their injured leader to bed (vol. 1, #5, May 1964: 2); indeed, he often appears physically or telekinetically manipulated, as when rescued from the ocean when the team's boat explodes (vol. 1, #6, May 1964: 14), or when Grey "speeds up" his movements, thinking, "To others he's just a helpless man in a wheelchair! But, when I see him like this, I sense courage . . . and *power* . . ." (vol. 1, #13, Sept. 1965: 4, all emphases and ellipses in original).[13]

One also observes, as aforementioned, a distressingly high number of instances in which Xavier appears splayed out on the floor, spilled ignominiously from his chair: whether horizontally confronting Lucifer (vol. 1, #9, Jan. 1965: 8), awkwardly unbalanced on the pavement before Juggernaut (#13: 2), or, as a caption puts it, "desperately, painfully, disregarding the agony of his injured body, the crippled mutant tirelessly crawls inch after inch, until he reaches" a highway (#16: 3). Even when he heroically hurls himself from his chair to save Beast from a booby-trapped door, Xavier comes off as wholly inadequate; again collapsed on the floor, his speech is maudlin and pathetic: *"Leave me!* I'm no good to you any more! The explosion deadened my mutant power! I can no longer read minds—or throw my thoughts! Go after the evil ones—forget me!" (vol. 1, #4, Mar. 1964: 23, emphasis in original).[14]

But perhaps the most problematic aspects of Xavier's representation are the most banal. Firstly: the static, frontal imagery. Kirby mostly draws the chair directly facing the reader, even when the Professor moves under his own power (see vol. 1, #11, May 1965: 20 for a good example), depriving his figure of much dynamism and instead emphasizing its deliberate, quasi-immobile state. (One gets the distinct impression that Kirby, the genre's greatest master of superheroic action, doesn't quite know what to do with a non-able-bodied man who is not a villain.)

Second, Xavier's chair is almost always pushed by others, even into battle (vol. 1, #4: 22; vol. 1, #13: 16); we often see a helper or facilitator standing

5.4 Xavier often appears with his chair overturned or sprawled helplessly on the floor (*X-Men*, vol. 1, #13, Sept. 1965).

behind him. As argued by Michelle R. Hebl and Robert E. Kleck, such a posture subtly frames the "pushee" as socially subordinate:

> When one pushes the wheelchair of another person, for example, the normal physical context of the interaction between two people is disrupted. Rather than walking abreast, two friends become a "helper" and a "helpee"; eye contact and reciprocity of nonverbal behaviors are lost; and the nature of the interaction can change dramatically, often to the disadvantage of the person in the wheelchair. (421)

Xavier's visual depiction as a physically helpless man—passive, horizontal, static, despite being the "most powerful mutant on Earth" due to his mental prowess—perhaps best explains his conspicuous asexuality. The series' third issue reveals the professor harbors a secret, forbidden attachment to Grey— but immediately forecloses even the possibility of a romance: "Don't worry!" thinks Xavier. "As though I could *help* worrying about the one I love! But I

5.5 Kirby often depicted Xavier through static frontal imagery (*X-Men*, vol. 1, #11, May 1965).

can never *tell* her! I have no right! Not while I'm the leader of the X-Men, and confined to this wheelchair!" (vol. 1, #3: 4, emphasis in original). Such an attitude coincides all too smoothly with 1960s presumptions about the disabled's unsuitability (indeed, their taboo identity) as sexual partners.[15]

Once more, the Doom Patrol's Chief makes for quite the dramatic contrast to the prim depiction of a wheelchair-user in *X-Men*. Unlike Xavier, Caulder is a normal, non-superpowered man. We should place the emphasis on "man": hirsute, bearded, beefy, and very much the control freak, he does not allow his paraplegia to impede his active (even robust) participation in physical battles. Unlike with the baldpated Xavier, Caulder's aloofness and authoritarianism reads as much "manly" and patriarchal as cerebral.[16] Even when the Chief complains about his paralysis, the body language and expressions come off as "macho": "Faster! Faster! Oh, these cursed legs of mine—they could cost *Robotman* his life!" (vol. 1, #103, May 1966: 11, emphasis in original).[17]

Caulder often moves under his own power, even pulling himself up ramps (vol. 1, #88, Jun. 1964: 85); he almost always travels quickly, the wheelchair's progress depicted with "speed lines" (vol. 1, #89, Aug. 1964: 5 and passim); even when pushed by a surrogate, it is almost always at high speed, to deal with some emergency (ibid.: 15 and passim); he bursts through doors (vol. 1, #105, Aug. 1966: 2); his chair at times even merits the sound effects WHIRRR (#88: 21) and WHOOSH! (vol. 1, #108, Dec. 1966: 22). Premiani draws his movement

5.6 Premiani renders Caulder as a man of action, his fast-moving wheelchair even meriting a sound effect (*Doom Patrol*, vol. 1, #108, Dec. 1966).

chiefly across a diagonal, reinforcing the impression of fast motion across the panel (vol. 1, #120, Aug. 1968: 9 and passim).[18]

Furthermore, the redoubtable Caulder's paralysis is no impediment to love. Late in the series, he conducts an affair with the villainess Madame Rouge, who passionately declares after some careless roughhousing that nearly dislodges the Chief: "You—you *fools*! A man like zis—more man zan any of you! You could have *killed* him!" (vol. 1, #111, May 1967: 15, emphasis and unconventional spelling in original). The Doom Patrol's aggressive, domineering leader indeed behaved as "more man zan any of you" throughout the title's run.

Perhaps the sharpest contrast between Caulder and Xavier's depiction— and further proof of the more violent masculine image of the former—appears in their use of "special" chairs for unusual situations. In "Enter, the Avengers!" (vol. 1, #9, Jan. 1965), the Professor ventures into the bowels of the earth astride a tracked vehicle, in search of the villain Lucifer. This device proves capable of defensive action—when the floor suddenly gives way, it deploys "hydraulic extendo-arms" to brace itself against the cavern walls (4). But Lucifer's superior technology quickly overwhelms the "explorer chair" by whisking Professor X off it with a super-powerful "dust devil." We never see the chair again; for the rest of the story, Xavier confronts the villain while sprawled on the floor, and defeats him with his mental powers.

Compare this episode with a repeated motif in *Doom Patrol*: what Caulder calls his "wheelchair fortress" or "action chair," a conveyance he constantly renovates and improves like some men might work on a jalopy. The "action chair" comes fully equipped for battle, with concealed flamethrower, grappling hooks, ultra-sonic emitters, machine guns, antiaircraft rocket launcher, a giant steel claw, etc. The armored rig, in fact, resembles Cadavus or M.O.D.O.K.'s arsenals; Caulder is not above boasting of its capacities: "This souped-up motorized chair can do 25 miles an hour! And the fastest runner can't do better than 15!" (vol. 1, #117, Feb. 1968: 18).

In "The Chief 'Stands' Alone" (vol. 1, #94, Mar. 1965; note the title's ironic quotation marks on the word "stands"), Caulder pits his fortress against the absurdly avian villain Claw, who mocks him by branding the confrontation one of "man to *half* a man!" (11, emphasis in original). The Chief defeats his enemy's bird allies with his flamethrower and steel claw, then darts about on the chair to avoid the villain's lunges. Eventually Caulder, still seated, punches Claw unconscious (13).

The fight's conclusion underscores a consistent feature of Caulder's depiction: his physical vigor. He transfers from his accustomed conveyance to the "action chair" with the aid of his "powerful arms" (ibid.: 5); he strangles a giant condor with his bare hands when it tries to carry him off, bragging, "The power that a man loses in his legs is transferred to his arms. The law of natural compensation, bird! Now—*feel it!*" (#117: 11, emphasis in original). Again and again, Drake and Premiani present the Chief as anything but weak, and wholly self-sufficient—at times stubbornly so. In his battle with the Black Vulture and his birds, Caulder refuses to summon his teammates (with whom he's quarreled), musing, "The sensible thing would be to call the police! But that's an admission that I can't draw a breath without the aid of the *Doom Patrol*! The devil with that!" He then says out loud: "I'll stand alone—or fail!" (ibid.: 15, emphasis in original).[19]

For Xavier, then, the wheelchair constitutes a mere implement and marker of his disability, easily (and often) overturned—the better for him to wield his mental powers just when others see him as most physically helpless. Caulder's wheelchair, in contrast, functions as a prosthetic, a full-blown extension of him, his scientific genius and aggressive personality. (The flamethrower and rocket-launcher are reifications of the Chief's hyper-masculine cholera, while Xavier's bald head and lean body emphasize his disconcerting intellectualism and "intragender" status.) Secondly, Caulder's insistence on autonomy (the imposition of his will on others, eager participation in battles, and sexual liaison with Madame Rouge) makes him a full-fledged individual—and a fully *mobile* one—in ways Xavier does not achieve during the Lee/Kirby run. In other words, Caulder's autonomy is visually premised on his capacity to move, if not as easily as his comrades, certainly as readily and effectively. (His red hair—stereotypical signifier of a hothead—serves a similar purpose as visual shortcut.) Xavier, on the other hand, consistently appears physically hampered, stiff, and in need of assistance to get around—if not outright defenseless, spilled from his seat on the floor—rendering him a far more remote and "inhuman" figure.

5.7 Caulder dispatches one of the Black Vulture's minions — barehanded (*Doom Patrol*, vol. 1, #117, Feb. 1968).

It is Caulder who seems more starkly to exemplify the wheelchair-using scholar Simi Linton's 1998 contention that "as we are now emerging, upping the ante on the demands for a truly inclusive society, we disrupt the social order. . . . We further confound expectations when we have the temerity to emerge as forthright and resourceful people, nothing like the self-loathing, docile, bitter, or insentient fictional versions of ourselves the public is more used to" (3). For all that, it is simply one of *Doom Patrol*'s many dramatic paradoxes that the Chief's very individuality and independence make him as *dependent* on his "family" of teammates as they on him; indeed, the group's alternative model of community is predicated on interdependence, a crucial concept in disability theory and disability rights activism. Let us turn to a brief examination, as expressed through a more recent, related notion.

DISMODERNISM

Lennard Davis first proposed the term "dismodernism" in *Bending Over Backwards: Essays on Disability and the Body* (2002) as a discursive response to the double-edged problem of postmodernism's dissolution of fixed categories and identities, with its resultant threat to any unified identity politics. As argued by, among others, Rosemarie Garland-Thomson,

> the post-structuralist logic that destabilizes identity can free marginalized people from the narrative of essential inadequacy, but at the same time it risks denying the particularity of their experiences. The theoretical bind is that deconstructing oppressive categories can neutralize the effects of differences. (1997: 22–23)

By emphasizing disability itself as an unstable category and postmodernist subject position predicated on universal impairment, partial-ness and interdependence, in which bodies are often "completed by technology" (2002: 30), Davis inverts the traditional givenness of social relations on this question, declaring, "Impairment is the rule, and normalcy is the fantasy" (ibid.: 31). As he puts it,

> The dismodern era ushers in the concept that difference is what all of us have in common. That identity is not fixed but malleable. That technology is not separate but part of the body. That dependence, not individual independence, is the rule. The watchword of dismodernism could be: Form follows dysfunction. (ibid.: 26)

He goes on:

> The dismodernist subject is in fact disabled, only completed by technology
> and by interventions. Rather than the idea of the complete, independent
> subject, endowed with rights (which are in actuality conferred by privilege),
> the dismodernist subject sees that metanarratives are only "socially created"
> and accepts them as that, gaining help and relying on legislation, law and
> technology. It acknowledges the social and technological to arrive at func-
> tionality. (ibid.: 30)

Davis proposes three broad regimes for a twenty-first-century dismodernist ethics: care *of* the body (interpellation into society through consumerist
practices); care *for* the body (engagement with the healthcare sector); and
care *about* the body (emancipatory human rights activism), which supersedes
and ameliorates the negative aspects of the other two. He concludes:

> With a dismodernist care ethic, you realize that caring *about* the body sub-
> sumes and analyzes care *of* and care *for* the body. The latter two produce op-
> pressive subjection, while the former gives us an ethic of liberation. And the
> former always involves the use of culture and symbolic production in either
> furthering the liberation or oppression of people with disabilities. (ibid.)

With its ecumenical gambit to "[expand] the protected class to the entire
population" and movement "beyond the fixity of the body" (ibid.: 31), Davis's
vision serves as an inspirational riposte to quasi-Foucauldian notions of docile subjects suffering under the strictures of governmentality; a dismodernist
stance refutes such passivity, embracing "incompleteness" and inter-reliance
as the ideological underpinnings for demanding universal social justice.

In advancing *Doom Patrol* as a dismodernist text, I will emphasize three
things: the group's utter expulsion from "mainstream" normality and society;
the inner and outer pressures that consistently destabilize the group; and, especially, the model of caregiving/nurture which undergirds the characters'
relationships, "completing" them. (These precepts, incidentally, apply equally well to other "alternative communities" in the series, including the team's
arch-enemies, the Brotherhood of Evil.)

DOOM PATROL AS DISMODERNIST TEXT

As absolute outsiders, the Patrollers experience a painful rejection and separation from the socius familiar to many disabled people of the era. Trainor/Negative Man's origin story, "The Private World of Negative Man" (vol. 1, #106–107, #109, #111, 1966–67), typifies the quandary. After his disastrous flight, forcing his separation from others lest he kill them with his new radioactive body, Trainor is elated to receive the special bandages (secretly invented by Caulder) which allow him to safely rejoin the world. But almost immediately, the stares and mockery begin: walking in public, the "mummy-like" former pilot endures such perceived taunts as "he must be a publicity stunt for a monster movie!" (#106: 6). Even after rescuing a pretty, blindfolded blonde, Trainor suffers a cruel rejection when the woman at last catches a glimpse of his face (with the bandages slipped off): her pose and expression mirror those found in Edvard Munch's *The Scream* (1893) (ibid.: 8). Trainor's humiliation is so complete, he links his condition to the dehumanizing freak show tradition, in which the disabled made for mere spectacle: "I'm *free*! Like a circus freak is free! Like *Jo-Jo the Dog-Faced Boy*—and *Two-Ton Tilly*! Some *freedom*!" (6, emphasis in original).

Like Summers/Cyclops of X-Men, Trainor must grapple both with the world's repudiation of his self-worth and his own fears of harming others inadvertently. Where Summers must remain ever vigilant behind the ruby quartz lenses that hold back his eye blasts, Trainor is compelled to live in a sealed, lead-lined room (initially at his mother's house, no less). These various pressures, not surprisingly, push Trainor into unintended collaborations with the deformed villain, Dr. Death, who tells him: "You'll never make it in the outside world! Sooner or later, you'll see that I'm the only man you can do business with!" (#109: 8).[20]

As with other "borderline cases" discussed in the previous chapter, anomalous/monstrous physical specimens such as Trainor and Cliff Steele/Robotman invite public fear and loathing through superpowers that are themselves "unpoliceable" disabilities, and which ultimately drive them to moral grey zones. Indeed, Steele fulfills this paradigm perfectly: he begins as an outright villain, moved to vengeful rages against the man who saved his life by transferring his brain into an automaton's body, and against the world which alienates him.[21]

The verdict of that disability-denying world is clear: it demands physical conformity, control of one's body, exacting adherence to an illusory standard of independence that makes outcasts of radioactive men, brains encased in robots, "elastic" women, people in wheelchairs, and other such "dismoderns."

Another salient Marvel-derived feature of *Doom Patrol*—the team's frequent squabbles—points to a further innovation in the series' depiction of disability and a "dismodern" outlook *avant la lettre*. These quarrels erupt from the strong individual personalities of the characters, a refutation of Linton's "self-loathing, docile, bitter, or insentient fictional versions of ourselves the public is more used to." The interpersonal frictions and childish insults— Steele mocking Trainor with "my band-aid buddy"; Trainor retaliating with "nickel-head"; jealousies over Farr; Farr's frustrations with "the boys"; Oedipal strife with Caulder—are enacted not by passive "invalids" but by people with complex inner lives and emotions, who demand to get their way and fight for it, sometimes going too far. These are family quarrels; no matter how vituperative, at times even spilling into temporary "divorce," the conflict has as its subtext a (mostly) unquestioned foundation of love and mutual respect.

That subtext finds its most prominent expression in the ethic of community, mutual caregiving, and interdependence threaded throughout the entire series. As dismoderns, the Patrollers are indeed impaired and partial, "completed by technology and by interventions": Robotman's constant breakdowns, dismemberments and repairs by the blowtorch-wielding Chief; Trainor's need for weekly bandage replacements, provided also by Caulder; Farr's training to control her powers as well as need for a father figure. Caulder, a strong—at times insufferable—patriarchal leader, himself relies on the team as a bulwark against loneliness and for emotional sustenance, often referring to them as his children.

Alvise Mattozzi emphasizes the Doom Patrol's fundamental *esprit de corps* (often cast into relief by outside threats) as the title's key theme:

> Indeed, only as a group, working together, they are able to change their curses into superpowers. Along the series, the importance of the united group is often highlighted through the depiction of the four members together cheering for victory within one panel at the end of most stories.

I would add that the team even chooses to die in precisely that posture; our final image before Captain Zahl's bombs kill them shows the four hand and hand, defiant (vol. 1, #120, Sept.-Oct. 1968: 22). Long before that cataclysmic finale, the pattern indeed showed that the most severe threats to the group's integrity came from without: Steve Dayton/Mento's desire to marry Farr, retire her from the team and turn her into a homemaker; the orphaned Gar Logan/Beast Boy's repeated attempts to join the core group, destabilizing their dynamic; and of course the Brotherhood of Evil's constant existential threat.[22] The team faces them all, through accommodation, resistance, mutual respect, and in the end, by going down together.

Let us take the aforementioned story "The Black Vulture" (#117), in which the team temporarily disbands due to the Chief's distraction with Madame Rouge, as paradigmatic of the insider/outsider and interdependence themes. The piece opens with Caulder and the Madame, enjoying a calm night at home by the fireplace. Suddenly Robotman disturbs the peace, clanking in on one leg and missing an arm, the results of "battling a maniac with an atomic ray!" Rather than repair to the lab to put Steele back together again as usual, Caulder nonchalantly tells his dismembered comrade, "There's a torch and soldering iron waiting for you inside!" (3). A similarly dismissive attitude towards Trainor—who nearly dies when Caulder ignores Negative Man's pleas for help—explodes into a no-holds-barred screaming match that draws Farr from her marriage bed in the middle of the night. As Madame Rouge, the cause of this familial strife, looks away in irritation, the group goes at it:

FARR (entering): Are you out of your minds? I could hear your shouting from six blocks off! And what you said on the phone . . .
TRAINOR: We're grateful to Dr. Caulder for having just put us humptie-dupties back together again . . . but our former chief is too busy for nonsense like the *Doom Patrol*! Well, so am I!
STEELE: It's that dame! I tell you, the "Brotherhood" sent her here to bust us up!
CAULDER: You watch that talk, Robotman! Say what you want about me, but . . . (5, emphasis and ellipses in original)

Despite Farr's attempts at mediation, reminding the group of all Caulder has done for them, the contretemps escalates to fever pitch:

TRAINOR: That did it! Neg-Man, yank that phony beard from his chin, hair by hair!
CAULDER: Yes, like the primitive minds that you are, you understand only violence!
STEELE: Larry, cut it out! He'll sue us for assault and beardery!
FARR (punching the ceiling): Ohhhhh, you all give me a pain! (7)

The team fractures, each member going his or her own way, and leaving the Chief abandoned: "This is insane! They're all gone! They've all left me! I—I—I'm alone!" (9). As described in a previous section, this circumstance also leaves Caulder vulnerable to attack by the Black Vulture.

Yet, as the Chief battles alone in his "wheelchair fortress" against the villain and his coterie of winged predators, the others have a change of heart. After rescuing a blind man crossing the street in traffic, Steele has an epiphany, thinking: "That guy we called the *Chief* . . . He's a defenseless man in a wheel-chair—and you walked out on *him!*" (16, emphasis and ellipses in original). He rushes back home. Trainor too "chicken[s] out" and returns, along with Farr—only for them all to be incapacitated by disruptive bat sound waves. (As it happens, in a particularly ludicrous resolution, it is not the Doom Patrol but a "cavalry" of Native Americans led by the Caltech aerodynamics profes-sor/warrior White Feather who lend Caulder a hand in defeating the Vulture. Truly.)

In the end, the group convenes in its conventional "four together" final panels (with the addition of a smiling Madame Rouge), reaffirming the old communal order. (Even Robotman, who had fallen apart in the battle, is whole and reassembled.) Only rarely has the series' family dynamics been stated so explicitly:

> TRAINOR: Well, we've learned one thing! We've all gotta hang together . . .
> STEELE: . . . or we'll go hang!
> CAULDER: And I hope you've learned one other fact, *kiddies!* If I'm the fa-ther figure around here, then what I say . . . *goes!* I say, Madame Rouge stays as long as she needs to! What do you say?
> STEELE, TRAINOR, FARR: Yes—*Poppa!* (23, emphasis and ellipses in original)

"The Black Vulture" reiterates *Doom Patrol*'s governing principles of famil-ial bonds; interdependence for survival; ranking the group above outsiders; and subsumption (albeit never stable for long) to a patriarchal leader. Each lacking and imperfect in her own way, the team's members must support, nur-ture and complete the others for the dismodernist structure to prevail.[23]

CONCLUSION

While *X-Men* has earned a reputation as the preeminent disability allegory in superhero comics, *Doom Patrol* went further, earlier, and more entertainingly in this regard than the better-known title, constructing a vision of physical difference, alternative communityn and interdependence akin, I have argued, to Davis's more recent, post-ADA concept of dismodernism. As Wolk rightly identifies a critical aspect of the series: "Its characters were all 'superheroes' be-cause they had something terribly wrong with their bodies" (259). Davis's key insight—and no Silver Age series explored this notion more fully than *Doom Patrol*—tells us there is "something terribly wrong" with *everyone's* mortal, de-caying bodies; rather than simply deny this in deference to a physical ideal of

5.8 Many Doom Patrol stories end with mutual caregiving and reconsolidation of family ties (*My Greatest Adventure*, vol. 1, #82, Sept. 1963).

independence and plenitude, we must rely on each other for mutual care and love as the foundation of a truly just society.

Not all are convinced. Some deem such "feel-good" ecumenism as potentially corrosive of what they see as a marginalized group's core identity. In their radical critique of dismodernism, which they call "the process of normalization of disability" with all the baggage that assimilation has borne for other minorities, Mitchell and Snyder contend:

> The idea that postmodernism entails a recognition that we are all disabled to some extent—undermines our ability to pay attention to abject populations peripheral to the project of living. There is not a level playing field that all bodies occupy, and calling for all to recognize levels of insufficiency will do little to accomplish meaningful systems change. (2012: 48)[24]

5.9 The fugitive Robotman hides out with a family of "freaks," including a blind man, a hunch-backed man and a short-statured person (*Doom Patrol*, Vol. 1, #101, Feb. 1966).

Whatever dismodernism's "mainstreaming" proclivities—it does contain an element of bland bourgeois "inclusiveness"—*Doom Patrol* presents several examples throughout its run of Mitchell and Snyder's "abject populations" (with and without superpowers) that operate on the same principles of alternative, interdependent community. Before joining the Patrol, Trainor finds solace from his isolation by helping restore the Sunshine Club, a society of retirees (secretly led by Dr. Death) to financial viability. Through teamwork, tapping the expertise and experience of all its members, they succeed (#111: 1–4). Similarly, Steele in his fugitive period shelters with a group of physical misfits—hunchbacked, blind, small-statured—who live beneath an abandoned subway station. The odd "family" (which prefigures that in the 1971 Batman story "A Vow from the Grave," discussed in chapter 2), have established their own commune of mutual support and care. Without giving a reason, beyond their shared "freakishness," the group helps Steele procure the "brain food" he needs to survive, even at the cost of arrest, while Steele assists in repairing their faulty roof (#101: 4–8).

But the most striking interdependent "abject population peripheral to the project of living," of course, is the Brotherhood of Evil, in many ways a dark counterpart to the Patrol. The Brain (a sort of total quadriplegic) relies on his charges, especially the hyper-intelligent gorilla Monsieur Mallah, for transport and maintenance, while he provides leadership, medical technology, and (in parallel with Caulder) quasi-abusive fatherly support.[25]

Doom Patrol managed, more explicitly and trenchantly than any series before, to redefine the superhero as something other than a hyper-individual physical ideal and make his or her reliance on the care of others a central tenet of that redefinition. All this is to be expected; as Harold Braswell has argued, the expansion of the social circle to incorporate the dying and disabled as fully realized human beings entails a new understanding of cherished core values as expressed and lived by an astonishing variety of bodies:

> "Autonomy" means the substitution of a conception of the self that is defined by static, characterological consistency for one defined by the process of *development*; such development is measured via a great consciousness of one's dependence on other individuals as embedded in broader socio-historical processes. ... The goal of "autonomy," rather than upholding the pretense that individuals are isolated units, is to create the relational conditions for individual self-development. Such conditions are economic, social, psychological, and biological. It is not an idealized "goal" that one achieves, but rather a constant commitment to each other's mutual development. This development, it should be noted, can be described in terms highly particular to each individual, but the orientation of individual life will be toward a heightened recognition of the particular relationships constituting the self. In this view, there can never be a completely "autonomous" person, though some people can be relatively more autonomous than others. But "autonomy," conceived of as a process, is a commitment to our mutual flourishing as individuals and a society. (emphasis in original)

Jacobs and Jones, in their history of superheroes, state the matter more broadly, but they too acknowledge that Drake, Boltinoff, and Premiani's work produced characters "so very outlandish that the nature of their powers required a whole new approach to costumed-hero adventures" (102). *Doom Patrol* refashioned the genre and its approach to disability in ways even the pioneering Marvel itself had yet to assay.

6

HOW NOT TO BE A SUPERHERO
Narrative Prosthetics and *The Human Fly*

Compensation—or, rather, schemes of superpower overcompensation—rule the roost of neo-liberal explanatory systems. Such systems enshrine those bodies different yet enabled enough to ask nothing of their crumbling, obstruction-ridden infrastructure, continually naturalized as environments made for most but (unfortunately) not all bodies. Enhanced supercrips are celebrated by capitalist commodity cultures and social democratic governments alike as symbols of the success of systems that further marginalize their "less able" disabled kin in the shadow of committed researchers conjoined to "creaming" practices for the *non-impaired impaired.*" (Mitchell/Snyder 2012: 48, emphasis in original)

When is a superhero—not?

The short-lived Marvel Comics series *The Human Fly* (1977–79) featured a protagonist who flouted the genre's Silver Age conventions: he preferred Evel Knievel-type daredevil stunts and charity work to crime-fighting—but kept finding himself in situations where he had to rout crooks; adventured not in New York City but exotic locales such as Montreal, the American southwest, and Alaska; never appeared without his mask or revealed his secret identity; and possessed no superpowers, though he did boast a "metal skeleton" and overcame a devastating injury through sheer willpower. Finally, the Fly was not entirely fictional; Marvel, working under license from Human Fly Spectaculars, Ltd., based its nineteen-issue series on the exploits of a Canadian costumed stuntman, Rick Rojatt.

One of Marvel's more quixotic forays into the "relevance" movement of the 1970s (whereby superheroes explored social-activist topics such as race, feminism and the counter culture),[1] *The Human Fly* both challenged and reaffirmed accustomed notions of superheroism as well as disability. But despite its problematic depictions, the series was indeed unlike any seen before or since. True to its tag line ("the wildest superhero ever—because he's real!"), over the course of its run the title brought attention to real-world issues such as substandard medical care for Vietnam War veterans and the integration of the disabled into the workplace, just as the US disability rights movement was turning to a more activist phase. Above all, *The Human Fly* demonstrated the limits of combining "reality" with superheroics, and the ways in which disability, prominently foregrounded, redefines the genre itself.

"BECAUSE HE'S REAL!"

On October 7, 1977, a Canadian daredevil stuntman who called himself Rick Rojatt, aka The Human Fly, attempted to jump over twenty-six[2] buses in his "rocket-bike" at Montreal Olympic Stadium. Clad in the red and white costume he used for all his public appearances, the masked Rojatt told a reporter he wanted to break Evel Knievel's jump record of thirteen buses to prove himself the greatest daredevil of all. (According to witnesses and the engineer of the rocket-bike, Rojatt exhibited a death wish and flouted precautions on the jump.) Before a sparse crowd at the stadium, he careened into the air—though too high and at the wrong angle, causing his engine to stall—and crashed yards from the landing ramp, breaking several bones, but survived. He waved at the crowd as he was being carried away in a stretcher. The Fly did not perform again.

Part of the 1970s daredevil stunt craze, Rojatt (who kept his face hidden behind a mask) had a compelling "back story." He claimed to have suffered massive injuries in a car crash near Ashland, North Carolina in 1971, which killed his wife and children. With reconstructive surgery, steel-reinforced bones, and a fierce will to walk again, he made an astonishing recovery. Inspired by comics he read in the hospital, he decided to devote his life to raising money for the disabled through stunts and charity events as the Fly.[3] Though aspects of his story were exaggerated by his business partners, the Montreal sausagemakers Joseph and Dominic Ramacieri (who founded Human Fly Spectaculars),[4] and many accused him of fraud and baiting the media, Rojatt/the Fly did put his life in genuine risk on several occasions. His most celebrated feat: standing astride a DC-8 as it flew at up to 220 knots over the Mojave Desert in June 1976—which led to loss of consciousness and third degree burns on his legs.[5]

In 1977, under license from HFS, Marvel launched its comics series loosely based on Rojatt's story written by Bill Mantlo, with art by Lee Elias, Frank Robbins, and others. Though set in the Marvel universe, and featuring occasional guest stars such as Ghost Rider, the series generally removed itself from greater Marvel continuity, and the Fly never appeared in other titles. Most of the Fly's adventures involved not supervillains but stunts gone awry,

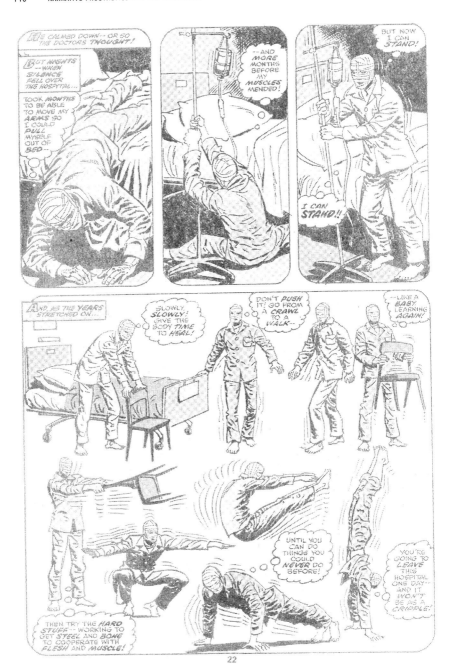

6.1 The Fly recovers from his injuries through sheer will (*Human Fly*, vol. 1, #1, Sept. 1977).

small-time hoods, and charity events.[6] (Marvel abruptly and without explanation cancelled the series in 1979, possibly due to alleged improprieties in HFS business practices.)[7]

The Fly's origin story in the Marvel series adheres to the general outline of Rojatt's legend, with some exaggerations for dramatic effect. For example, "Death Walk!" (*Human Fly*, vol. 1, #1, Sept. 1977) directly alludes to the Fly's real-life 1976 Mojave Desert stunt, though it depicts much more dangerous actions in and around a plane in flight and guest stars Spider-Man (a proven Marvel sales-driver). Rojatt's reported post-accident journey is similarly "heroicized" to conform to genre conventions. In Mantlo/Elias' telling, the mysterious, unnamed car crash victim overcomes his injuries through sheer personal drive, in secret self-therapy that lasts years—beneath skeptical doctors' noses.[8] Over the course of a page that covers years of chronological time, the Fly first struggles out of bed, then pulls himself by an IV stand back onto his feet, then (in a series of portraits without gutters) undertakes a clandestine calisthenic routine, thinking:

> Slowly, *slowly!* Give the body *time* to *heal!* Don't *push* it! Go from a *crawl* to a *walk*—like a *baby*, learning *again!* Then try the *hard stuff*—working to get *steel* and *bone* to cooperate with *flesh* and *muscle!* Until you can do things you could *never* do before! You're going to *leave* this hospital one day—and it *won't* be as a *cripple!*" (22, emphasis in original)[9]

The sequence amounts to a classic narrative of overcoming (examined in more detail below), reinforced immediately thereafter by a panel in which the Fly (his face still bandaged, but now walking freely), gazes at a despondent group of disabled men, brooding: "*Vets . . . workers . . .* most hurt *more* than me . . . all given *up* without *hope!* There's got to be *some way* of giving them *courage!* To show them that if *I* could triumph over *my* disability—so can *they* over theirs!" (23, ellipses and emphasis in original).

Hammering home the message is series writer Mantlo's essay "Who Is The Human Fly: A Tentative Explanation," which ran on the page which would accommodate readers' letters in subsequent issues. The screed spares neither verbiage nor ableist presumptions:

> He was released from the hospital, carrying with him a body partially rebuilt . . . and the memories of walking the hospital corridors unseen at night and witnessing, first hand, the hopelessness of others like him. Veterans, missing limbs, and maimed from Vietnam. Workers, torn in industrial accidents. Those born to disability and all separated from the mainstream of life. He had fought against that separation and won. They had lost, because

the motivation was not there and was not being supplied by the world without.

It was then that this victim determined to supply the motivation, the hope to the disabled of the world that they could rise above their disabilities, they could triumph over infirmity, they could succeed . . . for, hadn't he? (19, ellipses in original)

Setting the tone for the series, which Mantlo noted was targeted at younger readers (Yurkovich and Mantlo: 20), the essay ties personal sacrifice and "overcoming" disability to the superhero's mission in a "real-world" context: "The truly wondrous thing about him, though, is that he's *real!* We said that on the cover, we said it on the title-page; and, folks, we meant it!" (ibid., emphasis in original).[10]

REDEFINING THE SUPERHERO

Mantlo and *The Human Fly*'s appeal to the "real" would seem to overlay additional criteria onto the definition of the superhero, or at least try to substitute for generic elements absent in this unusual series. Indeed, superhero conventions often go missing or undergo considerable revision in the title's nineteen issues.

Recalling the work of Richard Reynolds and Peter Coogan, note that certain key attributes—mission, powers, and secret identity—"establish the core of the genre. As with other genres, however, specific superheroes can exist who do not fully demonstrate these three elements . . ." (Coogan: 39). In the case of the Fly, the generic markers of mission, powers, and secret identity go through significant modifications or, more radically, go absent—in ways directly attributed to its prominent disability theme.

Firstly, the Fly refuses to fight crime, instead devoting his efforts to stunts and charity fundraising. (Naturally, these activities often fall prey to saboteurs, criminals, and even the rare supervillain with which the hero must contend.) Coogan and Reynolds do identify the generic marker of "mission" as essential, since "someone who does not act selflessly to aid others in times of need is not heroic and therefore not a hero" (Coogan: 31) and "the hero's devotion to justice overrides even his devotion to the law" (Reynolds: 16). While neither says much about crime-fighting, the overwhelming majority of superheroes—certainly by the Silver Age—had sought out criminals to foil their plans and arrest them in the name of legal authorities; their mission is in effect to fight crime.[11] While the Fly has a definite mission (to help and inspire the disabled), his reluctance to proactively apprehend crooks and villains situates him well

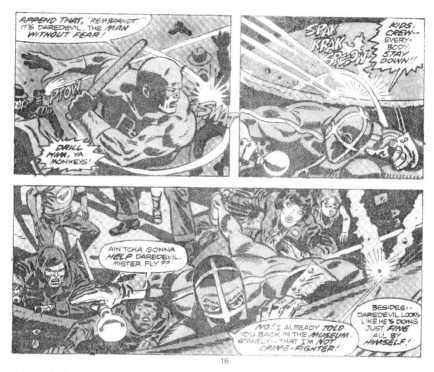

6.2 The pacifist Fly retreats, leaving the conventional superheroics to Daredevil (*Human Fly*, vol. 1, #9, May 1978).

outside the mainstream of the genre. (No "night patrols" or detective work for this hero.)

Just how far outside comes into stark relief in ". . . And Daredevil Makes Three!" (*Human Fly*, #9, May 1978, Mantlo/Robbins), when the Fly elects to stay behind and protect a group of children rather than engage in battle with the supervillain Copperhead. He leaves that job to a pair of "real" superheroes, guest stars Daredevil and the White Tiger.[12] Huddled inside an ancient urn with his young charges, he takes part in this exchange with one of the kids:

STANLEY: Ain'tcha gonna *help* Daredevil, Mister Fly?
FLY: *No!* I already *told* you back in the *museum*, Stanley—that I'm *not* *crime-fighter!* [*sic*][13] Besides—Daredevil looks like he's doing just fine all by himself! (16, emphasis in original)[14]

At various points in the series, in fact, the Fly declares himself a pacifist,[15] resorting to his fists only under the most extreme duress. "I'm not going to let you *harm* these kids, Copperhead!" he says, at last confronting the evildoer. "I don't believe in *violence*, but . . ." "It is better than *dying*, eh, señor Fly?" the

White Tiger completes the thought, as they engage their foe (ibid.: 26). Rarely has the genre expressed such self-consciousness about its violent, hyper-masculinist underpinnings.[16]

If the series' letters pages serve as any guide, many of the *Human Fly*'s readers not only welcomed but demanded such an unconventional portrait of superheroism, seeing in it a vital alternative to Marvel's tiresome, unthinking Bronze Age formulae. Rich Fifield of Presidio of Monterey, California, writing in the "Fly Papers" letters column of issue #3 (Nov. 1977), argued:

> The Fly is *not* a crime-fighter. He should not be facing criminals and super-villains in every issue. He has no *need* or reason to fight crime.
>
> His stories should be centered around his stunt exhibitions, on his helping people in need or trouble, on his adventures to mountaintops or jungles, and so forth. The possibilities and locales are endless. The Human Fly has the potential of becoming the first truly *nonviolent* adventure hero in comics, as well the first who doesn't rely on rehashing the perpetual battle between a simplistic *good* and a simplistic *evil*. (19, emphasis and ellipses in original)

Several letters, some supposedly written by people with disabilities,[17] expressed similar opinions throughout the series' run; fans routinely asked that he not be made into a regular crime-fighter and that he avoid bludgeoning wrongdoers. "There must be other ways to be a hero beside beating people up," wrote Betsy Jacobs of St. Louis (#7, Mar. 1978: 19). One correspondent even groused the Fly should not be called a superhero at all, even on the covers (#10, Jun. 1978: 19).

The (within limits) avoidance of violent set pieces freed up the series to explore a more "humanitarian" side of the Fly's personality, as well as the interdependence built into his relationships with his crew (in ways not dissimilar to *Doom Patrol*, discussed in chapter 5). The pacifist frame also seems to have contributed to making *The Human Fly* one of Marvel's more consistently politicized titles of its era.

For example, the series linked the disability rights movement's demands for dignity and fair treatment to other minority civil-rights struggles of the 1970s. At the start of "The Tiger and the Fly!" (*Human Fly*, #8, Apr. 1978, Mantlo/Robbins), our hero performs jet-powered skateboard stunts in front of New York's Metropolitan Museum of Art, in full view of Hector Ayala, aka The White Tiger (billed as Marvel's "first Hispanic superhero"). Exercised by the adoring crowd, which includes Latino youth, Ayala seethes, "*Look* at him! That *anglo* is cheering up *my* people—giving them something to *live* for—the way *I* want to be able to *do!*" (2, emphasis in original). In his final, two-part

6.3 The Fly contends with disgruntled Vietnam War veterans in "War in the Washington Monument!" (*Human Fly*, vol. 1, #15, Nov. 1978).

storyline before cancellation, the Fly, provocatively, battled corruption on a Native American reservation in New Mexico.

As seen in the origin story, the series touched on another painful issue of the 1970s: the country's shoddy treatment of injured veterans home from the Vietnam War. Tackling this reality full tilt, "War in the Washington Monument!" (*Human Fly*, #15, Nov. 1978, Mantlo/ Elias) depicts a pair of disgruntled Vietnam vets—one of whom is in a wheelchair—who threaten to blow up the eponymous national icon to protest corruption in the Veteran's Administration and substandard VA hospitals. "We been *lied* to enough, Locke" growls Larry, one of the terrorists, "in '*Nam*—an' in that *butcher shop* they called a *VA hospital!*" (14, emphasis in original).[18] The series did not shy from controversy; the episode recalls not only the neglect of war veterans but also an April 1977 forced occupation of the Health, Education and Welfare offices of the San Francisco Federal Building by over 100 activists, including people with disabilities. They were protesting bureaucratic intransigence in enacting sections of the Rehabilitation Act of 1973, legislation aimed at improving access (in various senses) for the disabled. The protesters occupied the building's sixth floor for twenty-five days.[19]

More disappointingly, the Fly's adventures often led him to rescue disabled kids, thus perpetuating the old association of disability with infantilization.[20] The title establishes the kids/disability link early; in Mantlo's inaugural essay, he quotes Rojatt: "I've got 50,000 kids out there depending on me. I've got a lot of people to support . . . youngsters in hospitals, struggling against cancer, polio, cerebral palsy or whatever. I've got a lot of people to support. And this is *my* way of doing it!" (#1: 19, ellipsis and emphasis in original).

In practice, the series had the Fly consistently rushing to pluck disabled children out of danger; in "Castle in the Clouds!" (*Human Fly*, #3, Nov. 1977, Mantlo/Elias), he agrees to undertake the rescue of a kidnapped little girl—for the sole reason that she is "a *polio victim*, isn't she, sir? A *cripple?*" (17, emphasis in original). Other stories see him rescue a blind boy from a bear (*Human Fly*, #7); disabled kids from a crazed wire-walker (#5); two mute children stranded on a rogue dirigible (#14); and a wheelchair-using boy from drowning at Niagra Falls (#16). And while the depiction of these children at times defied the synecdochic linkage of disability and infantilism,[21] the motif's near-obsessive recurrence made for the series' most retrograde representational strategy from the perspective of disability rights.[22]

Another area in which *The Human Fly* mildly reconfigures superhero conventions involves teamwork. The Fly's backup team includes techie Ted Locke (a double amputee Vietnam vet), pilot Blaze Kendal, and publicist Arnie Berman (and later a critic converted to his cause, the reporter Harmony Whyte), who work closely with him to execute his dangerous stunts (jumping a canyon on a motorbike, breaking out of a tank filled with sharks). The Fly recruits Locke and Kendal after they too suffer traumatic injuries and find themselves on the verge of giving up hope (addressed below); their common triumph over misfortune serves to bond the group in ways more intimate than in a standard superhero series. Several stories show how the stunts work only through careful planning and cooperation (as well as subterfuge)—often, it's the Fly's friends who save him![23]

For example, in ". . . Race to Destruction!" (*Human Fly*, #2, Oct. 1977, Mantlo/ Infantino), the Fly explains in detail how "today's *stunt* went off like *clockwork*, team!" which allows him to escape a death trap. This cheery dialogue ensues:

KENDAL: You made it sound so blasted *easy!*
LOCKE: It *is*—when you're the *Human Fly!*
FLY: And when you've got *three friends* standing by you! (11, emphasis in original)

The Fly later echoes this sentiment when bystanders praise his victory over some thugs, saying: "*No,* kids! *Anyone* could have done what *I* did—with the *proper training*—and with *three friends* who know what to *do* in a jam!" (#6: 31, emphasis in original).[24] The collective ethos pervades even those moments when the Fly—along with his crew—must engage in physical combat. In the opening splash page from "War in the Washington Monument," depicting a full-on brawl between the good guys and some corrupt hospital security guards, the Fly seems merely part of an ensemble rather than the lead fighter. (In fact Locke is the largest figure shown.) The series, in short, consistently subverted the hyper-individualistic masculine fundament upon which much of the genre rests.

But no superheroic convention undergoes as radical a reinscription in *The Human Fly* as the secret identity motif; this is a series whose protagonist has no alias—no one knows his alter ego or even his true name, and at no point do we see his face unmasked. As discussed in chapter 2, such an approach has normally applied to supervillains such as Dr. Doom—and like him, the Fly does reveal himself to friends (his crew) and even strangers (a group of Native Americans in *Human Fly*, #18), but not the reader.

As with the title's non-violent "humanitarianism" and teamwork creeds, the Fly's odd anonymity has much to do with the foregrounding of his "triumph" over disability. His visage never appears in the series because he has made himself a living symbol of hope and perseverance,[25] visually underscored by depicting his countenance in black silhouettes or off-frame.[26] Indeed, though unseen by readers, its "nobility" is never in doubt. Reflecting on how he first glimpsed it (surreptitiously), Berman remarks: "You can *imagine* how I *felt*, Harmony! The *Human Fly* stood before me *unmasked*! I didn't know his *name*—but I knew I would *never* forget that *face*! It was the most *honest—strong—decent—courageous face* I'd ever seen!" (*Human Fly*, #12: 20–21, emphasis in original).

For all its "inspirational" burden, however, the Fly's unseen face and unknown alter ego forced the series' creators to seek subjects for drama other than their "inhuman" protagonist—with uneven results. As blogger Tim O'Neil put it:

The odd part about the Fly's set-up is that not only is his secret identity a secret to the world, but it's a secret from the readers as well. . . . It's intended as a metaphor for the Fly's universally inspiring message. He could be *any-one*, so he could be *everyone*, is the logic. . . . But the problem is that while this is undoubtedly a good idea for a potential masked daredevil, it's a *hor-rible* idea for an ongoing superhero comic book. The driving engine behind most modern superhero books is soap-opera stuff. A character who isn't a character so much as an abstract ideal is, in storytelling terms, a cipher. (emphasis in original)

6.4 Through "ensemble" splash pages such as this, *Human Fly* consistently subverted the hyper-individualistic masculine fundament of the superhero (*Human Fly*, vol. 1, #15, Nov. 1978).

Worse, over time the "anonymous" Fly comes to take on aspects of a cult leader, inspiring nigh-religious devotion (as evinced by Berman's breathless description of his face). The narrative arc of the cynical reporter Harmony Whyte, in fact, functions as a conversion narrative when she decides to quit her job to join his team, as a new believer in his cause (*Human Fly*, #12). In any case, the series never adequately addressed the non-dramatic "inhuman protagonist" issue, which puts into question its long-term viability even had it not been cancelled after 19 issues. As a 1982 *Marvel Index* article drylynoted, not revealing the main character's identity "may ultimately have contributed to the comic's demise" (95).

THE TROUBLE WITH "OVERCOMING"

". . . while every night, under cover of darkness, the victim of an accident that would have left most others dead or paralyzed for life began to secretly exercise his unresponsive body . . . until it *became* responsive, until it became *his* body once again . . . and perhaps something *more* than it had been before." (*Human Fly*, #1: 19, ellipses and emphasis in original).

"The Human Fly is me," Mantlo begins his first issue essay. "He's also you and millions of other people you've encountered every day of your life since the day you were born. The Human Fly is a concept, an idea."

The concept, the idea, as elaborated over the next 500 words under the heading—"The Making of a Hero!"—involves the surmounting of tragedy (the death of his family in an accident, the crushing of his body beyond medicine's reach) to stay "determined to prove his doctors wrong—or die trying."[27] Four years later, after countless operations, the steel reinforcement of his skeleton, and tricking doctors into thinking he had "accepted" his condition, the triumphant Fly amazes everyone by standing up and walking *through force of will alone*—then having unimaginable adventures in Milan, Montreal, above Mojave's desert sands.

The Fly's origin shares much with earlier Silver Age iterations of the "overcoming narrative," including their "supercrip" ableist logic and drive to "inspire."[28] Indeed, for all the attention it pays to the real-world problems of the disabled—and in ways that often empower its subjects—the series largely perpetuates the notion of disability itself as a problem that needs solving and transcending rather than an identity to be embraced and celebrated. Worse, it places the onus for such "transcendence" on the individual rather than the

6.5 The ever-anonymous Fly recruits Ted Locke to his cause (*Human Fly*, vol. 1, #1, Sept. 1977).

social forces that stigmatize and devalue a disabled subjectivity in the first place.

It does so, oddly, even as it presents disabled characters notable for their level of comfort with their own physical differences, such as crewmember Ted Locke. He doesn't start out that way, however. Locke's first chronological appearance is in a 1967 wartime flashback: we see him, a U.S. soldier, sacrifice both hands to save Vietnamese civilians from a bridge demolition. After the accident, his technical expertise makes him an attractive hire for Tony Stark, but an embittered Locke only replies, "Tell him to *save* his *pity*, doc—I don't *need* it!" (*Human Fly*, #1: 11, emphasis in original).[29]

The Fly then makes his appearance (in silhouette) before the angry "handless engineer,"[30] pulling up his own sleeves to reveal his forearms: "Look at these *scars*, Ted! Almost *60%* of my *bone structure* had to be *replaced* . . . with *steel!* If *we* give up, we're *nothing!* But if we *succeed*—we'll give others *like* us the *hope* to go on!" (ibid.: 14, emphasis and ellipsis in original). Strikingly, the Fly's use of his own body to make his point—as if his disfigurement were a simple affliction he has surmounted—compels Locke to come onboard; he never again bemoans his outcast state.[31] He soon discovers his artificial hooks' advantages in doing his job; at one point, the toolkit hidden inside his prosthetic arm helps effect the Fly's escape from confinement (*Human Fly*, #15: 5).[32]

Still, despite such affirming portrayals, *The Human Fly* proceeds from a stigmatizing logic that sees physical difference as an unworthy condition to be overcome. Disability-rights movements (in the 1970s and today) have striven for just the opposite: to compel the investment of resources so that one's self-fulfillment is facilitated by egalitarian social environments (in various senses), rather than making it contingent on well-meaning individuals with agendas such as the Fly. "Overcoming"—the tactic of "special," supremely motivated individuals who buy into the logic of winners and losers—thus has no place in a just social order. One of the more eloquent voices in the disability rights movement, Simi Linton, argues along these lines in her important 1998 manifesto *Claiming Disability*. In a section titled "Speaking About Overcoming and Passing," she writes:

> The ideas embedded in the *overcoming* rhetoric are of personal triumph over a personal condition. The idea that someone can overcome a disability has not been generated within the community; it is a wish fulfillment generated from the outside. It is a demand that you be plucky and resolute, and not let the obstacles get in your way. If there are no curb cuts at the corner of the street so that people who use wheelchairs can get across, then you should learn to do wheelies and jump the curbs . . . When disabled people internalize the demand to "overcome" rather than demand social change, they shoulder the same kind of exhausting and self-defeating "Super Mom" burden that feminists have analyzed. (18, emphasis in original)

She goes on to compare popular expressions related to overcoming (such as "I never think of you as disabled") to once-common "compliments" such as "he/she is a credit to his/her race"—such phrases imply that the "complimentee's" community is "somehow discredited and needs people with extraordinary talent to give the group the credibility that it otherwise lacks . . . To accept it, one must accept the implication that the group is inferior and that the individual is unlike others in that group" (ibid.).[33]

Tobin Siebers goes even further, diagnosing the cultural emphasis on overcoming and cure as a symptom of what he calls "the ideology of ability," the unconscious aversion to any disabled paradigm for living.[34] Premised on an appealing ableist lie of human worth, the overcoming narrative causes incalculable psychic and physical damage within and without the disabled community:

> The value of people with disabilities to themselves does not lie in finding a way to return through medical intervention to a former physical perfection, since that perfection is a myth, nor in trying to conceal from others and themselves that they are disabled. Rather, embodiment seen complexly understands disability as an epistemology that rejects the temptation to value the body as anything other than what it was and that embraces what the body has become and will become relative to the demands on it, whether environmental, representational or corporeal. (2008: 27)

In its unexamined "inspirational," "no griping" model of overcoming (the hollow core of the series), *The Human Fly* resembles "The Case of the Disabled Justice League" (*Justice League of America*, vol. I, #36, Jun. 1965, Fox/ Sekowsky), one of the retrograde "counter-examples" of disability's representation in early Silver Age superhero comics noted in chapter 2. That also had plenty of disabled kids and much bandying-about of the word "overcome" and its variants.

In sum: *The Human Fly* helps us to think through the paradoxes evoked by disabled "supercrip" identities (Mitchell/Snyder's "non-impaired impaired") and the ableist superhero genre in general. In seeking to negotiate these paradoxes, the series indeed holds claim to being the "wildest of all"—not because it's "real," but because it goes further than any before it in exploring how the very notion of disability disrupts the modus operandi of the superhero. While it did ultimately fall prey to privileging narratives of "overcoming" (prevalent in the 1970s, less so today) rather than embrace alternate empowering identities, the *Human Fly* nonetheless presents (at moments) a surprisingly progressive (if flawed) vision of disability rights "in action."

CONCLUSION: "THE BELIEVE-IT-OR-NOT DISABILITY STORY"

On the cusp of its third decade, the "Marvel Age of Comics" saw both major publishers struggling to present even-handed and positive new depictions of disability in their superhero series. Rather than consolidate the gains of the 1960s—as exemplified by landmark characters such as Ben Grimm/the Thing, Matt Murdock/Daredevil, and the Doom Patrol—DC and Marvel largely opted for retrograde, pre-Silver Age formulae privileging sentimentality, overcompensation for lack, and "inspirational" narratives of surmounting. Even the boldest and most radical of the 1970s creations, *The Human Fly*, found

6.6 Hal Chandler, polio victim, manifests the 3D Man (his brother Chuck Chandler) (*Marvel Premiere*, vol. 1, #36, Jun. 1977).

itself too often weighed down with a previous generation's prejudices, among other things associating disability with infantilism.

Other Marvel series fared worse, in effect revisiting a Golden Age outlook toward the subject. Not without its charms, the short-lived revisionist *3D Man*, which debuted mere months before *The Human Fly* in 1977, nonetheless bore hallmarks of a Freddy Freeman/Captain Marvel, Jr., understanding of disability.

Written by Roy Thomas and Jim Craig in full nostalgia mode, the brief series set in 1958 looked back at the early Cold War era with backhanded affection. Through the usual ludicrous plot devices (e.g., Skrull technology), test pilot Chuck Chandler gains three times the strength, speed, and agility of a normal man, becoming the crime-fighter and "red-buster" 3D Man—but only for three hours at a time. The rest of the day he is reduced to a red and green double image on the glasses of his "nerdy" brother Hal, who has been rendered a "cripple" by polio (*Marvel Premiere*, vol. 1, #35, Apr. 1977).

The 3D Man stories shrewdly re-examine the 1950s, celebrating their (facile) sense of innocence and fun with numerous period references—"I hope I'll do as a *Lucky Strike Extra!*"; "Feels like *Marciano* clobbered me!" (ibid.: 3 and 19, emphasis in original)—but also critiquing the repressive, paranoid witch-hunt atmosphere of the Red Scare (Communist infiltrators rub elbows with the reptilian shapeshifting Skrulls). Hal, the timid, feminized polio victim, is loyal to his dashing brother to the point of absurdity.[35] Once more, superpowers not only compensate for, but obliterate physical disability, as Hal falls unconscious whenever Chuck swings into action. With his frail brother safely *hidden away*, 3D Man is free to vanquish the country's enemies (foreign, alien) with flourishes of red-blooded American manliness: "*All right, Skrull!* Show's over!*" (Marvel Premiere*, vol. 1, #36, Jun. 1977: 27, emphasis in original).

Precisely this erasure of disability in a nationalist setting offers a retrospective clue to the genre's fixation on a tidied-up physical difference. America may seem weak, even "crippled," but through the superheroic alchemy of overcompensation/erasure, it is strong, virile, and manly. 3D Man thus acts as a parodic disclosure of the Silver Age's prehistory and formative anxieties—but in the process it also reinscribes the subordinate subjectivity of the disabled for a new generation.

Another Marvel hero, the Shroud, combined elements of Batman and Doctor Doom's origin stories: the murder of his parents leads an unnamed boy to seek out the "Cult of Kali" in the Himalayas, where he absorbs mystical knowledge but must render himself blind through a gruesome branding. The "kiss of Kali" brings *"eternal darkness forevermore!"* in exchange for extrasensory powers (*Super-Villain Team-Up*, vol. 1, #7, Aug. 1976, Englehart/Trimpe: 10, emphasis in original).

As conceived by writer Steve Englehart, the Shroud functioned largely as a parody of Dick Sprang-era Batman—in his battle with Dr. Doom he uses "bomb-a-rangs," "parallo-mist," and a titanium net, all produced from inside his dark cloak; unlike with Daredevil/Matt Murdock, we have no window into his life as a blind man.[36] Later writers endowed the character with the ability to access the "Darkforce Dimension," in effect rendering others blind by immersing them in inky black. As discussed in previous chapters, the "they want to make us like them" contagion model of disability has a long pedigree; the Shroud merely perpetuates it.

Similarly empowered, Cloak of *Cloak and Dagger* likewise yields little insight into the lives of the disabled, despite its "relevance" moves to address drug abuse. In the duo's origin issue,[37] Cloak (berobed similarly to the Shroud, and also wielding control over a "dark force") reveals his true identity: Tyrone Johnson, a poor black kid from South Boston who stutters.[38] This speech impediment leads the young man to fail his best friend Billy at a crucial moment: because Johnson can't explain away a misunderstanding, a policeman shoots the fleeing Billy, killing him. Deeply traumatized, consumed by guilt, Johnson becomes a runaway, and eventually easy prey for mobsters testing a new synthetic drug—which grants him superpowers (*Cloak and Dagger*, vol. 1, #4, Jan. 1984, Mantlo/Leonardi, n.p.).

Yet this power (the ability to immerse others in a cold, dark void) triggers the same associations with disability as the Shroud's: that of "vampiric"

6.7 The origin of the Shroud (*Super-Villain Team-Up*, vol. 1, #7, Aug. 1976).

infection, of casting the able-bodied into the purgatory of impairment through contagion. Recalling Paul Longmore's characterization of ableist fears: "disabled people resent the nondisabled and would, if they could, destroy them. . . . the unacknowledged hostile fantasies of the stigmatizers are transferred to the stigmatized" (2003: 133–34). As if to underscore the link, Cloak in his early manifestation "hungers" for "light" which he consumes from his partner, the able-bodied (white, blonde) Dagger/Tandy Bowen, as well as from victims he has swallowed up in his cloak. Incidentally, once transformed into Cloak, Johnson no longer stutters.

By scholarly consensus (and any fair-minded measure), Marvel and DC's "relevance" movement—what Bradley Wright called "a proliferation of self-consciously leftist comic book explorations of political and social issues" (233)—proved a decidedly mixed bag for the disabled. As they had with other

6.8 Tyrone Johnson's stutter leads to the death of his best friend (*Cloak and Dagger*, vol. 1, #4, Jan. 1984)

ham-handed stabs at feminism (late-1960s Wonder Woman, Valkyrie) and race (Luke Cage, Black Lightning), mainstream superhero comics in the 1970s struggled with progressive depictions of disability, resorting more often than not to outdated formulae. The 1980s fared somewhat better, with sensibility-challenging, button-pushing figures like She-Thing/Sharon Ventura and Cyborg/Victor Stone; to that list I would add *Alpha Flight*'s Roger Bochs, a double-amputee scientific genius as comfortable using a wheelchair as he is controlling his robot strongman alter ego, Box; and the *Teen Titans'* Jericho/ Joseph Wilson, after Black Bolt the most prominent mute character in the genre, often shown using sign language.[39]

The 1970s heroes, in contrast, mainly resorted to David Mitchell and Sharon Snyder's "narrative prosthesis" representational tactic, whereby the disabled figure is subjugated within an ableist epistemology. Shoehorned into an acceptable discursive frame, disability is rendered into "tolerable" deviance available for pity, inspiration, or disappearance. Eli Clare, in attacking such rhetorical obfuscations of the disabled community, references one of its most despised figures:

> Supercrip stories never focus on the conditions that make it so difficult for people with Downs to have romantic partners, for blind people to have adventures, for disabled kids to play sports. I don't mean medical conditions. I mean material, social, legal conditions. I mean lack of access, lack of employment, lack of education, lack of personal attendant services. I mean stereotypes and attitudes. I mean oppression. The dominant story about disability should be about ableism, not the inspirational supercrip crap, the believe-it-or-not disability story. (2–3)

As I have argued throughout Part I, the genre in this era wavered between a "supercrip"-like paradigm and something more complex, inclusive, and human. Too often disability as mere incidental physical/cognitive difference had to be worried over, spectacularized, explained away, ushered out of view, thrust into the closet, or discursively "overcome." Never just let be.

Disability in the Silver Age and beyond: what the superhero can never just let be.

7

THE DISMAL TRADE
Death, the Market, and Silver Age Superheroes

It would be a really sleazy stunt to bring him back. (O'Neil 1988)[1]

As we have seen, the superhero genre is a disability-denying representational practice which privileges the healthy, hyper-powered, and fetching body over the diseased, debilitated, and deformed body. The superhero, by the logic of the narrative itself, through his very presence, enacts an erasure of ordinary, mortal flesh in favor of a quasi-fascist physical ideal, an ideal complicated in the Silver Age but by no means transcended.

This does not mean that superheroes never die. Though as the comics blog Quarter Bin puts it, for them "mortality, it seems, never sticks" (2001). In an amusing column called "The Revolving Door of Death," the blog for years railed against the genre's "trivialization of death that saturates most episodes where comics choose to kill, then revive, a superhero" (2000) in ways ever more baroque and insulting to the reader's intelligence. Striking—at least to those accustomed to the idea of death as non-negotiable and permanent—is how ubiquitous this aspect of the genre has grown since the Silver Age, and particularly in recent years. Commenting in early 2011 on the latest spate of superhero "deaths" and (for the most part) speedy resurrections—including those of Bruce Wayne/Batman, Steve Rogers/Captain America, Barry Allen/ The Flash, and Johnny Storm/The Human Torch—George Gene Gustines dryly noted, "the smarter question is, 'how long before the deceased returns?'"

Many critics of the superhero's revolving door of death, like Gustines, tend to follow two rhetorical conventions in addressing the topic: 1) it is evidence of the genre's steady decline (things used to be better), and 2) market demand compromises realism (characters come back from the grave for crass commercial reasons):

In 1980, when Jean Grey, the super-powered mutant known as Phoenix, died in *X-Men* No. 137, it was a cosmic adventure with deadly consequences and a bittersweet love story (her soul mate was Cyclops, the X-Men's leader). She returned in 1986 when Marvel wanted to unite the original X-Men members in a spin-off book, *X-Factor*, and she died again in 2003.

Ta-Nehisi Coates, writing in 2009 in the *Atlantic Monthly* blog, emphasizes the diminishing returns of such an approach to drama: "At some point brand degradation kicks in. If you're going to kill main characters, only to resurrect them later, why should we care in the first place?" The comments section to Coates's post neatly encapsulates many of the arguments pertaining to superhero death. One commenter grouses, "It's not quite the same when you know someone will be back in a year or so—especially when it happens *every time*" (emphasis in original), while some compare the routinely resurrected superhero to other genre figures who "died" and returned from the grave: Sherlock Holmes, Gandalf the Grey from *The Lord of the Rings* series, Spock from *Star Trek*, and Aslan from the *Narnia* series. Going even further back, some mention the rebirths and resurrections of mythological figures such as Dionysus, Osiris, and Jesus.[2]

Still, as products of ongoing serial narratives, mainstream superheroes seem to experience the "death"/resurrection cycle more routinely than characters in other genres, even soap operas, and with accelerating frequency.[3] That fact has, for some fans and readers, belied post-Silver Age claims to greater psychological realism. At least some industry figures agree; when I asked Paul Levitz, former DC president and longtime DC writer, how "the majors" handle the theme of death, he replied diplomatically:

Well and badly. When you're writing drama—or melodrama, as is most often the case in comics—consequence is an important concept, and I think over the years when there've been points in individual comics where the peril of death was made more real because a character genuinely died, and didn't mystically get reborn two seconds later or something like that, you enhance the feeling of peril and risk in the serial, and to some extent enhance the potential depth of the story. When you do that where there's no emotional consequence for the survivors, where there's no change, or you wave the magic wand somehow and the person pops right back up like you're playing Whack-a-Mole, you're denigrating the emotional experience and you're diminishing the story value. And we've certainly seen that done an awful lot of times as well. (2011)

Others are more blunt. Writing in 2009, Tom Spurgeon of the *Comics Reporter* website concluded, "I'm not certain the Marvel writers (or the DC ones) as a collective have ever handled well how astounding it would be to have certain people in any fictional world even half-way designed to resemble our own outright cheat death."

In short, the Silver Age superhero has been not only a disability disavower and overcompensator—he is also a world-class death-denier.

This introductory chapter on death and the superhero, as well as the case studies that follow, trace the mechanism of that denial; its role as a central organizing convention of the genre; and the influence of market pressures on the depiction of death in mainstream superhero comics up to 1993. The commercial considerations seem straightforward. In the most obvious sense, heroes never die because it makes no business sense—one doesn't kill the cash cow. But how has that economic given "warped" the superhero? What accommodations does the genre make to that reality, what "price" does it pay for that denial? In a psychoanalytic sense, what "neuroses" has this repression of death's ineluctability spawned? And what happens when that repression, occasionally, cracks?

Furthermore, the subject of death in literature entails a discussion of the particular problems it poses to strategies of representation, as well as how its depiction relates to societal attitudes on death and dying in a given period. These we explore in the next sections.

DEATH, REPRESENTATION, AND BODY POLITICS

> Strictly speaking, we no longer know what to do with them, since, today, it is not normal to be dead, and this is new. To be dead is an unthinkable anomaly; nothing else is as offensive as this. Death is a delinquency, and an incurable deviancy. (Baudrillard: 126)

The study of death and bereavement in the Humanities, as social phenomenon and ideological construct—or, following the sociologist Clive Seale, "an attempt to construct a refuge of meaning and purpose" (1998: 11)—has exploded in the last thirty years.[4] This attention is owing to various cultural changes in postwar American life, particularly since the 1960s, which I can here treat only schematically. In brief, death in this period evolved—from a subject little-discussed and treated as impolite (even likened to pornography)[5]—to a (rather queasily) accepted part of the social fabric.

In this evolution, two US figures stand out: the muckraking journalist Jessica Mitford, whose jeremiad against the funeral industry, *The American Way of Death*, appeared in 1963, and the Swiss-American psychiatrist Elisabeth Kübler-Ross, for her pioneering Death and Dying seminars at the University of Colorado Medical School, in which terminal patients were invited to answer questions on their experiences, fears, and disappointments with their care. Their complaints—insensitive doctors; feelings of abandonment; taboos on speaking about death—started a national conversation after Kübler-Ross published her findings in the landmark *On Death and Dying* (1969). Its now-famous "five stages of grief" model—denial, anger, bargaining, depression and isolation, and acceptance—entered the popular culture lexicon. In addition, the modern, technologically based legal criterion of "brain death" (defined by a 1967 Harvard Medical School committee to study artificial life support) superseded millennia of thought and custom on the border between the living and the dead.[6]

Throughout the following decade, the rise of the death with dignity, death awareness, and hospice movements[7] agitated for more humane terminal care, while the trauma of the Vietnam War and, later, AIDS further sensitized the populace to such discussions. Also dating back to this era, increasing media and popular discourses regarding "near-death" and "out of body" experiences in part filled the spiritual vacuum left by an increasingly secular society that had come to treat death as a medical, scientific, and institutionalized process (see Webb: 244–49; Davies: 156; and Smyrniw).

Indeed, a vogue for the subject spread throughout the 1970s, spurred by books such as the cultural anthropologist Ernest Becker's *The Denial of Death* (1973), which depicted death-terror in a psychoanalytic frame as a fundamental human drive (elaborated upon below), and, more controversially, Derek Humphry's *Jean's Way: A Love Story* (1978), which advocated assisted suicide. Discussions of euthanasia and right-to-die cases proliferated, including that of Karen Ann Quinlan, a young woman in a vegetative state whose family succeeded in convincing the New Jersey Supreme Court to permit removal of her ventilator, and Nancy Cruzan, who had lain in a coma since 1983, and was allowed to die in 1990 after the US Supreme Court ruled constitutional the withdrawal of her feeding tube, as argued by her parents. Both cases proved influential in the development of advance directives laws, including living wills, culminating in the Patient Self-Determination Act of 1991.[8] In short, by the time of the 1992–93 "Death of Superman" storyline (discussed in chapter 9), America had been engaged for at least three decades in an at times acrimonious conversation on death and dying.

In what remains of this brief sketch, I want to emphasize the ways scholars have figured the dead body as a politicized object open to multiple purposes, as well as how death's resistance to interpretation lends itself to such appropriations. Precisely these aspects of death, as well as the bizarre ways in which the market realities of published serial narratives have influenced the genre's approach to the topic, seem the most relevant to a discussion of superheroes.

What does it mean to represent death, something by definition unknowable?

The radically other dead body, as semantic "void" (a simultaneous absence and presence), both demands and deflects all attempts at representation;[9] once human, it can never be wholly "inhuman," wholly "thing"—at least until it decomposes. (This is why people talk to the dead, why they close the unseeing eyes of cadavers.) Elisabeth Bronfen (referencing Maurice Blanchot) sees the dead human body as a polyvalent signifier unparalleled in its power to disrupt the social status quo, and therefore must be contained by representation *of some sort*:

> The corpse initially marks a moment of total destabilization of categories like position, site and reference . . . the cadaver is not in its place, not here and yet it is not elsewhere. A stability of categories must again be recuperated, namely in the act of representation, so that we move from the experience of decomposition to composition, from the dying body/corpse to a representation and narration of the dying body/corpse. (1992: 52)

Furthermore, as Bronfen and Sarah Goodwin write in *Death and Representation*, the cadaver's semantic polyvalence, its resistance to stable categories of reference, its "here and nowhere" make it a (warped) mirror upon which culture views its own desired reflection: corpse as tragedy, corpse as tranquility, corpse as indictment, corpse as national rebirth. In this sense,

> every representation of death is a misrepresentation. Thus the analysis of it must show not only how it claims to represent death, but also what else it in fact represents, however suppressed: assertion of alternative power, self-referential metaphor, aggression against individuals or groups, formation of group identities or ideologies, and so forth. Whether as state or as event, death cannot be represented. Attempts at representation therefore seek to appropriate that resistant power. (20)[10]

The anthropologist Katherine Verdery, in *The Political Lives of Dead Bodies*, reads the corpse in much the same way, with an emphasis on its ideological uses:

> A body's symbolic effectiveness does not depend on it standing for one particular thing, however, for among the most important properties of bodies,

especially dead ones, is their ambiguity, multivocality, or polysemy. Remains are concrete, but protean . . . Different people can invoke corpses as symbols, thinking those corpses mean the same thing to all present, whereas in fact they may mean different things to each. All that is shared is everyone's *recognition* of this dead person as somehow important. In other words, what gives a dead body symbolic effectiveness in politics is precisely its ambiguity, its capacity to evoke a variety of understandings. (28–29, emphasis in original)

In the US, a culture known for its pragmatism and optimism, the specter of death holds profound anxieties. Simply put, its sheer unknowability and the material nature of its evidence (the corpse), combined with its stark terror for a society inured to the "good life," necessitates a robust sociocultural response to contain death's destabilizing power; these responses are open to being shaped by various political actors, for different ideological aims. Who represents death, narrativizes it, or tells its story, can direct a culture's strong emotional recoiling from mortality's "bottom line."[11]

Moreover, in the deaths of our most revered national figures—some politicians, soldiers, some athletes, superheroes—we see an intensified cultural compulsion to, as it were, narrate our way out of death's blind alley. Heroes, in fact, seem tailor-made for such posthumous ideological repurposing. As Verdery argues, they "come with a curriculum vitae" which, through proper handling, can itself serve to authorize particular values and delegitimize others—with, of course, no resistance from the dead person: "Words can be put into their mouths—often quite ambiguous words—or their own actual words can be ambiguated by quoting them out of context. It is thus easier to rewrite history with dead people than with other kinds of symbols that are speechless" (29).

Superheroes, no less than their esteemed real-life counterparts, through their "deaths" (can be made to) ritualize, render meaningful and exorcise cultural trauma. Their resurrections—so contemptible to certain elements of the fan base—likewise help inject a sense of hope and new beginnings into storylines, at the same time tacitly reassuring readers of the durability and continuity of the values they embody. Yet superheroes—quasi-fascist physical and moral paragons—also seem to communicate something deeper through their utter intolerance to death: an underlying fear and motivation amounting to the genre's structuring disavowal itself. This line of reasoning—death-fear as psychological undergirding for all human thought and action—was pursued the furthest by a late-twentieth-century thinker on mortality particularly germane to our analysis.

BECKER'S MECHANISM OF DEATH DENIAL

For Ernest Becker, death denial serves a critical function in the formation of human character. In *The Denial of Death*, Becker plants the fear of mortality upon the supreme throne of human drives. In a reinscription of basic psychoanalytic concepts, he reorients the instincts from the pursuit of sex and pleasure to the avoidance of annihilation through vast networks (both individual and collective) to disavow the conscious knowledge of man's finitude. The specter that haunts humanity, writes Becker in a pessimistic, neo-Kierkegaardian vein, is its own mortal body, with its demoralizingly banal needs:

> Man's body is a *problem* to him that has to be explained. Not only his body is strange, but also its inner landscape, the memories and dreams. Man's very insides—his self—are foreign to him. He doesn't know who he is, why he was born, what he is doing on the planet, what he is supposed to do, what he can expect. His own existence is incomprehensible to him, a miracle just like the rest of creation, closer to him, right near his pounding heart, but for that reason all the more strange. (1973: 51, emphasis in original)

Caught between biology and symbol, the human animal, if it is to gain a proper self-knowledge, must reconcile itself to the scandalous cosmic joke of being a "god that shits":

> This is the paradox: he is out of nature and hopelessly in it; he is dual, up in the stars and yet housed in a heart-pumping, breath-gasping body that once belonged to a fish and still carries the gill-marks to prove it. His body is a material fleshy casting that is alien to him in many ways—the strangest and most repugnant way being that it aches and bleeds and will decay and die. (ibid.: 26)

Rather than face this horrifying paradox, Becker argues, cultures erect psychic defenses (the afterlife, religion, humanism, self-esteem) to convince man of his "special" symbol-producing powers, his superiority and uniqueness in the animal kingdom. But what Becker calls the "vital lie" of human character involves much more than mere body-hatred and shying away from thoughts of one's own surcease. The individual, he insists, must "repress globally"; it is a retreat from life as well as death. Like Freud before him, he paints man's relationship with reality as fundamentally "dishonest"—in a very real sense, *he cannot exist without illusion*. As he writes, "the core of psychodynamics, the formation of the human character, is a study in human self-limitation and in the terrifying costs of that limitation" (ibid.: 51).

For all its gloom and medieval contempt for the flesh,[12] Becker's concept of the "vital lie" has some clearly relevant applications to the superhero. Indeed, the idealized super-body (the "best" humanity has to offer) manages to repress more "globally" and more successfully than anyone else: to him death has (can have) no meaning at all, certainly no credible threat. But his "admirable" repression of death is also a further retreat from life, a narrowing of real human experience, with a concomitant deflation of drama. Knowing superheroes can never die makes them more difficult to relate to, sympathize with; immortality cheapens them.

Among other things, this makes the superhero, like certain media or national figures, an ideal object for Becker's "transference heroics," the "natural fetishization for man's highest yearnings and strivings," which "gives man precisely what he needs: a certain degree of sharply defined individuality, a definite point of reference for his practice of goodness, and all within a certain secure level of safety and control" (1973: 155–56).[13]

For Becker, fictional death falls far short of what we need: it may remind moderns of the mortality they and the culture otherwise represses, and in a "safe space" that poses no real danger—but this very vicarious quality deprives the reader/viewer of a real, direct appreciation of death, the only thing that would make his life "meaningful." This is the double-edged nature of all art for Becker; fictional universes (such as those in superhero comics) both provide psychological "cover" to experience death "secondhand," but precisely this artifice trivializes what is for him always a very serious matter. Only an unflinching confrontation with death makes one a fully realized person, "born again" to the "terrifying paradox of the human condition, since one must be born not as a god, but as a man, or as a god-worm, or a god who shits" (58).[14]

Becker's arguments here recall Sigmund Freud's formulation on the psychological advantages of art for the human confrontation with death:

> [We] seek in the world of fiction, in literature and in the theatre compensation for what has been lost in life. There we still find people who know how to die ... In the realm of fiction we find the plurality of lives which we need. We die with the hero with whom we have identified ourselves; yet we survive him, and are ready to die with another hero. (1915A: 291)

Or, as it happens, with the same one, resurrected. Yet Freud, too, warns that, however psychologically useful, fictional deaths cannot wholly compensate for the need to face one's own mortality "honestly," be it in the field of battle or the hospital ward. He sees this as a central problem of a Western modernity, which has "outsourced" death to hospitals, nursing homes, and mortuaries: "Life is impoverished, it loses in interest, when the highest stake in the game of living, life itself, may not be risked ... the tendency to exclude death from our calculations in life brings in its train many other renunciations and exclusions" (ibid.: 290–91).

Thus, a Beckerian reading of superhero death-denial would emphasize its extravagant "dishonesty"—by callously flouting such a central component of human reality, the genre cedes its claim not only to realism but to true heroism as well. Every time they once again stroll back through death's "revolving door," good as new, thanks to another ludicrous plot device, superheroes only alienate the reader further. What's the point, Quarter Bin writes, of following characters for whom death is "no more incurable than a bad cold" (Sept. 2000)?

Hence, the market realities of the mainstream comics industry—which demands its moneymaking brands live on *ad perpetuum*—have led to a state in which the consumer steadily loses interest in fictive creations who have nothing to risk, in a genre where a fundamental aspect of being human has been scrubbed clean away. There is no death: this is the "vital lie" of the mainstream superhero genre; it cannot live without that illusion. All the same, since the Silver Age writers and editors, in keeping with their drive for greater verisimilitude in their stories, strove to address the reality of death, at least obliquely, through numerous stratagems, without jeopardizing their core company properties. These we examine in the next three sections.

DREAMS, MULTIVERSES, AND IMAGINARY STORIES

Perhaps the most expedient (some might say "cheapest") means to explore the ramifications of death for a character in an ongoing series—without actually experiencing it—was the simple dream story. "Robin Dies at Dawn!" (*Batman*, vol. 1, #156, Jun. 1963, Finger/Moldoff) exemplifies the more baroque extremes of this approach. Trapped on an alien planet, shorn of his utility belt and other weapons, with no memory of how he arrived, Batman is attacked by a plant monster whose tendrils threaten to squeeze the life out of him. "If only *Robin* were here to help me!" Batman cries. "*Robin! Where are you Robin? Robin!*" (Kawasaki 2005: 37, emphasis in original). Just in time, the dark knight's partner appears, to whack the monster with a shovel-like implement. Later, Robin again saves Batman from a stone giant, but loses his life when a boulder crushes him. Stunned by "the shock of a terrible catastrophe," as the caption puts it, Batman buries his friend under a hot alien sun: "*Robin*

sacrificed himself for me! He died so I could live! Oh, *Robin* . . . Robin . . ."
(ibid.: 40, emphasis and ellipses in original).

Despondent, driven to exhaustion on the strange world, Batman finally
succumbs to suicidal despair, welcoming a fanged monster's attack: "Let it
come! I don't want to live! It's my fault *Robin* died! I don't want to live . . ."
(ibid.: 41, emphasis and ellipses in original). At this point, through a "match-
cut" panel sequence, the scene shifts to Batman in a lab test chamber, outfit-
ted with scientific instruments. A live Robin and others appear—Batman has
been hallucinating the entire story while undergoing an experiment on how
stress and isolation might affect astronauts in space. As explained by a white-
coated "doc": "You imagined that you were guilty of *Robin's* death . . . your
constant concern about the boy's safety came to the surface in your hallucinations!" (ibid.: 42–43, emphasis and ellipsis in original).

Apart from its stark reminder of Batman's fear of abandonment (brought
on by young Bruce Wayne witnessing the murder of his parents) and its mythological echoes (Robin's fall in battle recalls the similar demise of the beloved
Enkidu in the Gilgamesh myth), "Robin Dies at Dawn!" demonstrates the incompatibility of death and superheroics: devastated by his loss, overcome by
guilt, Batman prefers to die himself rather than live on with the pain. As in the
Golden-Age "Case of the Honest Crook," when his belief that Robin has died
drives him to acts of blood-thirsty vengeance such that even the police fear
him, Batman here cannot maintain his moral authority or strength of will—
he merely collapses, wilting under the hot alien sun (identified later as the
view of scientists observing him during the experiment, but no less relatable
to the gaze of the Real, i.e., death, reducing him to cowardly powerlessness).

Despite the restorative "happy ending"—Robin is not dead—the story
conveys many disquieting clues to Batman's unsound state of mind, his psychological scars resulting from repeated encounters with mortality, a popular interpretation of the character's motivation which David M. Hart terms
"borderline psychopathic, driven . . . by an irresistible compulsion induced
by childhood trauma" (213). The oneiric mood of the alien planet scenes (the
wish-fulfillment fantasy of Robin's rescue, the nightmarish spectacle of his
sacrifice) indicates we are witnessing Batman's constant internal struggle
to ward off death, either through inflicting violence on others or giving in
to it once and for all. Even as the "doc" provides a scientific explanation for
Batman's hallucinations, the artist Sheldon Moldoff draws his portrait with
an odd crosshatch pattern across his face, darkening it, as well as a curiously wagging finger, all against a black background (9)—as if the authority of
medicine itself can only scold the reader over the "proper" rationale response
to death, even as the black background and crosshatch pattern tell us all such
accountings wither in the face of actual death. Finally, the story (part two

7.1 Batman gives in to despair in the dream story "Robin Dies at Dawn!" (*Batman*, vol. 1, #156, Jun. 1963).

of a loose trilogy) ends with the doctor worried Batman might suffer "after-effects" from his ordeal; indeed, part three shows the hero overcoming a form of post-traumatic stress disorder. Death is flouted, but it always haunts the edge of consciousness.

The "dream story" approach to mortality in the superhero genre (while capable of producing such discomfiting material as "Robin Dies at Dawn!") ultimately amounts to a very limited, even trite technique for addressing the topic. Any "genuine" readerly sympathy for the hero's loss is undermined by the revelation that "it was never real," that it was "only a hallucination." The "dream story" holds as much weight as a nightmare in the "real world": not inconsiderable as a window on our own death anxieties, but insubstantial when held up to actual death and bereavement itself. To the superhero, death really is a weird "alien" planet.

A different strategy advanced by DC senior editor Mort Weisinger starting in 1960,[15] the "Imaginary Stories," did not avoid the direct confrontation with death so valued by Becker and purportedly appreciated by many comics fans, but at the same time did not endanger core character continuity. Freed from the imperative to preserve the status quo of their commercial properties—since these tales did not formally redound to their history—creative teams could explore otherwise taboo topics such as life changes (marriage, birth, death, the revelation of secret identities), revise character backgrounds, even reverse heroes' morality or bring histories to a close. As explained by Umberto Eco, the "Imaginary Stories" provided an elegant quasi-solution to the superhero's entrapment in a timeless, ambiguous half-romantic/half-mythological mode:

> If Superman married Lois Lane, it would of course be another step toward his death, as it would lay down another irreversible premise; nevertheless, it is necessary to find continually new narrative stimuli and to satisfy the "romantic" demands of the public. And so it is told "what would have happened *if* Superman had married Lois." The premise is developed in all of its dramatic implications, and at the end is the warning: Remember, this is an imaginary story which in truth has not taken place. (154, emphasis in original)

Moreover, the raising of the dramatic stakes meant death became not only a possibility in these tales, but a common component. The "risk" that gives life meaning, which Freud complained had been lost in modernity, was restored to superheroes (albeit in an "imaginary" setting), with a concomitant heightening of readerly emotional involvement, as Levitz prescribed. In this regard, the "Imaginary Stories" tapped the wisdom of ancient myth and epic. As described by Jacobs and Jones:

Generally, many years were covered in these "what if" stories, which often followed characters along the full journey from birth to death. (Death ran rampant in these stories, but never as senseless annihilation; those who died usually did so in acts of heroic self-sacrifice.) They were extremely bittersweet in tone, and frequently modeled after the heroic epics of antiquity, in which defeat made the brave even braver and neatly rounded out their existence. Defeat, irony and tragedy were preponderant, and the intense sorrow often endured by the characters was both touching and elevating. (78)

The pervasiveness of the death theme—along with its emotional payoff—becomes apparent in reading the most famous "Imaginary Stories," such as "The Three Wives of Superman!" (*Superman's Girlfriend, Lois Lane*, vol. 1, #51, Aug. 1964, Schaffenberger), in which the man of steel marries and tragically loses his three great loves; "The Death of Lois Lane" (*Superman*, vol. 1, #194, Feb. 1967, Binder/Swan); and "Robin's Revenge!" (*World's Finest Comics*, vol. 1, #184, May 1969, Bates/Swan), in which an enraged Robin seeks Batman's killers.

In perhaps the boldest and most far-reaching of the Silver Age "Imaginary Tales," "The Death of Superman" (*Superman*, vol. 1, #149, Nov. 1961, Siegel/Swan), our hero is brutally murdered with a Kryptonite beam by arch-villain Lex Luthor, who straps him to a slab in the manner of a state execution (a glass partition separates him from his friends, who gaze on in horror). Over the next several pages, representatives of many nations, planets, and eras, as well as ordinary people, file past Superman's body in its glass coffin in solemn farewell. A crowing Luthor, meanwhile, throws a party for his fellow criminals. Here, we see the tragic dimensions and•global reach of the "imaginary" superhero death story as its chief dramatic advantage: it more "maturely" explores the reality of loss and grief through the behavior of those left behind, who lament, celebrate or otherwise react to the fallen figure.

The 1961 "Death of Superman" imaginary story—like its non-"imaginary"[16] 1992–93 counterpart—also serves as a snapshot of the public attitudes to mourning and capital punishment of its era, with concessions made to the ecumenism required for a large and diverse readership. Though Superman lies in state in a building that somewhat resembles a church, no religious service accompanies his friends' leave-taking, and only a monumental statue appears to memorialize the slain hero; there is no mention of the body's precise location (presumably inside the monument). Luthor, at his trial, is compared to none other than Adolph Eichmann, the Nazi functionary, linking Superman's murder to the Holocaust (Gold/Greenberger: 205). Finally, the story fosters a sense of intergenerational continuity in its bittersweet ending, impossible in

7.2 Imaginary stories such as "The Death of Superman" (*Superman*, vol. 1, #149, Nov. 1961) made it possible to examine the repercussions of events inadmissible to "core" continuity.

"canonical" tales: once she dispatches Luthor, Supergirl assumes the mantle of Earth's protector.[17]

In what would in effect turn out to be the last of DC's Weisinger-style "Imaginary Stories," "Whatever Happened to the Man of Tomorrow" (*Superman*, vol. 1, #423, Sept. 1986; *Action Comics*, vol. 1, #583, Sept. 1986, both Moore/Swan), irreversible grisly death predominates. Solicited by longtime DC editor Julius Schwartz as a "farewell" story meant to put a period to the character's mythos and tie up all loose ends before the wholesale continuity revamp of *Crisis on Infinite Earths*, this deeply pessimistic story culminates in a bloodbath worthy of Shakespearean tragedy, as Superman faces down virtually all his foes; Luthor, Lana Lang, Jimmy Olsen, Mr. and Mrs. Perry White, Brainiac, Mr. Mxyzptlk, Kryptonite Man, Bizarro, even Krypto the dog, all perish violently. The work, a bizarre conflation of heartfelt homage with macabre desecration, is made all the more perverse by Curt Swan's "innocent"-looking, Silver Age-y art. It seems as though, after forty-eight years, the opportunity for "real" dramatic closure unleashed a latent death and destruction for decades disavowed by the genre—a four-color Götterdämmerung.[18]

Andrew Helfer, incoming editor after Schwartz, captured the sense of possibility at a unique cultural turning point when he said:

> In that one moment, we were closing the book on Superman. And in that moment, it really was the last Superman story. It was not an imaginary story. You could utilize all the "real" things that preceded it and really create a definitive conclusion for the story of Superman. That only existed as a real story for a moment, because right afterwards, the first issue of [the post-Crisis series] *The Man of Steel* basically defined *all* of the previous Superman stories as imaginary stories. (Kahan 1997, emphasis in original)

Helfer touches on a key point regarding the contingent nature of the "imaginary"/canonical divide: every continuity revamp (or retcon) essentially consigns the previous, outmoded version to the limbo (Phantom Zone?) of the "imaginary story." Like a serpent shedding its old skin, retcons (of which there have been several in both major comics companies since the 1980s) propel the genre forward, keeping it up to date with cultural changes and (some) fan tastes.[19] This is why *Whatever Happened to the Man of Tomorrow?* is an elegiac piece not only for the characters but for their creators: Schwartz, who had edited the Superman titles since 1971, and was about to retire after forty-two years at DC, arranged for veteran artists long associated with the character (Curt Swan, Murphy Anderson, and Kurt Schaffenberger) to work on the storyline, drawing Superman effectively for the last time in their careers. It was the passing on of an entire generation of comics creators. Swan, in his cover to the final part of the story, even drew Superman weeping as he flies away forever from his friends. "The tears in Superman's eyes are really Curt's tears," noted Schwartz.[20]

Nevertheless, as with the "dream story," the "imaginary story's" claim to more realistically portray death in the superhero genre ultimately comes up rather hollow; any move to "honestly" depict it—even as transgressively as in Moore/Swan's tale—is undercut by some version of the familiar refrain, quoted here from the 1961 "The Death of Superman," with which such tales routinely end: "Well, let's not feel *too* badly! After all, this was only an *imaginary* story . . . and the chances are a *million to one* it will *never* happen!" (Gold/ Greenberger: 206, emphasis and ellipsis in original). As Eco reminds us, the drive to dramatic satisfaction in this context must always contend with "commercial necessities" (155).

"Imaginary stories" serve as the genre's subconscious dream material, which it revokes and denies in its "waking" canonical continuity—while that "official version" itself awaits expulsion to "imaginary" status in the next ret-con. All of which recalls Becker's critique of modern man's psychological re-lationship to death as fundamentally "dishonest." But the common "only an imaginary story" waiver also belies a curious tension: the whimsical dismissal of death's threat, meant to safeguard beloved characters, must be reiterated consistently so as to keep the "real" continuity safely segregated from the "non-real" alternative. The "imaginary stories" boldly explore the wide-rang-ing impact of such major life events as death, but must constantly reassure the reader—to protect company brands as well as, presumably, impressionable young minds—that this is not happening "in actuality."

In Marvel Comics' version of the "imaginary story," the gatekeeping func-tion falls to a character within the diegesis: the superego-like Watcher (aka Uatu), member of a race of superior beings tasked with monitoring events across different universes. Launched under editor-in-chief Archie Goodwin in 1977 and running for forty-seven issues, the original *What If?* series ex-plored the "alternate realities" created by divergent paths taken at critical pe-riods in Marvel history. Some ranged from the innocuous: "What If Jane Fos-ter Had Found the Hammer of Thor?" (*What If?*, vol. 1, #10, Aug. 1978, Glut/Hoberg); to the climactic: "What If The Avengers Had Become The Pawns of Korvac?" (*What If?*, vol. 1, #32, Apr. 1982, Gruenwald/Laroque), in which the universe is destroyed; to the absurd: "What If The Fantastic Four Were The Original Marvel Bullpen?" (*What If?*, vol. 1, #11, Oct. 1978, Kirby).

Once more, death plays a major role in these non-continuity stories, with creative teams seeming to relish the opportunity to "cut loose" with "no rules" about maintaining a series status quo. Several take on darkly tragic dimen-sions, perhaps none more than "What If the Invisible Girl Had Died?" (*What If?*, vol. 1, #42, Dec. 1983, Gillis/Frenz), notable for its unrelentingly pessimistic portrait of Reed Richards (Mr. Fantastic) after the death of his wife. Splitting off from events at a crucial juncture in "Let There Be . . . Life!" (*Fantastic Four Annual*, vol. 1, #6, Nov. 1968, Lee/Kirby), Peter Gillis's story explores the corro-sive effects of grief, the moral toll it exacts on even the noblest souls, crossing the line from superhero tale to grim revenge drama.

The original tale opens with a heated Richards frantically searching for a sample of antimatter to counteract the effects of cosmic radiation on his wife Susan Storm (the Invisible Girl), who is about to give birth. Without the sub-stance, found only in the dauntingly dangerous Negative Zone, Susan will die. When questioned, the normally calm and methodical Richards, a scientific genius, barks, "*Shut up! I know* what I'm doing!" (1, emphasis in original) at his teammates Ben Grimm (the Thing) and Johnny Storm (the Human Torch). When reminded of the peril they face, Richards replies, "*Forget it!* What does my life matter . . . *now?*" (2, emphasis and ellipsis in original). The three launch themselves into the Negative Zone, where they battle the insect-like villain Annihilus for the antimatter. Despite several setbacks, the trio makes it back to Earth just in time, with their prize, and Susan gives birth safely. Ecstatic, the super-family celebrates the arrival of their new member, a son.

As made clear by its title, "What If The Invisible Girl Had Died?" explores the opposite outcome with unusual candor: Annihilus delays the heroes long enough so that, though they make it home safely with the antimatter, they arrive too late. The remainder of the story—some thirty pages—is taken up with the question posed by the narrating Watcher at the outset: what if the Fantastic Four "incurred a tragedy too great to be endured . . . a tragedy which even their fabled resolve could not overcome?" (ellipsis in original). The question answers itself.

The *What If?* story starts at the same point as its predecessor: a stern Richards leads his partners into the Negative Zone on their urgent quest. The artist Ron Frenz duplicates many of Kirby's original compositions, while Joe Sinnot, longtime *Fantastic Four* inker (who had worked over Kirby's pencils in "Let There Be . . . Life!"), inks Frenz. This imparts an "authentic FF look" to the proceedings;[21] like Swan's pencils in "What Ever Happened to the Man of Tomorrow?" the familiar artwork, characters and situations make the introduction of "real" death seem even more shocking and transgressive.

Departures from the Lee/Kirby original soon become apparent, and long before Storm's death; interestingly, these changes both announce Gillis/Frenz's command of their revered forerunners' work and reflect changes in public attitudes (including to death and dying) since the 1960s. In this version, Richards is more cold and obsessive about curing his wife from the outset; he even orders Grimm and Johnny to sacrifice team members if need be to secure the antimatter. Back on Earth, meanwhile, several lengthy scenes feature Susan— a striking divergence, as she appears only once in the original, to present Reed with his son.

If, in the former story, Susan seems mainly an off-panel pawn of fate— a wombed object to rescue—in the *What If?* variant she expresses her fears and longings, recounting for the Inhuman Crystal how she met Richards and Grimm in college. This poignantly humanizes the character, as does the explicit revelation that Sue knows of her pregnancy's real dangers. When a doctor tells her about the gravity of her condition, she replies, "Thank you for not hiding the risks from me" (n.p.). These scenes function as a remarkable corrective to the original's avoidance of the personal in favor of action set pieces, and mark the cultural transition from a period when doctors and families often did not tell dying patients about their situation to a post-Kübler-Ross (and post-feminist) era when such conversations were becoming normalized.[22]

But the most salient feature of "What If The Invisible Girl Had Died?" is how far it goes in depicting the impact of "real" death on the superpowered and normal communities. In a tale that could have been called "Let There Be . . . Death!" the world reacts with horror and grief to Sue's passing. Even age-old rivalries come to a pause for reflection; chief villain Doctor Doom, gazing from his Latverian fortress, muses:

And so, fate has inflicted on my greatest enemy a defeat—a loss far more agonizing than any which Von Doom might give him. And Richards must live the rest of his days with that knowledge. It is a time for even enemies to cease their conflicts . . . for now. (ellipsis in original)

As in "The Death of Superman" (1961), luminaries from all parts of the globe converge to pay their respects, as narrated by the Watcher: "And so they gather—to pay tribute and to mourn.[23] Whether they come from Chicago or from sunken Atlantis. Whether they are honored Avengers—controversial mutants, or simple mailmen [i.e., the Fantastic Four's postman Willie Lump-kin] . . . they are one in their grief" (ellipsis in original). The page design here signals deep emotional trauma: Uatu's words appear in lower case (unlike in the rest of the Watcher's captions), in a style of lettering appropriate to funeral announcements. The page itself is composed of four vertical panels (like gravestones) hanging "loosely" in a space dominated by white—as if the comic book were literally decomposing. The design evokes Christophe Dony and Caroline Van Linthout's observations on comic language's resonance with states of mourning and trauma:

Both comics and . . . traumatic memory can be understood in terms of frag-ments and totality because they construct a whole (a narrative or story) by assembling multiple parts (such as panels, testimonies, or memories). Moreover, both the comics medium and traumatic events shatter notions of time and space as they are perceived under "normal" conditions. (180)

Indeed, the sense of time and space remains in suspension as the "mourn-ing" chronotope comes to predominate: Johnny, Grimm, and Richards each give eulogies in monotonous nine-panel grids, with silent funeral attendees in the central panels. The story then settles into a bifurcated structure recalling Freud's "Mourning and Melancholia" (1917): we see an illustration of "healthy" mourning (Johnny, Grimm, Namor) and "unhealthy" melancholia leading to self-)destruction (Richards).[24] Inconsolable, the one-time Mr. Fantastic erases his data tapes, soliloquizes on how his life is over and how Sue "was the only

And so they gather--to pay tribute and to mourn.

Whether they come from Chicago or from sunken Atlantis.

Whether they are honored Avengers--

--controversial mutants,or simple matlmen...

...they are one in their grief.

7.3 Page design evokes the trauma and grief of loss in "What If the Invisible Girl Had Died?" (*What If?*, vol. 1, #42, Dec. 1983).

thing keeping me from ending up like Von Doom." He then sets out, without his teammates, to avenge himself on Annihilus.[25]

What ensues shows the depths plumbed by a once-heroic personality shattered by loss. Dead-eyed, unshaven, appearing often in shadow, Richards methodically destroys his enemy's defenses; an inhuman figure of retribution, he speaks tonelessly: "I've come for you, Annihilus. You're going to die." In a bizarre reversal, the once-terrifying supervillain is reduced to mostly begging his implacable foe for his life: "I'll torture myself—mutilate myself—only please don't kill me!! Death—Death is the end! The end of everything! Anything is better than death! All I did was defend myself! It's all I've ever done!" (a slightly edited version of the truth).

Johnny, Grimm, and Namor, who have followed their friend into the Negative Zone, at last confront him at the dimensional interface between the two universes—where matter and antimatter constantly meet in mutual destruction. With Annihilus groveling at Richards's feet, the following dialogue ensues:

GRIMM: Reed—Reed—This ain't gonna bring Susie back.

RICHARDS: *Don't you think I know that!?!?*

NAMOR: Hear me, Reed Richards. My grandfather—my father, my mother— all of them died because of the stupidity and malice of surface men. I have a hundred times more cause to grieve than you. And I loved Susan, too. You know that. But I learned, Reed Richards. I learned that life continues to unfold, despite death. And I learned that love—never loses its meaning, even with death. Even with death. Come back with us.

RICHARDS: (in tears) *No!!* You can't take this *last thing* away from me! I *have* to have my revenge! It's all I have *left!* (emphasis and ellipses in original)

The ideal reader of this exchange would be all the more moved by a longtime familiarity with the Fantastic Four mythos—Namor's tragic confrontations with the surface world, his near-love affairs with Susan Storm, Grimm's own unrequited affection for her, the nuances of the Fantastic Four's extended family dynamics, and so on—after some twenty-two years of continuity. The *What If?* scenario capitalizes on such presumed knowledge for its affective power; Richards's behavior, out of character, extreme and appalling though it is, makes "sense" based on that history—which might even make it difficult for some readers *not* to identify with him.[26]

As boldly as any "imaginary story" can, "What If The Invisible Girl Had Died?" explores the devastation of grief, how it ripples through whole communities no less than through the self left behind in tatters. As noted by Judith Butler in *Precarious Life: The Powers of Mourning and Violence*:

> If I lose you . . . then I not only mourn the loss, but I become inscrutable to myself. Who "am" I, without you? When we lose some of these ties by which we are constituted, we do not know who we are or what to do. On one level, I think I have lost "you" only to discover that "I" have gone missing as well. (2003: 22)

Indeed, Richards the superhero loses himself. Tellingly, while on his mission of vengeance the former Mister Fantastic almost completely forgoes the use of his stretching powers; they in fact disappear completely in the last several pages. He defeats Annihilus solely through technological superiority and dogged persistence, while he holds off his friends with only a laser pistol—until the completion of his gruesome murder/suicide.[27] Again, we see "real" death and superheroics as irreconcilable.

The "imaginary stories," despite (or because of) their non-canonical status, serve as a venue for delving into such taboo subjects as beloved characters dying and committing atrocities "safely," thanks to the gatekeeping function of the "it's not real" (whether stated explicitly as an editorial comment or personified in the Watcher). Their preoccupation with death speaks to its paucity, indeed the psychological deficiency, wrought by the routine absence of such material in the "official" continuity. Even if it's "all pretend," death in the "imaginary stories" since the Silver Age performed a valuable function as an outlet for the genre's otherwise repressed truths.

Another stratagem for addressing such truths as death strikes its own balance between the requirements of ongoing serial fiction and the need for realistic portrayal of life changes, while removing the "it's not real." The multiverse concept, introduced in the Schwartz era at DC in "Flash of Two Worlds!" (*The Flash*, vol. 1, #123, Sept. 1961, Fox/Broome), posited a separate "Earth-2" inhabited by the Golden Age superheroes of the 1930s–40s, distinguished from the "Earth-1" of the current era, where dwelt the revamped heroes of the new Silver Age. Inadvertently traveling to the alternate "predecessor" universe through his super-vibration powers, the current Flash (Barry Allen) encounters his childhood idol from the comics, the original Flash (Jay Garrick), now middle-aged and retired. Many more alternate earths soon appeared.[28]

The parallel universes are not dreams or "imaginary," but ontological givens within the diegesis, observes Karin Kukkonen, "fully parallel, equally actualized realities" (40) that offer "counterfactual scenarios involving alternative developments of the story of a known superhero" (41). In the multiverse (comprised of many realities), superheroes can grow old, marry, die, and even be evil, without affecting the core reality of Earth-1 (except in crossover adventures). So as to tell apart the myriad versions of a character, in what over the decades developed into a "labyrinthine complexity of the superhero mul-tiverse"(41), artists resorted to iconographic elements and costume variations: for example, Garrick's Flash wears a helmet with wings, Allen's a red-yellow suit, and the Earth-2 Superman (also now middle-aged and married to Lois Lane) still dons a costume with the distinctive "S" shape of the character's original 1938 appearance.

In Marvel's own "alternate realities," death preponderates, as seen in the thanatocentric history of the Squadron Supreme, initially a thinly veiled ver-sion of rival DC's Justice League of America. First appearing in "The World Is Not For Burning!" (*The Avengers*, vol. 1, #85, Feb. 1971, Thomas/Buscema), the "Earth-712" heroes starred in their own miniseries, *Squadron Supreme* (Sept. 1985–Aug. 1986, Gruenwald/Hall), in which they establish an authoritarian state on their world. In the internecine battles that result (as some members object to the utopian scheme), several characters perish. Dystopian alternate futures also appeared at Marvel, inaugurated by 1982's "Days of Future Past" storyline in the *Uncanny X-Men* (vol. 1, #140 and #141, Claremont/Byrne), which features the violent deaths of Storm, Colossus, Wolverine, and others in a totalitarian 2013 America under the sway of the Sentinels.

The multiverse model offers an elegantly postmodern solution to character stasis in a market-driven serial publishing system which privileges constancy over major change; it is also a particularly "scientific" version of death denial.[29] Now there exists, in theory, no "official" reality, but many, in which quite liter-ally anything can happen—including the death of our hero. (Not to worry—we have many "spares.")[30] At the same time, the lay public will not lose sight of the primary brand, since the only consumers who care to know the difference between an Earth-X and Earth-Y Superman or a present and future variant of Wolverine[31] are the subculture of "comics geeks." (For the most part, the Superman appearing in films and lunch boxes remains the familiar Earth-1 version, and he never really dies.)

At the same time, the daunting complexity of the multiverse model (with its ongoing proliferation of character versions and histories)[32] has proven among the leading factors in discouraging new readers.[33] This very complex-ity, in fact, eventually led DC to streamline continuity in the limited series *Crisis on Infinite Earths* (1985–86), a superhero holocaust of "real death" on a multiversal scale (as elaborated below). Again we observe that, when it does not "count," the genre gravitates towards death as a dramatic and "house-cleaning" device. ("Kill all you like—we're retconning anyway . . .") This holds even in the "official" universes, in the cases when "real" death has taken place since the Silver Age. As so often with superheroes, however, the meaning of "real" death fluctuates—which we shall see as we turn to its examination in non-dream, non-alternative, non-"imaginary" tales.

"HEROIC" DEATH

First and foremost, to perhaps belabor the obvious, *if* death ever befell a superhero in "real" continuity in the Silver Age and beyond, it had to be *heroic*. (Nihilistic material like Richards's *What If?* mission of vengeance is out of the question.) As opposed to supervillains, who routinely escaped the reaper through ludicrous plot devices and technicalities so as to strike again,[34] superheroes had to exhibit such noble qualities as self-sacrifice and selflessness, in the process saving their fellows or even the universe. Their deaths not only had to *mean* something, they had to *accomplish* something.

As in the "Imaginary Stories," these deaths reverberated throughout the fallen hero's community, often for several issues.[35] We may take as paradigmatic the Legion of Superheroes story "The Stolen Super-Powers" (*Adventure Comics*, vol. 1, #304, Jan. 1963, Siegel/Forte), in which Lightning Lad falls to an alien threat. This and subsequent issues exhibited an odd form of death-anxiety; several tales in this series, set in the thirtieth century, featured characters obsessively seeking to forestall death, sacrificing themselves to save their teammates, trying to undo death, and experiencing survivor guilt. Such is the case in this tale: when Saturn Girl learns of a computer's prediction that a legionnaire will soon die in battle, she does everything in her power—including taking over and deceiving the team—to ensure she will be the one. All the same, Lightning Lad sees through her ruse, and wins the bizarre "competition" to perish instead of the others. He expires, uttering: "Don't cry, *Saturn Girl!* . . . Better me . . . —Gasp!— Th-than you . . . Goodbye . . ." (Kawasaki 2008: 29, emphasis and ellipses in original).

An elaborate funeral and leave-taking follow, of the sort encountered in the "Imaginary Stories." Encased in a glass coffin, with eternal lightning bolts powered by a "perpetual motion device," the dead hero's body is hailed by representatives of various nations, planets, and galaxies, while his closest friends pledge to "never, never forget him!" (ibid.: 29). Artist John Forte's pained expressions on the faces of the survivors, Jacobs and Jones note, exemplified the "rage and pathos that ran riot" through this and other *Legion* stories (83). Yet "The Stolen Super-Powers" ends with its own sort of disclaimer, a quasi-reassurance not all that unlike those of the "imaginary" tales: "Is *Lightning Lad* really dead . . . separated from his gallant companions for all time? Or is it possible that the super-science of the 30th century can restore his life? See forthcoming issues of *Adventure Comics* for the surprising answer!" (Kawasaki 2008: 30, emphasis and ellipsis in original).

Indeed, over several subsequent stories, culminating in "The Super-Sacrifice of the Legionnaires!" (*Adventure Comics*, vol. 1, #312, Sept. 1963, Siegel/

Forte), the Legion obsessively strives to return their fallen comrade to life, through illusion (his sister Lightning Lass impersonates him briefly), exposure to a revivifying alien sun's rays, and research into an alien life form's phoenix-like powers of resurrection. At last, they strike upon a method pioneered on Mon-El's homeworld, Daxam, in which one member must sacrifice his/her own life in a lightning strike to bring Lightning Lad back. As in the previous story, a team member (Mon-El) seeks to keep the procedure secret, so that he can be the one to give up his life. His subterfuge discovered, the Legionnaires argue amongst themselves over who should take the fatal dose of electricity for their friend. In the end they agree to leave it up to chance – though even here Saturn Girl seeks to trick the others, disguising the lightning-attracting powers of her wand (Kawasaki 2008: 45). As it happens, the putty-like life form Proty fools them all, impersonating Saturn Girl so that it dies from the lightning strike, successfully resurrecting Lighting Lad. (Curiously, upon its death, the inhuman Proty receives no immediate commemoration of the sort dedicated to his human counterpart; only several issues later is it so honored.)

The death and resurrection of Lightning Lad would set the rough pattern for superhero death in the Silver Age and beyond: demise in battle, funeral, emotional fallout, attempts at revivification, and return from the dead. The sheer inadmissibility of real death, superheroes' (and the genre's) literal inability to live with it—neurotic forms of mourning, to say the least—color such tales.[36]

Which made it all the more remarkable when creators broke the pattern. Jim Shooter, a thirteen-year-old wunderkind hired by DC's Weisinger, scripted the unusual *Legion of Superheroes* story "The Doomed Legionnaire" (*Adventure Comics*, vol. 1, #353, Feb. 1967, Shooter/Swan), in which a member gives up his life to save the galaxy.[37] Shooter explained that as a reader he had found superhero death/resurrection intensely unsatisfactory, even offensive.[38] He took it as a personal goal to inflict real death and injury on the Legion "for the sake of verisimilitude":

> Before my run, Lightning Lad had died at one point, but after a while, was brought back to life. Later, Lightning Lad—him again, poor guy—lost an arm! But, the arm was ultimately restored. Triplicate Girl had lost one iteration to become Duo Damsel, but . . . come on! I wanted to do it meaningfully, for real. Permanently. (Kawasaki 2009B: 165)

Knowing the DC editorship would resist killing any well-established character, Shooter decided to sacrifice one of his own creations, Ferro Lad (aka Andrew Nolan of Earth), only recently inducted into the Legion in "One of Us is a Traitor!" (*Adventure Comics*, vol. 1, #346, Jul. 1966, Shooter/Swan). Faced with the apocalyptic threat of the galaxy-devouring Sun-Eater, at a critical moment Ferro Lad knocks out a weakened Superboy so that he might carry an "absorbatron bomb" into the anomaly's core in hopes of destroying it. The kamikaze ploy works, at the cost of Ferro Lad himself (Kawasaki 2009B: 98–99). His fellow team members look on in awe at his act of supreme courage: "He gave his life willingly . . . as any *legionnaire* would!" (ibid.: 99, ellipsis and emphasis in original). As with the aftermath of Lightning Lad's demise, the fallen champion receives a memorial: a cenotaph on the cemetery asteroid, Shanghalia. "*Ferro Lad's* sacrifice will be remembered *forever!*" sounds the familiar refrain (ibid.: 102, emphasis in original).

The similarities with Lightning Lad's death, however, more or less end there. The heroes make no attempt to revive their slain comrade (a difficult prospect, as his vaporized particles were scattered over millions of miles of space), and the very next issue, in a story set decades after the battle with the Sun-Eater, a commemorative statue confirms Ferro Lad is still dead (ibid.: 106). The Legionnaires do register various degrees of survivor guilt over several issues; Superboy blames himself for the death: "*I* should have gone on that suicide mission. . . . Did I subconsciously fear the *Sun-Eater* so much that I let poor *Ferro Lad* overpower me . . . only to doom himself doing *my job?*" (ibid.: 144–45, emphasis and some ellipses in original).

Such guilt complexes reached a pinnacle in stories where Ferro Lad "haunts" the Legion, either in the guise of his vengeful twin brother Douglas (who has identical powers) in "The Adult Legion!" (*Adventure Comics*, vol. 1, #354, Mar. 1967, Shooter/Swan) or as a faux "ghost" berating its former team members for letting him die in "The Ghost of Ferro Lad!" (*Adventure Comics*, vol. 1, #357, Jun. 1967, Shooter/Swan). In the latter, a series of apparition-like events convinces most of the Legion's core members that their dead comrade is haunting them, and decide to hold a séance to learn why. A ghostly image of Ferro Lad appears, angrily accusing his old teammates of murder; pointing at Superboy, he rails, "*You* took my life! As acting leader, it was *your* duty to deliver the bomb . . . But you pretended weakness . . . Tricked *me* into carrying it into the Sun-Eater's heart! And the rest of you *saw* this, yet did nothing to *stop* it!" (Kawasaki 2009B: 156, emphasis and ellipses in original). As his penalty, the ghost demands the Legion disband in disgrace—astonishingly, they do.

By negative example, "The Ghost of Ferro Lad" says a great deal about the representation of death in superhero comics of its era, as well as the parameters for discussion of mortality in a pre-Kübler-Ross America. First of all, it functions as a melodramatic illustration of Freud's "law of ambivalence of feelings," whereby unconscious death wishes collide with conscious love of the object, producing monstrous psychic projections as a warped "solution" to the finality of death: "It was beside the dead body of someone [primeval man]

7.4 "The Ghost of Ferro Lad!"
(*Adventure Comics*, vol. 1, #357,
Jun. 1967) explored survivor guilt
after a "heroic" death.

loved that he invented spirits, and his sense of guilt at the satisfaction mingled with his sorrow turned these new-born spirits into evil demons that had to be dreaded" (1915A: 294).[39] Superboy, Cosmic Boy, and others constantly torment themselves over their friend's demise and their own possible role in it, which expresses itself in feelings of culpability. Their demobilization therefore amounts to a tacit admission of blood guilt. This guilt had rendered them vulnerable to the machinations of the Controller, the supervillain secretly engineering the Legion's downfall through subtle mind control—a demonstration of Verdery's argument that heroes' deaths can be made to serve ideological interests. He who "controls" the death (with its potent emotional fallout) controls the mourners.

The story also serves as a raucous allegory for how the specter of death uncannily "haunts" the superhero genre. Denied, outmaneuvered, subjected to bad faith, it keeps appearing at the gate, waving its "key" of reality, in a repetition compulsion which the genre habitually exercises only to once again disavow. Let us recall Freud's definition of the Uncanny: "[It] is in reality nothing new or alien, but something which is familiar and old-established in the mind and which has become alienated from it only through the process of repression" (1919: 241). Like Edgar Allan Poe's revelers in "The Masque of the Red Death" (1842), who carouse all the more frenziedly to keep the knowledge of the plague out (in vain), the legionnaires in "The Ghost of Ferro Lad!" scramble to appease the apparition, even disbanding on its orders—anything to forestall (read: repress) the truth the Ghost symbolizes: real, irrefutable death, returned from banishment, come to claim its due.[40] Significantly, it points at Superboy, the progenitor of the genre (in a vigorous, youthful phase of his career), as the one most "guilty" for its exile.

On another level, of course, this scenario itself refutes the very reality the "Ghost" personifies: the idea of an afterlife (which a ghost represents) goes a long way toward defusing the fear of death as nihility ("at least it's not the end"), while the story, despite Brainiac-5's skeptical, "scientifically"-minded, thirtieth-century refusal to accept the supernatural, in the end is resolved through the *deus ex machina* of Ferro Lad's *actual ghost* helping the team to beat the Controller. Unseen, it activates a communicator ring on the paralyzed Superboy's finger, thereby summoning aid, and ultimately gives the supervillain a heart attack (Kawasaki 2009B: 161, 163).

In all these overdetermined ways, then, "The Ghost of Ferro Lad!" recapitulates the incommensurability between superheroes and death. The encounter here leads to a crisis that temporarily destroys the legion as an institution, only to, in the "end," reassure the reader once again that the hero still "lives on" as a spirit. The final panel even shows the translucent green figure of Ferro Lad, its back turned, stalking the corridors of the Controller's fortress. The accompanying caption amounts to another version of the well-worn, death-denying disclaimer: "Do you still doubt that ghosts *can* return from the dead? Then *who* turned the L on *Superboy's* ring?" (163, emphasis in original). To which we can answer, only half-facetiously: the invisible hand of the market.

It perhaps comes as no surprise that the death of Ferro Lad, the most infamous and far-reaching instance of "permanent" superhero mortality in the early Silver Age, took place 1,050 years in the future, in a series that had minimal overlap with the rest of the DC Earth-1 universe. In fact, we can take the *Legion of Superheroes'* thirtieth-century setting, despite the presence of the twentieth-century Superboy and Supergirl, as in essence another alternate-future "safe zone" for death, not unlike the X-Men's "Days of Future Past" setting, in which heroes can die (as long as they are lesser-known or variant versions of established heroes) without affecting core continuity. Furthermore, as explained to me by Paul Levitz, who would write the series after Shooter, the sheer number of Legionnaires made them in a sense more "expendable": "If you have a cast as large as the Legion of Superheroes, one of the advantages for a writer is you can show change. People can marry, people can unmarry, people can get wounded, people can die. . . . You can't do that nearly as easily in *Superman*" (2011).

Beyond that, even if a Legionnaire did die (always in exemplary heroic fashion), he would soon be resurrected, and failing this, he would come to haunt the series in all sorts of ingenious and baroque ways (including as a literal ghost), until, if all else failed, he could return in the multiverse-wide "reboot action" of a retcon. This turned out to be the case with Ferro Lad (re-christened Ferro), versions of which have proliferated since the 1970s.[41]

The "heroic death" model for superheroes has endured to the present. Notable Marvel examples from the Silver Age and later include that of Wonder Man (Simon Williams), who in "The Coming of the . . . Wonder Man!" (*Avengers*, vol. 1, #9, Oct. 1964, Lee/Heck) joins the Avengers so as to infiltrate them. Dying as a result of the process that granted him his superpowers, he initially cooperates with the villains Baron Zemo, the Executioner and the Enchantress, but in the end betrays them, gallantly saving the heroes at the cost of his own life. But the story only begins there: over the years, Wonder Man would have these thought patterns used as the basis for the Vision's; be quasi-resurrected thrice as a sort of super-zombie, including for a stint in the Legion of the Unliving; all before being fully resurrected (several times) as a being of "ionic energy."

Even the apotheosis of the "heroic death" model, the conclusion of the classic Phoenix saga in "The Fate of the Phoenix!" (*X-Men*, vol. 1, #137, Sept. 1980, Claremont/Byrne), does not significantly alter the pattern cemented by Lightning Lad. Faced with the return of the Phoenix force, whose uncontrollable destructive power had already led her to murder billions, Jean Grey chooses to sacrifice herself through suicide rather than risk killing again.[42] Another major death, of the antiheroine and Daredevil/Matt Murdock love interest Elektra, in "Last Hand" (*Daredevil*, vol. 1, #181, Apr. 1982, Miller), while not quite "heroic," does immediately follow upon a selfless act of mercy, when Elektra foregoes killing Murdoch's partner Foggy Nelson. Both Grey and Elektra were resurrected (more than once) within a few years.[43]

Well before then, by 1968, the convention had grown so familiar as to become the object of an outlandish, lacerating parody, "The Death of the Doom Patrol?" (*Doom Patrol*, vol. 1, #121, Sept. 1968, Drake/Premiani).[44] In this unprecedented ending to a (low-selling) series, the super-team of misfit "freaks" braves certain doom by explosion on a desert island so as to save "14 useless fishermen" from Codsville, Maine, whom they've never met (21). Introducing the issue with artist Bruno Premiani, editor Murray Boltinoff tells the reader in direct address: "Only you can save the *Doom Patrol* now—and *I kid you not!"* (1, emphasis in original). Despite its tongue-in-cheek mood, the story carries a dark undertone of creeping mortality, as the team is methodically driven out of their headquarters by the supervillains Madame Rouge and Captain Zahl (as well as by the city that now fears the destruction they attract), their superpowers nullified, their options and movement reduced to their last stand on the island's shore. In the aftermath, the world mourns the fallen warriors and celebrates their "lesson in courage"; Codsville is renamed Four Heroes, Maine in their honor (23).

Closing the tale (and the five-year-old series), the creative team[45] follows through on the convention, in their own version of the open-ended "death-denying" disclaimer. Breaking the "fourth wall," they proclaim:

> PREMIANI: Then it *is* true! They are dead! The *Doom Patrol* will never fight again!
> BOLTINOFF: It would take a miracle to change that ending, Bruno! A tougher job than even the DP ever faced!
> And only you out there—the reader—could do it! You always wanted to be a superhero, didn't you? Okay, *Charlie,* let's see you try!

A caption declares: "The end—or *is* it, *Charlie?*" (24, emphasis in original). The droll direct appeal (with its cutting reference to the Vietnam conflict) underscores the brutal commercial reality behind the series' demise: only readers—with their nickels and dimes—determine whether superheroes "live" or "die." The message was incorporated into the issue's cover by Joe Orlando. In an image framed by a thick black border (of the sort used in funeral announcements), the team members appear in a cemetery, hunched over their own gravestones. "Is this the beginning of the end of the Doom Patrol?" the cover asks. A single yellow and white beam pierces the black border, with the words *"you decide!"* (emphasis in original) bursting at its end.[46] The market had, of course, already decided by then: the Doom Patrol would remain "dead" well into the next decade, when the first of several revivals was launched.

The rise in depictions of superhero ultra-violence in the 1980s, particularly with the advent of more "mature" titles such as Marvel's *Epic Illustrated*, DC's Vertigo imprint, the direct market series *Omega Men* (1983), and the British series *Marvel Man/Miracle Man* (published in the US by Eclipse), only accelerated after the 1986 releases of the revisionist *Dark Knight Returns* and *Watchmen*. The upsurge affected the portrayal of heroic death, with the storyline "A Death in the Family" (*Batman*, vol. 1, #426–429, Dec. 1988–Jan. 1989, Starlin/Aparo) an odd case in point, due to the circumstances whereby DC killed off the second Robin, Jason Todd. Editor Denny O'Neil, in a notable publicity stunt, gave readers the opportunity to vote by phone on Todd's

7.5 The heroes' last stand in "The Death of the Doom Patrol?" (*Doom Patrol*, vol. 1, #121, Sept. 1968).

survival in an explosion engineered by the Joker. The final vote, held on September 16, 1988, was 5,271 for, 5,343 against survival (Starlin and Aparo).[47]

The episode holds considerable interest also for the extended—sadistic—manner in which the demise is represented: over several pages Robin is betrayed by his own estranged mother, then beaten to a grisly pulp by Joker and his thugs in Ethiopia, then left to die in a warehouse explosion. Batman, too late to save his partner, stumbles on Todd's mother in the rubble, mangled but still breathing. She tells Batman that her son threw himself in front of the blast in a bid to save her; she dies anyway. The Dark Knight then locates Todd's corpse, to the accompanying affectless captions: "One look tells the story. There's no need to check for a pulse. But I do anyway. Nothing. I've lost him. He's already getting cold to the touch. Gone" (*Batman*, #428: 9).[48] The

7.6 Batman discovers his partner's body in the "Death in the Family" storyline (*Batman*, vol. 1, #428, Dec. 1988).

7.7 The multiverse model allowed for the death of "alternate" characters, such as Earth-3's Ultraman (*Crisis on Infinite Earths*, vol. 1, #1, Apr. 1985).

art, however, carries more emotion: the scene's final splash page shows a devastated Batman, holding Robin's bloodied remains, in an image recalling the pietà cover to "Robin Dies at Dawn!" The scene appears nearly nihilistic; in his ineffectiveness at resisting the villain and saving his mother, Robin seems more victim than hero.

Another multi-issue storyline in the *Spider-Man* titles sought the opposite strategy: injecting as much "meaning" as possible into a death. In "Kraven's Last Hunt" (1987)[49] J. M. DeMatteis and Mike Zeck depict the last days of the Russian-born supervillain Kraven the Hunter (Sergei Kravinoff) and his twisted scheme to assume Spider-Man's identity. In an overwrought, near-Wagnerian tale suffused with death symbols, Kraven drugs the hero, buries him for two weeks, impersonates him, and eventually chooses to commit suicide by shotgun as a sign of his supreme will. Kraven's final act seems both illustration and parody of Becker's contention that it takes more than an ordinary being to unflinchingly stare down one's own death: "It takes men of granite . . . automatically powerful, 'secure in their drivenness,' we might say . . ." (58). Yet, for all its bathetic overreach and its painful puns on William Blake, "Kraven's Last Hunt" touches on the dark subconscious of the genre, how death structures it, so that the villain's forthright, extreme *causa-sui*[50] self-destruction comes to bear a tinge of nobility.

It bears repeating that, as sidekick and villain, Todd and Kraven were given more leeway in terms of their susceptibility to death than the "marquee" protagonists whose titles they inhabit. And both eventually returned from the dead to normal continuity, fulfilling the pattern shared with the "star" superheroes.

Despite considerable critical and fan obloquy, the heroic-downfall-and-resurrection model remained the standard treatment of death in mainstream superhero comics, even through such extraordinary continuity events as the wholesale slaughter (The Flash/Barry Allen, Supergirl, scores of non-Earth-1 figures) in DC's *Crisis on Infinite Earths* (1985–86) and "Death of Superman" storylines (1992–93), as well as in the Marvel examples cited. Creative attempts to introduce more naturalistic approaches to the theme (for superheroes) had to contend with the inexorable pushback of market economics, which demanded the eternal return of valuable commercial properties—no matter how "final" their demise seemed. In this respect, the genre stood like the defiant Doom Patrol on the beach, facing down the inevitable: not that they die, but that they come back.

"STICKY," "NORMAL" DEATH

All the same, capital D death, the kind one cannot come back from, did take place in the Silver Age, as, indeed, it had since the earliest superhero narratives. Death played a crucial role in the origin and founding motivations of many major characters. Such was the case when the ordinary mortal friends, relatives, and loved ones of the superhero perished: Uncle Ben Parker (Spider-Man), "Battling" Jack Murdock (Daredevil), the Castles (Punisher), Una (Captain Marvel), to say nothing of the Waynes (Batman), and in the 1938 urtext of the genre itself, Jor-El and Lara[51] (Superman).[52] This, paradoxically for such a death-denying practice, places mortality at the heart of the superhero project—the "launching point" of many characters' trajectories—a role similar to what it plays in other genres. As the Soviet formalist theorist Vladimir Propp noted, the "absentation" of the main figure's family members formed a key function of dramatis personae in myriad fairy tales, with "an intensified form of absentation" represented by the death of parents (26) at the start of such stories.[53]

What Quarter Bin calls "sticky death"—which, not unlike death in the "real world," lasts indefinitely, scars the surviving hero (often setting him on his mission) and resonates throughout his journey—lends dramatic weight to what otherwise seems to be a caricature of the facts of life:

> Death, used properly, can add importance to a story by showing that human failings can have real consequences. It can provide a springboard from which to launch a character driven by the death of loved ones to achieve as penance for some failing, as in the early design for Spider-Man. (Apr. 20, 2002)

Like the "meaningful" heroic death of superheroes already discussed, the sacrifice of the non-superpowered loved one often involved a selfless act to save others. The deed was rendered even more heroic, we might say, by the very fact that those who undertook it had no powers but only normal human courage—the sort accessible even to readers of the comics themselves. Earl Wells describes the reaction to the exemplary death scene of a "normal" person in the Marvel Silver Age:

> The sacrifice is usually acknowledged and validated by other characters, who declare it to be noble, heroic, and/or the act of a *man*. Often, the sacrificed character's last or dying words indicate acceptance of his fate; sometimes, the dying character feels he has redeemed himself for past sins or failings. (82, emphasis the author's)

Wells here is making specific reference to the demise of Franklin Storm, father of Johnny and Susan Storm of the Fantastic Four, which did much to cement the pattern in the early Silver Age. In "Death of a Hero" (*Fantastic Four*, vol. 1 #32, Nov. 1964, Lee/Kirby), Storm, a world-class surgeon (as well as inveterate gambler, convicted felon, and prison escapee) takes the full brunt of a Skrull explosive device to shield his family from the blast. Off-frame, in a drawn-out, moment-to-moment panel sequence, Storm tells Sue and Johnny as he expires: "Think kindly of me, my children . . . Always remember . . . I loved you . . . Never forget how proud you made me . . . With your honor . . . Your valor . . . Your selfless love . . ." (21, ellipses in original).

The "normal" heroic death (as distinguished from its superheroic counterpart), typically allowed for a leave-taking from the dying, as well as acceptance of the tragic turn of events (as noted by Wells). Such a depiction thus tended toward the more maudlin and sentimental. (Because they often died in more violent or explosive situations—or, more cynically, because they were expected to return before long—superheroes tended not to deliver a final statement when they "passed.") Finally, normal dead people tended to stay dead, lending a patina of credibility to stories filled with outlandish costumes and preposterous plots.

Notable examples of such normal "bystander" deaths include that of the DC heroine Black Canary's husband, the detective Larry Lance, who takes a fatal arrow to save his wife in "Where Death Fears to Tread!" (*Justice League of America*, vol. 1, #74, Sept. 1969, O'Neil/Dillin); Iris Allen, wife of the Flash/Barry Allen, in "The Last Dance!" (*Flash*, vol. 1, #275, Jul. 1979, Bates/Saviuk); and Marvel's "And Death Shall Come!" (*Amazing Spider-Man*, vol. 1, #90, Nov. 1970, Lee/Kane), in which another major supporting character, former police captain George Stacy (father of Peter Parker's girlfriend, Gwen)

7.8 Johnny and Sue Storm in "Death of a Hero" (*Fantastic Four*, vol. 1, #32, Nov. 1964).

dies heroically, saving the life of a child threatened by falling rubble. With his last breaths, Stacy reveals he knows Spider-Man's secret identity: "After I'm—gone—There'll be no one—to look *after* [Gwen]—No one, Peter—except *you!*" (Youngquist 2004B: 63, emphasis in original). In the context of Spider-Man's broader continuity, this landmark event enacts another example of Freud's "repetition compulsion": Stacy clearly represents a father figure who (like Uncle Ben) is killed (however indirectly) by Spider-Man's actions. This represents an excruciating "rebirth" for the character of Spider-Man /Parker; nothing will ever be the same again.

Stacy's death would further the pattern for many other supporting "normal" characters: they are usually killed in the line of duty, trying to help their superpowered friend, which accentuates the gap between the fantastical feats of the meta-humans and the very real consequences of their battles for ordinary people. By mid-decade this pattern had solidified, as seen in the death of the Hulk's paramour in "Do Not Forsake Me!" (*Incredible Hulk*, vol. 1, #205, Nov. 1976, Wein/Buscema). In the story, the Hulk's alter ego, Bruce Banner, and his love interest, the alien queen Jarella, are spending a relaxed afternoon shopping in Santa Fe, when they stumble upon the super-android Crypto-Man committing a robbery. In the ensuing battle, Jarella saves a child from a collapsing wall (in circumstances and blocking similar to those of the Captain Stacy episode), at the cost of her own life. Broken and bleeding in the Hulk's arms, she weakly intones her leave-taking: "Maybe it is . . . *better* this way, my love. I was not a . . . *part* of your world . . . I did not *belong* here . . . But you made my time here . . . a *happy* one . . . Please . . . be kind to yourself . . . my darling . . . until we meet *again* . . ." (27, ellipses and emphasis in original). It

7.9 The Hulk's paramour Jarella succumbs to death in "Do Not Forsake Me!" (*Incredible Hulk*, vol. 1, #205, Nov. 1976).

is a scene that would not seem out of place in many a sentimental Victorian novel.[54]

But the Hulk, in a nod towards the sort of real-world denial that often flares in such cases, refuses to accept the death, even after the physicians at Gamma Base say they can do nothing more for the deceased Jarella. Over the next two issues, he seeks out and finds his friends, the super-team The Defenders (albeit by cutting a swathe of destruction from New Mexico to New York), in hopes that their leader Dr. Strange can revive Jarella with his magic. But by the conclusion of "Alone Against the Defenders" (*Incredible Hulk*, vol. 1, #207, Jan. 1977, Wein/Buscema), Strange must regretfully explain to his jade teammate the unavoidable reality:

STRANGE: Try to *understand*, Hulk—there are things in this life beyond the *ken* of even the *wisest* men. Why those we love are *taken* from us in fury

is perhaps the *darkest* question of all. Jarella is *gone,* my friend, and there
is no way to summon her *back.* You must try to go on *without* her—as
she would *want* you to.

HULK: Jarella is . . . dead? (27, ellipses and emphasis in original)

In response to this unusually blunt exposition of the facts, the Hulk's usual
childlike demeanor serves as a marker for the overwhelming power of grief in
death's wake, of the numb helplessness experienced by those it touches. And
yet, after another uncontrolled rage, and breaking down in tears, the Hulk
does, in the end, with a stone-faced look, accept his love's passing—and apolo-
gizes for the damage he has caused (29). On the other side of grief, the story
concludes, lies the reverse of its infantilizing force: a somber maturity.[55]

Despite such pathos, the heroic death of normal loved ones at least held
meaning; something was still accomplished, usually somebody was saved
through the loved one's sacrifice. Meaningless death, however, would pose an
additional burden on the psyche of survivors, who as mourners are always
engaged in (to return to Clive Seale's description) "an attempt to construct a
refuge of meaning and purpose." The genre only reluctantly and belatedly arrived at such depictions in 1973.

EXISTENTIAL DEATH

Tragedy struck again for Spider-Man in the most notorious and reverberant
killing of a "normal" loved one, the milestone story "The Night Gwen Stacy
Died" (*Amazing Spider-Man,* vol. 1, #121, Jun. 1973, Conway/Kane), in which
Parker's girlfriend Gwen follows her father in death, at the hands of the insane Green Goblin (Norman Osborn). Gwen's death is radical in several ways:
without warning[56] it brings to a violent end the main character's long-standing
love interest; it serves to fulfill the vengeful motives of a villain who (rarely
for the genre) knows the secret identity of his arch-rival; it violates the "heroic
(normal) death" model, in that Gwen is simply murdered (off-panel) with no
chance at redemption or speechifying; and it implicates Spider-Man himself
in her killing.[57] While later in the storyline an enraged Spider-Man stops short
of killing the Goblin with his bare hands, the supervillain perishes anyway in
graphic fashion: impaled by his own glider in a failed attempt to defeat his foe
(as discussed in the present study's conclusion).

Here, death took on an existential quality—the beloved, innocent but weak
Gwen is merely a victim, the casualty of a war between superpowered rivals—
and as such the episode proved a turning point in the genre's depiction of
mortality (which conferred on the tale a "classic" status). For some critics, it

7.10 Spider-Man/Parker's pivotal moment in "The Night Gwen Stacy Died" (*Amazing Spider-Man*, vol. 1, #121, Jun. 1973).

single-handedly launched the darker "Bronze Age."[58] As described by Brett M. Rogers:

> In death, the Goblin becomes both a symbol (along with Gwen Stacy) of the lost innocence of Silver Age comics readers and a martyr ushering in a new age of comic narrative in which no character is safe. Spider-Man the hero leaves the scene of the battle and returns home with no boon or elixir to bestow—just suffering and death. (85)[59]

The existential "meaningless" death model for "normals" would manifest in later Marvel events, such as the "Death of Jean Dewolff" storyline, in which a police detective ally of Spider-Man is brutally dispatched in bed by shotgun blast, in "Original Sin" (*Peter Parker, The Spectacular Spider-Man*, vol. 1, #107, Oct. 1985, David/Buckler); in the person of Tom Thumb, who succumbs to cancer in the *Squadron Supreme* miniseries (1985–86, Gruenwald/Hall), set on a counter-Earth; and the miscarriage of Susan Storm's second child due to radiation poisoning in "A Small Loss" (*Fantastic Four*, vol. 1, #267, Jun. 1984, Byrne).[60] Occasionally, the passing took on a more overtly political tone, as in the death of the Hulk's former sidekick, Jim Wilson, in "Let Darkness Come" (*Incredible Hulk*, vol. 1, #420, Aug. 1994, David/Frank). Wilson, a 1970s working-class African-American replacement[61] for the Hulk's first sidekick, Rick Jones, reappears after a number of years, only to shortly die of complications due to AIDS (he had revealed his HIV-positive status some thirty issues earlier). Despite Wilson's pleadings, Banner/Hulk refuses to compromise his medical ethics by providing an experimental treatment for the disease or conducting a transfusion of his Gamma-irradiated blood (14).

Along with its subject matter, this issue of the *Incredible Hulk* contains some very unusual design elements in keeping with its theme. The cover depicts Hulk/Banner standing over Wilson's hospital bed (IV, monitors), holding his friend's hand, both illuminated by the cone of an overhead light that cuts through the deepest darkness, which takes up fully 60 percent of the illustration. Just visible below the cover title, printed in an off-black gray against the murk, is the phrase "In the Shadow of AIDS." A red AIDS ribbon illustration lies to the side. Finally, for this issue the letter's page, Green Mail, was replaced by several short testimonials from industry professionals who had lost loved ones to the disease. All of this denotes, once more, a move away from the "heroic death" model, so as to more directly reflect the real-life epidemic of AIDS (though unlike the Gwen Stacy case, the impact of Wilson's demise is somewhat diffused by unfolding episodically alongside other major and minor storylines).[62]

As is made clear by the stories of Larry Lance, Franklin Storm, Captain Stacy, Gwen Stacy, Jarella, and Jim Wilson, the death of a "normal" loved one since the Silver Age proved an emotionally powerful and authentic means to relate the high-risk stakes of superhero experience in a more realistic fashion, without bringing harm to the superhero franchise itself. Readers could more easily relate to their heroes, not because they could die, but because, like the rest of us, they could experience a tragic loss. Whether "heroic" or "existential," then, what we might call "superhero mortality by proxy" (a compromise of sorts between the genre and lived reality) came to represent the most consistently conscientious means of depicting death in mainstream superhero comics.[63]

Much less consistent—in fact, positively rare in this era—is what I have been calling existential death (death which *means* nothing and *accomplishes* nothing) applied to superheroes themselves in a continuity-driven context. This, in many ways, represented the final taboo for the genre, an utter abnegation of Becker's "transference heroics"; what good are superheroes if they can die as randomly and senselessly as any one of us?

It happened—as far as market-based serial fiction would allow it to happen—in a storyline featuring the Canadian team Alpha Flight, in which team leader Guardian (James Hudson), after beating the villain, succumbs to a fatal momentary distraction as his malfunctioning cybernetic suit is about to explode. The conclusion to ". . . And One Shall Surely Die!" (*Alpha Flight*, vol. 1, #12, Jul. 1984, Byrne) shows Heather Hudson (the hero's wife and inadvertent cause of the distraction) bearing shocked witness to her spouse's graphic self-immolation to ashes.

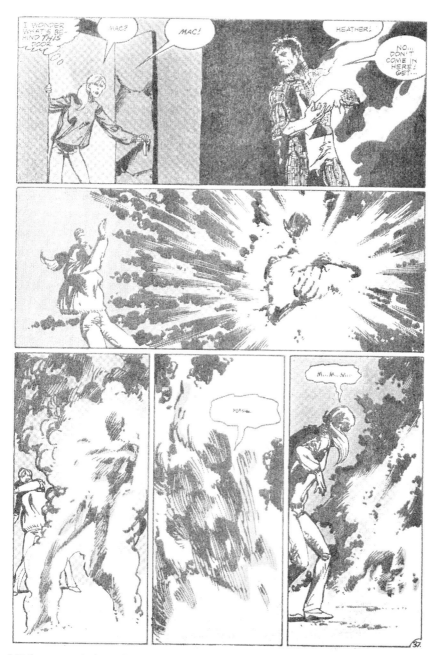

7.11 The rare example of a superhero's existential death: Guardian/James Hudson in ". . . And One Shall Surely Die!" (*Alpha Flight*, vol. 1, #12, Jul. 1984).

In some respects, this was hardly unexpected; the death had been "pre-sold" in an advertisement published throughout Marvel's titles. It depicted a lineup of the team in a spotlight, with the headline: "Soon, these heroes will face their greatest challenge . . . One of them won't survive it" (ellipses in original). Moreover, in a by now familiar tactic, the death was used as a selling point on the cover, which shows the various members of Alpha Flight in target sights with the heading: "And One Shall Surely Die!" Then, of course, there is the issue's title. The only suspense, then, lay in discovering precisely *who* would "surely die,"[64] and the writer/artist Byrne keeps up the guessing game until the surprise ending.

He also teases the reader, lulling him/her into a sense of "business as usual" as a battered Hudson muses over his victory in discourse familiar from countless past superhero battles: "It . . . worked. It was a heckuva risk. I might have been *killed* by the blast. But then, I was *certain* to be killed otherwise" (35, emphasis and ellipses in original). Byrne then heightens the tension by depicting time as a countdown: in panels shaped like the numbers nine to one in descending order, Hudson works quickly to defuse his suit's power pack before it blows. Unfortunately, Heather intrudes at the last critical second, lending the event a tragicomic, horrific tone—none of those past battles ended anything like this. (In subsequent issues, the widow is consumed with guilt for her unwitting role in the accident, repeatedly experiencing a gruesome nightmare in which Hudson's burning form accosts her.) The Guardian episode thus represents a stunningly bold depiction of superhero death not as heroic or self-sacrificial, but as mere bad luck.[65]

It seemed all the more remarkable for taking place in a regular series (albeit a relatively new one with less-established heroes, and set in Canada), in the ordinary "floppy" format (in an era when trade paperback collections of story arcs were not yet the norm).[66] ". . . And One Shall Surely Die!'s" obvious precedent in depicting the existential death of a superhero, however, had come two years before, and made for such a momentous publishing event that it even—fortuitously—launched a new format: the Marvel graphic novel.

THE DEATH OF CAPTAIN MARVEL

For all its notable milestones, the foregoing survey of death representation in superhero comics since the dawn of the Silver Age in some sense only serves as prologue, casting into sharp relief Jim Starlin's innovations in the remarkable *Death of Captain Marvel*, released as noted in Marvel Comics' first graphic novel format to widespread critical and fan acclaim in 1982. To the present it remains the most radical representation of superhero death in a mainstream, continuity-driven series, in large part because Starlin chose to have the long-standing hero die not in battle but by a most common wasting disease which had taken the author's own father: cancer.[67]

In this excursus I want to examine various key aspects of the work: its unusual genesis and format; its creator's peculiar reputation as "undertaker" to the genre;[68] its radical rewriting of the superhero plot through the conventions of death literature and thanatography, reflecting death and dying discourses of the 1970s; its depiction of the cancer patient's body as abject, as well as of a subtly antagonistic patient/doctor relationship; and its use of religious imagery to figure the superhero as modern messiah, all of which played a hand in attaining its renown as the "death degree zero" point for the genre in its mainstream incarnation.

Starlin (b. 1950) began his professional career in 1972, working at Marvel in a style derivative of Gil Kane, Steve Ditko, Barry Windsor-Smith, and, to some extent, underground comix. In the mid-1970s he took over writing and art chores on second-tier Marvel titles *Captain Marvel* and *Strange Tales* (featuring Warlock), whose unconventional layouts, mannerist visuals and strikingly philosophical "space-opera" plots established his reputation as the rare auteur working in the mainstream comics industry.[69] In both series, mortality would come to take on an outsize meaning, either in the form of the supervillain Thanos (whose name recalls Thanatos, the personification of death in Greek mythology, and whose motivations involve an obsessive desire to please his "lover," death figured as an unspeaking woman in a cowl) or the (anti-)hero Warlock, who commits "cosmic suicide" to save the universe from his own future evil self.

With the *Death of Captain Marvel* graphic novel and the later "Death in the Family" storyline, which as noted violently dispatched Batman's second Robin, Jason Todd, Starlin secured the title of "official slayer of superheroes" (Quarter Bin 1999) for many in the fan community. In 2002 the curmudgeonly Quarter Bin, who as we've seen tends to look on death in superhero comics with a jaundiced eye, praised him thus:

> To readers of my generation, folks who began to gain an appreciation of the possibilities of the medium in the mid-1970s, Jim Starlin stands out in the specialized field of writers handling death in comics. In more than one decade, more than one company, more than one franchise, and more than one storytelling level, he played the role of pioneer in taking the subject of death and improving its treatment in comics, making it meaningful, ethically significant, and, for a limited time, *binding* ... A view of selected pieces shows a body of work permeated with death and its themes—not the shallow slaughter of men typical of some gore-infested throwaway rag where

writers fail to make distinctions between heroes and mass murderers, but deaths of significant players in the stories where they occur. (emphasis in original)

Such declamations, hailing Starlin's status as the one writer/artist to depict superhero death with "integrity," rest most especially on his work in *The Death of Captain Marvel*, featuring a minor hero with less than stellar sales since Starlin had left its title, and whose circumstances of creation involved a legal imbroglio between Marvel and its chief competitor DC.[70] As it happened, the decision to kill the hero also had much to do with commerce and intellectual property rights; in brief, Marvel by the late 1970s had decided to eliminate the character so as to create a new one with the same name that would retain Marvel's trademark and attract more readers.[71] (The foregoing goes a long way towards explaining why the first Marvel graphic novel was not called, say, *The Death of Captain America*; like Ferro Lad and the Doom Patrol before him, Captain Marvel was deemed second-class and therefore "expendable.")

The hero first appeared in "The Coming of Captain Marvel!" (*Marvel Superheroes*, vol. 1, #12, Dec. 1967, Lee/Colan): Mar-Vell, a warrior of the alien Kree, betrays his imperialist masters to fight for his adopted home, Earth. Later, he assumes an alter-ego partnership with the human Rick Jones, whereby—through the action of Kree "nega-band" bracelets—the two exchange places: one remains on Earth, the other is vanquished to the Negative Zone. When Starlin fully controlled the title (starting with *Captain Marvel*, vol. 1, #25, Mar. 1972),[72] a mysterious entity named Eon endowed Marvel with "Cosmic Awareness" (vol. 1, #29, Nov. 1973), after which he became, in the words of Jon Morris, "Marvel's first spandex-suited saint" (2007): a warrior who tried to renounce violence. As Starlin put it, "I wanted him to go through a metamorphosis, becoming a sort of peaceful figure, a kind of Shaolin monk, if you will" (2011). Though it sometimes puts his life in jeopardy, Mar-Vell's new star-spanning insight makes him a better person, a sort of über-hippy: "He's beaten *vanity* and *pride* by seeing the *universe* as it is! He *knows* what must be *done* and *does it*, but does it with a *great sorrow!* For this man knows *truth* and *peace!*" (vol. 1, #30, Jan. 1974: n.p., emphasis in original).

To some extent a reflection of 1960s–70s "flower power," the warrior became a "protector," at times going to absurd (and genre-defying) lengths to avoid a fight. In "The Beginning of the End!" (*Captain Marvel*, vol. 1, #31, Mar. 1974), rather than leap into a battle between the Drax Destroyer and the Avengers, he decides to *shout* them into submission, using "sudden *shock* and strong *vocal cords!*" (n.p., emphasis in original) to jolt them to their senses. In "To Be Free From Control!" (*Captain Marvel*, vol. 1, #30, Jan. 1974), he first

7.12 Mar-Vell accepts his fate in *The Death of Captain Marvel* (1982).

tries talking reason to the supervillain, in a farcical exchange taking up a page: "You squander your *entire energies* upon fleeting dreams of *grandeur* and let the *priceless treasures* of inner *peace* and *truth* elude you!" (n.p., emphasis in original). It doesn't work.

In "Blown Away" (*Captain Marvel*, vol. 1, #34, Sept. 1974), an otherwise unremarkable story featuring the exploding hunchbacked supervillain Nitro, a battle exposes Mar-Vell to a deadly gas which slowly begins to overwhelm the power of his mystic nega-band bracelets. (Starlin would later cite this as the carcinogenic which eventually dooms his hero.)[73]

The *Death of Captain Marvel* graphic novel picks up the story several years later, when Mar-Vell comes to realize his terminal diagnosis, and gradually succumbs to illness, his body visibly wasting away until he is confined to bed, a breathing tube in his nostril. Various scenes recount his friends' and loved ones' disbelief and sense of powerlessness before the disease, which cannot be fought off with fists, laser blasts, or scientific genius. As he tells his stunned former partner Jones:

> I'm afraid all my powers are *useless* in this situation, Rick. I can't punch, kick or fly away to escape this cancer. It just doesn't work that way. It's my *body* that's betrayed me. It's my *own biology* that's killing me. There's *nothing* my powers can do to save me. All they can do is help me to *accept* my fate. (emphasis in original)[74]

Mar-Vell himself experiences all the frustration, depression and settling of accounts which many patients in his situation go through, before accepting his fate and taking leave of his companions (including most heroes of the Marvel Universe). He descends into a coma. After a hallucinatory "final battle" with his arch-enemy Thanos (the genre's pound of flesh), Mar-Vell comes face to face with the age-old figure of death as a woman, and here *The Death of Captain Marvel* arrives at a rare transcendent moment for superheroes: he waves his hand before the woman, saying, "It's not that I fear her. It's just that . . . I no longer need . . . *the illusion*" (ellipses in original, my emphasis). As his hand moves away, the woman's face is revealed as a skull. Mar-Vell walks off, hand in hand with Thanos and the woman, into a bright light, as his former nemesis tells him this is "only the *beginning!*" (emphasis in original). Back in "reality," Mar-Vell has died; his physician Mentor drapes a sheet over the corpse, intoning, "He's gone."

In forty-four years of mainstream superhero stories, none had unfolded anything like this. Yet *The Death of Captain Marvel* does bear much in common with other discursive practices which had attained considerable prominence by 1982: thanatographies, autothanatographies, pathographies, and related "death literature," among them A. Alvarez's *The Savage God* (1971, on suicide); the surgeon Richard Selzer's *Mortal Lessons: Notes on the Art of Surgery* (1976/96); Raymond A. Moody's *Life After Life* (1975), on near-death "visions"; and Victor and Rosemary Zorza's *A Way to Die* (1980), on their deceased daughter's journey through hospice.[75] The graphic novel, in fact, functions as an idiosyncratic hybrid of superheroics with death discourses of the post-Kübler-Ross/Becker age, which saw their popularity peak just as Starlin was producing his landmark work.[76] The result is a profound radicalization of the super-body, the tropes of superhero "death," ultimately of the superhero itself—in ways so corrosive to the genre's commercial viability as to necessitate a unique, unrepeatable, "one-shot" treatment. (Like a cancer, the fatal tissue had to be isolated from the rest of the corpus to maintain the latter's health.)

Let us begin with the title: *The Death of Captain Marvel*. From the outset, Starlin leaves no doubt as to the proceedings, indeed, purpose of the book; there is no mystery or ambiguity as in the headings "The Doomed Legionnaire!" or even "The Night Gwen Stacy Died!" (which was not used until the end of that story, the better to shock the reader). This "seriousness" of intent is mirrored in the production values: a sixty-four-page oversized format soft-cover book with superior glossy paper akin to a European graphic album,[77] labeled "Marvel Graphic Novel" with the title and author's name on the cover, for the unheard-of price of $5.95. The regular, disposable thirty-two-page(with ads), cheap newsprint "floppies" in which Mar-Vell had previously appeared were then selling for 60 cents.[78]

Moreover, the cover bears no "Imaginary Story" or "Elseworlds"-type disclaimer, but rather an image of the hero sprawled in the arms of a skeletal death-figure in a parody of Michelangelo's *Pietà* (1499), against a backdrop of Marvel characters springing into action, themselves against a blank white background. We will return to that image later, but for now I want to emphasize the book's weighty literary presentation; aesthetically, commercially, materially, and ontologically, this publication strained against the definition of a superhero comic book as understood in 1982 America[79]—and, as a reader would discover upon cracking open its pages, so did its contents.

The first thing she would see is not "comics" at all, but a title page similar to that of a text novel: author, production credits and indicia; in type (not comic-book lettering) on a white page. Turning the leaf, she would read a brief preface by editor Al Milgrom, in white letters against a stark black background, thanking Starlin "for his extraordinary portrayal of Mar-Vell's adventures, including this, his last."[80] Facing opposite, the story proper begins: the costumed hero appears beneath the title—but not in an action pose. He is sitting at a console on a Titanian ship, *dictating his memoirs.*

In *Constructing Death* (1998), the sociologist Clive Seale accentuates the role played by narrative in helping the ill and dying cope with their condition and adapt to new corporeal realities. What Seale calls cultural scripts (official discourses about what death signifies in a given socius) "provid[e] people with rhetorical resources for explaining and justifying their actions" (1998: 21), in other words, for how to "be" a dying person. Drawing on the work of Pierre Bourdieu (particularly his concept of hexis, the bodily enactment of cultural scripts) and Anthony Giddens, Seale draws a distinction between "practical consciousness" (tacit, unexamined mental modes of being) and "discursive consciousness" or the "capacity to comment upon, justify and explain activities, including the shaping of self-identity" (ibid.: 23), in other words a self-awareness and stocktaking of one's own life often set off by health

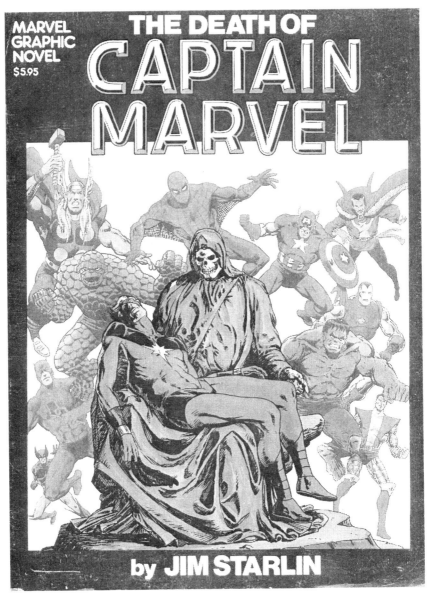

7.13 Starlin's cover marries "high" and "low" in *The Death of Captain Marvel* (1982).

crises. "Occasioned by the 'fateful moment' of illness," Seale writes, "in which the body acts as a reminder of human finitude, [the dying] demonstrate a switch from practical to discursive consciousness, in order to repair disrupted routines, and to construct new ones" (ibid.: 24). He calls this process "narrative reconstruction."

Mar-Vell's "recap" of his origin, adventures and life journey through his dictated memoirs acts as just such a reconstruction; it brings a self-conscious meaning, order, and narrative arc to random events. More than that, coming at the very opening of the novel and unfolding over several pages, the "recap" serves a familiar generic purpose: to inform the reader of things he/she may have missed. Mar-Vell's narrative reconstruction here, at the beginning of the end, goes hand-in-hand with the strategies of superhero comics, with their complicated, years-long continuity paths, to keep fans "in the loop."[81]

Furthermore, throughout the novel Mar-Vell explains his new condition to both himself and others, seeking to come to terms with his own imminent demise through a "discursive consciousness" mode. Some of these explanations come across as pedestrian and straightforward, even blunt: "I've got *cancer*, Rick, and it's *inoperable*. I've less than four months to live" (emphasis in original). Others utilize comics' textual/visual techniques in more complex ways.

At one point, Mar-Vell reminisces on meeting his lover Elysius, and sorrowfully laments the life together they will never have. His reverie is violently interrupted by an onslaught of bodily pain. Over four panels along the bottom of the page, showing Mar-Vell clasping his torso and head in agony (the background color shifts from red to yellow), captions declare: "Pain . . . Overwhelming pain . . . It burns . . . It tears . . . It twists and bends . . . It kills. It kills slowly . . . A little piece at a time . . . and then it fades. Yes, the pain comes and it goes . . ." (ellipses in original). Turning the page, a caption concludes, ". . . But the anger always remains" (ellipsis in original), as Mar-Vell angrily demolishes a control panel, screaming, "*Damn!*" (emphasis in original).

Over seven thin, vertical panels on this same page, the hero rants a soliloquy, stalking the hallways of Mentor's compound. He enters progressively darker chambers until he appears in utter gloom, lit up only by a spotlight, his face in shadow:

Alien invaders, super-villains, monsters, mutants, they *all* tried, but *none* of them could kill me. I fought them all and I won! *I survived!* Who would have thought that, in the end . . . it'd be my *own body* that would turn on me and do me in.

But what are you carrying on so about, Mar-Vell? It's not as if you've been *singled out* for this. *Everyone* has to die someday. Or did you think you were *unique?* Yes, I guess that's what it's all about. I just never figured it would happen to *me*. Deep down inside me I felt that those *special things* that make me who I am would just live *forever*. It's hard to *accept* that the world is going to go on *without* me. Damn. (emphasis and ellipsis in original)

The Death of Captain Marvel, more than any other work examined in this chapter, operates on an archetypal, mythological level; the mythology it interrogates—and brutally deconstructs—is that of the American superhero. In this scene, pain assaults Mar-Vell, with an invisible power he can neither resist nor escape, leaving only the option to lash out blindly at some futuristic scenery. Like the unseen, unrepresentable (but felt!) pain, the captions pronounce their decree with all their unquestioned authority: "Pain . . . overwhelming pain . . . it kills slowly . . ." The same textual device whose convention once declared, "With great power comes great responsibility" (*Amazing Fantasy*, #15, 1963)[82] and "Well, let's not feel *too* badly! After all, this was only an *imaginary story* . . . and the chances are a *million to one* it will *never* happen!" (Gold/Greenberger: 206, emphasis and ellipsis in original) now renders a very different, non-negotiable verdict.

That classic superhero pose (Mar-Vell demolishing the equipment) which opens the second page of the sequence, the widest and brightest panel, is ultimately deflated by the seven narrower ones which follow, plunging the hero progressively into darkness. The second panel depicts an enraged Mar-Vell in close-up, brandishing his fist directly at the reader, as if in appeal: "*All* tried, but *none* could kill me." The fifth shows him, back to the reader, entering a rectangular black doorway; the image suggests he is being swallowed up by a coffin. His figure gradually diminishes, until reduced in the final panel to a distant, downcast body in gloom. The sequence functions as the polar opposite of the Mole Man origin page from *Fantastic Four* #1 examined in chapter 2: if in that example the villain has constituted his identity by the last panel (signified by a close-up portrait) out of several smaller panels/views, in this case the hero finds himself steadily eclipsed, decomposing, shrunk, helpless. The first panel's excoriating *"Damn!"* hurled at the ether finds its counterpart in Mar-Vell's soliloquy-closing "damn," calmly uttered in the murk; the page visually evokes an inner journey from (futile) superheroic bombast, the urge to "Rage, rage against the dying of the light,"[83] to submission, resignation, acceptance. The superhero's courage, redefined, lies not in violence but stoic forbearance in the face of the inevitable.

Furthermore, Mar-Vell's ruminative soliloquy partakes of a long Western tradition of death contemplation, known as the *timor mortis-memento mori* (fear of death—remember you will die) lyric, initiated by the Latin poetry of St. Bernard of Clairvaux (1090-1153). Its components included the strong

7.14 Mar-Vell's soliloquy on death in *The Death of Captain Marvel* (1982).

implication or declaration of a fear of death, imagery of death (skulls, dark chambers), a catalog of the famous dead (e.g., Absalom, Caesar, Cicero, Aristotle, Alexander), and the *ubi sunt* (where are they?) motif (Harry Morris: 1035). Perhaps the most well-known example of the *timor mortis-memento mori* lyric appears in Hamlet's graveyard speech (Act V, Scene 1), in which he tells his best friend, "To what base uses we may return, Horatio! Why, may not imagination trace the noble dust of Alexander till a find it stopping a bung-hole?[84] . . . Imperious Caesar, dead and turn'd to clay, / Might stop a hole to keep the wind away" (387).[85] As evident here, by the time William Shakespeare wrote and performed *Hamlet* in the early seventeeth century, the tradition was so well known that he could easily mock it, by humorously demonstrating how Alexander the Great and Julius Caesar could decompose and be refashioned into crude insulation and beer-barrel stoppers.

In his realization that "*Everyone* has to die someday," Mar-Vell is tapping into a centuries-old rhetorical convention, "cataloguing" those who have fallen before him, asking where they have gone, and bemoaning his own fate—while trying to accept its finality ("Damn."). *The Death of Captain Marvel*, a modern, secular *memento-mori* work, does not admonish the reader to repent of his sins to gain everlasting life as did its Christian predecessor, but as Mar-Vell concludes in his soliloquy, it does appeal for a stoic acceptance of death as *natural*. In this way it participates in an age-old dialogue in the West on the mysteries of mortality. Just as Thanos entreats after the climactic "final battle," when he introduces Mar-Vell to Death, "*She* is the bridge to *eternity*. *Her* caress is *peace*. Do not fear *her* for she is merely that which awaits us all" (emphasis in original), so does Michel de Montaigne, in his essay "To Philosophize Is to Learn to Die" (1580) declare,

> It is uncertain where death awaits us; let us await it everywhere. Premeditation of death is premeditation of freedom. He who has learned how to die has unlearned how to be a slave. Knowing how to die frees us from all subjection and constraint. (18)

Of course, we often find such acceptance hard won; parting with life, to say nothing of devotion to an afterlife, often seem objectionable or irrational in a post-religious modernity with its variegated materialist pleasures and individualism. Hence, Mar-Vell's bewildered, "I just never figured it would happen to *me*." Leo Tolstoy's *The Death of Ivan Ilyich* (1886), the first modern literary depiction of death and dying,[86] anticipates such protests. Its eponymous hero, an unthinking Everyman with a terminal illness, discovers the depths of his denial:

The syllogism he had learnt from Kiesewetter's Logic—"Caius is a man, men are mortal, therefore Caius is mortal"—had always seemed to him correct as applied to Caius, but by no means to himself. That man Caius represented man in the abstract, and so the reasoning was perfectly sound; but he was not Caius, not an abstract man; he had always been a creature quite, quite distinct from others. (93)

Ivan Ilyich frantically asserts,

If I were destined to die like Caius, I would have known it; an inner voice would have told me. But I was never aware of any such thing; and I and all my friends—we knew our situation was quite different from Caius's. Yet now look what's happened! It can't be. It just can't be, and yet it is. How is it possible? How is one to understand it? (94)

These are utterances on death from a post-Enlightenment, materialist worldview much closer to our own. Indeed, they are a short step from Sigmund Freud's psychoanalytic writings of a generation later, on the unconscious' inability to accept the concept of mortality: "It is indeed impossible to imagine our own death; and whenever we attempt to do so we are in fact still present as spectators" (1915A: 289). Mar-Vell's frustration, his struggle to understand his own looming quietus, touches upon a very modern version of death fear, itself rooted in centuries of philosophic scrutiny.

The twist lies in the soliloquy's next passage: "Deep down inside me I felt that those *special things* that make me who I am would just live *forever.*" While this could apply to any contemporary death-denying reader's personal attributes (don't we all feel "special"? therefore "safe" from the Reaper?), in the present context the *"special things"* Mar-Vell refers to can mean only one thing: superpowers. The thoughtless presumption he would "just live *forever*" resonates with us all, but here it first and foremost pertains to his having a super-body, a chief attribute of which is its invulnerability and immortality; recall Scott Bukatman's description of Superman as someone with a "body that retains no marks, on which history cannot be inscribed" (2003: 197). *"Special things"* that make you *"just live forever"* amounts to a concise summary of the qualities possessed by superheroes since their inception, certainly since the dawn of the Silver Age—and now, for the first time, they are failing. *The Death of Captain Marvel* therefore functions as an allegory for a genre painfully "growing up": compelled to abjure the "super-," it desperately strives to retain the "-hero." Mar-Vell's grudging resignation at the end of this page is its answer; the superman made human at last.

With the foregoing in mind, let us requote and recapitulate Mar-Vell's soliloquy, annotating as we go:

Alien invaders, super-villains, monsters, mutants [sci-fi, superhero conventions], they *all* tried, but *none* of them could kill me [generic masculinist bombast]. I fought them all and I won! *I survived!*[87] [presumption of invulnerability, immortality]. Who would have thought that, in the end . . . it'd be my *own body* that would turn on me and do me in [death/nature as irresistible force]. But what are you carrying on so about, Mar-Vell? It's not as if you've been *singled out* for this. *Everyone* has to die someday *[timur mortis-memento mori*, with catalogue of previous fallen, *ubi sunt* motif]. Or did you think you were *unique?* Yes, I guess that's what it's all about. I just never figured it would happen to *me* ["Caius is mortal" . . . psyche's inability to accept its own demise]. Deep down inside me I felt that those *special things* [superpowers] that make me who I am [superhero] would just live *forever* [genre, market presumption of immortality]. It's hard to *accept* that the world is going to go on *without* me [difficulty of jettisoning the "super-"]. Damn [grudging acceptance].

Mar-Vell's words constitute a "narrative reconstruction" patchwork comprising not only his own journey but over a thousand years of Western thought on death, filtered through the genre conventions of the very twentieth-century superhero. In this sequence, Starlin has erected a verbal/visual monument to its decline, fall, and transcendence. Crucially, it is Mar-Vell the man in his "unheroic" life-support tunic (not Captain Marvel the mask) who sings its swan song.

Difficult as our hero finds coming to terms with his own passing, it triggers nothing short of existential shockwaves that reverberate throughout his community of friends, enemies, the Marvel universe itself. His ex-partner/alter ego Jones (as pointed out by Elysius, an orphan), explodes at Mar-Vell, whom he perceives as "giving up" the fight against his disease: "You're *part* of my *life!* I'm not going to quietly sit by and *watch* you *die!*" (emphasis in original). (They later reconcile in a maudlin, tear-filled deathbed scene, though not before the hotheaded Jones excoriates the Avengers for not properly focusing their energies on cancer research.)[88]

Another episode at Mar-Vell's sickbed further illustrates the profound helplessness and inadequacy of the superhero before a threat he can neither see nor repel through violence, as well as the role played by continuity in "deepening" the novel's dramatic impact. Spider-Man, one of the attendants at the deathwatch, finds himself caught off guard when Ben Grimm, trying to lighten the mood, says of Mar-Vell: "I tell you, Elysius, this is one *tough cookie*

you got. Ain't that right, Spidey?" (emphasis in original). In two narrow vertical panels with a blank white background, an uneasy Spider-Man mutters, "I
...I mean...Sure...Please...Excuse me..." (ellipses in original), then walks
off in embarrassment. Out in the corridor, Spidey tells his fellows: "This just
can't be happening. Captain Marvel is one of us. A full-blown, card carrying
superhero. We die from *bullets* and *bombs*...not from something like *cancer*.
It just can't be" (emphasis and ellipses in original).

The brief speech expresses the genre's own befuddlement before the unprecedented banality of "real" death. But what will not escape a reader familiar
with Spider-Man's history is how the character's own death-scarred past—the
violent killings of Ben Parker, Cpt. Stacy, Gwen Stacy, and so on—informs
his misgivings and inability to cope. His mask and inarticulacy hide Peter
Parker's true emotions, but a Marvel reader's "continuity literacy" fills in the
emotional blanks. (His character history—World War II veteran, tough guy—
also explains the older Grimm's greater comfort level with death.)

Both Jones and Spider-Man exhibit Becker's "transference heroics," their
blithe reliance on a "higher power" as a psychological bulwark against the cer-
tainty of their own deaths, but also against full responsibility for their lives
(what he calls the "*causa-sui* project"). As Becker describes it in one of several
such passages in *The Denial of Death*:

> The comfort, the trust, the relief in one's chest and shoulders, the lightness
> in one's heart, the sense of being sustained by something larger, less fallible
> ...To melt oneself trustingly into the father, or the father-substitute, or even
> the Great Father in the Sky, is to abandon the *causa-sui* project, the attempt
> to be the father of oneself. (1973: 116)

Commercial imperative aside, the mainstream genre routinely disavows
death precisely for this reason: to allow for the very possibility dismantles
its ableist, immortalist foundations, exposes its feet of clay; the conventional
wisdom that superhero comics serve as male adolescent power fantasies can
hardly be reconciled with the sort of mortality which defines its readers' actual, fallible lives. In Becker's terms, the "father-substitute" superhero cannot,
should not die—not unless its "sons" want to put aside childish things and
grow up.

On another level, the Spider-Man and Rick Jones vignettes simply illustrate
Mar-Vell's trite remark that "death touches us all in different ways." More precisely, they demonstrate the poet/undertaker Thomas Lynch's *aperçu* that

> any damage or decency we do accrues to the living, to whom your death
> happens, if it really happens to anyone. The living have to live with it. You

don't. Theirs is the grief or gladness your death brings. Theirs is the loss or gain of it. Theirs is the pain and the pleasure of memory. Theirs is the invoice for services rendered and theirs is the check in the mail for its payment. (8)

To one extent or another, the various supporting characters' reactions (some dozen spread throughout the novel) embody Lynch's point; their grief, anger, and irresolution are the ripples through which Mar-Vell's death "happens" to the living—and metafictively, the genre. They also elucidate the difficult task of "narrative reconstruction," for the mourners no less than the dying.

One scene in particular returns us to the role played by community commemoration of the dead/dying in a wider—nationalist—sense, which is to say, to the political dimensions of death. Shortly before lapsing into a coma, the ailing Mar-Vell receives a representative of his longtime foes, the Skrull Empire, on an official affair of state. General Zedrao, before stunned witnesses, salutes the dying man, lauds Mar-Vell as the Skrulls' *"greatest enemy"* (emphasis in original) and presents him with the Royal Skrull Medal of Honor. As Zedrao leaves, the ever-hotheaded Rick Jones grouses bitterly that while Mar-Vell's enemies do him honors, his own people, the Kree, shun him in his time of dying, since, as Mar-Vell says, "They don't give medals to *traitors*" (emphasis in original).

The bizarre Zedrao episode further integrates the story into the greater continuity of the Marvel Universe, but more than that, it casts into relief how Mar-Vell's death (the death of any famous person, with attendant trauma and affect) is rendered "useful" in/by a socius. As the anthropologist Katherine Verdery explains, "[Dead bodies] help us to see political transformation as something more than a technical process . . . The 'something more' includes meanings, feelings, the sacred, ideas of mortality, the nonrational—all ingredients of 'legitimacy' or 'regime consolidation'" (25). In other words, the Skrull Empire cannily "legitimates" itself by eulogizing its greatest foe at the hour of his passing, reinforcing its claim as a great state precisely through recognition of such a worthy opponent. In its turn, the Kree empire likewise "inoculates" itself from Mar-Vell's destabilizing threat by spurning a turncoat son. Finally, the community of superheroes participates in a sociopolitically crucial enactment of values through rituals of leave-taking, mourning, community support, and burial at a time of loss, to contain death's meaning-corroding power. Widening our scope, Zedrao's encomium bears yet another symbolic burden germane to 1970s America: Starlin noted to me that he inserted the scene (the one overtly political message in the novel) as a protest against what he perceived as the US government's abandonment of Vietnam War veterans, including himself (2011).

The Death of Captain Marvel, the "death literature" heir to centuries of Western thought on human mortality and its representation, abounds in death symbols and iconography, only a portion of which I will touch on here. From the skull that appears in Mar-Vell's eye in the laboratory scene as he discusses his terminal prognosis; to the dark chambers he stalks while delivering his Hamlet-like soliloquy (in particular recalling the "to be or not to be" speech from Act III, Scene 1); to the gigantic "Heart of the Universe" which in a moment-to-moment panel sequence ceases to beat, signaling Mar-Vell's "crossing over"; to the preponderance of narrow vertical, tombstone-like panels—some them even rounded at the top, as discussed below—much of this death imagery seems fairly obvious, even hackneyed. Other visuals derive from a specifically Christian symbology, especially the association of Mar-Vell's body with that of Jesus on the cover and the appearance of a "halo" around his head, formed by an overhead lamp in the laboratory scene.[89]

But the most sustained thanatopic image (taking up nearly 20 pages) is Mar-Vell's deathbed, a chronotope familiar from sentimental Victorian fiction and engravings, which comes to dominate the final third of the novel. Its maudlin reconciliations, pained regrets, loss of words, awarding of Skrull medals, declamations about a life well-lived, as well as its heroic culmination, recall yet another Christian contemplative tradition, the *Ars Moriendi*, or "art of dying." Introduced by the Catholic Church in fifteenth-century Europe, these Latin booklets (sometimes illustrated with woodblock prints) instructed the sufferer—pictured in bed—on how to die well, resist demonic temptations to renounce Christ in his final hours, and successfully ascend to Heaven. As David Stannard notes in *The Puritan Way of Death*, such spiritual counsel proved invaluable to believers living through the horrors of the plague-filled Middle Ages, in which death "was a ghastly visitation upon the body of man, but fear of the soul's fate . . . remained blunted by the Christian tradition" (19).

Ars Moriendi prints depicted the dying Moriens surrounded by demonic figures who struggle with angels over his soul, as Mary and Jesus look on. In the end, his faith in Christ vanquishes the devils, and his soul rises out of his mouth towards salvation. Several panels from the graphic novel's deathbed scenes recast *Ars Moriendi* imagery in secular terms, perhaps none more elaborately than the large panel which first shows Mar-Vell after he has fallen into a coma. Under covers, a nimbus-like spotlight setting him aglow, the dying man is surrounded by shadowed "angels" (Nighthawk, Thor's winged helmet, Quicksilver's locks), and "demons" (Gargoyle, Ghost Rider, Nightcrawler, Devil-Slayer, the "horned" Scarlet Witch, Beast). A partly opened curtain over his head reveals a void, figuring his ultimate destination. The coffin-like horizontal panel above, depicting the hoary Mentor against another field of black, could even be read as a portrait of God the Father, floating above the earthly

7.15 Mar-Vell's deathbed: a superhero *Ars Moriendi* (*The Death of Captain Marvel*, 1982).

scene, awaiting Mar-Vell's soul (though read on for a complication to such a reading).

A final age-old emblem of death employed by Starlin has a more problematic ideological pedigree, particularly from a modern feminist perspective. The linkage of woman with mortality (e.g., the novel's cowled dark lady) has deep misogynistic roots. As pointed out by Elisabeth Bronfen and Sarah Webster Goodwin, it is the product of anxieties that cut to the heart of the male imagination:

> Death, as the limit of cultural representation, has been associated with that other enigma, the multiply-coded female body . . . Death and femininity appear in cultural discourses as the point of impossibility, the blind spot the representational system seeks to refuse even as it constantly addresses it . . . The kinds of power attributed to death are also those associated with the woman, because they are the confounding power of the body. Just as woman *is* the body, she is also the body's caretaker, the nurse, the layer-out of the corpse. If death is a kind of return to her care, then she is also contaminated by it, so that rituals must be found first to enable her care and then to dissociate her from the corpse. Like the decaying body, the feminine is unstable, liminal, disturbing. Both mourning rituals and representations of death may seek strategies to stabilize the body, which entails removing it from the feminine and transforming it into a monument, an enduring stone. (13–14, emphasis in original)[90]

Indeed, Starlin's novel does precisely this: figures the annihilating threat of death in gendered terms (as a silent female for whom the male Thanos always speaks); oddly sexualizes it by symbolizing Mar-Vell's passing as a sort of perverse "wedding" with Thanos as "best man," in which the hero kisses the ghastly skeletal bride; and ultimately "converts" Mar-Vell's dead body into a suggestively shaped stone obelisk (seen in the book's back cover). Still more strangely, the "skeletal" version of the cowled figure, which appears when Mar-Vell waves his hand and says he no longer needs "the illusion," disappears immediately after the conjugal kiss; the womanly avatar returns to lead the hero on into the bright light. It seems Mar-Vell does indeed still "need the illusion"; Thanos's own necrophiliac obsession becomes "legitimized" by Mar-Vell's participation in the ceremony. (Whose death is this, anyway?) The scene therefore suggests that there exists something "inevitable" about men seeing death through the lens of gender; its "Otherness," as argued by Bronfen and Godwin, redounds to the feminine.[91] It is true that Starlin inherited the woman-as-death convention along with most of the novel's tropes. It is also true he does little to complicate or ironicize it as he does the others. The privileged signifier of death in the novel is an eroticized, necrophiliac vision, Thanos's "dark and deadly *beauty*" (*Captain Marvel*, vol. 1, #31, Mar. 1974: n.p., emphasis in original), the age-old conflation of womb with tomb.

The most prominent female avatar of death greets the reader before he even opens the book: the skeletal personage that sits in for Mary, mother of God, in the cover's *Pietà* parody. The image, among the most iconic in the history of the genre, in some respects merely extends the convention of "fallen comrade" or "*pieta*" covers which announce a (supposed) death in the storyline, e.g., Batman holding up the defunct Robin in "Robin Dies at Dawn!" or Superman holding the deceased Supergirl in his arms on the cover of *Crisis on Infinite Earths*, vol. 1, #7.[92] But in crucial ways it is very different. Not a fellow hero, nor even his love interest Elysius, but *Death itself* bears Mar-Vell in her/its arms. The portrait announces the irrevocability of the superhero's passing, the sense of "this is for real," underscored by the black border that frames it, as in traditional funeral announcements, and the utter lack of editorial clamor: no exclamation points, no breathless cries of the "This Issue: Captain Marvel Dies!" variety. Once more, the tone of expression is "serious," literary—also once more, it falls along gendered lines. The Mary/Death figure (the Other, the Monstrous Maternal,[93] the supervillainness none can defeat, if you will) has Captain Marvel in her clutches, signal to a presumed male fandom that the end truly has come. (On the other hand, the cover slyly leaves the door open to a resurrection, since Mar-Vell after all assumes the messiah's pose.)

In another sense, of course, the cover is not "serious" at all, since for some the very act of conflating fine art and superheroics amounts to ironic appropriation ala Pop Art, or else outright kitsch. As promulgated by Marxist-leaning art critics and intellectuals, most notably Clement Greenberg in his essay "Avant Garde and Kitsch" (1939), the term, in brief, describes mass cultural artifacts of the postindustrial age usually consumed by citizens uneducated in the fine arts.[94] While some see in kitsch a benign if mindless upholding of the status quo, others have characterized it as a sign of Western civilization's decline; Milan Kundera defined it as "a folding screen set up to curtain off death" (1984: 253), a cheery brand of thanatopic disavowal. For my present purposes I want to stress Greenberg's initial formulations of kitsch as a species of bottom-feeding cultural parasitism, expressed most concisely in the oft-quoted dictum:

> The pre-condition for kitsch, a condition without which kitsch would be impossible, is the availability close at hand of a fully matured cultural tradition, whose discoveries, acquisitions and perfected self-consciousness kitsch can take advantage of for its own ends. (12)

Scholars such as John Morreal and Jessica Loy echo this sort of discourse: "When Leonardo's *Last Supper* is executed as a five-inch glow-in-the-dark sculpture . . . it is destroyed" (71). Kitsch, they argue, "looks for images from traditional art that have already become icons, such as the *Mona Lisa,* the *Last Supper,* and the Eiffel Tower. It tries to tap their established acceptability and value to get a predictable reaction" (69). And: "That's why we prefer works which have subtlety and multiple meanings which cannot be taken in at a glance. By eliminating these features, kitsch eliminates the potential for aesthetic experience of any worth" (68).[95]

We can certainly read Starlin's engagement with one of the singular images of Western fine art in his cover to *The Death of Captain Marvel* as "parasitic," though this would seem to be only the beginning, not the end, of a worthwhile reading. The question is whether his "kitsch" appropriation and parody of Michelangelo's *Pietà* "destroys" it, robs it of "subtlety and multiple meanings which cannot be taken in at a glance"—or rather co-opts its status so as to interrogate it; translates it into ironically modern terms; opens up new avenues of interpretation; and signals a turning point for the superhero genre. In other words, is the appropriation productive rather than "cheap" (to use one of any number of derogating terms), in dialogue with its source rather than beholden to "top-down" hierarchies of taste?[96] I argue the former.

Aware not all will be swayed, I offer these considerations on, if you will, the productivity of the Starlin/Buonarroti "team-up." To begin with, the cover self-consciously, and humorously, allegorizes the very antagonistic relationship between fine art and popular/mass culture we have outlined. Beneath the *Captain Marvel* of the title, with its garish yellow bespoke font, the grey "skeletal Mary" supports the red-blue-and-yellow-clad, dead Mar-Vell. Behind: a squadron of scrambling heroes bolt forward as if to strip their friend and ally from her grasp—though this interpretation is belied by the fact that they uniformly stare not at her but out at the reader. Their conventional "action" poses therefore mark a strong contrast between the received idea of superheroics (pure masculinist dynamism—no superheroines appear), the classic seated female figure of Michelangelo's (vestigial) Mary, and the recumbent, "feminized" Mar-Vell. This is the "new reality" introduced by the novel, with its "mature" approach to death. Gender anxieties of the sort we have discussed lie at its heart: the "dark lady" authorizes this new reality; her body creates a formidable "maternal" barrier between the Captain and putative rescue. The image is of course not bereft of humor: we feel a certain ludicrous hilarity at seeing the ineffective Hulk, Thing, Captain America, the non-Christian Thor, and others frozen in place, like decorative Pop wallpaper, but also seeming to radiate from "Mary" like a nimbus. (Perversely, Spider-Man emerges mid-groin from "her" head, like Athena.) To follow the Greenbergian line, then, a preestablished work of Catholic fine art *(Pietà)* "gives birth" to degraded pulpy American kitsch (superheroes); in return, kitsch "kills it," transforming Mary into a traditional figure of death that long predates Michelangelo's sculpture. But this is an internecine process: at the same time, fine art "kills" Mar-Vell—even as it also intimates his resurrection as the savior messiah.

Second, we should recall that, broadly speaking, not that wide a gulf separates Starlin and Michelangelo's projects in terms of their labor with what we might call antecedent mythology: the Tuscan worked in dialogue with a long lineage of conventions for portraying Biblical figures (often inflected to reflect patronage), themselves derived from an ancient oral tradition with many facets, while the Detroiter earned his reputation, like most in the mainstream comics industry, revamping and reinventing characters he himself had not created, with extensive histories that preceded him, while staying (more or less) within a recognizable "house style."

The cover thus functions as both homage and amalgam; it reifies in gaudy hues the commonalities of artistic work and "continuity" in the Renaissance and postindustrial stages of capitalism. Each and every character depicted has a rich mythological background/backstory and context (New Testament, Silver Age, paganism) that makes such an outlandish "crossover" all the more plausible. In this regard, the "doubled" figures in particular catch the eye: Mary/dark lady unites in one body Christian and pre-Christian myth, just as Captain America has Golden Age as well as Silver Age incarnations, while Thor exists simultaneously as superhero and Norse god. They are all syncretic image-texts, in W. J. T. Mitchell's term, pictures carrying an embedded narrative (see in particular 1986: 40–42). Similarly, as David A. Lewis (2002) has shown, *midrash*, the Judaic tradition of Biblical exegesis and (re)interpretation, has much in common with the ebbs and flows of superhero retconning. The Greenberg-inspired high/low split between "transcendent" fine art and "parasitic" kitsch tends to obscure or disregard such overlaps.[97]

Finally, and most germane to the superhero at this critical juncture in its development, is the cover image's bizarre, paradoxical deep flatness or flat depth. The heroes appear in a curious half-tone, contrasting with the full-tone of the Mar-Vell and Skeletal Mary subjects and the complete black of the border. The art thus produces an effect of three-dimensionality.[98] On the other hand, the blank white background against which the heroes stand out accentuates their fundamentally flat, artificial, and illusory nature. Adding to their irreality, the coterie of "action-ready" figures defy gravity, they overlap unnaturally (Thor looks larger than the Thing, though "behind" him) without a unifying visual perspective; as noted they resemble illustrations on wallpaper.[99] We might imagine that Death has just plucked Mar-Vell from the wall's gallery of heroes, and endowed him with a paradoxical life-death: he no longer seems two-dimensional and half-tone like the others, but he is also not living, in repose. The heroes, though flat, seem more dynamic and alive; Mar-Vell, though more "real," is inert. In this respect the image rehearses the primary "there and not there" of the corpse, its simultaneous presence and lack; as Bronfen and Goodwin note: "In any representation of death, it is strikingly an absence that is at stake, so that the presentation is itself at a remove from what is figured" (7).[100]

There is more. The cover's "foreground" and "background" are suspended in a fraught spatial tension enhanced by the skeletal figure's dull grey-white color; her "full-tone" quality notwithstanding, she seems the most statically statue-like, partly because a reader conversant in art history recognizes her first and foremost *as* a statue or *the spoof of* a statue: Mary from Michelangelo's *Pietà*. The picture therefore comes off as multiply artificial. It resembles a (caricature of a) set of mannequins against a diorama—in close relationship and continuity with their background, yet set apart from it. And yet, due to her position between the colorfully garbed Mar-Vell and the also colorful (if muted) costumes of the "wallpaper" heroes, she manifests as a visual vacuum around which the heroes swirl, orbiting a hollow grey void—Death, the master trope of nihility. A disconcertingly procreative void, for the skeletal lady, as the lone female presence, also denotes maternity, in part because in *Pietà* Michelangelo strongly evokes Madonna and Child visual conventions. There it is again: femininity and death, womb and tomb.

The cover's "mash-up" quality of multiple image-text registers, simultaneous illusionistic depth/flatness, and other aspects which I have been trying to describe produce an effect that recalls—though is by no means synonymous with—the Japanese modern artist Takashi Murakami's anime and manga-derived Superflat, which relies on similar graphic strategies for its critique of a homogenizing postmodern consumerist culture, as well as "propos[es] formal historical connections between classic Japanese art and the anime cartoons of today to a Pop Art-like cross-contamination of high and low to a social critique of contemporary mores and motivations" (Darling: 77).

As Thomas Looser describes it, Superflat brings disparate objects (e.g., different historical epochs) together in the same visual/psychological space of the viewer, to engender "a retheorization of possibilities in the present":

The "Superflat" layering and juxtaposing of different worlds, in ways that retain the unique organization and coherence of each media world or each layer—though still grounded within some kind of common order—are already a new image of history, or a new way of imaging history. It is one that, on the one hand, can bring out the singular set of relations and conditions that make up our own time, without grounding them in a determinative origin. And on the other, it also still insists on some larger picture of history, or a kind of relationality, extending beyond the non-historical singularity of any given time. (108)

Something much like this plays out in the various tensions of Starlin's *Pietà*, with its ecumenical commingling of multiple cultural registers difficult to reduce to one interpretation. All this as we realize: at the end of the day, it is still only ink on paper, a flat (printed, mechanically mass-produced) representation which, however subtle its nuances, ultimately falls far short of the actual three-dimensionality—and, were it accessible, sensuous tactility—of Michelangelo's original sculpture.

Returning to earth, so to speak, and to the cover's purpose beyond serving as an eye-catching set piece to lure the buyer, we can further say that Starlin's oppositions in this image—male/female, high/low, sculpture/caricature, death/life, flatness/depth, light/dark, color/grey, text/image, superhero/villainness, uniqueness/mechanical reproduction, stillness/movement, among others—coalesce about a primary aim: to mock the "eternal return" of the dead superhero, who routinely strides through Quarter Bin's "Revolving Door of Death," by conflating it with Christian faith in the resurrection of the Savior. Further, as noted, we see here a complex allegory of moribund high culture ("dead Mary") overtaken, encrowded by raucous, superficial kitsch. I would only reiterate that—as one discovers upon actually opening and reading the book—the superhero is also diminished ("half-toned") by the introduction of "real" death to the traditionally ableist, masculinist genre.

If I have by now belabored my arguments, I have done so in an attempt to show that, whatever else the *Death of Captain Marvel* cover is doing, it is not merely filching from the aura of a Renaissance masterpiece so as to crassly or simplistically yield "vicarious experience and faked sensations" (Clement Greenberg: 12), or as Morreal and Loy put it, "eliminat[e] the potential for aesthetic experience of any worth." Far from it. Rather, the cover reveals that, even before delving into the story proper, Starlin's work is already delivering a complexity, self-awareness and aesthetic pleasure worthy of the amusingly lofty new marketing term, "Marvel Graphic Novel."

Let us now turn to a more detailed examination of how this new, more "mature" publishing format transforms the standard post-Silver Age superhero plot. As with the cover, does the "contaminating" influence of literary and ideological content customarily thought anathema to the genre result in a thorough dismantling of its key presumptions—and ultimately, its undoing? The unsurprising answer: a provisional yes.

Certainly many conventions remain in place: costumes, double identities, climactic violence and a triumph of sorts for the hero. Moreover, readers of other superhero "death" stories will recognize some familiar elements, such as discourses of family, honoring a fallen comrade, reactions across many quarters (in this case, throughout the galaxy),[101] leave-taking, and ritual commemoration of the passing.[102] Among the best examples that bring together most of these elements: the splash page showing more than forty heroes disembarking on the Saturnian moon in a show of support for the dying man. As the varicolored assemblage descends a staircase, the accompanying caption reads:

> They are the family of super-man. Theirs is the task of protecting a universe they call home. Many have fought beside Mar-Vell, a few have fought against him, but now, all think of him as a brother who is dying. They've come to Titan to say goodbye to one of their own.

The page has no speech balloons, and does not need them: each clearly recognizable character comes with its own history and preconfigured personality which allows us to read much into their interactions; the image, comparable to the "Catalog of Ships" in Book 2 of Homer's *Iliad* and the Gigantomachy frieze on the Pergamon Altar, is a master class in how serial continuity invests even the simplest exposition (the arrival on Titan) with elaborate meaning. Throughout we see various sparks and sputters of drama: Hercules has an altercation with Devil-Slayer; Human Torch greets his old pal Spider-Man; Nightcrawler looks startled; the lascivious Tigra flirts with Hulk, apparently to Namor's offense; Janet van Dyne (the Wasp) seems to restrain the striding Hank Pym (Yellowjacket), perhaps hinting at the couple's marital strife, and so on.

Curiously, the only figure with her back to the reader is Black Widow (Natasha Romanova), who gazes in the foreground at the oncoming heroes. A suggestive choice: is she a stand-in for the "dark lady" whom she, largely in shadow, so resembles in this portrait—and whose sobriquet likewise blends femininity with death? She stands in an odd pose, as if scratching her back with her left hand. Could this intimate a deceitful mien, as if she were "holding something behind her back," i.e., the threat of annihilation? In any case, the mass portrait serves several functions at once: it advances the narrative; further opens up the novel to the wider intertextual continuity of which it forms a part;[103] upholds a major convention of superhero "death" tales; and, again, taps gender to subtly undermine the genre's "immortalist" proclivities.

Of course, *The Death of Captain Marvel* is at its most gripping when it actively works to rewrite, ironicize, and raze those proclivities. The early melée with Thanos's followers aboard a derelict ship exemplifies Starlin's revisionist approach, a carryover from his run on the series. In the fight, a reluctant semiretired Mar-Vell uses his Cosmic Awareness to apply the precise amount of force so as not to cause excessive harm to his non-superpowered opponents. Indeed, he exhibits as much concern for his foes' welfare as for that of his Titanian comrades-at-arms—two supporting characters, who (uncharacteristically for a superhero story) take the lead in battle.[104] Furthermore, these figures flout the genre's masculinist, agist status quo: Eros (as his name implies) is as much lover as fighter, while his father, the white-haired Mentor, is that rare thing: an elderly superhero. Finally, their adversaries' motivation for the skirmish—they worship the dead Thanos as a god and await his resurrection—alludes to the misguided pursuit of eternal life, precisely what the superhero implicitly promises.

It is therefore significant that after the battle, Mentor lambastes these disciples for their blind faith in fantasies of immortality, telling them to go and live their lives in the real world, because his son Thanos's death "has freed you to do so." As Mentor says this, Mar-Vell (strangely winded after the battle) is holding his hand up to his mouth; in the very next panel he succumbs to a violent coughing fit that brings him to his knees. Theme here neatly imbricates with plot: Mar-Vell's first sign of physical distress is "brought on" by Mentor's stern reproach about the futility of thinking one can live forever.

From this point, Starlin inverts much of the standard superhero narrative to assault its ideology. Captain Marvel's nega-bands, part of his arsenal and source of much power, are revealed as the very instrument of his death, since they repeatedly repulse attempts to save him. As explained by Dr. Strange, Mr. Fantastic, and Beast, in retarding the cancer over the years, the bands have made Mar-Vell's body dependent on their energy: "The one thing that's keeping Marvel *alive* is also keeping us from *curing* him!" (emphasis in original).[105] Here, translated into the genre's terms, is an illustration of Becker's point about the over-reliance on illusion and fantasy (read: superpowers) as a shield against despair-inducing death: "It is fateful and ironic how the lie we need in order to live dooms us to a life that is never really ours" (1973: 56).

The Herculean labor that befalls Marvel, then: to live his life "honestly" in the face of death, to "no longer need the illusion." In this process, which Becker describes as the greatest challenge of the mature individual, the body plays a paramount, unequivocal role. Let us return to the moment just before Mar-Vell's soliloquy on accepting his fate. Recall that the extended bout of introspection is provoked by an intense attack of "Pain . . . Overwhelming pain . . . It burns . . . It tears . . . It twists and bends . . . It kills. It kills slowly . . . A little piece at a time . . . and then it fades. Yes, the pain comes and it goes . . ." Note how closely the captions parallel lines from the founding document of modern death literature, Tolstoy's *The Death of Ivan Ilyich*, in which a judge suffers similar pangs on the path to self-awareness:

But suddenly, in the middle of the session, the pain in his side, disregarding the stage the proceedings had reached, would begin its gnawing proceedings. Ivan Ilyich would focus on it, then try to drive the thought of it away, but the pain went right on with its work. And then *It* would come back and stand there and stare at him, and he would be petrified, the light would go out of his eyes, and again he would begin asking himself: "Can *It* alone be true?"... And the worst thing was that *It* drew his attention not so that he would do anything, but merely so that he would look at *It*, look It straight in the face and, doing nothing, suffer unspeakable agony. (95)[106]

When Tolstoy writes of *looking* at the pain he is of course using a metaphor; by definition pain cannot be visualized – in fact, part of its terror is that it cannot be adequately communicated; only its effects are accessible to the senses: grimaces, grunts, cries, breaking into a sweat. Elaine Scarry describes pain as the "unmaking of the world" because of its fundamental opposition to the construction of meaning; where pain is, language is not. When the attack hits, Mar-Vell can only clutch his torso and yell an inarticulate "ARH!"; the scene reminds of the corpus' (anti-linguistic) challenge to narrative reconstruction, of the mind's onus to a body in revolt, of how the mind *is* that body. Once the pain has passed, Mar-Vell's ensuing speech, as noted, serves as a summation of his dilemma, of being a hero who cannot win. Heroism therefore undergoes redefinition: first and foremost, as the capacity to die well.[107]

The rest of the novel in essence makes plain Mar-Vell's new mission, as those around him react in their individual ways. The "non-heroic" dying and death which he carries out—with its life-support vests, sickbed, oxygen tubes, wasting physique—hurls a profound challenge not only to long-established models of heroism, to say nothing of superheroic death, but to the meanings of manhood and life itself in postwar US culture. We see this reflected in some of the critical responses to the novel; as Quarter Bin writes, "The Kree soldier died of a common ailment that afflicts ordinary people: cancer. In fine *unsuperheroic* fashion, Mar-Vell passed on from the confines of a bedroom, not on a battlefield, *as a man would*" (Ouzamandias 1999, my emphasis).

Inevitably, then, Western culture is primed to read Mar-Vell's dying—with all its props—as his quasi-feminization. Since the dawn of civilization, such deaths have traditionally been received with disquiet, if not repulsion. So it is for ancient heroes such as Enkidu in the Babylonian epic *Gilgamesh* (ca. eighteenth century BCE), cursed by Ishtar to die not on his feet in glorious struggle, but in bed: "My friend, the great goddess cursed me and I must die in shame. I shall not die like a man fallen in battle; I feared to fall, but happy is the man who falls in the battle, for I must die in shame" (93).[108] Ancient Greek,

Roman, Norse, and other standards of heroism likewise privileged a violent death in war over a contemptible withering away under the covers,[109] and the "heroic death" had long been the only one acceptable for mainstream superheroes—even in "imaginary" tales!

A scene between Mar-Vell, now bedridden, and his lover issues a stern rebuke to such hypermasculine pieties, rendered all the more powerful for the softness and gentleness of its delivery. In her only speech of the novel, Elysius says, "Perhaps this way is best . . . I feared your end would be *violent*. I dreaded you dying *alone* on some distant planet surrounded by enemies. At least this way *I* can be with you to the end" (emphasis in original). The time spent together as the sick man's health deteriorates allows the couple to share their deepest intimacies; at one point Mar-Vell tells Elysius (directly addressing the reader), "I've never loved anyone as I have you." Such scenes exemplify not only the advantages of "un-heroic death" (for emotional and social bonding, reflection, bidding farewell), they also expose the blindness, vapidity, and pathological individualism of the "heroic" death model it replaces.[110]

Instead of a quick, anonymous end on a faraway battlefield, a gradual, managed decline in conditions of humane caregiving, leave-taking, and love reimagines the dying experience—for society as a whole no less than for the individual. Just such an ethic, argued Elisabeth Kübler-Ross, leads to an appreciation of death as a "meaning, growth-inducing aspect of life" (1975: 145)—and not only for the individual. As Harold Braswell maintains, recent debates on "death with dignity" and euthanasia make apparent a constitutive social interdependence, crucial to recognize since "such relationships are more illustrative of the human condition than the notion of the autonomous individual—an idea that masks the inevitable and constitutive vulnerability of existence."[111] Mask vulnerability—along with a host of other truths—is precisely what the hyper-autonomous superhero does. Mar-Vell shows another path; to paraphrase the Watcher at the conclusion of the Dark Phoenix saga, it was more important to him that he die a human.

All the same, as mentioned, the genre will have its pound of flesh. And the "final battle" between our hero and Thanos which closes *The Death of Captain Marvel* certainly delivers the sort of Kirby-ish slugfest and pulse-pounding action which superheroes cannot live (or die?) without. On the edge of death, Mar-Vell opens his eyes one final time. We see his point of view: his friends and loved ones gathered about his bed, a transparent skull floating in the air. The last words he hears, Mentor's "so unfair," echo across the page, as in the bottom tier the sick man "transforms" through a five-panel dissolve into Thanos's statue. This statue comes to life and confronts Mar-Vell, now alone in his sickbed: "It *pains* me to see you so. Frail, ill, decayed, slowly withering away . . .

For one such as you, death should not come gnawing like some vermin. For you, death should be . . . a *glorious event!* So *rise, Captain Marvel!*" (emphasis and some ellipses in original). Thanos strips Mar-Vell of his bedding, to reveal the hero made whole again, in costume and healthy, braced for combat.

The Titan then leads the captain to a strange psychedelic dimension reminiscent of Steve Ditko's Dr. Strange settings (as well as of Marvel's encounter with Eon, the being who granted him Cosmic Awareness), where resides a gigantic "Heart of the Universe" which the villain means to destroy "because . . . I am *Thanos* . . . and because you are *Captain Marvel*, your job is to stop me." "Then stop you I *will*, madman!" Marvel replies (emphasis and ellipses in original), leaping into the fray. Over the next several pages, many made up of large panels and one splash, the hero spectacularly clashes with an army of his slain foes, now risen, and smashes them to stone-bits.

Such an ending prompts serious questions—first and foremost for some readers about Starlin's apparently mixed messages. Why does a depiction of a quietly dying man—albeit superpowered—end in an orgy of violence? Does the conclusion undo the existentialist critique of the "heroic death" which up until then the author had been advancing? Does the ending's reliance on cliché compromise the novel's revisionist stance? Does Marvel's dynamic showdown—replete with shattering bodies, jagged-edge speech balloons, and "loud" exclamation points *("Crush him!!")*—trivialize the sober contemplation of dignified dying that precedes it?

Starlin himself says he found the denouement necessary for purposes of satisfying dramatic expectations and respecting the character. As he told me:

> The reason I went for him fighting it out with Thanos at the end was, it was a book about death. I didn't want him to just perish and die and have a really downer ending to it. He had to die, but I wanted to give him a moment of triumph. Part of the point of the story was to give him exactly that: a moment of triumph. I think the success of the book has a lot to do with the fact that it's not a downer ending. He dies, but he dies triumphant . . . [Without it] [y]ou would've walked away hollow. This ending is a testament to his life, so you leave on an up-note rather than a down-note. (2011)

Like so much else in *The Death of Captain Marvel,* the "triumphant ending" has its precedents in death literature of the past and present, no less than in superhero convention. Once more, Tolstoy's *The Death of Ivan Ilyich* provides the most salient example: in the protagonist's final hours, the novel's representation shifts to the subjective, ultimately incommunicable experience of dying "from within." Ivan Ilyich, for the first time, comes to feel genuine compassion for those around him, and this provides the key to ecstatically overcoming his terror of death:

> There was no fear because there was no death.
> Instead of death there was light.
> "So that's it!" he exclaimed. "What bliss!" (133)

Illness compels Ivan Ilyich to walk his personal Golgotha on the way to a transcendent self-awareness portrayed as a joyful effulgence, just as he dies.[112] His rediscovered faith leads him to see this process in terms of a spiritual rebirth. Similarly, the Confederate sympathizer Peyton Farquhar in Ambrose Bierce's short story "An Occurrence at Owl Creek Bridge" (1890) heroically escapes his Northern executioners and exultantly rejoins his family, only to discover as his neck snaps that he has imagined the entire thing. In a more recent cinematic example, the bawdy Broadway choreographer Joe Gideon in Bob Fosse's All That Jazz (1979) pictures his own subjective death as a loud, flashy "farewell concert" to the tune of "Bye Bye Life." All these depictions have two things in common: the unrepresentable experience of death envisioned in accordance with the protagonist's subjectivity, and the delinking of the corporeal from the ineffable at the moment of passing.[113] I'll have more to say about the latter in my conclusion; for now let us return to Marvel's last face-off with Thanos and other "risen" dead villains.

On one level, the final battle, complete with "triumphant ending," indeed fulfills the genre's compulsion to address problems and resolve storylines through violence and hyper-masculine display. Mar-Vell's unavoidable death must be translated into terms codified over the decades: superheroes fight and win. Hence, Starlin's contention that anything else would have made for an unsatisfying "downer ending." So Thanos is absolutely correct when he says he must do evil "because . . . I am *Thanos* . . . and because you are *Captain Marvel*, your job is to stop me"; Marvel likewise speaks true when he replies with the superhero cliché: "Then stop you I *will*, madman!" In this respect they are marionettes manipulated, sans irony, by genre.[114]

But a closer inspection of the Marvel/Thanos showdown reveals something much more subversive than merely a gaggle of superpowered yahoos knocking each other about. A metaphysical dialogue (of the sort Starlin had pioneered in his work a decade earlier) is threaded through the scene, eliciting a spirited dialectical tension between the visuals and the speech balloons—the two very much at odds. Mar-Vell, in hyperbolic, standard-issue superhero poses, exclaims lines such as "*No! The light* and *life* have always been my gods! My pride is that of the *never vanquished!* If I am to *die,* I shall die *fighting!*" and "*No! I refuse to accept that!* As long as there is *life* there is *hope!"* (emphasis in original). The latter delivery is compellingly crafted: as he shouts, Marvel assumes a classic stance, left arm extended as if in flight—against a blank white background which emphasizes the illusory nature of such super-bombast.

To such trite homilies, dry-eyed Thanos responds, "So you refuse to acknowledge death's kind *mercy*—but even *you* must accept its *inevitability!* . . . Because its nature is universal! You may strive against it. You may even close a few doors to it. But in the end, *nothing* can halt its *cool touch*" (emphasis in original). He concludes, as Marvel's blow reduces him to fragments, that to deny the infinite means "to find that your victories are the stuff of dreams . . . illusions" (ellipsis in original). Moreover, throughout the battle Thanos's off-panel voice appears in text-boxes, not balloons, lending his death-acceptance rhetoric the "authority" customarily accorded captions; this occurs when he intones to a desperate Marvel beset with foes, "Put an end to this childish myopia of reality."

Other factors distinguish this sequence from the standard superhero brawl: when Marvel utters "I shall die *fighting!"* the background immediately behind him consists of sleek purplish abstract lines, while Thanos's side of the same panel has a backdrop of organic structures, like veins or synapses; principle, idealism, culture, vs. body, mortality, the return of the repressed. Finally, the clash ends untypically, with no resolution; the other enemies have vanished, but a reintegrated Thanos remains, saying, "Like all men, I am *finite* and *accept* it. Your arrogance is noble, but *futile*; just, but *useless*. It is the way of man, the only way we know how to play the *game*" (emphasis in original).[115]

As nearly half a century of superhero comics had amply demonstrated, a fanciful repudiation of mortal truths was indeed "the way of man, the only way we know how to play the *game*." Starlin indicates that must change: precisely at this point, with hero and villain at a stalemate, equal before death, the non-male "dark lady" appears, once more effecting genre change through the catalyst of gender.

The Death of Captain Marvel's spectacular final showdown certainly delivers the superheroic goods: colorful costumes, energy blasts, overwhelming odds, good vs. evil, noble platitudes, Richter-scale punches, "explosive" mise-en-page, energetic poses, villainous rants, "Kirby krackle," and so on. But it also functions as, firstly, an arch allegory of the genre's endless recycling of its dead (the returned villains) endlessly repulsed by the hero, and, more poignantly, through metafictive dialogue relayed alongside the mayhem, as a meditation on death recast in terms of the superhero plot—the genre speaking to itself, striving as a human mind strives to grasp the supreme mystery of its own imminent demise, to the point where denial breaks down and acceptance looms.[116]

7.16 Mar-Vell and Thanos debate life and death in the mighty Marvel manner in *The Death of Captain Marvel* (1982).

Before concluding, I want to briefly touch on two more facets of Starlin's novel which seem particularly illustrative of his radical new vision, the mortal superhero: its poetics of abjection and subtle reorientation of the "good vs. evil" trope to a patient/medicine dichotomy. Again, both bespeak the influence of death literature and wider debates on end-of-life care in the late twentieth-century US.

The depiction of Mar-Vell's body over the course of the story, from begarbed and brawny to bare-chested and weak, breaks new ground in the genre, and can best be understood through Julia Kristeva's concept of the abject. In her oft-quoted formulation, the abject represents a state of "in-betweenness" or appalling dissolution between subject and object which "draws me to the place where meaning collapses." In short, it is "death infecting life" (1982: 2–4).[117] Jackie Stacey applies Kristeva's philosophy to the experience of cancer, a disease of uncontrolled cellular growth in which life processes go haywire, threatening the very organism of which they themselves comprise a part. (Unlike a virus or other foreign threat to the body, cancer is produced from "within.") As she notes:

Cancer invites an unwelcome visitor into the land of the living. By exaggerating the reproduction of life, cancer introduces the threat of death. Too much life; too many cells; the work of a deadly enthusiast. The body's natural processes of regeneration miss a beat and turn into their opposite. Cancer thus not only promises death but it promises death by means of life, death by reproduction. Cancer is "death infecting life" by the means of life itself . . . The treatments for cancer extend this confusion further; radiotherapy destroys as it heals, chemotherapy pollutes as it cleanses. To kill the cancer cells the body is pumped full of poison. (79–81)

Abjection made flesh, cancer exposes as illusory the "immutable" boundaries between self and other, as well as our fundamental, ever-present, built-in vulnerability (76); as psychological "collateral damage" to its overwhelming existential threat, the "demonic pregnancy" (Sontag 1989: 14) of cancer overthrows the tidy categories by which the healthy live their lives.[118] Clearly the portrayal of Mar-Vell's decline in the novel reflects the Kristevan abject, as when he says, "It's my *body* that's betrayed me. It's my *own biology* that's killing me." Other episodes convey it in more nuanced ways.

In seeming to police its boundaries so as to ward off the "contaminating" threat of abjection, the genre as manifest in *The Death of Captain Marvel* progressively strips the protagonist of his superheroic accoutrements—literally so, in that halfway through the novel he discards his red and blue leotard, saying, "I'm afraid I've lost too much weight to look anything but *silly* in it" (emphasis in original). Instead, he dons a life-support tunic created by the computer Isaac, whose unflattering "leisure suit" design of green and beige, with an enormous turtleneck, seems to be a parody of the sleek battle uniform. Later, in his sickbed, Mar-Vell goes shirtless. But the question suggests itself: given the economy of abjection, can we not say it is rather Mar-Vell's body that has been rejected by his costume, not the other way around?

In the same vein, key plot points depicting events out of keeping with traditional notions of superheroism are oddly elided through Starlin's dramaturgy. When Mar-Vell collapses, too weak to further stand on his own, and has to be carried to bed, we only hear of it as reported by Eros. Several pages later, when Mar-Vell falls into a coma, again it happens off-panel, with Eros once more filling the role of messenger. These unshown incidents, along with the elision of Mar-Vell's corpse after his death (only part of its head appears, in shadow), betray a genre reluctance to permit the effects of "real," incurable sickness a place on the stage of representation—seemingly as a stratagem to keep them tidily quarantined lest they contaminate the "purity" of the proceedings. Precisely at those moments Marvel presumably appears at his most vulnerable and helpless—a state out of keeping with the ableist definition of the superhero, and thus taboo. Even Mentor's assertion upon learning of his friend's loss of consciousness reflects this genre anxiety, as he says, "We're too late. We have failed you, Captain Marvel." He uses not the dying man's Kree name, as has been his wont, but his superhero alias; it is not *Captain Marvel* who has failed, but his *friends* who could not manage to save him.

The "abjection apprehension" I have so far described reaches its pinnacle in the vexed issue of how to render Mar-Vell/Captain Marvel's physique in the final pages, once the evidence of his illness can no longer be occluded through scriptwriting sleight-of-hand. His body, in fact, becomes nothing less than a site of contention between the novel's urge to "realism" and "honesty" on the true effects of cancer, on the one hand, and the genre's resistance to destabilizing morbid depictions of the superhero on the other.[119] Starlin "solves" this aesthetic conundrum through a sort of compromise: he draws Mar-Vell in his deathbed somewhat gaunt, hollow-cheeked, with dark circles under his eyes, a sallow complexion, and black, "deadened" pupils. The catheters running to his nostril and chest, along with a medical monitor by the bed, complete his portrait of infirmity. But for all that, Mar-Vell, with his blond coif, broad chest and straining biceps, still cuts a strapping figure, even in repose. Adding to this impression is his robust chest hair, a staple of 1970s/early 1980s US manhood (e.g., Burt Reynolds, Tom Selleck). In short, for some readers Mar-Vell still looks awfully vital and hardbodied for a man about to meet his maker. Such was the verdict delivered by the blog Bronze Age Babies: "Starlin left him a bit too hero-looking as we were told he was failing" (2011).

For his part, Starlin defended his strategy by referring to his father's own multi-year journey with cancer and the disheartening toll it took on his body:

> [Mar-Vell] never came out looking as bad as my dad did. My dad lost a tremendous amount of weight before he passed away. I just didn't feel like I should get him down to a 98-pound, scrawny skeleton by the end of the story, because I think that would have been *a little too hard on the reader.* Plus, not everybody goes that way. A lot of folks perish before they become completely emaciated. . . . I consciously decided I didn't want to go that far down the line. I thought it would actually take away from the story. (2011, my emphasis)

Starlin insisted no one at Marvel Comics censored him or forced this representational decision—he chose it for the reasons given. Mar-Vell's body as seen in the final portions of the novel thus takes on aesthetic, ideological, and, for Starlin, autobiographical resonances which overlap—to some extent clash—on the issue of "how far to go" in one's explicit mission to show Death and Dying with a capital D, while observing a personal (as well as generic) injunction not to unnerve the reader "gratuitously." Precisely such objections, Kübler-Ross reported, exemplified the vehement resistance to her work, since "death is viewed as taboo, [and] discussion of it is regarded as morbid" (1969: 6–7), all the more so when presented in graphic terms. In weighing these various considerations, Starlin arrives at, one might argue, an uneven trade-off with abjection.[120]

Important to mention, however, is the "glass half-full" portion of this outcome. Within the parameters set by Starlin and the genre, a potent message is conveyed: in *The Death of Captain Marvel,* in the new reality the author depicts, the villain is not Thanos, not the body, not cancer. Death is a natural process, no more "villainous" than the ocean tide. The challenge, the radical new role for the superhero, as we have mentioned, is not to defy death (as if he or any of us could!) but to die well—as far as genre interdictions allow, to embrace abjection.

All that said, and moving on to the last major facet of the novel I want to treat in brief: does Starlin's reordering of the superhero plot really leave no place for the supervillain? Indeed it does not—not even for Thanos, ultimately. (Thanos, Death, and Marvel all walk off, hand-in-hand, into the light at novel's end.) And yet there is a "villain" in *The Death of Captain Marvel*: the institution of modern medicine as represented by Mar-Vell's physician Mentor. This is the work's most obliquely expressed theme, a veritable counter-text operating parallel to the primary narrative, in its shadows. After all, Mentor is also Mar-Vell's friend and ally, who takes the lead in seeking a cure for his cancer. Hence, I base my "against-the-grain" reading on subtleties of mood and dialogue, character expression, and Starlin's choices in mise-en-page. These, I argue, reflect anxieties related to the care of the dying widely discussed in the 1970s, thanks largely to Kübler-Ross, whose work sought to sensitize doctors to patients' human needs rather than look on them as mere collections of symptoms.

The dehumanizing, hyper-rational apparatus of the healthcare system, in which people routinely hooked up to machines died in sterile hospitals, cared for by doctors and staff who due in part to their own thanatophobia often avoided the topic of death, was subjected to severe critique by Kübler-Ross in *On Death and Dying*, as well as by the Death with Dignity and other movements gaining prominence in mainstream America just as Starlin was beginning his career—a process which eventually led to the widespread adoption of palliative and hospice models of care at the end of life.[121] The danger—as discussed by Dennis Waskul and Pamela van der Riet, one still present today—is that "[a patient] may experience self as a disconnected and impotent spectator to a body that everyone treats as a passive object. In this way medical interventions can easily contribute to an experience of powerlessness and alienation" (492).

The modern paternalism of medical practice, though historically recent, grew pervasive in postindustrial Western culture; as discussed in this book's introduction, an Enlightenment-era "medical gaze" in essence constructed the body though discourse as passive, moldable, legible, in short completely subordinate to the scientist/physician's trained eye. David Armstrong, channeling the Foucault of *The Birth of the Clinic*, concludes:

> The modern body of the patient, which has become the unquestioned object of clinical practice, has no social existence prior to those same clinical techniques being exercised upon it. It is as if the medical gaze, in which is encompassed all the techniques, languages and assumptions of modern medicine, establishes by its authority and penetration an observable and analyzable space in which is crystallized that apparently solid figure—which has now become so familiar—the discrete human body. (2)[122]

Along with the awe-inspiring advances of medicine in the last two centuries, then, a focus on reductive, quantifiable "cases" has removed a critical human dimension from the age-old, meaning-laden process of dying. Doctors are trained to avoid emotion, notes Deborah R. Gordon, since "as a 'thing,' the body is neither a person nor something sacred ('a thou'), but run by mechanisms and best approached objectively through the purest and most objective of languages—numbers" (30). In the twentieth century, dying itself migrated from the home (where family and community took on caregiving) to the hospital ward or nursing home (where caregiving becomes anonymous, state-driven), leaving patients to, as Waskul and van der Riet write, "negotiate a self that is pinched between the institution of medicine and the abject body itself" (491).

George Orwell, in an essay called "How the Poor Die" (1946), paints a particularly stark, class-inflected picture of the reductive "medical gaze" view of the body. Describing his experiences in a Parisian public hospital in 1929, Orwell recounts how a doctor would absently use a cirrhosis patient as a prop while he lectured to students:

As usual he neither spoke to his patient nor gave him a smile, a nod, or any kind of recognition. While he talked, very grave and upright, he would hold the wasted body beneath his two hands, sometimes giving it a gentle to and fro, in just the attitude of a man handling a rolling-pin. . . . Utterly uninterested in what was said about him, [the patient] would lie with his colourless eyes gazing at nothing, while the doctor showed him off like a piece of antique china." (357)

Michael Taussig sees more than mere callousness in such treatment; in *The Nervous System* he calls the modern clinical situation "a combat zone of disputes over power and over definitions of illness and degrees of incapacity" (99) whereby the medical establishment achieves social control over its subjects, the patients, all while "concealed by an aura of benevolence" (87). Taussig's Marxist-derived analysis concludes by likening medicine's reordering of patients' epistemological horizons to those of commodity production and the alienation of labor; he boils its message down to:

Don't trust your senses. Don't trust the feeling of uncertainty and ambiguity inevitably occurring as the socially conditioned senses try to orchestrate the multitude of meanings given to otherwise mute things. Don't contemplate rebellion against the facts of life for these are not in some important manner partially man-made, but are irretrievably locked in the realm of physical matter. To the degree that matter can be manipulated, leave that to "science" and your doctor. (89)

In short, medicine forms a branch of the vast ideological machine of domination which renders the citizen/patient docile, unquestioning, inert—exactly like Orwell's cirrhosis case. Turning back to Starlin's novel, we see that Mar-Vell acts nothing like the Parisian patient—but, though by no means as inhumane, Mentor does share some characteristics with the Parisian doctor. As representative of the "medical gaze," he diagnoses the disease, expertly naming it in different languages—Titanian ("inner decay"), Kree ("blackend"), and English ("cancer")—then pronounces Isaac's prognosis: Mar-Vell has about three months to live. Later, we learn he is giving Mar-Vell radiation treatments, and that his various interventions have "reduced [the illness'] degeneration process by some 20 percent" (emphasis in original). And while he clumsily intrudes on Mar-Vell's private life by asking if he has told Elysius about his condition—which leads to an awkward pause—Mentor throughout the novel radiates paternal compassion.

From early on, however, the reader catches glimpses of how easily that paternal feeling slips into Oedipal tension between Mentor and the younger Mar-Vell, conveyed through blocking, composition, angle, facial expressions, and other subtle cues. For example, Starlin draws Mar-Vell and Mentor like the same man at different ages: both are lean and regal, while their hair, though styled differently, is of similar length. Mentor's cape and high collar, however, give him a more Mephistophelian mien; in some aspects he seems to be an aged version of Daimon Hellstrom, the Son of Satan. Moreover, as an immortal descended from the ancient Greek gods, Mentor cannot die; as the being who turned the dead moon of Titan into a lush paradise and rules it as a benevolent monarch, he resembles the God of the Old Testament. In comparison the dying Mar-Vell, an exiled long-term guest (or less generously, refugee) on Titan, in every way seems "disadvantaged."

Many elements of this understated antagonism between Mentor/medicine and Mar-Vell/individual converge in the laboratory scene. It begins with four panels depicting futuristic Titanian technology with the captions, "Examination. Analyzation. Computation. Diagnosis," and the subsequent reading out by Mentor of Isaac's results. Strictly speaking, though, the data are superfluous. Mar-Vell already knows everything about his grave condition, thanks to his Cosmic Awareness—which does not afford him the luxury of denial. (A cutting irony: super-powers, by definition a disavowal of reality, are here rendered a tool for learning the terrible truth.) To Mentor's offer of medical intervention, Mar-Vell only shrugs, "[I]'m not expecting *miracles* from you. I'd *welcome* one, but I don't expect any" (emphasis in original). One can picture Taussig nodding as Mar-Vell asserts his autonomy and self-awareness before his doctor.

Along with such vaguely adversarial dialogue, the lab scene depicts a virtual ballet of dramatic poses as the two men discuss the repercussions of the diagnosis. Yet, curiously, at no point in their exchange do Marvel and Mentor ever look each other in the face.[123] In fact, throughout the sixty-page novel, Starlin never pictures Mar-Vell and Mentor looking eye to eye, something that doesn't happen in Mar-Vell's interactions with any of the other characters.

7.17 Mentor as embodiment of the medical gaze: the lab scene (*The Death of Captain Marvel*, 1982).

However, Mentor does spy on Mar-Vell a number of times–again, out of "parental" concern. The "silent" page in which Mar-Vell informs Elysius of his cancer shows Mentor furtively keeping watch through an interesting device: the elder appears in black,[124] narrow vertical panels (resembling tombstones) inserted between the lovers' frames. The design produces an uneasy mix of emotions: pathos, romance, violation of privacy. Mar-Vell almost seems to sense they're being watched; at the bottom of the page his gaze goes out toward the final "tombstone" panel, now solid black—Mentor has walked away.

The final element in the ambiguous relational chemistry between the two men plays out on Mentor's wizened visage. In scene after scene, often in inappropriate moments, he appears with a sullen, penetrating, even nefarious expression. If not for the speech balloons, the reader might conclude he is savoring Mar-Vell's plight; moreover, judging from his own countenance,

Mar-Vell seems to sense this antipathy as well. An especially good example occurs when, just after the hero's coughing fit on Thanos's ark early in the novel, Mentor offers to run a medi-scan. The elder's eyes have dark shadows, his lips betray the beginnings of a smirk, his pointed eyebrows and high collar add to the "demonic" impression. Mar-Vell, meanwhile, has his back to the older man, and the reader can see the unease on his face, his eyes pointed in the direction of Mentor. (Compare this tense near-exchange of gazes to the clueless, bovine expression of Eros elsewhere in the frame.)

Starlin uses very similar blocking in the lab scene, when Mentor stands uncomfortably close behind Mar-Vell and says, "Whatever you need . . ." (ellipsis in original). Again, his appearance is sinister, the partly shadowed face vaguely threatening, whereas Mar-Vell's reaction seems recalcitrant. But Mentor gives perhaps his most disconcertingly "malevolent" expression—gritted teeth, arched brows, piercing eyes, in short a villain's baleful grin—when, against a jet-black background, he announces, "We're too late. We have failed you, Captain Marvel." Recall this portrait dominates the panel above the "Ars Moriendi" image of Mar-Vell in a coma surrounded by friends, already discussed. The clash creates an unnerving full-page picture: a dying, helpless, "holy" man seemingly towered over by a giant quasi-satanic figure baring his teeth straight at the reader.

Even in closing the novel, as he covers Mar-Vell's body with a sheet, Mentor looks evil. On this last page he is also the only character who does not appear partly or fully in soft blue tones (even Mar-Vell's hair has lost its customary hue). Mentor's green-and-yellow costume stands out as the page's only vibrant color (save the red flatline on the medical monitor, which he switches off). This and his expression in the last panel make him seem apart, almost exultant, just as the tragedy hits home. And indeed it is his words that replace the accustomed disclaimer at the end of so many superhero death stories—assuring the reader this was an imaginary tale, an alternate reality, a dream—with the hopeless, funereal (triumphant?) "He's gone . . ." (ellipsis in original).

My reader may object that the evidence I have picked is circumstantial—were there such a thing as circumstantial evidence in art.[125] A less generous interpretation would be that Starlin simply has trouble depicting subtle emotions.[126] Yet the consistency with which Mentor is portrayed as interloper, snoop, meddlesome father figure, with the look of a malefactor whipping Mar-Vell on his road to Golgotha, and furthermore his role as stand-in for the medical profession which was coming in for such abuse from the Death with Dignity movement at the very time Starlin was producing his work, strongly hints at a shadow text, a story within the story that reifies in radical terms the genre's wonted superhero-supervillain agon. Mentor, then, bears the considerable symbolic weight of Oedipal, medical, ableist hegemony—hence, the

7.18 The "split-page" layout separating Mar-Vell's spirit from his body in *The Death of Captain Marvel* (1982).

choreographic, emotive, and aesthetic oddities—which the hero must resist as part of his mission to face death honestly, embrace abjection, die well, and maintain his individuality, to resist, as Waskul and van der Riet write, becoming a "spectator to your own drama" (492).

To sum up: if, for Ernest Becker, the "vital lie" of human character demands a fatuous denial of death so as to repress a paralyzing thanatophobic anxiety, for the mainstream corporate superhero this "vital lie" is central to the logic of his very existence—but it also acts to his detriment as a subject of drama (to say nothing of his humanity). By explicitly giving up that illusion, Starlin's *The Death of Captain Marvel* restores—if all too briefly—a sense of real characterological depth and complexity to the much (and justly) maligned superhero.

The fact that this ultimate human vulnerability jars irremediably with the definition of the superhero is amply displayed by the novel's "split" last page: in the top half, the "super" Mar-Vell walks spectacularly, illusionistically, off into eternity—leaving behind in the page's bottom half his mortal remains, a flatlining monitor, and grieving friends as Mentor intones, "He's gone . . .": dream vs. reality, power fantasy vs. ultimate fate, spirit vs. flesh—irreconciled.[127]

CONCLUSION: "WE'VE ALL BEEN HANDED A LOT OF GARBAGE," OR THE FIVE STAGES

Toward the end of *The Death of Captain Marvel*, as the hero lies wasting in bed, between the Spider-Men and Skrull generals he welcomes another old friend: Drax the Destroyer. The costumed, bemuscled, green-skinned Drax (a Starlin creation) looks supremely confident and strutting as he greets the bare-chested Mar-Vell; the two launch into a curious exchange that reminds us Drax once died and came back to life:

> DRAX: As you know, *I've* been to where *you're* heading. We've all been handed a lot of *garbage* throughout our lives about what death is like. *No* description I've ever heard even comes close. It's indescribable and it's really not all that bad.
>
> MAR-VELL: Thanks, Drax. But you'll forgive me if I don't *rush* off to find out if you're giving it to me straight.
>
> DRAX: Of course, take your time. (emphasis in original)

As with so many set pieces in this work, the scene operates on a deeply allegorical level that ups its revisionist stakes. On one side we see Drax, the smug, hyper-masculine, ever-resurrected superhero. Strangely enough, in his

7.19 Drax's deathbed counsel to Mar-Vell in *The Death of Captain Marvel* (1982).

tight-fitting cowl he somewhat resembles the personification of death in Ingmar Bergman's classic *The Seventh Seal* (1957); he even sports a skull-shaped broach on his cloak. Rather callously, he offers self-satisfied advice to his dying ally about the (so to speak) discovered country, making light of what everyone else considers a tragedy. Mar-Vell, on the other hand, appears as everything Drax is not: a cancer patient, stripped of his costume, about to shuffle off this mortal coil. Nonetheless, he faces down his visitor, saying with a grim or irritated expression, "You'll forgive me if I don't *rush* off . . ." Drax, in turn, doesn't seem to appreciate the sarcasm, or ignores it, with a half-smirk ("Of course, take your time").

The episode illustrates the (when all is said and done) profoundly inhuman, illusory underpinnings of the superhero, its false promise of perfectibility and eternal life—generic and ideological precepts the novel challenges in myriad ways. Drax comes off as especially absurd: in his purple "Grim Reaper"-ish get-up, he seems clownish, a walking conflux of thanato-clichés merely playing at death. Quite a contrast with Mar-Vell: horizontal to Drax's vertical, bedridden but human-looking, fallible, elsewhere in the scene reminding the reader, "There's pain and that uncertainty . . . and the fear" (ellipses in original). The dichotomy prompts the query: which is more alive, more "real"?

Partly through a structuralist approach, in this chapter I have argued that death lies, paradoxically, at the sweepingly immortalist, ableist core of the superhero project, as the crucial "other" against which the genre defines itself. The progressively more "realistic" depiction of death in superhero comics in the period examined (rife as it is with contradiction, compromise, evasion, bad faith) itself only reflects a growing awareness of issues related to mortality which fitfully seeped into US culture within a generation after World War II.

The 1969 publication of Kübler-Ross's *On Death and Dying*, with its "five stages of grief," contributed immensely to this national conversation; the rise of the Hospice, Death With Dignity, Right to Die, Disability Rights, and Assisted Suicide movements in the 1970s, along with such seminal media events as the Karen Ann Quinlan case (which helped legalize the right to withdraw life support from comatose patients), the Vietnam War, and AIDS epidemic all contributed to an atmosphere in which the old standby of simply denying death—in art and culture as well as ordinary life—proved less and less tenable. The change in public perceptions took decades and did not happen without controversy. Many Americans still struggle with these questions today.

The superhero genre, operating under an economic imperative which precluded the killing of its main characters but also necessitated topicality, greater psychological realism, and "relevance," responded in the Silver Age by introducing capital-D death through supporting figures, such as friends and loved ones. The existentialist "Death of Gwen Stacy" storyline proved a landmark for this sort of depiction, as well as an anomaly; even vulnerable "normal" characters, with whom readers had established a rapport, could not be subjected to such grisly, meaningless deaths—at least not too often. Mortality, to the extent it applied to superheroes themselves, continued to follow the formulaic "revolving door" death/resurrection model. Few heeded Jim Shooter's injunction: "Death should be handled with care. There's no formula to it, any more than there is in real life" (2012).

Jim Starlin (in fans' estimation the most death-obsessed writer in the genre) would take the Gwen Stacy formula one step further in 1982 with *The Death of Captain Marvel*, committing an act anathema to the very identity of the superhero as practiced since its inception; in the words of Quarter Bin: "Our hero died in bed, from cancer, as various immensely powerful beings looked on in bafflement at their own inability to prevent it" ("Starlin's Explorations of Immortality" 2002).

Yet as Bronfen and Goodwin remind us, "every representation of death is a misrepresentation" deflecting from the actual aesthetic and ideological issues which a given depiction truly has at stake; similarly, as Becker insists, the denial of death forms a variegated, fundamentally "dishonest" aspect of modern life. How do these insights apply to *The Death of Captain Marvel*, to the acutely problematic treatment of death in the genre as a whole? Significantly, for all Starlin's innovations, despite the novel's respected place in the canon, and perfectly in keeping with market logic—no one has followed the captain to that place "from whose bourne no traveler returns." They *do* all return, routinely. After 1982, the vast majority of superheroes continued to resemble Drax rather than Marvel, even down to their anatomy. After all, why should a genre based in fantasy and adolescent wish fulfillment obey real-world rules (especially involving such disagreeable matters as death) with any degree of consistency?

An odd kenosis, then, is effected—Captain Marvel as sacrificial lamb: "And that he died for all, that they which live should not henceforth live unto themselves, but unto him which died for them, and rose again" (2 Corinthians 5:15).[128] Only, uniquely in this case, without the "rose again." More than any other superhero, Mar-Vell—a sort of Super-Moriens—took on that radical, deconstructionist (soteriological?) mantle. Goaded by Thanos, a figure more stern guide than supervillain, he abandoned illusion in a genre *of* illusion, on the difficult journey to the acceptance of death—the ultimate "Cosmic Awareness." He died so no one else has to. So no one else does.

In closing let me offer a Kübler-Rossian outline of what this survey has covered: death representation in the genre since the advent of the Silver Age. Call it the "five stages of super-grief": anger (total inadmissibility of death; vociferous disapproval of any such depiction); denial (dreams, imaginary stories); bargaining (multiverse, alternate futures, heroic death); depression ("existential" death of normal loved ones); and acceptance (*Death of Captain Marvel*, with caveats).[129]

Mar-Vell's demise—the high watermark for this sort of representation and rightly lauded for it—proved to be a one-time feat, a pawn sacrifice inapplicable to the genre as a whole. Like Dr. Manhattan at the conclusion of *Watchmen*, the industry smiles on beatifically: "*Nothing* ends, Adrian. Nothing *ever* ends" (vol. 1, #12: 27, emphasis in original).

We mull further evidence for assessing death in the genre in the next two chapters, which examine the representation of mortality in superhero tales in more specific, contrasting contexts: the cult 1980s series *Strikeforce: Morituri* and the mega-selling early 1990s "Death of Superman" storyline. The reader should rest assured, however, that for the mainstream "spandex league," mortality remains safely, forever, denied. We may each of us, as Freud wrote, "owe nature a death" (1915A: 289),[130] but it is testament to the superhero's *unnatural*, quasi-fascist condition that he can and does escape all such earthly accountings.

8

FACING DEATH IN *STRIKEFORCE: MORITURI*

Morituri (as I originally wanted to call it) was definitely a reaction to the problems that mainstream comics had with death: I was hanging around with Chris Claremont when he was forced to kill off Phoenix—and rose to the occasion by making it powerful comics; I remember when my friend and collaborator Gene Day[1] died, which hit us all hard, and how Chris told me that that was the point when he laid to rest all his ideas about bringing Phoenix back; and how the same forces that had demanded her death now brought her back in *X-Factor*. Clones, Alternate Worlds, Time Travel, alien shapeshifters, robot simulacra—nobody ever had to die—except (like *Supergirl in Crisis on Infinite Earths*) if their movie had bombed. And if one writer wanted to really, truly, no takesy-backsies kill a character—well, after a while another writer would take over the book and bring them back. And if you certainly can't write about sex and can't write about death, what can you write about? Superheroes devolved into professional wrestling, where characters bellowed at each other and fought because they were defeated the last time. I realized the only way to write convincing comics about death (and therefore heroism) was to write death into the premise itself. (Gillis: 2013)

It begins as usual.

One group of superheroes confronts another, and due to misunderstanding and conflicted loyalties, a melée erupts. The goateed, foppishly garbed Wildcard, whose abilities allow him to sap the superpowers of others, confronts his opponent Blackthorn, sprawled on the ground.

Suddenly, something odd starts to happen: Wildcard doubles over, all aglow. The strange combustion quickly spreads, intensifies—"No*" he chokes out, "no*it's*too soon*I've*only*had*weeks—*weeks* . . ."; over four panels, before his horrified comrades, his flesh liquefies. Wildcard melts to death, screaming, "Helllplplllllllllll . . ."[2]

The fight grounds to a halt.

Created by writer Peter Gillis and artist Brent Anderson, the late 1980s Marvel team series *Strikeforce: Morituri* took on a radical organizing device for a superhero story: the persistent, inescapable surcease of its main characters—who gain their powers through an eventually fatal process. They all know they have at most a year to live. The series premise allowed for "real" death to occur routinely, a remarkable flouting of genre conventions (a denial of denial, so to speak), though its segregation from Marvel continuity—set in an "alternate" future, it mixes science fiction and war story conventions with superheroics—makes *Strikeforce* a marginal experiment without repercussions for the genre as a whole. Or does it?

This chapter examines key episodes and figures in the Gillis/Anderson original run for a consideration of death's genre-warping role in a very unusual superhero "anti-series," one which provocatively made capital-MM mortality the rule. In thinking through *Strikeforce*'s complications of the Bronze Age status quo, I will proceed from the work of two scholars, both influenced by psychoanalysis, both deeply invested in the question: what do we think about when we think about (our own) death?

THE SCREEN

In *The Denial of Death*, the cultural anthropologist Ernest Becker discusses the "vital lie" of repression, the critical disavowal of mortality which allows the "healthy-minded" to function. Yet this necessary psychological retreat from death is also a retreat from life—a self-castration not unlike an animal gnawing off its own member to escape a trap: "The irony of man's condition is that the deepest need is to be free of the anxiety of death and annihilation; but it is life itself which awakens it, and so we must shrink from being fully alive" (1973: 66).[3]

For all that, and crucially for a discussion of *Strikeforce*, Becker sees the unflinching confrontation with death—or at least what one thinks of as death—as the heart of the heroic project in the West:

> Heroism is first and foremost a reflex of the terror of death. We admire the courage to face death; we give such valor our highest and most constant adoration; it moves us deeply in our hearts because we have doubts about how brave we ourselves would be ... since primitive and ancient times (the) hero was the man who could go into the spirit world, the world of the dead, and return alive. (1973: 11–12)[4]

Yet Becker goes on to argue that our instinctual rejection of death—the "vital lie"—functions so powerfully in human psychology that it veils the awful truth no matter how "authentically" we believe ourselves to be facing it:

Even in our flirtations with anxiety we are unconscious of our motives. We seek stress, we push our own limits, but we do it with our *screen against despair* and not with despair itself. We do it with the stock market, with sports cars, with atomic missiles, with the success ladder in the corporation or the competition in the university. . . . Even in our passions we are nursery children playing with toys that represent the real world. Even when these toys crash and cost us our lives or our sanity, we are cheated of the consolation that we were in the real world instead of the playpen of our fantasies. We still did not meet our own doom on our own manly[5] terms, in contest with objective reality. It is fateful and ironic how the lie we need in order to live dooms us to a life that is never really ours. (ibid.: 56, emphasis in original)

For man inured by modernity to a "dishonest" relationship with his own mortality, even the attempt to incorporate the knowledge of final things into his psyche is doomed to failure, to inauthenticity, his valiant strivings reducible to empty projections on a "screen."

The art historian Hal Foster speaks in similar terms on visual representations of death. In his discussion of Andy Warhol's *Death in America* series, he rejects the standard "image as referential or simulacral" reductive approach to most postwar photographic art, instead reading Warhol's repetitive photoworks as in a sense both referential and not. They are obsessive repetitions of the same graphic images (real-life car crashes, disasters, mangled bodies) as a strategy to drain affect from the Real, defined in Lacanian terms as *trauma* (or a "missed encounter" with the Real):

As missed, the real cannot be represented; it can only be repeated, indeed it *must* be repeated. . . . Repetition in Warhol is not reproduction in the sense of representation (of a referent) or simulation (of a pure image, a detached signifier). Rather, repetition serves to screen the real understood as traumatic. But this very need also *points* to the real, and at this point the real ruptures the screen of repetition. It is a rupture less in the world than in the subject—between the perception and the consciousness of a subject *touched* by an image. (132, emphasis in original)[6]

This screen, a manifestation of the symbolic, or perhaps "the cultural reserve of which each image is an instance," disarms the threatening gaze from the object[7] into a tolerable image: "Call it the conventions of art, the schemata of representation, the codes of visual culture, this screen mediates the object-gaze for the subject, but it also protects the subject from this object-gaze" (140). Without this screen, Foster adds, we would be "blinded by the gaze or touched by the real" (ibid.), so that most sublimative art seeks to "tame" the violent force of the alien object-gaze at the level of the screen/image.[8]

In modern thanatophobic America, Foster argues, abject images of grisly death such as Warhol's tear at the prophylactic screen; by repeating the images the artist cements their repulsion/allure, like the proverbial act of slowing down to glimpse a highway accident: "Such images evoke the body turned inside-out, the subject literally abjected, thrown out. But they also evoke the outside turned in, the subject-as-picture invaded by the object-gaze." (149)

Foster's model of the ruptured screen helps us understand the precise nature of the dread inspired by images of a "live" corpse (in the sense of "live wire"). As *objet par excellence* of the "blinding" Real—hence its awesome power to terrify—the dead body carries its own signifying "high voltage," exactly because it presents the viewer with a human-looking absolute nothingness. Its void, contained in its horrifying object-gaze, swallows up the subject. Like the gorgons, it freezes, symbolically kills, with a look.

Little wonder, then, that for both Becker and Foster, the psyche reflexively builds defenses against "despair itself," "the Real"—in a word, death. To do otherwise . . . but then the point is that, as healthy-minded individuals, we can't do otherwise. Death haunts, threatens always to rive the mental partitions we erect against it, grinning through the gaps.[9]

AVE IMPERATOR, MORITURI TE SALUTANT[10]

In the future envisioned by *Strikeforce: Morituri*, Earth has fallen victim to alien invaders, the Horde, viking-like pillagers with an odd fixation on terran kitsch. Content to terrorize the planet from orbit, sometimes on perversely meaningless raids (e.g., causing much mayhem and loss of life to secure supplies of chocolate or old movie reels), the Horde delight as much in sadistic games and casual cruelty as in adorning themselves with mass culture "bling" (can tabs, Captain America buttons, crayons, safety pins). The Earth's ruling government, the Paideia, resolves to fight back against the vaguely scrotum-faced, militarily superior barbarians through the "Morituri process," which bestows unpredictable superpowers on those genetically suitable, even as it leaves them an extremely short lifespan.[11]

Our initial guide to this world, through whose eyes we see, is Harold Everson, a young, impressionable would-be writer mulling the thought of joining the Morituri, who are lionized as beacons of hope by a war-weary Earth. "I was getting ready to turn my life into a weapon hurled at the invaders from space," he narrates (*Strikeforce: Morituri*, vol. 1, #1: 2). In a self-reflexive nod by the authors, Everson's naïve notions of heroism are fed by *The Black Watch*, a comic book based on the real-life exploits of a Horde-blitzing trio (the first group to brave the process and gain superpowers). The story-within-a-story, full of Golden Age-y dialogue ("So what are we waiting for? Let's *hit em!*")[12], concludes with the black-clad team going out in a blaze of glory after assassinating a Horde commander, the word "Earth!" on their expiring lips (10).[13]

Like the Blackwatch, Everson wants to earn eternal glory, so that his death will "mean" something. Moreover, he sees signing up as a great literary career move. As he explains to Morituri commander Beth Luis Nion, pre-op: "I'll admit it—I intend to write about all this—maybe that way I'll become immortal" (12).[14] The jaded Nion and Dr. Kimmo Tuolema, inventor of the process, soon disabuse him of such blithe youthful notions. They rather flintily play him the "video telemetry" from the Blackwatch's actual last mission: grainy footage shows the recorded death of member Woodrow Joshua Green—not valiantly in battle, but spontaneously combusting (like Wildcard, due to the highly imperfect procedure that granted him his powers). A grim close-up presents Green's blazing skull, black flesh sloughing off, red eyes shooting sparks as he dies in agony.

"The Morituri metabolism is fundamentally incompatible with the human," Tuolema sheepishly offers, "—and Woody's body rejected it catastrophically. As any body must" (14). A stunned Everson, gazing wide-eyed at what amounts to a snuff video, cringes at his commonality with the monitor's image (should he join the team), his own "screen" savagely torn by the display of unembellished death. Significantly, he touches his still-intact cheek in a visual echo of Green's last throes, as if his own flesh might melt off at any moment (ibid.).

The grisly portrait from Green's death video haunts Everson for the rest of his days. We could say it has been haunting the Western imagination since at least the Middle Ages; the image strongly recalls the *transi*, half-decomposed corpse effigies which the historian Philippe Ariès calls "the most important minor character in the macabre iconography of the 14th to the 16th centuries" in much of Europe (113).[15] Intended as objects for the contemplation of mortality, the *transi* signifies the ineluctability, tragedy, and *grossness* of one's own physical death—the better to reorient the mind towards Godly salvation. In this they resemble the Christian *Ars Moriendi* tradition discussed in the previous chapter. Indeed, Green's blasted face (a recurring image throughout the first part of the series) serves precisely such a meditative purpose—minus the God part.

In a notable splash page, Everson sits in pajama pants (his pose a cross between Rodin's thinker and Munch's screamer) against a black background. Also standing out in the abyss, floating above him: portraits of his parents; Green's "transi" face; a scowling Horde warrior against which Everson had fought that day. The *Blackwatch* comic book lies uselessly at his feet. His interior monologue cascades in captions down the page, its language the age-old plaint of a soul pondering its lot:

> I saw my death on a video monitor! It was *nothing* like I had thought. Nothing. Death. Death is it, kid. The end of all stories. You want your stories—to shine in the light of glory—or just to be. Life is sweet, isn't it, when you flirt with death? Excitement—beauty—? But you're not flirting—you're marrying death. Guaranteed. No refunds or exchanges. And you're scared. You simply don't want to die—! But you do want to author the ultimate heroic story—to be immortal through your art. (21–22, emphasis in original)[16]

The splash amounts to a visual/verbal projection of Everson's inner struggles and fears; like much Christian art, it is spatially coded. Reading from top-left, we see the parents, representing biological connection, continuity, the march of generations, interrupted by the twin death figures of Green and the Horde (both reaching out towards the reader, one with its light rays, the other with its hand). Down at bottom-right: the hollow dream of "immortal[ity] through your art," the caption not only floating in a black void but at precisely the same level as the discarded comic book.

This complex image also contains a significant double portrait: of teammate Aline Pagrovna/Blackthorn. In one we see her terrified, recalling an earlier scene in which she suffers a panic attack, pleading, "Oh, Dr. Tuolema, I don't—I don't want to *die*—I don't want to die—!" (11, emphasis in original).[17] Another shows her after her recovery, when she confidently declares that thanks to the Morituri process "[I]'m going to be a *hero!* This *means* something, Harold!" (15, emphasis in original). Aline—the series' most torn, anguished character—appears twice as an emblem of the divided self, lost to death/life's terror, but also self-deluding, foolhardy, and brave. The brooding Everson appears precisely between the two Alines, agonizing over his choice.

Immediately after this page—reconciling himself (for now) to the object-gaze of death—Everson approaches Nion to declare he has decided once and for all to undergo the Morituri process. A panel shows him leaving the black void through a lighted doorway, seeming to step on (or step out of, transcend) the *Blackwatch* comic book he has clearly outgrown (23). The story thus signals that the rules for this series will be different from those in Marvel's mainstream (read: death-denying) titles.

Just how different would become obvious by the sixth issue, when Everson himself (now operating under the code name Vyking) falls victim to the same Morituri pitfalls as Green—and unexpectedly "burns up" while on a mission. Moreover, he expires in particularly "unheroic" circumstances, as the team

8.1 Everson confronts his death fears for the first time (*Strikeforce: Morituri*, vol. 1, #1, Dec. 1986).

pilots a hijacked Horde craft into space. Gillis and Anderson depict Everson's end with brutal economy: without warning, within five panels, his last words not exactly inspiring: "Oh no please no! Please! Not before I'm finished!" (*Strikeforce: Morituri*, #6: 16).

The fact that the series had up until then been largely focalized through Everson, and that he's grown to assume leadership of the team, does not ameliorate his fate, nor the harsh lack of sentimentality in its representation. For a fan of conventional superhero comics, the effect is one of profound shock— akin to that produced some thirty minutes into Alfred Hitchcock's *Psycho* (1960). As with Marion Crane's (Janet Leigh) scandalous murder in the shower in that classic of audience alienation, Everson's sudden demise leaves the reader with no idea what will happen next, nor with whom to identify. As disoriented, in fact, as the spacecraft with a hole blown open by Everson's stunning immolation (which his teammates have to remedy or die themselves).

Other characters in *Strikeforce: Morituri*'s original six-member lineup undergo similar journeys, though as with Vyking, Gillis and Anderson derive much of the series' power not only from the genuine suspense generated (will someone die in this issue? will it be my favorite character?),[18] but also through the very different ways in which each hero confronts his/her demise (or in Becker and Foster's terms, from the "screens" they erect to ward off existential angst). Let's turn to three examples and how they interact.

Through the Morituri process, the mild-mannered Adept/Jelene Anderson attains vast analytical powers, nearly to the point of "cosmic awareness." Her heightened senses of perception reinforce a deep Christian faith, as Anderson comes to feel increasingly "at one" with the universe. Anderson's worldview finds expression in her rather demure costume, which bears a cross along the chest and abdomen, and through scenes showing her reading the Bible. "Healing" (*Strikeforce: Morituri* , #5, Apr. 1987) opens with Adept going over John 3:2: "Beloved, now are we the sons of God, and it doth not yet appear what we shall be; but we know that, when he shall appear, we shall be like him; for we shall see him as he is."[19] She does this in remembrance of fallen teammate Lorna Raeburn/Snapdragon, saying, "You're with our creator now, Lorna, and his mercy will grant you the rewards this world is unable to offer" (1).[20]

The sociologist Clive Seale, among others, has written on the role of religion in the shadow of imminent death. He notes that, though often deemed slightly out of keeping with modernity, a stance such as Anderson's may prove advantageous for meaning-making and "heroism" at the end of life:

Religious narratives once sustained the hopes of individuals as they approached their deaths or contemplated the deaths of others. Human lives could then be cast in narratives, as at funeral orations, in which the individual was judged according to whether s/he had met the demands of a higher purpose. In this respect, the religious society is . . . an "heroic society." That is to say, it offers the individual the chance to understand his/her life as standing outside the mundane concerns of everyday life, giving the individual the opportunity to define his/her own fate by engaging in moral behavior, sacrifice, bravery and spiritual adventure in the service of a higher purpose. (1995: 598)

As the least violent Morituri (her powers geared more towards analytics and healing), Anderson in some sense has the good fortune to practice warfare according to her conscience. As her skills become highly valued by the Paideia, her teammates have to increasingly protect her in battle (*Strikeforce: Morituri*, #9: 17)—throwing her superheroic identity into some doubt. But as Gillis and Anderson insist, Adept has no easy journey: "Even though my life is with Christ, it's hard to face my own death—with calm," she broods (*Strikeforce: Morituri*, #5: 2).

What Anderson's Christianity does give her—which the others largely lack, which Everson coveted and which Seale observes—is a meaning and pattern to her existence. The others, for the most part, "don't see the common threads—the universal constants in the basics of all things as I do. I see so clearly his grand design in all things" (ibid.).

These divisions grow apparent when Anderson tries to communicate her faith to comrades, in (mostly futile) attempts to comfort their death-fears. Witness this exchange with Radian/Louis Armanetti:

> ARMANETTI: I wish I could believe as firmly as you do that there's an afterlife, Jelene, but—
> ANDERSON:—But it's true, Louis! We're God's children in Christ. All you have to do is open your heart and let him in. (*Strikeforce: Morituri*, #5: 10)

Such bald-faced expressions of religious belief—which could easily come off as caricature—nonetheless lead blogger Gabriel McKee to write:

> Though the volume of her faith is perhaps a little bit louder than one usually sees in the real world (witness the cross motif on her costume), Gillis handles it with much more subtlety than most other writers would. It's an important aspect of her character, but it's not the only aspect of it, and it never becomes a punchline. . . .
>
> In Adept, Gillis paints a picture of faith blending with science to create a deeply unified understanding of the universe, and her final moments are among the series' strongest.

8.2 Everson/Vyking's death due to the Morituri process (*Strikeforce: Morituri*, vol. 1, #6, May 1987).

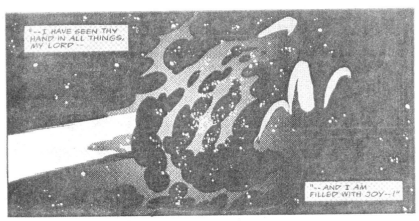

8.3 An abstract representation of the devout Adept/Anderson's death (*Strikeforce: Morituri,* vol. 1, #13, Dec. 1987).

Indeed, it is precisely the confrontation with death that represents the greatest challenge to faith (or the lack of it). Anderson's takes place just after the series' one-year mark, in issue 13, while racing to Earth on a Horde spacecraft. As the nearness of her demise dawns on her, she bids farewell to a devastated Pagrovna:

PAGROVNA: God, no, no, no, no—!
ANDERSON: Don't cry, Jelene [*sic*].²¹ He's very close—come to take me home. My true life is about to begin—! . . . I want you to know I love you all, and I'll be waiting for you all to join me.
PAGROVNA: Jelene, no—! (*Strikeforce: Morituri,* #13, Dec. 1987: 3).

As death approaches, Adept's powers surge, leading to a supreme sense of oneness with all things—which only cuts her off further from her mourning teammates. White crosses fill her pupils, serving as a somewhat kitschy Christian symbol, though also as a classic signifier of death in comic strips and cartoons (ibid.). Anderson's dignified death (oddly, she does not burn up like the others) would seem to seal her bona fides as Kierkegaard's ideal "knight of faith": "Humanly speaking, he is mad and cannot make himself understandable to anyone . . . [He] knows that it is inspiring to give up himself for the universal, that it takes courage to do it, but that there is also a security in it precisely because it is a giving up for the universal" (76).²²

But in the end (so to speak), Gillis and Anderson resort to a (perhaps) symbolic, abstract representation of Adept's off-frame death. In a page-width rectangular panel, we see what could be Anderson's astral-form hand in space, caught in some sort of screentone energy shape, a yellow beam (possibly the ship's contrail) bisecting it; two captions read: "I have seen thy hand in all things, o lord—and I am filled with wonder and contentment" (#13: 4).[23]

Critically—and in contrast to a "Christian" portrayal—the series' authors leave what precisely happens to Adept at the end of her life open to speculation. Did she go to heaven? Was she clasping God's hand? Were those shapes in space just random energy bursts? All we have to go on is our heroine's body, "miraculously"(?) un-immolated, brought home. Gillis and Anderson leave it to the reader to ponder this inert flesh—did it ever house a soul? Has it fled? Did it ever exist? Was Adept enlightened or deluded? Much of *Strikeforce: Morituri*'s dramatic power (and perhaps, its fond remembrance by fandom as a cult series ahead of its time) rests on just such grown-up ambiguity and opportunities for readerly agency.[24]

If Adept's case represents the religious "screen" against death, Marathon/ Robert Greenbaum embraces a more nihilistic approach. No character undergoes a greater personality shift in the series. As the group's "strong-man" figure, Greenbaum starts off as a gentle giant; not unlike Steve Rogers before becoming Captain America, he was a "mousy" skinny kid, pre-Morituri process, and remains self-consciously bashful (*Strikeforce: Morituri*, #3: 10). Scarred by battle and the untimely death of Vyking, however, Greenbaum transforms into a bloodthirsty killer.[25] His only purpose is endless revenge against the Horde. Grim, driven, robotic, he comes to spout such Punisher-worthy dialogue as: "Deterrence isn't enough. Annihilation is enough" (*Strikeforce: Morituri*, #9: 18). His violent single-mindedness starts to disconcern his teammates, including Pagrovna as she watches him train (*Strikeforce: Morituri*, #6: 5) and Armanetti, who witnesses Marathon coldly brand an M on his face with a laser (*Strikeforce: Morituri*, #11: 11). Then there is this exchange with Adept:

> GREENBAUM: Nothing's wrong, nothing's right. There's no room for any of that. We fight and die, and all that matters is how many of the enemy we can kill first.
>
> ANDERSON: Oh, no, Robert, no! There's time for everything even if life is only a day! We are God's children, and he loves us! Please don't despair!
>
> GREENBAUM: Oh, Jelene, if only I could believe that. (*Strikeforce: Morituri*, #6: 10)

Like Achilles, Marathon's wrath ultimately leads him to turn against his superiors; when Strikeforce Commander Nion's strategy clashes with his own agenda, he emotionlessly informs her: "Strikefore Morituri's mission is to attack and destroy the alien Horde. If the Paideia tries to get in the way of that, we will no longer serve the Paideia" (*Strikeforce: Morituri*, #9: 13).

Greenbaum's creed, as he tells his closest friend, is "No, Jelene, no hope. But no fear either" (*Strikeforce: Morituri*, #7: 22), a renunciation of conventional heroism in favor of a hyper-masculine death drive—which recalls Becker's dictum: "We push our own limits, but we do it with our *screen against despair* and not with despair itself" (1973: 56, emphasis in original). By embracing fearlessness, hatred, and sadism, Marathon has only burrowed deeper into his own disavowal of personal death and projected that fear into destructive acts against others.[26]

That something "not right" is going on in Greenbaum's psyche—which directly affects his actions as a nominal superhero—is visually coded by artist Brent Anderson through "abjected" portraits which depict Marathon with limbs or head protruding from the panel (as in the two examples just cited). Another striking instance of "abjection" occurs when he confronts a pair of Horde warriors—almost his entire body lies outside the frame (*Strikeforce: Morituri*, #5: 18).

I have discussed the Kristevan abject at length in chapter 7, in relation to Jim Starlin's *The Death of Captain Marvel*; here I only wish to emphasize how such "off-kilter" portraits signal Marathon's unhinging—mental as well as moral—from the superhero's expected role, in effect threatening it. By stepping outside the panel borders' confines into the white space beyond, he is rupturing not only the page's modular design but, in the terms of anthropologist Mary Douglas, inviting the danger of social pollution that emerges from "transgressing the internal lines of the system" (141). In sum, Marathon's death-fetish disrupts the myth of the superhero as "good" and "life-affirming"—his "self-abjection" from the page design represents that disruption's aesthetic correlative.[27]

Furthermore, over the course of the series he appears increasingly villain-like (another marker of something being "wrong"). Thus, when he overrules any suggestion that the team withdraw from battle against the entire Horde space fleet by declaring, "We fight—and die," not only does Marathon's muscled, armored arm exceed the panel border, but his face is shadowed, his stance menacing, all against a black background that fades to white as it nears the much diminished Armanetti (*Strikeforce: Morituri*, #6: 20). At such moments, Greenbaum is not merely suicidal; he is jeopardizing the entire team's lives for the sake of his bloodlust.

If death is truly what Greenbaum wants, like all super-soldiers in *Strikeforce: Morituri* he soon gets it. Yet the depiction of Marathon's final moments represents one of the most bizarre and paradigm-shifting sequences of this or any mainstream superhero series.

In one sense, the scene comprises a standard heroic death: like Ferro Lad, Marathon sacrifices himself to destroy a Horde ship while his comrades

8.4 One of many Marathon/Greenbaum "abjected" portraits (*Strikeforce: Morituri*, vol. 1, #6, May 1987).

escape to space. Feeling the Morituri effect start to overwhelm his body, he elects to release his pent-up energy in one annihilating burst. "I don't want— need–anything more than this!" he tells Armanetti (*Strikeforce: Morituri*, #12: 19). But Gillis and Anderson choose to "intercut" this more conventional depiction with the mundane death of Commander Beth Luis Nion back on Earth, also due to the Morituri process (she had secretly undergone the procedure to no avail, as the superpower gained is useless for battle). The climax unfolds over three extraordinary pages, whose designs grow increasingly unorthodox.

8.5 The deaths of Greenbaum and Nion (*Strikeforce: Morituri*, vol. 1, #12, Nov. 1987).

Page twenty: In three disjointed tiers, Greenbaum's crackling body spills out of his costume; Pagrovna (who has just learned she is pregnant) is comforted by Everson's mother; the team heads to the escape craft—and taking up the central panel in the middle of all this, Dr. Tuolema holds vigil at Nion's death-bed. Captions, presumably communicating Greenbaum's last thoughts, read: "It will be—it will—be a good—a good way—a good way to—."

Page twenty-one: Three tiers show the team boarding their ship; Greenbaum starting to explode; Adept engaging the warp drive; and Tuolema and Nion bidding farewell (their panels of "calm" death no longer central, but imbricated with the superheroic action). Captions read: "It will be—it will be a—a good—a good way—a good way to—." The expected verb ("die") is never uttered. But more intriguingly, it is no longer so clear this discourse emanates from Greenbaum's frenzied consciousness. Couldn't these words apply just as well to Nion's leave-taking with the man she loves? More weirdly, the final panel, a close-up of Greenbaum's face as he starts to burn up, is "split" by a portrait of Anderson, who in the previous panel declares, "The Lord keep you, Robert—." That "Robert" is repeated in the final caption, over Greenbaum's face, which moreover seems to answer back, "Jelene—!" (An "abjected" sound effect—"SRIP"—signals Greenbaum's imminent immolation.) We thus have the strong implication through dialogue and page design that Anderson and Greenbaum make telepathic contact – more than that: they achieve an overlapping of their identities.

Page twenty-two: In one of the most challenging comics page designs I have ever encountered, twenty-two panels (or seventeen, depending on how on one counts) depict Greenbaum's detonation, which destroys the Horde ship, as the others fly away; several characters' expressions; Nion's death; Tuolema mourning over her body; both Anderson and Jelene in astral form (?); and the last expression of Nion's superpower—to make a field of flowers bloom. The artist renders all this through two overlapping "panel-ripples": twin circular shapes, like targets, which intersect each other, creating additional smaller panels where the gutters meet. The top "target's" bullseye depicts the ship's explosion (in black), while the lower bullseye is comprised of Tuolema weeping over Nion's body in "long shot" in a green-dominant field of verdure and blossoms.

These rounded, "maternal" shapes constituting panels actualize a boundlessness and transcendence, a supreme breakdown of barriers at the moment of death, which the previous two pages only imply; like the flowers opening their petals, this page gloriously fulfills its predecessors' potential. (At the same time, paradoxically, the "targets" are contained by a "coffin-like" rectangular outer border.) Aside from its amazing symmetry—the top explosion and bottom blooms mirror each other; the faces of Lisieux, Anderson and

Nion form a sort of feminine totem pole; the relationship of dark and light elements recalls a yin-yang symbol—this wordless "mandala-page" advances several tantalizing ideas about . . . in a sense, about everything: life, death, birth, love, hate, male, and female principles, and many other mysteries.

For one thing, Jelene and Robert form twin astral portraits facing away from each other across the second "tier," their expressions similarly ecstatic, even eroticized, like a meditating caryatid and telamon supporting the structure of the page, visually and telepathically linked. (There is no death.) Counterposed to them, immediately below, we see in succeeding panels a weeping Tuolema, Nion's lifeless visage, and their clasped hands. (There is death.) Connection and contradiction freely co-exist through the page's architectonics: mechanical (ship), organic (flowers); twin bursts of explosion and bloom; violence and death coalescing with new life—the birth of the flowers; the "birth" of the ship, barreling away from the explosion-flower like Kal-El's rocket-crèche in the genre's urtext. A close-up of Anderson (in her material form) occupies a central position in the "mandala's" architecture—her analytical powers taking in the vast complexity of the design, seeing the endless connections which the page opens up to the reader's gaze. (Spiky lines shoot directly out of her head, almost as if she were projecting the page's content itself.) The composition even seems to "revive" deceased characters: are those Everson and Raeburn looking on from "interstice" panels on the extreme middle-right and -left? Has the life/death barrier definitively been severed? (This is implied by the story's title: "The Birthgrave.")

Though only scratching the surface, I hope the preceding ekphrasis conveys some of this image's complexity. Its page design, itself evocative of blooming flowers/explosions, enacts a dissolution of borders (in various senses); taps an ancient mode of figuring death in terms of birth;[28] all the while announcing that there is no abjection here—everything is ordered, universal, belongs, in the scheme of things, symmetrical, self-contained, every piece in relation to every other piece. It is a dramatic reminder that, in the words of Joseph Witek, "panels on the page always create narrative meaning both as sequences and as spatial arrangements" (2008: 153).[29]

The "simultaneous" "telepathic" death of Nion and Greenbaum, figured thus, likewise explodes gender dichotomies—recalling recent scholarship on comics' image/text pairing as a fundamentally feminist practice.[30] As Hillary Chute argues, "While we may read comics' spatializing of narrative as part of a hybrid project, we may read this hybridity as a challenge to the structure of binary classification that opposes a set of terms, privileging one" (2010: 10).[31]

We may therefore read the sequence's subversion of conventional comics form as heralding an alternate "feminine" mode for depicting the end of life, identified by sociologist Seale as "aware dying":

The heroic script of aware dying contains specifically female elements . . . [It] contains elements of the traditional masculine heroism . . . whereby dying people fought external and internal enemies, courageously passing through stages of anger, fear and denial to eventual acceptance. However, the emotional labor in reaching acceptance of death and the caring talk and emotional accompaniment . . . became opportunities to demonstrate a female heroics of care, concern and emotional expression. (1995: 611)

Greenbaum's affectless hyper-masculine will-to-violence, Nion's powerlessness and "failed" life—their "screens"—are thus transformed through the figuration of their deaths into something grander, richer, universal, beautiful.

As we have seen, each character in *Strikeforce: Morituri* faces death on her own psychological terms. But only one's journey yields any evidence, albeit ambiguous and tantalizing, of an afterlife—in a sequence arguably even more aesthetically radical than Greenbaum/Nion's "mandala-page."

Scaredycat/Pilar Lisieux, a second-generation Morituri, considers "spiritual energy" the true source of her powers (*Strikeforce: Morituri*, #9: 2). With her rather silly sobriquet, bouffant-like hairstyle and eclectic "New Age" beliefs, Lisieux is the closest the series comes to an outright religious caricature.[32] Note this repartee with a bemused Anderson:

LISIEUX: So you're a Christian, Jelene? Great! I'm a mystic!
ANDERSON: Do you—believe in the Christ, Pilar?
L: Oh, of course! He was one of the great masters! My guide always speaks about him with reverence!
A: Your . . . guide?
L: Uh-huh . . . My guide on the other side. (*Strikeforce: Morituri*, #9: 6, ellipses in original)

But things get more serious—or at least much more abstruse—upon Lisieux's death in battle on the Serengeti Plain. As she passes, the last two pages of *Strikeforce: Morituri* #19 "open up" to a borderless, increasingly white spacedominated expanse superficially reminiscent of those in reported "near death experiences" of the 1970s and 1980s.[33] Line borders break down, comprising only part of some panels. As Lisieux walks into this "white space," an unidentified man greets her, speaking not in word balloons but in quoted dialogue contained within his featureless body (not unlike Richard Outcault's Mickey Dugan, aka the Yellow Kid, from the turn-of-the-century strip *Hogan's Alley*). "Welcome, Pilar!" he says, "Welcome to the true adventure!" (n.p.).

Promising that all Lisieux's deceased teammates are waiting for her, the smiling stranger beckons on. "Is it everything I imagined it would be?" she

8.6 Scaredycat/Lisieux meets (hallucinates?) her "spirit guide" (*Strikeforce: Morituri*, vol. 1, #19, Jun. 1988).

asks. The man winks, answering, "Oh, it's completely different!" (ibid.). On the next and final page, Lisieux and the stranger (both clad in white) set off hand in hand into the featureless void, now entirely emptied of panel borders. Their "floating" sequential figures diminish in a top-left-to-bottom-right diagonal, growing more abstract, until they "vanish." Only a washed-out clump of Serengeti grass at top-left marks the material world Scaredycat leaves behind forever.

Of the many things to say about it, the first is obviously that a two-page sequence such as this is exceedingly rare (both formally and content-wise) in superhero comics. (Though Thanos, Death, and Mar-Vell walking together into a bright light at the end of *The Death of Captain Marvel* seems to be a direct predecessor.) Its open-endedness, in which it outshines even the death representations of Anderson, Greenbaum, and Nion, so utterly subverts both the genre's conventional page design and logic as to render any message of "heroism" moot. In other words, if in the "mandala-page" nothing is abjected but conveyed as part of some universal order, here we see a space of *total* abjection: Lisieux has ventured beyond the confines of the panel, life, the generic borderline itself. Everything becomes potential, undetermined, almost Suprematist in its absolutism, hence the white garb and "empty" final page.

In other words, the sequence represents the "triumph" of the comics margin. As Thierry Groensteen notes: "Reduced to the circumference of the page, the margin remains far from indifferent on the aesthetic plane, or even on the semantic plane. Even empty, the space of the margin cannot be totally neutral. . . . This space is defined by its area or, to be more precise, by its breadth." (31). Gillis/Anderson's evocation of an "afterlife" constitutes the expansion of the margin to a supernal, totalizing "breadth." But what precisely does it *mean?*

Firstly, we may dispense with the notion that the sequence definitively settles for a "heavenly," life after death depiction—rather than simply another example of a Morituri seeing what they want to see projected on her subjective screen. Gillis himself strongly prefers such an ambiguous, "balanced" reading, as he explained to me:

> I didn't intend for that scene to be an answer at all. I always intended to do a white light sequence in the book—but leave open the possibility that it's just the brain engaging in a last flare-up before ceasing to function.[34] So it was carefully (as far as I'm capable of it) balanced . . . I don't know whether there's life after death in our world, and that certainly shapes my life. The only way the strip could have life for me is to have that doubt, fear, and hope in there as well—and to forego writerly omniscience. (2013)

8.7 Lisieux walks off into "eternity" (*Strikeforce: Morituri*, vol. 1, #19, Jun. 1988).

Thus, in a rush of endorphins and imagination as she expires, Lisieux (perhaps—the matter remains ever-open) has her metaphysics confirmed, the stranger reveals himself as her "spirit guide" and she launches on her "true adventure," a realization of Herman Hesse's poem "Stages": "Even the hour of our death may send / Us speeding on to fresh and newer spaces, / And life may summon us to newer races. / So be it, heart: bid farewell without end" (444). To put it another way, we can simply read the sequence as literal. Yay, afterlife!

But something else, what we might term the sequence's self-reflexivity, merits attention. Are we to simply elide the fact that Brent Anderson's naturalistic portrait of the "stranger" bears more than passing resemblance to none other than *Strikeforce: Morituri* editor Carl Potts?[35] Or that the Serengeti battle scene, even before Scaredycat's death, contains an unusually high number of white, "empty" backgrounds—a comment, perhaps, on mainstream comics' breakneck production schedule and its concomitantly "crude" aesthetics, absurdly borne out by the "white void's" economy of depiction? (How long does it take to pencil, ink, and color a "white void," after all?)[36] Does not the stranger/pseudo-Potts's balloon-less dialogue betoken an earlier, seminal period of comics history, evoking nostalgia for a more primal, "innocent" stage of the medium's development? (And so on.) Such touches lend the episode a metatextual, quasi-Morrisonian tinge that itself mocks notions of a "serious" treatment of life after death.

In sum, Lisieux's afterlife vision is pathetic, deluded, affirming, inspirational, sly, naïve, intertextual, hermetically sealed, self-undermining, transcendent, subjective, objective, as welcome to any potential reading as its white expanse. Above all, it is unfinalizable. It forecloses nothing (least of all death) without resorting to such narrative dodges as a caption announcing, "Well, let's not feel *too* badly! After all, this was only an *imaginary* story . . . and the chances are a *million to one* it will *never* happen!"[37]

More "honest," over-determined depictions of death and its screens, such as those in *Strikeforce: Morituri,* partake of Elisabeth Bronfen's paradoxical point that mortality lies at the event horizon of the real—only making it all the more "fictive":

[Death] is the one privileged moment of the absolutely real, of true, non-semiotic materiality as de-materializing or de-materialized body; it is a failure of the tropic. Non-negotiable and non-alterable, death is the limit of language, disrupting our sign system and image repertoire. Signifying nothing, it silently points to the indetermination of meaning so that one can speak of death only by speaking other. As the point where all language fails it is also the source of all allegorical speaking. (54)

CONCLUSION: DEATH COMES TO THE GENRE

This chapter has examined several characters from *Strikeforce: Morituri* as case studies of the varying psychological responses to imminent death. In this regard the series belongs very much in the tradition of "facing death" narratives, which stretches from medieval morality plays (*Everyman*) to Leo Tolstoy's *The Death of Ivan Ilyich* (1886) to Leonid Andreyev's "The Seven Who Were Hanged" (1908) to Stanley Kubrick's *Paths of Glory* (1957) to Ingmar Bergman's *The Seventh Seal* (1957) to Sam Raimi's *The Quick and the Dead* (1995)—to name but a few.

But in essence *Strikeforce* and its predecessors all retell (in endless variations) one of the oldest stories of human civilization: that of Gilgamesh, the ancient Babylonian warrior who must first see his beloved friend Enkidu fall in battle, then bitterly resign himself to the inevitability of his own death: "My beloved friend has turned into clay – / my beloved Enkidu has turned into clay. / And won't I too lie down in the dirt / like him, and never rise again?" (Stephen Mitchell: 168).

How does the novel introduction of irreversible mortality in Gillis/Anderson's superhero tale warp the genre? I argue that it does so along the following interlocking registers:

Feminization of a Traditionally Masculine Heroic Project[38]
Intensification of Religious Tropes
Classic Death Symbols[39]
Foregrounding of Neurotic Screens Against Trauma
Experimentation with Form (Nion, Greenbaum, Lisieux's deaths)
Ambiguity
Heightened Suspense (will my favorite character die in this issue?)

Above all, *Strikeforce: Morituri*'s premise—its *raison d'être*, Gillis contends—functions to repudiate the market-driven, drama-sapping elision of death in mainstream superhero comics. It flouts an industry practice whereby, as the "Revolving Door of Death" blog series puts it, "these tales involve little more than a narrative justification for a death (including commercial concerns like the desire to spike sales of a title), a pretext for undoing it, and a convoluted explanation for the vacated coffin" (Quarter Bin: Oct. 2002).

All the same, Gillis/Anderson's inversion of expectations[40]—apart from the series' ancillary pleasures and pitfalls—ultimately has little to do with "death." As discussed, the authors are hardly interested in exploring what that is "in reality." What they are after, as Gillis had previously attempted in his "What

If the Invisible Girl Had Died?" (*What If?*, vol. 1, #42, Dec. 1983, Gillis/Frenz) is a return to the dramatic stakes which only real, "no takesy-backsy" death confers.

Solely under such conditions, in the words of Sigmund Freud, has "Life ... indeed, become interesting again; it has recovered its full content" (1915: 291).

9

DEATH, BEREAVEMENT, AND "FUNERAL FOR A FRIEND"

We did eight issues of Superman's funeral, where he was literally a dead body, and we thought that was the most daring part of the whole plan. There was a strong analogy for how we felt, which was that Superman was being taken for granted. We wanted to remind people that some of the values that Superman stands for are still important. (Mike Carlin, quoted in Daniels: 168)[1]

Superman died on November 18, 1992. America paid attention.

The event, picked up by news outlets throughout the country and world, reported the end of an era; after fifty-four years, the DC comics hero with the forelock, garbed in red, yellow, and blue, who fought for nothing less than "truth, justice and the American way," had perished as befits what one commentator called a "secular American messiah" (Daniels: 19): fallen gloriously in battle, saving his hometown Metropolis from a monstrous menace.[2]

Of course, like many superheroes before and since, Superman did not *die*—he "died." Six months later, he came back to a grateful world and notably apathetic press—setting off a pattern of reportage which has continued up until the late 2000s "deaths" and returns of Batman/Bruce Wayne and Captain America/Steve Rogers—and beyond.

But the 1992–93 "Death of Superman" storyline, whatever its level of penetration into US mainstream consciousness, has definitively emerged in fan discourses of the last twenty years as a touchstone for everything gone wrong in the superhero comics industry of the 1990s, with its obsessive focus on speculator-driven, media-stoking "mega-events"; lack of respect for beloved, decades-old characters and long-devoted fans who bristle at seeing their icons tarnished; and crass commercialism leading to a mid-decade comics collectibles bubble and crash.

Chuck Rozanski, president of the retailer Mile High Comics, minced no words in 2004: "Frankly, I view that particular marketing event as being the greatest catastrophe to strike the world of comics since the Kefauver Senate hearings." Aside from linking it to 1950s government scrutiny which led to the industry-wide Comics Code, and acknowledging other factors which led to the 1990s collector's market crash, Rozanski noted that "the *Death of Superman* promotion inadvertently exposed to the general public (many of whom ignorantly bought into the prevailing delusion that all comics were collectibles that infinitely rose in value) the 'Ponzi Scheme' reality of the market for recent back issue comics" (Rozanski).

Writing in 2011, blogger Avi Green summed up the hard feelings with which many in the fan community now regard the storyline: "It's been nearly two decades since that farce, and nobody's going to pay diddly for the story today; it's utterly worthless and just clutters the bargain bins. But more alarming is the kind of attitude cultivated at the time—to care more about monetary than entertainment value" (Green). The storyline's title thus acquired a double meaning: the "death" of the character Superman as well as—goes the argument—the demise of a pre-1990s model of superhero comics production that privileged nostalgic reverence over short-term profit.

More than that: the "Death of Superman" story arc stands accused of trivializing death, through a cheap dramatic gimmick with no real repercussions, since publisher DC and its parent company Time Warner would never seriously consider eliminating one their best known corporate emblems, with its merchandising, TV and movie revenue stream.[3] Quite the opposite: the storyline—in part through the press-baiting strategies mentioned—temporarily revived a comics series that had found itself in a serious sales decline since the end of the Christopher Reeve film series; the "death" issue (*Superman*, vol. 2, #75, Jan. 1993) sold an astonishing six million units. (Comics shops across the country reported lines out the door, made up of fans and opportunists eager to buy multiple copies.) And as media events go, it certainly wasn't subtle: the better to capitalize on the collectibles mania, DC sold the issue in various formats, including a Direct Market Memorial Collector's Edition, which featured the comic book in a black polybag with the "S" logo dripping blood (others featured a tombstone façade with the engraving "Herein Lies Earth's Greatest Hero"), containing a commemorative card, poster, stamps, *Daily Planet* death edition/obituary, and black armband.[4]

All the same, over time critical regard for the storyline was not uniformly negative. While calling it "a calculated stunt to be sure" and "the latest in a series of concerted DC efforts to revive the Man of Steel's lackluster commercial performance," Bradford Wright noted the storyline served all the same as "a powerful metaphor for American culture and the comic book industry in the post-Cold War era" (283).

Indeed, as the best known example of superhero mortality and its repercussions in the genre, the "Death of Superman" arc serves as a valuable case study in, among other things, how a supposedly death-averse society like late twentieth-century America addressed mortality and bereavement through its popular culture. The storyline offers a compelling snapshot of US attitudes to grief and the "celebrity funeral" at the dawn of the 1990s, a period when those attitudes—due in part to the Death Awareness and Death with Dignity movements; the AIDS epidemic; and reassessments of the Vietnam conflict—were in flux. (As we will see, Superman's demise also displayed some marked continuities with earlier periods' death representations.)

"If human social life is an attempt to construct a refuge of meaning and purpose against the meaningless chaos that is nature," wrote the sociologist Clive Seale, "then study of the human approach to death and bereavement affords an unusually clear opportunity to perceive some of the most fundamental aspects of these constructions" (1998: 11). This chapter examines the landmark (if much maligned) "Death of Superman" storyline as one of those opportunities: for what it says, fifty-four years after Superman's debut, about the public nature of grief and the superhero in a media-saturated US at the end of the twentieth century.

THE DEATHS OF SUPERMAN

For all the media and fan outcry, Superman and his loved ones had faced death and near-death long before. Mortality, in fact, functions as a specter haunting the character from the very beginning; he came to Earth, after all, as a result of his home planet Krypton exploding, a holocaust that killed nearly every one of his race. Loss forms the subject of such early Silver Age stories as "The Last Days of Superman" (1962), "The Last Days of Ma and Pa Kent" (1963) and, as discussed in chapter 7, "The Death of Superman" (1961).

Superman's relationship to death has endured through decades and genre trends. Several stories by Elliot S. Maggin in *Superman*, vol. 1, #400 (Oct. 1984), celebrating the character's forty-fifth anniversary, explored questions of old age, nostalgia, and immortality, the stubborn refusal of this figure to succumb to time and death, along with the persistent structuring threat of just such an outcome. The Reaper himself makes an appearance in a stand-alone work, *Superman: Where is Thy Sting?* (2001), in which the Man of Steel, having outlived everyone and everything, witnesses the end of the Earth in despair. Finally, Grant Morrison and Frank Quitely made the hero's confrontation with death the motivating theme in their winkingly retro *All-Star Superman* series (2005–08).

The best essay on the character (perhaps the best ever written on superheroes), Umberto Eco's 1962 "The Myth of Superman,"[5] is in some sense an elaborate explanation for why he cannot die, yet remains haunted by death:

caught between a mythological and a romantic mode of serial narrative, Eco maintains, the superhero acts, but in acting "consumes himself," "takes a step toward death"—yet "Superman cannot consume himself, since a myth is 'inconsumable'" (150), or timeless. As a result, Superman's writers concocted various ways around that paradox, including an "extremely hazy" relationship to time and the "Imaginary Stories," in which such "consumption" constraints do not apply.[6]

Another way scholars have framed the question of Superman's "immortality" is through the trope of human perfectibility; Douglas Wolk, for example, calls him "a perfect person," though "the catch is that he's not actually human" (2007: 97). Richard Reynolds calls Superman a "man-god" (12). This signals religious, especially Christological associations, as argued by, among others, Koosed and Schumm: not unlike Jesus, they contend, "Superman always gets back up, his body heals from injury almost instantaneously, and even death is only temporary." Daniels compares him to Moses and Jesus, "sent from above to redeem the world" (19).[7] Thus, in 1992, the seemingly real prospect of the Man of Steel fallen and, so to speak, not rising on the third day, seized the imagination.[8]

It goes without saying that a deceased Superman is not like just any dead body. Recall anthropologist Katherine Verdery's reading of the "famous" corpse and its powerful affective influence on the masses, which renders the distinguished dead body a powerful, manipulable, "living" symbol ripe for ideological exploitation: "Words can be put into their mouths—often quite ambiguous words—or their own actual words can be ambiguated by quoting them out of context. It is thus easier to rewrite history with dead people than with other kinds of symbols that are speechless" (29).

In short, the famous deceased—such as America's first and greatest superhero—bear an outsize weight in how they affect the "national narrative." This makes them irresistible to appropriate for myriad overt and illicit aims. Tellingly, throughout the "Death of Superman" storyline Superman's body appears precisely as an object to be "appropriated," whether physically by Lex Luthor and rogue US government agents, or symbolically, be it by a mourning nation or commemorative funeral merchandise hawkers.

"FUNERAL FOR A FRIEND"

Dispersed over some thirty issues of continuity in various Superman and non-Superman publications, the "Death and Return of Superman" story arc (as it came to be called) dealt with an apocalyptic villain, dubbed Doomsday, whose Hulk-like bulk, stony jagged protuberances, and brutish asociability carve a path of destruction across the country. Superman, together with several other much-mangled superheroes, makes his last stand in downtown Metropolis, battling the monster to a standstill in the (in)famous *Superman #75*. Through a series of single-panel splash pages, this landmark issue depicts an exhausted and battered Man of Steel, desperate to save his friends and loved ones, sacrificing himself to finally deliver the knock-out punch; hero and villain collapse together among the rubble. Caught up in a weeping Lois Lane's arms (an allusion to Michelangelo's 1498–99 *Pietà*), Superman breathes out his last words: "Doomsday . . . is he . . . is he . . ." (Kahan 1993B: n.p.).

While the death seemed a standard (if unusually prolonged) heroic sacrifice, what unfolded over the next eight issues of the *Superman* title, in an arc called "Funeral for a Friend,"[9] proved a radical departure from the generic norm. Superman the person recedes, replaced by an inert object—his corpse—wrangled over, poked, manipulated, and interred (and almost immediately stolen). The impact of his unimaginable death on his friends, family, and enemies takes center stage: his fiancée Lois weeps inconsolably, but insists on working through her sorrow at the *Daily Planet*; photographer Jimmy Olsen agonizes over the sale of a career-making scoop, his picture of Superman's final collapse; the corporate magnate Lex Luthor (in his cloned, red-haired body) publicly praises the Man of Steel and finances his memorial, but secretly seethes at having been robbed of his just vengeance ("Try as I might, I couldn't *kill* Superman, but sure as *hell* . . . I'm going to *bury* him" [Kahan 1993A: 58, emphasis in original]); Superman's adoptive parents, Ma and Pa Kent, mourn helplessly in Kansas as their son's body receives a lavish state funeral in faraway Metropolis. "We lost a son," utters a heartsick Jonathan Kent, "but the world lost a *hero* . . . and they're gonna bury that hero with *full honors*" (59, emphasis in original).

As that quote announces, a major theme woven through these episodes is the authenticity of private grief (Lane, the Kents, Lana Lang, Bibbo Bibbowski) contrasted with the cynicism and theatricality of public mourning (Luthor, the merchandise hawker,[10] Agent Westfield). Page design underscores that distinction at several points. The Luthor and Kent dialogue cited above appears on facing pages, with Metropolis depicted in sunny tones, while the Kent home interior appears in shadow (its inhabitants' dejected faces never clearly seen). Most starkly, the page depicting Superman's actual interment, as Wonder Woman and Green Lantern slide the stony lid over his sarcophagus, the panels bordered by the faces of mourners (77), confronts its opposite: the Kents alone, sorrowfully burying some mementos of the deceased in the field where they first found him, as an infant (76). Crucially, Lois, the link between public and private grief, appears among the above-mentioned border portraits (evocative of nineteenth-century funeral cards), though she actually is

9.1 The "pietà" pose opens the "Funeral for a Friend" storyline (*Adventures of Superman*, vol. 1, #498, Jan. 1993).

9.2 The mourners look on as Superman is laid to rest by his comrades (*Superman: The Man of Steel*, vol. 1, #20, Feb. 1993).

not at the funeral; disgusted by the ceremony, she at that moment is telephoning the Kents.

Lois's there/not there depiction as regards her public lamentations attests to the ways societal rules of "proper mourning" shape—but are also resisted by—private grief, amounting to a blurring of the two. The British sociologist Tony Walter has critiqued what he considers the too-neat formulation of grief as private, "natural" emotional expression over loss and mourning as public "cultural" expression over loss, arguing that culture affects, polices, and determines "private" grief to no less a degree than it does public mourning. It is a process not without a degree of oppression: "Many . . . mourning rituals seem designed more to assist the dead and the power structure of society than the bereaved individual," he notes (29).

In contrast, "Funeral for a Friend," with its insistent juxtaposition of the extravagant burial ceremony "with *full honors*" and Superman's loved ones keening in isolation, inventing their own private rituals of commemoration, seeks to maintain a dichotomy between private (authentic) and public (inauthentic) for the reaction to loss. Jonathan says, "We'll say goodbye to our son in *our* way . . ." (73, emphasis in original).

In one sentimentalized scene, Lois returns to the apartment she had shared with Clark Kent/Superman; tall, thin panels, many dominated by black, underscore her sorrow. Captions, figuring her thoughts, read: "Don't cry, Lois" and "I'm alone. So terribly lonely . . ." (85). Inside, she discovers the Kents, come to Metropolis to join her (they embrace on the next page, made up mostly of more conventional square panels): they are a private community of grief. Their rectangular "reunion" panel bears the same thick black border as the covers (86).

As evident from such sequences, in "Funeral for a Friend's" rigid moral hierarchy, two unavoidable aspects of modern American life come in for considerable abuse: the media and the public. The former comes off as coarse and mendacious: a broadcast news anchor, mere hours after the death, declares, ". . . So I *guess* that *Superman* wasn't so *super* after all!" (13, emphasis in original). This prompts José Delgado, aka the superhero Gangbuster, to toss his helmet through the TV screen. More than once, the Kents switch off their set, infuriated and saddened at the sensationalistic coverage. "They just want a *piece* of him," sighs Martha Kent (ibid.: 73, emphasis in original). At least one of Olsen's coworkers compliments him on his photo, telling an embarrassed Jimmy, "Lighten up, guy. It's gonna make you *famous*. After this, you can write your *own ticket*" (59, emphasis in original).[11] Intriguingly, this distrust and indignation over the media belies how everyone in the story (as well as ourselves, the readers) relies on it for news.[12] At the end of the climactic Superman/Doomsday battle (*Superman*, #75), our hero's fall itself appears reflected

9.3 Public versus private grief: the Kents (*Superman: The Man of Steel*, vol. 1, #20, Feb. 1993).

in Jimmy's camera lens, while Lois's embrace of her doomed lover after the fall is seen on the Kents' television screen before being depicted "in the flesh." The ubiquity of television, a year after CNN's ratings triumph with its Persian Gulf War coverage, is reflected here through such tensions.

But "the people" also misbehave. "Funeral for a Friend's" main theme is that public styles of mourning fall far short of the propriety required to register such a momentous passing; America has forgotten how to grieve with grace. "Where's the *dignity?*" Martha Kent exclaims, watching the televised funeral deteriorate into a "circus" (73, emphasis in original). The unruly masses turn into a mob requiring superhero crowd control; in the aftermath of Superman's demise, innumerable frauds step forward to claim some link to him, including a "Mrs. Superman" who purportedly lived with him in secret in a New York penthouse (83); others declare themselves his tailor, business manager, and so on (84);[13] and the aforementioned funeral merchandise salesman peddles his wares at the ceremony—though a confrontation with Bibbo reveals he is just a family man out of work, who needs to make a buck (69).

Everyone, in short, seeks to profit from, reinterpret or otherwise appropriate Superman's body, to (in Verdery's terms) make it "speak" for them.[14] Institutions—the press, the corporation, the government—as well as the man on the street seem engaged only to compete over, regulate, and, if possible, exploit the reality of death. The people, it must be said, come out looking the best in the end: along with the frauds and cynics, anonymous crowds leave tokens of affection, such as cards, photographs, and flowers at Superman's monument; Jimmy calls it "a very solemn place" (96). This sort of spontaneous public tribute had become especially pronounced at the Vietnam War Memorial in Washington, D.C. (dedicated in 1982), where by 1993 visitors had left up to 250,000 objects commemorating their loved ones (Doss: 66).[15] It should come as no surprise, then, that Doomsday victim Mitch describes the crowd's impromptu shrine at Superman's monument as he does: "Just like the Vietnam Memorial" (97).

Yet for all "The Death of Superman's" emphasis on the new—the telepath Dubbilex declaring Superman dead using the eleven-year-old criteria of "brain death";[16] Pa Kent's near-death experience, modeled on many a 1970s/80s media report of briefly glimpsed afterlives; Superman actually *staying dead* for eight issues; his monument fashioned after modern memorials to national tragedy—the storyline is suffused with nostalgia, with familiar aspects of the legend reinterpreted in the tragic light of current events. As noted by journalism critic Carolyn Kitch, "News coverage of a death is partly the retelling of the story of a life" (299); so, too, is the portrayal of a defunct Superman an opportunity to re-traverse his legacy.

All its well-known elements are there. The Christological theme reasserts itself: the storyline unfolds at Christmas time; Superman's fan mail is implicitly compared to prayers of the faithful (87); Wonder Woman describes her fallen comrade in Christ-like tones, as "a man willing to give of himself" to help those "unfortunate souls" who "often go unheard" (ibid.); actual Superman worshippers make an appearance (142); and of course, he rises again, as evidenced when Lois and Henderson discover his empty coffin, with a caption that reads, "The Beginning" (237).

So, too, does Superman's past and half-century's worth of stories assert itself through innumerable allusions and homages,[17] another way to "[retell] the story of a life." While burying their son's mementos, Ma and Pa Kent relive the moment when they discovered the infant Kal-El, landed in their cornfield. The elegiac mood is signaled by a "dissolve" from the present-day panel to another, sepia-toned, bordered by what looks like a wooden frame, in which the younger Kents welcome their new baby. The effect is of an old photograph or newsreel,[18] though the Kents' positions and size are the same in both panels, suggesting continuity (75). At least two classic covers are invoked during the storyline: Superman's monumental portrait of himself with an eagle on his left hand directly references the wartime *Superman*, vol. 1, #14 (1941), while *Action Comics*, vol. 1, #1 (the first appearance of the character and one of the most parodied covers in comics history) makes an appearance in *Action Comics* #685, in which Supergirl demolishes a car.

Finally, as noted in chapter 7, "The Death of Superman" (1992) echoes many of the plot and visual details of the earlier "Death of Superman" (1961): the hero's body on a slab; Supergirl taking over his "defender" role; scenes of leave-taking and repercussions for friend and foe alike; the role of media (though much more prominent in 1992); a monument to Metropolis' hero, and, oddly, no religious sermon at his burial ceremony.[19] Nostalgia, as ever, is the pumping heart of the superhero narrative.

CONCLUSION: THE BEST AND THE BRIGHTEST OR, THE 500

"Death universally calls into question the order upon which most societies are based," write Michael Leming and George Dickinson. "As a marginal experience to everyday life, death not only disrupts normal patterns of interaction, but also challenges the meaningfulness of life" (172). The deaths of public figures whom most of us have never met in person nonetheless have the potential, through our mediated reality, to touch more lives. But whether anonymous or famous, death is experienced as a trauma in a community; this is what the poet Thomas Lynch means when he writes that it is the living "to

9.4 The monument to the Man of Tomorrow (*Superman*, vol. 2, #76, Feb. 1993).

9.5 The "Kennedy-esque" funeral procession (*Superman: The Man of Steel,* vol. 1, #20, Feb. 1993).

whom death happens, if it really happens to anyone . . . Theirs is the pain and the pleasure of memory" (7).

Over a century of anthropological observation construe mourning as a painful liminal period, encumbered with social obligations. Writing in 1909, Arnold van Gennep described it as a rite of passage that for a time sets the survivors off from the rest of the socius: "During mourning, the living mourners and the deceased constitute a special group, situated between the world of the living and the world of the dead" (214). At the same time, age-old structures assist in the labor of mourning and reintegration with the world. As Robert Jay Lifton and Eric Olson discern, "Societies and social institutions—when people believe in them—are able to aid in mastering death anxiety by generating shared images of continuity beyond the life of each single person" (39).

A crucial role here is played by the tales a people tells itself. As Tom Lutz puts it, "Making a narrative out of the competing emotions of grief makes therapeutic sense—it is a way for people to name, give shape to, and help manipulate their own experience" (222). Lutz is writing of personal grief narratives, but clearly popular cultural productions like "The Death of Superman" function similarly (if perhaps modestly) to help us grapple with such overwhelming questions as death, mourning, and carrying on in the face of loss. When the scope of death encompasses an entire country, as in the death of a sitting president, the work of culture, its deployment of nostalgia, and national symbols for healing (and, it need be said, social control) become of critical concern.

As Kitch elaborates when discussing media coverage of "large-impact" deaths:

> Such stories take on mythic qualities when they allow discussion of cultural ideals, when the real "story" is that of . . . the passing of an era, the punishment of greed and evil, the triumph of the underdog, the loyalty and sacrifice of patriots, or the loss of American innocence but resilience of American spirit. (305)

The foregoing, I believe, goes far to explain why a reader of "Funeral for a Friend"—particularly the burial issue, "Funeral Day" (*Superman: The Man of Steel*, vol. 1, #20, Feb. 1993, Simonson/Bogdanove)—might wonder why Superman's coffin is carried by horse and carriage rather than a hearse (or, for that matter, Green Lantern's power ring) and why the entire funeral sequence looks so familiarly, oddly (in short, uncannily) "nostalgic."

Whether by chance or morbid marketing, *Superman* #75 appeared in stores almost exactly twenty-nine years after November 25, 1963, when the assassinated president John F. Kennedy was laid to rest at Arlington National Cemetery in Washington, D.C., in a state ceremony. Clues abound that that ceremony served as the basis for the look of Superman's own funeral: the carriage (though true, Kennedy's body was borne by a gun carriage, not the coach depicted in the story); the closed casket[20] with an American flag draped over it;[21] the eternal flame; even the massed crowds and park setting for the monument recall photographs and newsreel footage of that day.[22] A further hint occurs after the funeral, when Lois places her engagement ring in her slain lover's coffin (197)—recalling the same gesture made by Jacqueline Kennedy with her wedding band (Laderman: xxxiii). The Kennedy funeral, like Superman's, even spawned a collectibles craze; for example, Time-Life, Inc., still enjoyed brisk sales of commemorative photographs, reprints of memorial editions of *Life* magazine, and other wares twenty-five years after the event (Zelizer: 166).

Why Kennedy?

Part of the reason must be the extraordinary impact of that particular national tragedy, as well as the way it was covered. As the historian Gary Laderman explains:

> The dramatic impact of the funeral and the outpouring of grief and sorrow across the country was unparalleled in US history. Although there are obvious grounds for comparison with Lincoln's assassination and funeral ceremonies, the presence of the media at the ceremonies, and the mediated

presence of Kennedy's dead body in the lives of millions of television view-
ers, created an instantaneous sense of common suffering on a scale never
seen before. (xxxi)[23]

But a deeper answer lies more specifically in the way Americans (certainly in 1992, and much more so today) consume national tragedies as media
events, which by the nature of their presentation take on familiarly "mythic"
grand themes of "American resilience" and the "American spirit," as noted. In
other words, the big news stories carry a strong sense of déjà vu, an "I've seen
this movie before" quality, as described by Kitch:

> When the significance of a news event lies in past events (especially events
> the news media has covered), the storyline of current news is threaded into
> an existing tapestry. In its coverage, memory is simultaneously invoked and
> constructed ... The "story"—whether it is the death of a celebrity, a political
> sex scandal, a World Series victory, soldiers' departure for war, or even a ter-
> rorist attack—is one we at least partly already "know." (304)

This national repetition compulsion, cultivated by the press, entered its modern phase with the Kennedy funeral, whose pattern we follow to the present
day; as Zelizer argues, news correspondents do far more than simply report
the facts, particularly at times of national upheaval: "The media's coverage of
Kennedy's funeral made them into *masters of ceremonies* who were celebrated
for their active part in healing the nation" (37, my emphasis).

As further noted by Kitch, use of the first person plural in coverage of national or celebrity deaths fosters the image of the press as part of an imagined community, and fabricates a "death in the American family" master trope
(295).[24] Something very similar is seen in President Bill Clinton and First
Lady Hillary Clinton's appearance at the Superman funeral service; the president (compared by some to Kennedy, incidentally) uses the first person plural
quite liberally in his remarks: "Superman himself would probably remind us
to care for the many victims of Doomsday's attack. And so we do" (Kahan
1993A: 74). It is an expected moment, familiar, clichéd, banal—and we (we!)
would miss it were it not there.

I submit that the writers and artists of "The Death of Superman," especially
the primary focus of this essay, "Funeral for a Friend," integrated (probably
unconsciously) these enduring tropes, conventions, and clichés dating back
to the Kennedy funeral to lend the proceedings a tone of solemnity, gravitas,
and—perhaps most of all—nostalgia. In doing this, they throw into relief the
assumptions, expectations and blind spots of American culture's engagement
with death and bereavement in 1992.

In closing, I want to touch on one of those blind spots.

The consumption of national deaths as packaged, digestible units (a process of which "The Death of Superman" is a fictional, pop culture example), relates to art historian Erika Doss's analysis of national sites of mourning erected since the Vietnam War Memorial, such as the Oklahoma City National Memorial (1999), built to commemorate the 168 victims of the terrorist bombing of the Alfred P. Murrah building on April 19, 1995, by Timothy McVeigh and Terry Nichols. For Doss, these modern monuments shed light on the "complicated narratives and processes that surround . . . public commemorations of tragic and traumatic events, of events that Americans have generally refused to consider critically in terms of cause and sociopolitical consequence" (66). Her thesis holds that, in these monuments, "memory overwhelms history" by "encourag[ing] forgiving and forgetting, rather than the urgency of facing the cause of bereavement"; they are "largely anaesthetic because the historical and political context of why these deaths occurred has been effaced" (78).[25]

(Depoliticized) memory overwhelms (haunting) history, too, in "Funeral for a Friend": the Big Death eclipses, for the most part, the little deaths. Doomsday's human victims, which number at least 500 (Kahan 1993A: 25), receive scant attention, save for Clinton's speech and some rebuilding done by the superheroes. No public outcry follows the near-leveling of Metropolis, or great swathes of America, by the monster. No questioning of superheroes' right to operate outside the law, or their ineffectuality, colors the proceedings.[26] Much less does the public witness the government's machinations behind the scenes, and the reader only sees institutions of power in the form of outsize personalities, such as Westfield the rogue government agent, Luthor the corporate fiend, and garrulous news anchors.

It would, of course, be misguided to require the "Death of Superman" to address questions it was never intended, nor all that keen, to answer. (But it would not be wrong.)[27] Rather, the storyline depicts the memorialization of a hero, tragically fallen, with all the attendant pathos—naturalizing what Doss terms the effacement of political context through powerful emotions, dramatic force, in short, the anaesthetic of storytelling.

All the same, "The Death of Superman" is a cathartic work, venturing deeper (albeit in bad faith) into taboo territory than most mainstream continuity series—and uncovering valuable insights into grief, superheroic paradox and the visual culture of national trauma in the 1990s USA.

10

CONCLUSION
Vital Lies, Vital Truths

It's not alive! It's not even a monster! It's just a . . . a *thing!* (Gold/Greenberger: 118, emphasis in original)[1]

In this book I have sought to demonstrate the centrality of death and disability in mainstream superhero comics of the so-called Silver Age and beyond, spanning the late 1950s to the early 1990s. I have argued that such representations—what Charles Hatfield calls "heroes whose superpowers were counterbalanced by deformities, disabilities or social stigmas" (2012: 116)—did much to define the second phase of the genre. Indeed, they did more than that: the highlighting of bodily/cognitive difference, frailty, and mortality not only heightened realism and diversified the *dramatis personae* in welcome fashion, but in so doing they cast into relief as never before anxieties lying at the heart of the superhero project itself. If, as Friedrich Weltzien writes, "the problem of masculinity in the superhero genre is the constant and invariable pubertal problem of *becoming* a man" (246, emphasis in original), to the extent that the Silver Age's new approach fanned postwar anxieties over sociocultural changes pertaining to gender, race, and physical infirmity—especially as they threatened traditional male power—it constituted a direct assault on the white phallocratic order in the US of this era.

The various conventions, clichés, and narrative prostheses regarding death and disability which I've identified in these pages emerged as strategies to contain said threat, leading to paradoxes, absurd compromises, disavowals, and bad-faith "resolutions" as fascinating to the reader, I hope, as they are to me. That said, we have observed some differences in the ways the major publishers approached such essential, unavoidable aspects of human life as physical vulnerability and mortality. While in both cases responding to a greater visibility of the differently abled in this period, superhero comics explored the theme of disability in ways considerably more complex (as noted, by in many cases making the disability of protagonists' alter egos an organizing trope "baked in" to the series); however, the market realities of serials severely limited the genre's treatment of death—at least, as it pertained to the "marquee" characters. In addressing this problem, the majors resorted to the disheartening "Revolving Door of Death" (heroes "dying" only to return forthwith) or else invited the Reaper to visit the "real thing" upon non-superpowered loved ones and acquaintances of the hero. The precious few exceptions only proved the ineluctable rule.

By the time of DC Comics' subsumption under Time Warner in 1989 and the 1991 public offering of Marvel Entertainment Group—events which signaled the beginning of the "collectibles craze," as discussed in the last chapter—these clichés and conventions had hardened; increasing consolidation, commercial pressures, and stockholder demands would mean still more sales-boosting death/disability-related "mega-events" such as "The Death of Superman" (1992–93), "Batman: Knightfall" (1993–94), and "Heroes Reborn" (1996–97) storylines. The result, in many cases, was fan alienation; an acceleration of the mainstream genre's decline in readership; further ghettoization in the Direct Market; and financial "blowback" exemplified by the collectibles crash and Marvel's own bankruptcy in December 1996.[2]

Nonetheless, the genre's engagement with death and disability cannot be reduced to the mere callous exploitation of commercial properties (themselves built, as documented elsewhere, on profoundly unfair industry labor and intellectual property practices directed at creators).[3] These stories tell us much about twentieth-century attitudes to bodies; about nostalgia and dread; in short, as Scott Bukatman puts it, about "the fragile niche that fantasy occupies within the waking experience of the real" (2009: 109).

Take death. What more can we make of the genre's repetition compulsion to revive those who have passed—indeed, to never let them rest in peace, certainly not for long? How does it relate to the superhero worlds' "oneiric" sense of time identified by Umberto Eco as a defining feature, or to the "multiverse" model with its proliferation of character "versions" and identities which explodes in the Silver Age, keeping mortality at yet further remove? (Another Earth, another Superman.)

How baroque, how ingenious the many ways the genre has devised to keep bringing them back—like a mind ever-striving, as Ernest Becker avers, to barricade itself against that final, horrible knowledge, to erect a "screen against despair" (1973: 56). Among my favorites: The Legion of the Unliving, deceased villains and heroes plucked from a time before their death by Kang the Conqueror to wage war on the Avengers (*Avengers*, vol. 1, #131, Jan. 1975, Englehart/ Buscema). A second iteration, assembled by the Grandmaster after assuming control of Death's realm, manages to kill nearly the entire team in the first round of a perverse "contest" in "The Day Death Died!" (*Avengers Annual*, vol. 1, #16, Dec. 1987, Defalco/Various).[4] Similarly, the climax to the Korvac saga sees a veritable bloodbath, with over two dozen heroes cut down by cosmically powered villains—only to have the massacre undone as a redemptive act by the antagonist before he himself succumbs, in "The Hope . . . And the Slaughter!" (*Avengers*, vol. 1, #177, Nov. 1978, Shooter/Wenzel). And as discussed in chapter 7, *Crisis on Infinite Earths* (1985–86) wipes out universes by the bushel, only to have most of their denizens eventually return in innumerable versions and variants. Multifarious, endlessly inventive are the ways to keep death "an easily appealed condition" (Quarterbin: Oct. 2002) in this milieu.

As lax and "dishonest" (in Becker's terms) a picture as this treatment of mortality undeniably presents, I don't believe we can dismiss it solely as a declining industry's compulsive recycling of tired properties (though in part that's so), or indeed as necessarily harmful. What psychic wounds might this "easily appealed condition" salve? As Henry Jenkins has poignantly explored in his essay "Death-Defying Heroes," on reading superhero comics at his dying mother's bedside, the genre's mystifications of life's eternal questions can indeed serve a therapeutic function in coping with loss:

> One could understand the reading of comics as entering into a psychological space that . . . denies death and mortality, that encourages a nostalgic return to origins. . . . Yet, I want to suggest that we cannot escape or forestall such dreaded feelings altogether, and that in their own way, both as texts and as artifacts, comics become reflective objects that help us think about our own irreversible flow toward death. (66)[5]

Chapters 7–9 of the present study examined how several examples of the genre functioned, in essence, as just such "reflective objects" in the Silver/Bronze ages. Meanwhile, in their negotiation of disability (as seen in chapters 2–6), superhero stories coped rather spectacularly in this era: Don Blake's cane metamorphosed into Thor's hammer, Matt Murdock's cane switched into Daredevil's billy club—potent narratives of transformation. Unlike the previous Golden Age, bodily difference was not merely wished away, made to vanish from sight (if it was ever there), but thrust to the center of the action: Tony Stark and Cliff Steele both agonize over superpowers that simultaneously make them demi-gods and "freaks." No figure better exemplified this quandary, nor more deeply tapped the dramatic vein it opened up, than Ben Grimm, whom Matthew J. Costello called the progenitor of flawed antiheroes: "Blessed with strength but cursed with ugliness, Grimm presents a paradigm of the Marvel hero who must pay a price for his power" (5).

Disability in the Silver Age: a crucial element of being a hero.[6]

I need hardly restate here the importance of such representations, not only to the disabled community itself. The inclusion of such imagery and characters into superhero business-as-usual reflected and helped shape a vast social movement, a civil and human rights struggle to acknowledge the fundamental dignity of all people, continuing to this day. It continues because of the ongoing need to make such utterances as this by Susan Wendell anachronistic:

> use the terms "rejected body" and "negative body" to refer to those aspects of bodily life (such as illness, disability, weakness, and dying), bodily appearance (usually deviations from the cultural ideals of the body), and bodily experience (including most forms of bodily suffering) that are feared, ignored, despised, and/or rejected in a society and its culture. (85)

Popular-culture depictions of disability such as those which burst forth in the early Silver Age show we are (it is fervently hoped) nearing an epoch when there will be no "rejected" or "negative" bodies; they herald a time, as Mitchell and Snyder declare, when disability "[will come] to occupy the status of a misnomer—no more and no less than the variable body operating in flux" (2012: 49).

We're not there yet. And (to deviate from what may sound like an overly triumphalist tone thus far in this chapter) it remains incumbent on me to remind that too often superhero comics even in the Silver Age and beyond have been part of the problem rather than the solution. This book has primarily dealt with how the genre reflected the sorts of social changes that made such relatively empowering depictions as Ben Grimm (commercially, narratively) possible. In closing, however, I want to return briefly to another important facet of disability's representation in the world of superheroes: how it has actively participated—despite the best intentions, perhaps—in the culture's dehumanization of the disabled.

"BESIDES, YOU'RE NOT A *LIVING* CREATURE!"

Let us examine three episodes, spanning as many decades, in superhero comics' treatment of mental disability.

In "The Boy of Steel Versus The Thing of Steel" (*Superboy*, vol. 1, #68, Nov. 1958, Binder/Papp), Smallville is terrorized by Bizarro, a quasi-duplicate of Superboy created by a Professor Dalton's faulty technology. The strange chalk-complexioned creature, possessed of all Superboy's powers but with an "imperfect imitation of *Superboy's* mind" (Gold/Greenberger: 119, emphasis in original) goes on a rampage when citizens, peers, and even Clark Kent's mother cruelly rebuff him: "Don't call me 'Mom'! I . . . I . . . don't know who . . . or *what* you are, but please go . . . please . . . gasp!" (120, emphasis and ellipses in original). The despondent creature ("Why they hunt me? Me not bad! Why they hate me? . . . choke!" [118]), despite clumsy attempts to placate the populace, inspires only fear, revulsion and extreme violence—at one point, Superboy and the military even try *an atomic bomb* against the invulnerable "lifeless imitation" (127).

Three chief discursive modes govern the depiction of Bizarro. Firstly, he is an "it," an agglomeration of non-living matter manufactured through a 1950s version of 3D printing, which can only crudely mimic human behavior; as Dalton says, "And it can even talk mumblingly, as if it has a mind! Well, electronic-brains can think, too, even though they are not 'alive'!" (117). Throughout the story, the "counterfeit Superboy" (122) is described in terms of incompleteness, artificiality, and mere derivation from life. Secondly, Bizarro is, ultimately, not unsympathetic; captions refer to him as "perilous, yet pathetic" (131), a "pitiful creature" (137) and "invulnerable to harm but not to scorn" (126). He even weeps in self-pity (120, 137), a super-nuisance: misunderstood, but not evil.[7] Finally, an intertextual mode: Bizarro as a twentieth-century Frankenstein's monster. Numerous references mark the source: just as Frankenstein's creation befriends an old blind man (Shelley: 156), Bizarro receives kindness from the blind girl Melissa (Gold/Greenberger: 12); like his predecessor,[8] Superboy's "dangerous double" is appalled and enraged by his "ugly" reflection (118); in both stories the "normals" rally to destroy the monster.[9]

For Mike Conroy, Bizarro in both his initial and later "adult" versions represents a shadow-Superman, "a kind of breaking up of the meaning embodied in the whole idea of the character" (244), "a Superman without radiance" (245). One of his creators, Alvin Schwartz, even called Bizarro a full-blown "deconstruction" of the Man of Tomorrow (244).[10] Nonetheless, for all the creature's pathos and literary pedigree of the persecuted outcast, the resolution to "The Boy of Steel Versus The Thing of Steel" only underscores the heartless economy of difference in which the cognitively different find themselves: the unfortunate brute is finally disintegrated to molecules by his version of Kryptonite. Though not without a—highly qualified—apology from Superboy: "Sorry, *Bizarro* . . . I have to destroy you with this glowing metal, for Smallville's sake! Besides, you're not a *living* creature! Don't try to escape!" (137, emphasis and ellipsis in original).

But Bizarro's death comes with an odd, "heroic" twist: in suicidal despair, he rushes headlong to his doom. The resulting explosion produces a shock wave which . . . cures Melissa of her blindness. Superboy muses, "Did poor *Bizarro* somehow have *one flash* of super-inspiration? Did he *sacrifice* himself

10.1 Bizarro, the duplicate Superboy, is persecuted by Smallville's citizens (*Superboy*, vol. 1, #68, Nov. 1958).

for his only friend, the blind girl?" (138, emphasis in original). In other words, a symbolic exchange has taken place. As in the ending to Franz Kafka's "The Metamorphosis" (1915), in which the dead Gregor Samsa is "replaced" by his sister Grete, "bloomed into a pretty girl with a good figure" (89), Bizarro's sacrifice secures Melissa's entry into the able-bodied, seeing world. Such narrative legerdemain authorizes the monster's execution; his life for her vision, his deviance for her normality. A poignant ending, no doubt; like Atticus Finch gunning down a mad dog: a sad situation, but necessary to safeguard the town. Besides, as we're constantly reminded, Bizarro is "not a *living* creature!" He embraces his fate "unwanted, unloved, shunned by all" (123, emphasis and ellipsis in original), but the neurotypical can rest easy knowing it was the best outcome for everybody.

A similar karma informs the aftermath to what Ben Saunders calls "the single most traumatic event in superhero history" (96), what Arnold Blumberg considers "the end of innocence for the series and the superhero genre in general" (199), the landmark story "The Night Gwen Stacy Died" (*Amazing

10.2 The schizophrenic Norman Osborn in "The Night Gwen Stacy Died" (*Amazing Spider-Man*, vol. 1, #121, June 1973).

Spider-Man, vol. 1, #121, Jun. 1973, Conway/Kane). In chapter 7, I discussed that work's significance as a breakthrough in the depiction of "existential death" and its reputation as the defining pivot from Silver to Bronze in the problematic "ages" model; here, I want to address the *other* death of a major character in that storyline. In "The Goblin's Last Stand" (*Amazing Spider-Man*, vol. 1, #122, Jul. 1973, Conway/Kane), an enraged Spider-Man hunts down his girlfriend's killer to his lair for a final climactic showdown.

That man, Norman Osborn, is subject to bouts of schizophrenia; in his Goblin persona, he knows Spider-Man's secret identity and blames him for his son Harry's drug abuse. Like Bizarro, Osborn remains a sympathetic figure: several scenes show him sweaty-faced, angst-ridden, suffering from severe stress and hallucinations, struggling against his transformation into a green-garbed homicidal maniac (Kahan 2004A: 18, 19, 66, 69). As Brett M. Rogers notes, the storyline "emphasizes the internal conflict between father and villain in the same character" (84). Osborn loses that battle once and for all in a panel depicting his mental collapse: over images of cast-members' faces gazing at the terrified businessman, captions read, "And then, all at *once,* the delicate tissues of Norman Osborn's memory *collapse*—and a flood of images, past and present, rushes through his pressured *brain*—*reminding* him—*tormenting* him—*until he can stand it no longer!*" (70, emphasis in original).

10.3 Osborn's death in "The Goblin's Last Stand" (*Amazing Spider-Man*, vol. 1, #122, July 1973).

Yet even as the Goblin wreaks havoc in the city, Spider-Man/Peter Parker feels for the older man's plight: "The *reason* he was so deadly is—he was mentally *sick*—"; "He's *ill*—desperately ill" (8); "I've got to pierce the cloud of *madness* in his brain—" (44). He tries to reason with the villain as they do battle over New York's rooftops: "You're *sick*! I—want to *help* you" (26), while authorial captions echo Parker's diagnosis, noting Osborn's "twisted, tortured *brain*" (44, all emphases in original).

All that "understanding," though, evaporates in the wake of Gwen's death: with the Goblin cornered at last, Spider-Man unleashes his full fury in four of the most ultra-violent panels limned in the genre up to that point. The vengeful hero bludgeons the villain nearly to death, screaming, "*Filthy—worm-eating—scum!*" (97).[11] And although Parker does come to his senses before dealing a fatal blow, the Goblin soon dies gruesomely nonetheless—accidentally impaled by his own remote-controlled flyer. In three disturbing panels show-ing his death throes, captions declare, "So do the *proud* men die—crucified, not on a cross of *gold*—but on a stake of humble *tin*" (98, all emphases in original).

Sympathy once more reveals its limits when faced with madness. The evil, insane Goblin commits the genre's one unpardonable sin upon the innocent Gwen Stacy, making her a sort of symbolic sacrifice to the reality principle.[12] Scripter Gerry Conway makes matters even more odious and traumatic by having the Goblin exhibit not a whit of remorse for his act; as he tells Spider-Man: "What *worth* is there in the paltry existence of one *useless female*? A simpering, pointless *girl* who never did more than *occupy space*—" (96, em-phasis in original). Such monstrosity justifies the villain's death by *lex talio-nis*—whatever the extenuating circumstances of Osborn's plight before his transformation. Atticus Finch shooting the dog again.

But what often gets elided in discussions of this episteme-shifting storyline is that Osborn/Goblin himself represents no less a "sacrifice" than the beauti-ful young girl; as Rogers puts it, "in death, the Goblin becomes both a symbol (along with Gwen Stacy) of the lost innocence of Silver Age comics readers and a martyr ushering in a new age of comic narrative in which no character is safe" (85). This gets at part of what I mean, but notice again the operative mechanism by which justice is visited (or, if you will, the sacrifice made); as in Bizarro's case, the only possible dramatically satisfying response to the threat of rampant unreason, psychosis, and mental imbalance is death.[13]

The final episode I want to examine, Alan Moore and Brian Bolland's cel-ebrated 1988 graphic novel *The Killing Joke*, likewise depicts an act of unfor-giveable, gratuitous cruelty exacted upon an innocent. As part of a perverse campaign to prove the meaninglessness of life (and madness as the proper response to it), the arch-villain Joker kidnaps Commissioner James Gordon and displays him naked in a cage at a derelict carnival before a crowd of "hu-man oddities" (people with varying disabilities). In a carny barker's tone, he describes humanity as grotesque: "Most *repulsive* of all, are its *frail* and *useless* notions of *order* and *sanity*. If too much *weight* is placed on them . . . they *snap*" (n.p., emphasis and ellipsis in original). Iconographically and ideologi-cally, the scene is a remarkable turning of the tables, worthy of Tod Brown-ing's *Freaks* (1932) or Katherine Dunn's *Geek Love* (1989).

But by far the most notorious scene in *The Killing Joke* (like Stacy's death often touted as a "turning point" for the genre) is the Joker's paralysis-by-gun of Barbara Gordon. In one of the most graphic series of panels up to that point in superhero comics, Barbara is shot, falls backward spewing blood, and crashes through a glass coffee table in "slow motion." Sprawled on the floor, she clutches her midsection in agony before her stunned father.

10.4 The Joker gun downs Barbara Gordon, paralyzing her, in *The Killing Joke*, 1988.

Moore and Bolland's "exploitational" moment-by-moment rendering of a woman[14] gunned down is enhanced by the Joker's sadistic banter punning on the fact that Barbara works as a librarian: "Mind *you*, I can't say much for the volume's *condition*. I *mean*, there's a *hole* in the *jacket* and the *spine* appears to be damaged. *Frankly*, she won't be walking off the shelves in *that* state of repair" (emphasis in original).

Fan and critical discourses have established the novel as a precursor to the ultra-violent spectacles of the 1990s and later, with Barbara's victimization representing both the revealed misogynist underbelly of superhero narratives as well as the start to her journey as Oracle, the genre's most developed disabled hero. Geoff Klock cleverly sees *The Killing Joke* as a post-*Watchmen*, post-*Dark Knight Returns*, postmodern recapitulation of Batman's history, with the Joker as "emblematic of contradictory tradition and influence, of the madness of oversaturated continuity" (61).[15] While partial to this metafictive reading, I do think it risks overly abstracting the Joker's cognitive difference, of turning it into a "metaphor [that] floats completely free from the actuality of the condition itself" (Stuart Murray 2008: 208), a common caveat in Disability Studies.

For the Joker, as chalk-white as Bizarro, as megalomaniacal as the Green Goblin, is also portrayed sympathetically in flashback sequences detailing his (possible)[16] origins as a villain: an unnamed engineer loses his pregnant wife in a freak accident, then gets framed by the mob before immersion in chemicals deforms him and drives him insane. The Joker's plots to exact a similar fate on Gordon, and to expose Batman as similarly deranged, are thus best interpreted as perversely Oedipal, evocative of a desire to kill these substitute father figures and/or turn them into versions of himself.[17]

But once more I draw the reader's attention to the ways in which the hero deals with the threat of mental imbalance gone "too far"—he tries to annihilate it. When Batman sets out on his final confrontation, only Gordon's admonition—"[I] want him brought in by the *book!*" (emphasis in original)—constrains his vigilante drive to vengeance. The scene is nigh Biblical in construction: the hero entering the mouth of Hell (a House of Mirrors), the white-haired Gordon intoning the Law of the Father after him.

Yet the novel in fact opens with Batman conceding the inevitable outcome; it's either him or the Joker: "We're going to *kill* each other, aren't we? Perhaps you'll kill me. Perhaps I'll kill you. Perhaps sooner. Perhaps later" (emphasis in original). Death again: the sole response to madness commensurate with its hazard.[18]

To sum up: we have traced a spectrum of the cognitively different super-antagonist, from confused to evil to beyond redemption, one shading into the other. These are men, as Ato Quayson describes, whose disabilities are first and foremost "markers of a sharp otherness and moral deficit" (38). We have seen the effect of these aberrant figures' actions on three white, "saintly" females: cured, killed, maimed, and tortured. The lesson, reinforced over the decades with their fluctuating mores, is that these villains will act in ways more and more grisly, more and more unconscionable, more and more inhuman—unless we stop them. Cold.

Perhaps this explains why, in pondering ways to conclude this book, I found myself fixating on the case of Adam Lanza. As the world learned on December 14, 2012, the twenty-year-old Lanza killed first his mother, then twenty-six children and adults at Sandy Hook Elementary School in Newtown, Connecticut, before turning a firearm on himself. Though this is not the forum to explore such aspects of the event, in the wake of the tragedy I along with the rest of the nation actively engaged in debates over gun violence in the US. But the ways in which much of the news media focused on Lanza's mental health in the immediate aftermath of the murders, reporting that he had possibly been autistic, diagnosed with Asperger's Syndrome and Sensory Integration Disorder (SID) as a child (Estes), does merit our attention here.

Such linkages between mental disability and mass shootings had been made before, as in the cases of Jared Loughner in Arizona and James Holmes in Colorado (to take only two recent examples). With all three men, cognitive difference—schizophrenia or some manifestation of autism—too readily served as a catalyst for their demonization, the pointed-to "reason" for evil, violent acts. Schizophrenia, in fact, is now "more commonly related to media stories about crime or state health policies," notes Stuart Murray (2008: 207). Responding to the Lanza slayings, some even called for a national registry of the mentally ill, the better to keep "us" safe (Bachman).

Such rhetoric prompted a response from mental health and human rights organizations, such as the Autistic Self-Advocacy Network (ASAN). A press release from the day of the shootings read:

> Recent media reports have suggested that the perpetrator of this violence, Adam Lanza, may have been diagnosed with Asperger's Syndrome, a diagnosis on the autism spectrum, or with another psychiatric disability. In either event, it is imperative that as we mourn the victims of this horrific tragedy that commentators and the media avoid drawing inappropriate and unfounded links between autism or other disabilities and violence. Autistic Americans and individuals with other disabilities are no more likely to commit violent crime than non-disabled people. In fact, people with disabilities of all kinds, including autism, are vastly more likely to be the victims of violent crime than the perpetrators.[19]

What makes these linkages so "easy"? Surely part of the answer involves public misapprehensions of mental disability. In the case of autism, a particularly heterogeneous condition that covers a broad range of behaviors and symptoms,[20] mystification, metaphor, and moral panic all too readily arise. As Murray notes, "The uninterrogated nature of autism that exists in the popular imagination . . . feeds upon a diffuse sense of wonder and latent notion of threat" (2010).

This "latent notion" leads to such ableist calumnies as "retard," "psycho," "robot," and "mindblindness," and the characterization of autistic people as "a dead soul in a live body" (quoted in Solomon: 238). Indeed, some see autistics as deficient in those qualities which make people people; Murray points out that in many autism-related narratives the impaired figure "seems to point to that which is absent from the condition of being human" (2006: 41). These attitudes go beyond the lay public; Emily and Ralph Saverese argue that

> the field of Disability Studies has been slow to take up cognitive disability, and it has done so with some discomfort – in part because notions of social constructions, while important, seem inadequate to the task of assessing physiological differences in the very organ of perception, and in part because these differences seem such a threat to what most makes us human.t

If someone's personhood is in doubt (or seen as lacking), all the easier to direct death wishes at them. When a tiny minority of them transgresses, their crimes of violence only confirm their abjection from the human, making it all the more likely the various systemic factors involved in such tragedies as Newtown will be ignored, and the quicker the call for "protective measures" like national registries, institutionalization, and selective abortion.

Does the representation of imagined crimes by the mentally disabled, like those of Bizarro, the Green Goblin, and the Joker—along with the "mad dog" response to them—in some small measure govern public reaction to national tragedies such as the Lanza shootings? Perhaps even to the willingness among some quarters to lock up autistic people? Superhero comics, with their decades-long slide in readership, can hardly take all the blame. But I do believe these stories and their resolutions—the pattern of the cognitively exceptional going too far, authorizing extreme reprisals—form a voice in the chorus of oppression visited on actual disabled people in real life.[21] As Susan Squier argues, such depictions transform the anomalous "into the abnormal, the impaired and ultimately the disabled, through the enforcement of social norms that fail to accommodate difference" (86).[22]

In his brilliant discussion of the Gwen Stacy storyline and its effect on the genre, Ben Saunders notes, "The problem that needs to be explained is why it is so often the pointless death of a young woman that throws the surviving characters of the story, or the audience of that story, into a traumatic encounter with life's 'absurdity'" (99). His explanation goes beyond considerations of gender, but I wish to highlight a point by the feminist scholar Elisabeth Bronfen that I think is key here: "Femininity and death . . . stand as the absence, the ground and the vanishing point of our cultural system of representation" (433).

What Saunders calls "absurdity," what the Joker terms meaninglessness, what I have been describing as mental disability, autism, schizophrenia, neurodiversity—a way of relating to the world that goes beyond the rational as defined by ableist culture—is itself such a cultural "vanishing point" as well. Saunders (and many others) highlight the obvious victim in this encounter, Stacy, but give short shrift to the other victim (scapegoat, really): the mentally ill Osborn. Yet he, too, is a "sacrifice" to the genre's confrontation with the Real no less than to the socius' need to "defensively" punish cognitive abnormalcy. Not just innocent dead young women, but "madness"—in a non-negotiably malign aspect—often turns up when we talk of "traumatic encounters with life's 'absurdity.'" The only response to that madness, time and again, is to kill it—even, in the case of Bizarro, with atomic weapons. As Michel Foucault wrote about the insane (criminal or not) in eighteenth-century Europe:

> Everything was organized so that the madman would recognize himself in a world of judgment that enveloped him on all sides; he must know that he is watched, judged, and condemned; from transgression to punishment, the connection must be evident, as a guilt recognized by all. (267)

I do not mean to say that the writers and artists of these works consciously enact discrimination, but as Mitchell and Snyder argue (and I advanced in chapter 2), the narrative prosthesis is a pervasive epistemic frame for relating to disabled people, perhaps none more so than the inscrutably insane, autistic, schizophrenic, mad, other. Anxiety, threat, dread, fear, and prejudice feed into the explanatory mechanisms that construct them as somehow beyond human, beyond mercy—mechanisms awaiting the trigger of tragedies such as Newtown. The fictions examined in this book both reflect and refract the greater culture's values, thus they always run the risk of exacerbating preexisting apprehensions—always to the greater detriment of the physically/cognitively different.

10.5 *Christopher Reeve,* 2004. National Portrait Gallery, Smithsonian Institution; gift of Mr. And Mrs. Sacha Newley; ©
2004 Sacha Newley.

THE END: VITAL TRUTHS

In Sacha Newley's portrait *Christopher Reeve* (2004), the quadriplegic star appears nearly ten years after his accident, his back to a curtainless window, seated in his motorized wheelchair. Reeve's expression, with its striking blue eyes, seems pacific, monumental, his oval head a play of light and shadows.[23] The chair looks imposing—gun-metal gray and black, with cables, treaded rubber wheels, an ostomy bag, and control panel—the effect heightened by its foregrounding through a low angle and Steranko-like forced perspective, which distorts the figure; the actor's sneakers appear much larger compared to his head than conventional realism would allow.

"[Newley] has attempted to capture the striking image of Reeve's terrible suffering since his catastrophic horse-riding accident," writes Sharon Feinstein, but it hardly seems so to me. If I had to describe the portrait in two words, they would be "peace" and "dignified." The calm gaze and well-appointed drawing room, with model sailboat perched on a wooden cabinet, bespeak security. The figure is stolid and powerful. Moreover, Newley slyly alludes to his subject's most famous role: the large window lets in the sunset or sunrise, which forms yellowish glints on arm, legs and shiny bald pate. Reeve is framed by that window, reducing the distance between him and open vistas of sky and clouds. Finally, a "star" pattern on the carpet seems an unmistakably comic-booky touch.

"On the one hand, he is imprisoned in the chair," Newley told an interviewer. "On the other, it's like a throne from which he looks out on the world" (Feinstein). Despite the ableist language, the portraitist does seize on something vital to this work: it is, oxymoronically, a calm contradiction, a peaceful paradox. For the image marries what Rosemarie Garland-Thomson calls "the cultural narrative of the famous, wealthy, quadriplegic actor Christopher Reeve . . . one of hopefulness—indeed of inspiration" (2004B: 778)[24] to the more disconcerting visual assault of the "man-machine" wheelchair-user (discussed in chapter 5). To many, Reeve appears both human and other, "inspiring" yet vaguely sinister.

Hairless, dressed in dark hues, he could in fact pass as a supervillain. Surely the reader has guessed what I will say next: Newley has reinvented Superman in the image of his longtime nemesis Lex Luthor. Actually, no: Newley has reinvented Superman in the image of his (and the genre's) very first recurring bad guy, the bald, wheelchair-using Ultra-Humanite.[25] *Christopher Reeve* is thus a brilliant compromise between the quasi-fascistic, aspirational physical ideal of the superhero, and the Gothic, disfigured abjection of the supervillain.

We arrive, ironically enough, somewhere in the middle, at something close to the lived reality of a man in a wheelchair.[26]

As Mitchell and Snyder note of the literary works they scrutinize, Newley's painting "expose[s], rather than conceal[s], the prosthetic relation" (2000: 8); it normalizes Reeve rather than exoticizing his condition (Garland-Thomson calls this the "realistic" mode of disability's visual rhetorics).[27] That Newley does this while at the same time subtly alluding to the character and genre which inspired Reeve's greatest success I think simply wonderful. Man of Tomorrow, indeed.

The stories and characters examined here have not always lived up to that degree of "honesty." The superhero, I have tried to show, is a figure that must "repress *globally*" (Becker 1973: 52, emphasis in original) to maintain its "vital lie" of corporeal vigor and plenitude. Death and disability function as the genre's subconscious, its dark matter whose gravitational effect is ever felt but, until the Silver Age, largely denied. Over the course of this book I've sought to strip back that denial, bearing in mind the goal of criticism as Mitchell and Snyder prescribe: "to undo the quick repair of disability in mainstream representations and beliefs" and *"make the prosthesis show, to flaunt its imperfect supplementation as an illusion"* (2000: 8, emphasis in original). To get at some of the genre's vital truths.

If, as Scott Bukatman argues, the superhero's invulnerable body "retains no marks," on it "history cannot be inscribed" (2003: 197, emphasis in original), then death and disability signal the return of history—the return of story— to Superman's flesh. If so, then I would say the trajectory of the superhero tracked in these pages casts into relief an aspiration.

Not us aspiring to them. They aspiring to all our diversity, incompleteness and humdrum reality. An aspiration to the frail, the mortal, the interdependent, the human.

To us.

NOTES

1. As Scott Bukatman puts it, Superman, popularly accepted as the first superhero, "entered a substantial tradition of hero AS America . . . In a country dedicated to propositions of progress and the 'new,' Superman appeared with his invulnerable body: the body that retains no marks, on which history cannot be inscribed" (2003: 197).

2. See http://adland.tv/content/aids-campaign-france-uses-superheroes for images of Superman and Wonder Woman wasting away in hospital wards. Unlike the Barbier piece, this ad campaign served an overtly socially conscious, rather than parodic, purpose.

3. See Johnson and Stars. A sample of the latter's contempt for the former Superman: "The concerns of the disabled community are valid. They are being killed off. They are not in pain; they are merely disabled, and most of them are cool with themselves and the way they are. They fucking HATE Christopher Reeve's self-loathing desperation for quacky cures" (emphasis in original).

4. On the controversy in the mainstream press and the disabled community after the ad aired, see McRuer 2003, especially pp. 150–51.

5. See Parille: 2012 for a recent treatment of the theme.

6. For one thing, as Friedrich Weltzien writes, "the successful performer of masculinity, as displayed in the superhero genre, is the one who is able to stay in control throughout the transformation. The superhero changes identities at will, and in this sense, failed masculinity is that which loses control over this process" (244).

7. See Saunders, especially pages 4–7, for a succinct treatment of this theme in a more philosophical key.

8. Even those who support the validity of comics as objects of serious study often "ghettoize" superheroes. In an appreciative 2008 essay for *American Art*, Katherine Roeder notes: "Comic art has always held popular appeal, but now it is spilling over increasingly into other forms of mass media and it is becoming intellectually and artistically respectable" (2), and "as mass-cultural products, comics often espouse dominant cultural values, yet their conflicted status as devalued 'low' art also encourages a strain of anarchic humor and anti-authoritarian sentiment" (4), yet pays scant attention to superheroes. (The essay's illustrations also favor other genres.) For a passionate call to greater inclusion of superheroes in Comics Studies, see the appendix to Saunders.

9. In addition, the superhero genre receives considerable attention in such scholarly journals as the *International Journal of Comic Art*, *ImageTexT*, *Image and Narrative*, the *Journal of Graphic Novels and Comics* and the *Journal of Popular Culture*; as well as at professional conferences including the International Comic Arts Forum, the Comic Art and Comics Area of the Popular Culture Association and the Comic Arts Conference.

10. In some respects, however, the academics are latecomers, as their work was itself partly built on long-standing fan, collector and comics journalism discourses going back at least to the 1950s, represented by such figures as Bill Blackbeard and Robert Beerbohm and fan publications like *Alter Ego* (1961), *Comics Buyer's Guide* (1971), *Back Issue* (2003), *The Jack Kirby Collector* (1994), and *The Comics Journal* (1976, previously known as the *New Nostalgia Journal*).

11. It bears mention, though no lengthy treatment in this study, that the superhero genre evolved directly from the pulp dime novels and adventure strips of previous decades. For a survey of that background, see Coogan, chapter 6.

12. Coogan's approach has resonances with (and advantages similar to) Thierry Groensteen's semiotics-derived "system" model for the comics medium. Such a model likewise presents a field of potentialities in which a given work need not fulfill all precepts of a definition in order to fall into the category of comics: "System defines an ideal . . . The comics system will be a conceptual frame in which all the actualizations of the 'ninth art' can find their place and be thought of in relation to each other, taking into account their differences and their commonalities within the same medium" (20). Such conceptualizations as Groensteen and Coogan's have done scholars the great service of, for instance, not having to define "the ninth art" at the start of each study (a Comic Studies rhetorical motif identified by Charles Hatfield and Joseph Witek) and not needing to tediously "prove" that the Hulk is, indeed, a superhero. This study, with gratitude, stands on their shoulders.

13. For compelling critiques of Campbell's monomyth model as applied to serial superhero comics, see Rogers and Saunders: 16–17.

14. Jewett and Lawrence's arguments extend beyond the superhero genre, though they spend a considerable amount of their 2002 book *The Myth of the American Superhero* on it.

15. Scholars such as Ian Gordon and Saunders (24–29) vigorously complicate Jewett and Shelton's linkage between superheroes and right-wing politics (7).

16. Witness the firestorm of fan criticism that swelled upon the release of *Man of Steel* (2013), the character's latest cinematic reboot, centered on the notion that "Superman does not kill." He has, a number of times, over the decades.

17. The term was popularized by Wertham and his adherents in, among other venues, his April 21, 1954, testimony before the US Senate Subcommittee to Investigate Juvenile Delinquency:

> I would like to point out to you one other crime comic book which we have found to be particularly injurious to the ethical development of children and those are the Superman comic books. They arose in children [*sic*] phantasies of sadistic joy in seeing other people punished over and over again while you yourself remain immune. We have called it the Superman complex.

See the online transcript at http://www.thecomicbooks.com/wertham.html.

18. During the Cold War Soviet cultural critics, I should note, did not hesitate to make such links explicit in their general attack on the American mass culture industry. In 1953, Isaak Lapitsky wrote scornfully of Superman, a "nationalist" character "who, of course, is a white 100-percent American defending the country against black people, Indians, communists and foreigners" (126). For more on Soviet and Russian reactions to the superhero, see Alaniz 2009 and 2010, chapter 4.

19. The essay was revised and translated into English in 1972.

20. On the superhero as an immigrant and "passing" narrative, see Fingeroth 2004: 53, Reynolds: 62, and Bukatman 2003: 217.

21. Note how closely this echoes the opening narration at the beginning of every episode of the 1950s *Adventures of Superman* television show with Steve Reeves: ". . . truth, justice and the American way."

22. Jules Feiffer, writing somewhat earlier than Berger, is similarly glum on the secret identity, noting, "Clark Kent was the fiction" (11), and further: "He is Superman's opinion of the rest of us, a pointed caricature of what we, the noncriminal element, were really like" (13).

23. Relating the device to Joseph Campbell's concept of "Atonement with the Father," Reynolds observes that in many superhero narratives "approval by the father is withheld time and

again by the absence or unavailability of the father-figure" (61). However, he does point out (rather cheerfully) that the superhero genre "can comfortably support a whole battery of contradictory interpretations, of which the Freudian/Oedipal element is only a single strand"(62).

24. Coogan sees the costume's simple iconicity as critical both for distinguishing superheroes from other pulp characters and as an ideogram for broadcasting identity, history, and national origin. Hence, Spider-Man wears a spider chevron on his chest (announcing the nature of his powers); Captain America dresses in what is essentially an American flag (indicating his patriotic mission); Batman dresses as his totem animal (to instill fear in the criminals he hates) and so on. See, especially, 33–39.

25. For Chabon, too, this process signals an ontological shift:

> In theory, the costume . . . forms part of the strategy of concealment. But in fact the superhero's costume often functions as a kind of magic screen onto which the repressed narrative may be projected. No matter how well he or she hides its traces, the secret narrative of transformation, of rebirth from the confines of the ordinary, is given up by the costume. (2008: 21)

26. For more on drag, see Berenstein, Marjorie Garber, and Butler.

27. This point had been made earlier, by Gillian Freeman in *Undergrowth of Literature* (1967).

28. In my bibliography see in particular Mauss ("Techniques of the Body"); Bourdieu (especially his concepts of "habitus" and hexis); Lock; Scheper-Hughes and Wacquant; and Gilman for key works and concepts in the Humanities and Social Sciences' by-now-vast corpus of literature on the body.

29. As outlined by B. Farnell: "Generally speaking, the Western model of person provides a conception of mind as the internal, nonmaterial locus of rationality, thought, language, and knowledge. In opposition to this, the body is regarded as the mechanical, sensate, material locus of irrationality and feeling" (345).

30. Taylor here is specifically addressing *los desaparecidos*, vanished and presumed victims of Argentina's "Dirty War." She continues, in what some might see as a quaint appeal: "Any attempt to think about the material facticity of the body poses problems. Nonetheless, I feel the urgency of holding on to the material body even if that body's existence and meaning cannot at the present be fully theorized" (149).

31. Golden Age heroes such as The Comet, killed in action, or Dr. Midnite, the first blind hero, serve as rare exceptions that cemented the rule.

32. On the latter, see http://www.comicsalliance.com/2011/09/22/starfire-catwoman-sex-superheroine/ and Parille.

33. Scholars continue to debate the validity and usefulness of the "ages" model (adopted from fan discourse) for comics history. My description of the Silver Age's development in this chapter follows convention. When the Silver Age "ended" is a more open question, with some scholars arguing for *Amazing Spider-Man*, vol. 1, #121 (Jun. 1973, the death of Gwen Stacy) as the beginning of the "darker" Bronze Age, as discussed in chapter 7. For a standard treatment, see Jacobs and Jones; for alternative views and critiques of the ages model, see Woo.

34. On the influence of the previous decades' Romance comics on the 1960s superheroes, see Hatfield 2012: 121 and passim.

35. See also Wright, chapter 5, on the anti-communist hysteria of the early Cold War as reflected in comics.

36. See, in particular, Kimmell, chapter 8.

37. On the changing paradigms for men and the anxiety they provoked, see Horrocks and Blazina: 91–95 and Badinter's discussion of the "mutilated man" in chapter 5; on superhero as two-edged compensation for male inadequacy, see Horrocks and Campling: 145.

38. On the mechanism of the "dominant fictions," she writes:

> Thus the male subject does not just spontaneously happen to believe that he is not castrated. That belief is instilled in him through the unceasing flow of paternal images and sounds within which he is encouraged to "find" himself; through the externalizing displacement onto the feminine subject of the losses that afflict him; and last, but by no means least, through his subordination to the dominant fiction by means of which his social formation coordinates its diverse discourses. Since this final operation generally necessitates a series of additional castrations, phallic male subjectivity might also be said to be predicated upon a massive cultural disavowal of the lack upon which it rests. (113)

Silverman further develops the concept of the "dominant fiction" (which pertains to comics as well as other media) through among other things Freudian and Althusserian notions of masochism, in her 1992 book *Male Subjectivity at the Margins*. On the application of such gender and psychoanalytic concepts to comics in another cultural context, see Alaniz 2009.

39. Danny Fingeroth, in *Disguised as Clark Kent*, notes that Stan Lee, Jack Kirby, and other Marvel Silver Age creators were middle-aged veterans by the early 1960s (115); this, too, could have influenced their choice to focus on physical vulnerability. He reiterated the point to me in interview (Fingeroth 2008).

40. Also in evidence, another genre marker: the youthful male superhero's Oedipal dynamics. Peter's collapse is recognized for what is—a rather juvenile overreaction to a common ailment—by paternalistic older men: Captain Stacy, who declares, "The boy is ill—feverish!" (10) and a garrulous doctor who diagnoses the hero.

41. In this regard, I strongly echo Ben Saunders's call to arms:

> If as comics scholars we want to continue to raise appreciation and awareness of the art form, then it would seem sensible to acknowledge the broad appeal of superheroes, and to encourage critical work that deepens our understanding of that appeal—in formal and aesthetic terms as well as psychological and social terms—rather than regard superhero comics with sniffy disdain, as if they were a shameful blot upon the otherwise immaculate landscape of contemporary sequential art. (149)

CHAPTER 2

1. As Lennard Davis wrote in the 1990s:

> The work of many scholars who have investigated aspects of the body is now being reassembled into the field of disability studies. . . . All these works might not have been seen as existing under the rubric of disability studies, but as the field evolves, it recuperates and includes this earlier work as a retrospectively organized set of originating documents. (1997A: 4)

2. Arguably, the disability rights movement since its beginnings (traced to quadriplegic Ed Roberts's struggle to enter the University of California at Berkeley's law school in 1962) attracted stares. On Roberts, the San Francisco sit-in and the rise of the Independent Living movement, see Shapiro, chapter 2. On the ADAPT (Americans Disabled Accessible for Public Transit) protest at Capitol Hill, see Shapiro, chapter 4.

3. A term coined by Simon Williams; see Williams, chapter 5.

4. Critics of the "disability as visuality" thesis, such as Davis and Stuart Murray, argue that the focus on plainly physical impairments has overly de-emphasized such cognitive and other disabilities as Tourette's Syndrome, deafness, epilepsy, Depression, Chronic Fatigue Syndrome, Environmental Illness, and, especially, autism. See Murray 2012 and 2006, where he notes, "The often hidden nature of cognitive impairment is, possibly, something that even scholars working in the field of disability and cultural narrative, or those utilizing the critical languages of neuroscientific enquiry, have failed to see" (25). For the neurodiversity model applied to comics, see Squier, Birge and Alaniz 2011.

5. Garland-Thomson developed these ideas further in her book *Staring: How We Look*, to which I turn in subsequent chapters.

6. Elsewhere they term the norm "an ideological abstraction based upon faulty empiricism" (2000: 29).

7. For more on the critique of normalcy, see Davis 2002, chapter 6.

8. See Birge: 194 for a useful summary of the concept of impairment (physical, physiological) vs. disability (social, constructed) in Disability Studies; see also Davis 2002: 23 and Engel/Munger: 52–53 for its critique.

9. See Berman and Davis 2012, chapter 1, for more detailed summaries.

10. Adds Shapiro: "While prodigious achievement is praiseworthy in anyone, disabled or not, it does not reflect the day-to-day reality of most disabled people, who struggle constantly with smaller challenges, such as finding a bus with a wheelchair lift to go downtown or fighting beliefs that people with disabilities cannot work, be educated, or enjoy life as well as anyone else" (17).

11. All these factors come into play when the appeal of superhero iconography (its "mysterious power") proves irresistible for the construction of a new, non-disabled self-image, e.g., the Christopher Reeve "super man" billboard. We might call this the "supercrip" paradigm taken to its literal, perverse extreme: Superman in a wheelchair. The California artist René Garcia's *Superman* (2002) literalizes it even further.

12. Davis estimates that 15 to 20 percent of the US population has a disability (2002: 4). On the vexed issue of measuring employment among the disabled, see Stapleton and Burkhauser, as well as its critique by Dinsmore. See Brueggeman, et al on the persistent barriers to the disabled in education.

13. Sigmund Freud, in *Beyond the Pleasure Principle*, refers to the children's game "fort-da" (here-there), a sort of "peekaboo" activity, as illustrative of his "repetition compulsion" concept. The insistent return and disappearance of disability in the superhero genre, I argue, functions as just such a repetition compulsion. For a discussion of Freud's use of the "fort-da" game, see Bronfen: 118.

14. Longtime editor/writer Jim Shooter characterized such Silver Age innovations to me this way: "I'm not taking anything away from . . . Stan [Lee], I think he revolutionized everything. On the other hand, I think that making a character sympathetic by giving him a disability or something like that is kind of an easy trick to pull" (2012).

15. Hatfield argues *X-Men* provided the "seed" (2012: 130) for a new "epic" approach to the superhero "'mythic' both in its scale and in its pantheonic complications" (ibid.: 138), which would eventually lead to Kirby's revolutionary 1970s "Fourth World" series at DC Comics. Also important to note: Lee and Kirby's Inhumans, a race of genetically engineered beings that debuted in *Fantastic Four*, vol. 1, #45 (Dec. 1965), a key bridge between the X-Men and the Fourth World. Sean Howe also notes the Inhumans' importance in Marvel's mythopoesis and bid to create a vast "universe" of continuity (2012: 71–72).

16. We need, of course, to take genre into account when discussing how disability "operates" in a given work. As fantastic narratives, superhero comics reify and negotiate the reality of

disabled bodies in outlandish and absurd ways—though as we see in the present study this often makes them more, not less, potent at broaching conversations about issues the society represses, especially for young readers. In *Aesthetic Nervousness*, Ato Quayson emphasizes, "It is in the totality of literary relationships established in the individual texts that . . . disability acquires distinctiveness, and a discussion of . . . the texts would have to pay close attention to such a totality" (35). He is specifically making reference to how disability "appears" differently in William Faulkner's work versus a magical realist novel such as Gabriel Garcia-Márquez's *One Hundred Days of Solitude*. The point applies no less to superhero narratives.

17. Other major Marvel Silver Age figures such as Spider-Man do not fall into this category (Peter Parker has no explicit disability besides astigmatism, unless one counts the "social disability" of being considered a nerd). Such characters therefore fit much more neatly into the realm of pure adolescent power fantasy, in which the superpowers merely overcompensate for a despised "normality." On the other hand, the otherwise non-disabled Captain America, a Golden Age figure revived by Lee/Kirby in the 1960s, was "given" an affective traumatic condition (survivor guilt over the death in action of his sidekick Bucky) to "humanize" him further.

18. On the "mortal" threat of domesticity to the superhero in the 1950s, see Best.

19. Though still widely used, the term "handicapped"—emblem of an earlier, badly regarded era—is today considered offensive by many in the disabled community. On language regarding disability, see Linton, chapter 2.

20. In fact, Fox recycled the general outline of this plot from a previous story he had published twenty years before, "A Place in the World!", which featured the Justice Society of America (*All-Star Comics*, vol. 1, #27, Winter 1945, Fox/Martin Naydel). In true Silver Age metafictive fashion, Flash cites the precursor Golden Age tale (519).

21. We see a more "serious" treatment of disfigurement and social isolation in the case of Ferro Lad (Andrew Nolan), a member of the Legion of Superheroes first introduced in 1966. In "The Adult Legion" (*Adventure Comics*, vol. 1, #354, Mar. 1967, Shooter/Swan), a flashback scene shows Nolan and his brother Douglas—who wear masks to hide their "grotesquely inhuman" (Kawasaki 2009B: 124) faces—mocked by two young girls.

22. O'Neil and Adams's late 1960s/early 1970s *Green Lantern/Green Arrow* series for DC represented their most sustained attempt at socially relevant comics, inspired in part by the counterculture. See Wright, chapter 8.

23. The representation of Flippy also participates in the nineteenth-and-twentieth-century freak show's frequent sensationalistic blurring between the human and animal; Adams's art makes the boy's appendages seem especially seal-like. See Bogdan for more on the social construction of freak shows, which had disappeared as an American cultural institution by the 1930s.

24. For more on bioethics and cochlear implants, and the resistance from some in the deaf community to the devices, see Komesaroff.

25. The original Green Lantern oath is, of course: "In brightest day, in blackest night, / No evil shall escape my sight / Let those who worship evil's might, / Beware my power—Green Lantern's light!" Other members of the Green Lantern Corps have used modified oaths, but only Fan's ignores the concepts of light and color.

26. For an account of accommodation traced back to section 504 of the 1973 Rehabilitation Act, see Garland-Thomson 2009: 197fn. On environmental modification as a concept in Disability Studies, see Hebl and Kleck: 434–35. On the failure post-ADA to create accommodating environments and integrate the disabled into education and work life as quickly and thoroughly as some would wish, see Longmore 2003, chapter 1.

27. They go on: "Disability studies does invite us all to at least consider the able-bodied agenda lurking in the way we make meaning through so many crippling metaphors, in the way we compose and communicate that disables even as it might be attempting to 'enable'" (369).

28. Moore, of course, is also punning on "ring" (an object worn on the finger, e.g., power ring) with "ring" (a resonating sound, and its figurative derivations, e.g., "ring of truth").

29. For an account of this "ultimate" instance of multiverse retconning and its aftermath, see Niederhausen.

30. Subsequent DC retcons restored the character to continuity.

31. It happened in *Hawkeye*, vol. 1, #4 (Dec. 1983), though the matter was subsequently milked for humor (see *Avengers*, vol. 1, #239, Jan. 1984) or dropped altogether, as elaborated by Suzanne Walker in her "Deafening Outcry: Hawkeye, Transformative Works, and the Re-Creation of Disability" presentation at "Fantastic! Heroic! Disabled?: 'Cripping' the Con" (Syracuse University, April 11, 2013). The casual jettisoning of a protagonist's disability without explanation has precedent in the Golden Age; see Daredevil (created by Jack Binder in 1940), whose muteness vanishes from one issue to the next.

32. Reynolds notes that

> heroes are generally obliged to defeat at least one supervillain per issue, but the events which lead up to the confrontation are normally initiated by the supervillain. The hero is in this sense passive: he is not called upon to act unless the status quo is threatened by the villain's plans . . . The common outcome, as far as the structure of the plot is concerned, is that the villains are concerned with change and the heroes with the maintenance of the status quo. (50–51)

On the villain as proactive and heroes as reactive, see also Coogan: 110–15.

33. As Fiedler writes, "In the throes of paranoia and projection, we convince ourselves that the crippledness of the cripple is an outward and visible sign of an inward invisible state" (1996: 41). Among the key literary figures he lists under such a heading: Shakespeare's Richard III, Captain Ahab, Long John Silver, Quasimodo, Captain Hook, and several James Bond villains. Incidentally, Quasimodo (Quasi-Motivational Destruct Organism) is also the name of a Marvel supervillain introduced in 1966 (see chapter 5).

34. For example, in his Lacanian reading, Christopher Murray sees the routine "castration imagery" humiliation of the villain by the hero as a form of therapy, "with the banishment and containment of the inner demons (fear, hatred, and impotence) represented in the villain" (202). Coogan's structuralist approach too sees the villain expressing "displaced aspects" of the hero (103–109).

35. As Francis Bacon observed in the early seventeenth century:

> Deformed persons are commonly even with nature; for as nature hath done ill by them, so do they by nature; being for the most part, as the Scripture saith, void of natural affection; and so they have their revenge of nature. . . . Therefore it is good to consider of deformity, not as a sign which is more deceivable, but as a cause which seldom faileth of the effect. Whosoever hath anything fixed in his person that doth induce contempt, hath also a perpetual spur in himself, to rescue and deliver himself from scorn; therefore all deformed persons are extreme bold. (296)

36. Mole Man visually stands apart from the Fantastic Four and "normal" bodies throughout the story, both physically and spatially: he appears in one panel in the opposite corner from a "beautiful" classical statue of a man (21); he is introduced in a separate, rather incongruous panel in medium close-up when Johnny and Reed discover the Valley of the Diamonds (19); his green costume contrasts sharply with the Four's magenta garb; and his five-panel action-to-action staff contest with Johnny (or Reed, the man is not identified) is staged such that the two remain in place even as they move dynamically, enhancing the impact of their stark physical differences.

37. Lee and Kirby's Mole Man owes a debt to the Franz Kafka short story "The Burrow" (1924, posthumous), about an unnamed creature's alienation and dread of the world beyond the confines of its subterranean home. Most readers have read the creature as an anthropomorphized mole.

38. It bears mention that, oddly, the Lizard's appearances correlated with instances of Spider-Man's body "destabilizing," as if the villain's own corporeal mutability had a contagion-like effect on the hero's. In one case, Spider-Man sprains his arm so that he must—absurdly—wear a sling as he fights (*Spider-Man*, #44–45, 1967) and in another, famously grows four extra arms (*Spider-Man*, #100–102, 1971).

39. The Kristevan abject, discussed in chapters 6 and 7, has useful applications to the super-villain as described here.

40. This episode's fraught Oedipal drama bears some mention, since later continuity would reveal that Doom had been trying to contact his mother, who lay trapped in the transdimensional realm of Mephisto, with the failed device. Reed Richards—whom Doom always blames for the experiment's catastrophic outcome—thus represents the interfering, domineering father that ever foils the son's desired return to the maternal.

41. This history leads Coogan to taxonomize Doom as a "mad scientist" and "renegade commander" brand of supervillain (61), and de-emphasize the role played by his disfigurement (85). As I argue in this chapter, he should also fall in the "monster" category.

42. For the fascistic overtones of this episode, and Kirby's seeming awareness of them, see the "Doom's Scratch" section of Fischer. On supervillain narcissism, see Coogan: 85–90.

43. The exception: John Byrne's "revisionist" account of Doom's origin story in *Fantastic Four*, vol. 1, #278 (May 1985). He depicts Doom's face after the experiment explosion, revealing that he had suffered only a scar along his cheek, thus reconciling Lee and Kirby's conflicting approaches to the character (for succinct accounts of this convoluted history, see Fischer and Jay's Fludd's article on Doom at http://www.ffplaza.com/library/?issue=ff@2). But Byrne does not represent Doom's face once he has donned the hot iron mask and seared his features, presumably beyond recognition.

44. For a different, non-queer theory approach to the horror cinema monster's ambiguity, see Carroll. His arguments pertain to Dr. Doom no less than do Berenstein's.

45. Compare these Silver Age villains to their pre-Cold War Golden Age counterparts: so many of them—Lex Luthor, Sinestro, Yellow Claw, Two-Face, the Penguin, Bizarro, Master Man, Lady Lotus, Mr. Mxyzptlk—go unmasked.

CHAPTER 3

1. In this regard, what I here call Daredevil's "hybrid" identity bears important similarities to the "borderline cases" of disabled superheroes discussed in chapter 4.

2. The reader, if she must, may see for herself in "Thou Shalt Not Covet Thy Neighbor's Planet!" (*Daredevil*, vol. 1, #28, May 1967, Lee/Colan).

3. Blogger Pat Curley pronounced, "It's an entertaining storyline overall, but it strains credulity to the snapping point"; while Robert of *The Matt Murdock Chronicles* site declared of *Daredevil*, #31: "some very good moments mixed with some really frustrating implausible plot points" (Jan. 8, 2009). On the end of the storyline, the latter opined, "Scientifically, a completely bonkers issue but still quite good fun. Especially with the promise of 'No More Mike.' Hurrah" (Feb. 15, 2009).

4. Though for a critique of Goffman's thesis as applied to disability, see the introduction to Brune and Wilson.

5. Writing on John Howard Griffin, whose *Black Like Me* (1959) represents one of the most notorious accounts of racial passing, Jeff Brune highlights the role blindness played in the author's

journey. He notes, in language pertinent to *Daredevil*: "Because a person's body can change so quickly and so often, disability can make identity especially fluid. The destabilization of Griffin's body contributed to the destabilization of his gender, sexuality, disability/nondisability status, and later, his race" (15–16). Brune's approach derives from intersection theory, explored at length in chapter 4. I thank Dr. Brune for sharing his unpublished essay. See also Brune and Wilson.

6. As Tobin Siebers points out:

> Temporary passing is empowering, producing brief moments of freedom from the prejudice and morbid curiosity often found to surround disability. Pretending to be able-bodied is one way of performing normalcy, of inserting oneself in society and escaping the alienating experience of being disabled. In the long term, however, disabled people who try to pass may feel guilty or become depressed about constructing their acceptance by society on the basis of pretense. They also internalize prejudices against disability, seeing their hidden identity as wrong, lacking or shameful. For the physically and mentally disabled, passing often requires overcompensation that exacerbates already existing conditions. (2008: 118)

7. Though eventually, Blake does disappear entirely, revealed by Lee and Kirby to have been an invention of Thor's father Odin, as part of his son's punishment in Earthly exile. The disabled identity amounts to a mere paternalistic lesson in overcoming for a brat thunder god in a sort of Midgardian penalty box (see chapter 2).

8. In contrast, no compunction pertained to the depiction of blind women's pupils, as evidenced by Ben Grimm's vision-impaired paramour Alicia Masters, introduced in *Fantastic Four*, vol. 1, #8 (Nov. 1962).

CHAPTER 4

1. Linking them to the Uncanny, which Sigmund Freud initially describes as that which "ought to have remained secret and hidden but has come to light" (1919: 225).

2. While the humanities have only relatively recently come to such associations, the link between the disabled and other marginalized groups has deep, entangled roots. As Mitchell and Snyder put it:

> Physical or cognitive inferiority has historically characterized the means by which bodies have been constructed as "deviant": the Victorian equation between femininity and hysteria; the biological racism that justified slavery and social subordination of racial minorities; psychiatry's categorization of homosexuality as a pathological disorder; and so on. This socially imposed relationship between marginalized populations and "inferior" biology situates disability studies in proximity to other minority approaches. (2000: 2)

For more on disability's intersections with other othernesses, see Baynton; Siebers 2008: chapter 4; and Davis 2002: chapter 1.

3. For example, Weinberg and Santana's 1978 sociological analysis of superhero comics found significant correlations between "evil" and "physical deformity" (57 percent), "head distortion" (71 percent) and "limb deformities" (75 percent) (328). Arthur Asa Berger, in his 1973 critique of comics, described the superhero genre as "abound[ing] with 'Hulks' and 'Things'—*grotesques* which are unnatural in shape and appearance—ugly, fantastic and incongruous" (199, emphasis in original). He maintained, "Its ugliness is an affront to society and suggests that something is wrong with the social order" (200).

4. When the team, due to the machinations of the shape-shifting Skrulls, become *personae non grata*, Grimm rails, "Well, maybe they're right! Maybe I *am* a monster! I look like one—and sometimes I *feel* like one!" (Sedlmeier 2011: 31, emphasis in original); later, sent back in time by Dr. Doom to the era of Blackbeard, Grimm assumes the pirate's identity (complete with beard and eyepatch), telling his teammates, "The future holds nothing for me! In the twentieth century I'm nothin' but a monster . . . a *freak!*" (ibid.: 119, emphasis in original). He proceeds to strand Reed and Johnny in a lifeboat at sea so that they won't interfere with his plans to remain in the past.

5. Lee and Mair also note that Grimm generated the most fan mail for the series (120), while Wright directly relates the Thing's physical state to the pangs of adolescence (205).

6. Grimm's problem-plagued traversal of Manhattan contrasts sharply with more "graceful" physically ideal heroes who soar over the city, such as Superman. As Scott Bukatman notes, "The best of them move with more than swift efficiency, their poise and elegance also speaking a kind of poetic appropriation of space" (2003: 190). In this, too, borderline Silver Age figures deviated from their Golden Age predecessors. I thank Charles Hatfield for the insight.

7. Lennard Davis relates the "one-size-fits-all" mentality regarding bodies to the demands of modern neoliberalism: "If all workers are equal, and all workers are citizens, then all citizens must have standard bodies to be able to fit into the industrial-political notion of democracy, equality and normality. Clearly, people with disabilities pose problems to work situations in which work is standardized and bodies are conceptualized as interchangeable" (2002: 111). See especially Davis 2002: chapter 6.

8. N.p.; page numbers refers to the original issue's pagination.

9. The term is Charles Hatfield's (2012: 116). While a detailed analysis goes beyond the scope of this chapter, Bruce Banner/Hulk (who debuted six months after the *Fantastic Four*, in 1962) clearly represents an even more fraught "borderline" case than the Thing, in that the former's physical/mental difference leads to even more profound social alienation—he eschews human society and team membership almost completely (leaving the Avengers in its second issue, preferring isolation in the southwest desert, later fitting in only with that team of misfits, The Defenders). Like other early Marvel series, *The Incredible Hulk*, an attempt by Lee and Kirby to create a "good-looking or sympathetic-looking monster" (Lee/Mair: 122), bore the strong influence of 1950–60s monster comics, as pointed out by Hatfield. Both Hulk and the Thing, he argues, were "pitiable fall guys whose power—basically, mind-boggling strength—came at the cost of monstrosity, social ostracism, and alienation" (2012: 117). Similarly, Bukatman describes the "really, really big guy" figure in many super-teams as "the most explicitly monstrous bodies in the superhero canon and often objects of self-pity—they are the strongest team members, but do they not bleed? Physical strength only hides the emotionally complex inner subject" (2003: 64). Furthermore, the borderline case, none more so than the Hulk, complicates any "purist" definition of the superhero. Tellingly, Peter Coogan's taxonomical approach struggles somewhat with the Hulk (who has no mission, costume, or motivation to do good), ultimately relying on recurring conventions (supervillains, a sidekick, super-teams) to "keep the Hulk within the superhero genre" (41). Even more so than with the Thing, then, the Hulk represents a case of the superpowers themselves functioning as a disability, which manifests itself in routine rampages. As discussed, such figures often serve as destabilizing forces; their "disabilities" threaten to escape their control—thus, the worldviews them with suspicion, alarm and (as the products of radiation accidents) Cold War dread. As Bradford Wright notes, "His very existence pointed to failures of modern civilization, and so the Hulk proved intolerable to society's controlling forces" (209).

10. As Haller notes, paraphrasing John Clogston:

The disabled person is portrayed as deviant because of "superhuman" feats (i.e., an ocean-sailing blind man) or as "special" because they live regular lives "in spite" of disability (i.e. a deaf high school student who plays softball). This portrayal reinforces the idea that disabled people are deviant—and so, for someone who is less than "complete," the accomplishment is "amazing."

11. As with much else in Grimm's story, this detail recalls the life (or its representation by others) of Joseph Merrick (1862–90), the severely deformed "Elephant Man" of late Victorian London. As surmised by his doctor Frederick Treves, "I fancy when he talked of life among the blind there was a half-formed idea in his mind that he might be able to win the affection of a woman if only she were without eyes to see" (Montagu/Treves: 32). Like Grimm, Merrick too complained that he had trouble using utensils made for more "human" hands, and that ordinary shoes didn't fit him (ibid.: 31).

12. On disability and narcissism, see especially Siebers 2008: chapter 2.

13. Among other things, a Kirby sketch (widely circulated on Hanukah greeting cards) depicted Grimm in skullcap and prayer shawl, holding a prayer book before a menorah. As Hatfield points out, many fans and colleagues saw much of Kirby (born Jacob Kurtzberg) in the Thing (2012: 118), a belief buttressed by "What If the Fantastic Four Were the Original Marvel Bullpen?" (What If, vol. 1, #11, Oct. 1978, Kirby), in which "the King" cast himself in the role. The conclusive revelation took place in "Remembrance of Things Past!" (Fantastic Four, vol. 3, #56, Aug. 2002, Kesel/Immonen), eight years after Kirby's death. See also Bower for an overview of the representation of Jews in the superhero genre. Christopher B. Zeichmann sees a different paradigm evoked by Grimm's outsider status and attempts to pass: the "tragic mulatto" type of racialized representation (78 and 87fn).

14. For a treatment of the Jewish body and abjection in comics, see Glaser.

15. In his discussion of "mutant bodies," Bukatman makes a critical point applicable to the borderline case: "[They] are explicitly analogized to Jewish bodies, gay bodies, adolescent bodies, Japanese or Native American bodies—they are, first and foremost, subjected and subjugated and colonized figures" (2003: 73).

16. As recounted in The Thing, vol. 1, #27–35 (1985–86).

17. See Captain America, vol. 1, #330–31, 1987. The strongly suggested gang rape occurred in #330.

18. In Fantastic Four #310, Ms. Marvel shows signs of mental imbalance and mania, prompting Grimm to think: "... You're not cuttin' it, Shary! Even though I luv ya—even though ya really do got a strong bod—I don't see ya gettin' any better in your head!" (7, emphasis and unconventional spelling in original).

19. The story, in fact, retells the Fantastic Four's origin in flashback (5–6), cementing the link.

20. The case was more complex than this: in response to the disability community's outcry, Bouvia issued a statement saying she was not acting under the influence of depression, but exercising her free will, and asked them to "express their support for me by agreeing that my choice, as a competent individual, is mine to make, however much any other person disagrees with that choice" (quoted in Mary Johnson 1997).

21. More recently, Tobin Siebers has detailed how such internalization of anti-disabled biases remains a serious issue in the twenty-first century. In discussing a hypothetical Iraq War veteran who has lost an arm and tries to adjust to his new reality back home, he writes:

How might we expect him to embrace and to value his new identity? He is living his worst nightmare. He cannot sleep. He hates what he has become. He distances himself from his wife and family. He begins to drink too much. He tries to use a functional prosthetic, but he loathes being seen with a hook. The natural prosthetic offered to him by Army doctors does not really work, and he prefers to master tasks with his one good arm. He cannot stand the stares of those around him, the looks of pity and contempt as he tries to perform simple tasks in public, and he begins to look upon himself with disdain. (2008: 26–27)

22. Schiavo was a Florida woman in a persistent vegetative state whose husband petitioned for the legal right to remove her feeding tube and end her life, despite the wishes of her parents. For a more thorough critique of autonomy in end-of-life decisions as they pertain to the disabled, see especially Braswell. For an alternative view on the issue, see Fadem, et al. See also Mary Johnson 1994 for more on disability and end-of-life issues.

23. Incidentally, Sharon Ventura was not the first romantic fixation for Grimm who turned to him after suffering a physical change. In "For Beauty Passed Away" (*The Thing*, vol. 1, #2, Aug. 1983, Byrne/Wilson), an old college flame, Alynn Cambers, returns to his life, her face and body showing the traces of a stroke. A movie actress now rendered a "hopeless cripple," her career ruined, she pleads with Grimm: "Tell me how you deal with it . . ." (21). The story makes for an interesting companion piece to "Lost Love," the 1985 Lori Lemaris/Superman story, also scripted by Byrne, examined in chapter 2.

24. Ventura, a highly conflicted but ultimately heroic figure, is brought out of her catatonia by Dr. Doom, who—true to his role of nemesis—offers to cure her so she might seek revenge on the Fantastic Four, those who "caused [her] affliction" (*Fantastic Four*, #311: 21). But, rather than repeat Grimm's old pattern, Ventura explodes, striking the villain. "I swore—to *deserve* the honor of joining the Fantastic Four!" she says. "I *promised* on my honor to make everyone *proud* of me!" (23). Later, she laments to Grimm: "I-I almost forgot—my *honor*, Ben! I would have—would have *failed*—!" (ibid., all emphasis in original).

25. Englehart mentioned in his personal interview that much of the staff in Marvel's "bullpen" despised She-Thing. The character, along with his other innovations—such as putting half the team into retirement—led to increasing creative clashes with editor in chief Tom Defalco, so that with issue #329 Englehart began using a pseudonym, "John Harkness," as his writer credit. Four issues later he left the series altogether.

26. For evidence of fans' displeasure, see the letter's page to *Fantastic Four* #314 (May 1988: 30–31), the first to register the change in Ventura's appearance. "What have you done to Ms. Marvel? Please turn her back to normal soon! I hate her like that! She's so ugly!" wrote one reader, while another opined, "Do you feel guilt? Shame? Or anything at all? Poor Ben! Poor Sharon! I can't imagine how they will carry on after this tragedy." At least one reader, however (Allen Bradford, writing in the letter's page to #317 [Aug. 1988]: 31) offered a more considered critique, wondering, partly in light of the Ventura storyline, "how wide a streak of misogyny" Englehart might have had, "and how much it is affecting your writing. . . . Give us women that are unique, sure, but that live, breathe love, that need not be troubled by trauma, odd sexual desires or experiences or physical transformation to be interesting and readable . . ."

27. See Garland-Thomson's portrait of McBryde-Johnson in 2009: 188–93.

28. Garland-Thomson's disability-inflected counterpart to the scopophilic male gaze, as discussed in chapter 2.

29. One of Aquilone's commenters even speculated on her "labia made of limestone."

30. The She-Thing case likewise evokes comparisons to the long-standing tradition in US horror cinema (also aimed at young males) of depicting the female body as monstrous; see especially Creed. For the application of a similar gendered psychoanalytic approach to comics, see Walton.

31. "Shulkie," as some came to call her, first appeared in *Savage She-Hulk* #1 (Lee/Buscema, Feb. 1980). Marvel at the time anticipated the producers of the *Incredible Hulk* television show

would create their own female version of the character, and wanted to seize the copyright first; see Vaughn and Howe: 220–21.

32. For the feminist critic Kelly Thompson, She-Hulk even comes to embody the over-sexualization of superheroines in the twenty-first century. In comparing male and female heroes in 2012, she writes (somewhat ahistorically):

> Men are still allowed to look a bit like "monsters" . . . on occasion. For women it's incredibly rare, unless they ARE in fact "monsters." And even when they are "monsters" . . . they're still frequently possessors of beautiful bodies and/or sex appeal. . . . Bruce Banner as The Hulk? Frequently drawn as a pretty terrifying monster and certainly not considered stereotypically handsome. Jennifer Walters as She-Hulk? Stone. Cold. Fox.

33. The episode also illustrates Reynolds's contention that

> in their simultaneous offering and denying of sexuality, plus their cool strength and determination in battle with supervillains, the superheroines offer a reconciliation of all the conflicting demands of adolescent male sexual desire. Sexuality is domesticated (i.e. made safe) and yet remains exceptionally exciting. Women are visually thrilling, and yet threatening and dangerous only to outsiders and strangers. (81)

Rebecca Wanzo similarly argues that "the challenge for those rendering the soft body of the female superheroine is to negotiate the tension between political progressivism and gendered conventionality" (23).

34. This language recalls a conversation with Grimm from eight issues earlier, evincing the gradual nature of Ventura's change of heart: "Don't you *see*, Ben? My problems all came because I was a *pretty woman*—but now I'm not *pretty*, and hardly even a *woman!*" (*Fantastic Four*, vol. 1, #313, Apr. 1988: 30, Englehart/Buscema).

35. Compare the fine art appropriation here to that of Michelangelo's *Pièta* on the cover of Jim Starlin's *Death of Captain Marvel*, discussed in chapter 7.

36. The sexuality of the disabled has received much scholarly attention in the last two decades; for an overview see Siebers 2008, chapter 7. See also Samuels for a deeper discussion of queer theory and disability. For a much more detailed treatment of sex and disability in comics, see my essay on Renee and Rich Jensen's 1975 underground classic *Amputee Love* (Alaniz 2012).

37. Among other things, Ventura's narrative arc elicits comparisons to the sex-positive poetry of the disabled Cheryl Marie Wade: "I'm a black panther with green eyes and scars like a picket fence / I'm pink lace panties teasing a stub of milk white thigh / I'm the Evil Eye/ . . . I'm the Woman With Juice" (408).

38. For all his woman-bashing, Aquilone stumbles on a similar point, albeit one expressed as only he can: "They made a female version of the monstrous Hulk damn hot. Would it have been so hard to make a huge, lumpy, orange rock creature sexy? Okay, so maybe they should have just left this alone."

39. Not surprisingly, black comics writers, including the late Dwayne McDuffie, have complained that such a uniquely heavy symbolic burden endlessly complicates their work. See the McDuffie interview in *The Comics Journal* #160 (Jun. 1993).

40. Singer identifies one genre convention as holding an unequivocal advantage for the depiction of the black experience in America: the "split identity" or "superhero as a mask which scars and splits the psyche" (2002: 116), something he relates to W. E. B. Du Bois's concept of

double-consciousness. But we can also easily link the "scar" with the internalized stigma and self-pity that can, as James Charlton puts it, "prevent people with disabilities from knowing their real selves, their real needs, and their real capabilities" as well as the true source of their oppression (27).

41. Or, as Aldo Regalado puts it: "How . . . should the transgressive potential of superhero fiction be understood in light of the genre's often racist underpinnings?" (86). For more on race in superhero comics, see Wright: 237–51 and Dyk, who argues, "Marvel black superhero texts of the 1970s are colonialist. They present an image of blackness mediated by white male capitalists. Superheroes of the Luke Cage/Black Panther variety are black men behind white masks" (468). Nama, Dyk, Regalado, Singer, and Brown all ignore Cyborg in their works.

42. As touched on in chapter 2, the character first appeared in 1980 as a member of the relaunched *Teen Titans* series, positioned to compete with Marvel's successful revived *Uncanny X-Men*.

43. Pérez pays homage to original *Doom Patrol* artist Bruno Premiani by drawing Stone's first glimpse of his new prosthetic hands as a "point of view" shot, as in Cliff Steele/Robotman's origin (see chapter 5).

44. In discussing the case of Roosevelt Dawson, a twenty-one-year-old African-American quadraplegic who ended his life with the assistance of Dr. Jack Kevorkian in 1998, Rosemarie Garland-Thomson contrasts his experience with that of the much more famous and wealthy Christopher Reeve: "What makes death preferable for Dawson and life preferable for Reeve, I argue, is that the narrative emerging from Dawson's life imagined him as incurable, but Reeve— including his extensive support system and positive media image—focuses a great deal of cultural, economic and racial capital on creating an optimistic narrative of cure" (2004B: 778).

45. Or, as Garland-Thomson puts it: "The prominent interest in hybrid theoretical figures such as cyborgs, monsters, and grotesques . . . squanders [a] critical opportunity by failing to recognize and politicize the relation between these figures and actual women with disabilities" (2005: 1565). See also Barbara Jo Lewis (2000), who subjects Cyborg, Marvel's Deathlok (1974) and other comics man-machine hybrids to an Adlerian analysis.

46. Oddly, Barbara Jo Lewis muses that Cyborg perhaps behaves so vituperously because of superhero comics' "teenage audience" (152), eliding the social reasons why a young black man in 1970s America might have some anger in his heart.

47. Stone's girlfriend Marcy also incites his race hatred. Urging him to "rumble" against a white gang, she explains, "My father was passed over for *promotion* for some *white* dude. The color of our skin *marks* us, Vic. An' like my father *says*, maybe we should start *doin'* something about it" (10, emphasis in original).

48. This places "Cyborg" squarely within a 1970s trend identified by Bradford Wright whereby superhero comics "endorse[d] a liberal civil-rights agenda but reject[ed] black separatism" (237).

49. Though somewhat simplistically and problematically described as the capacity to "*conquer* disability by looking for the hidden ability" (237, my emphasis), Packer's formulation seems applicable to Cyborg.

CHAPTER 5

1. See, in particular, Melrose's succinct account. Interestingly, Drake himself came to suspect Marvel "spies" had stolen his concept, though he did go on to write several issues of *X-Men* in the late 1960s (Epstein).

2. Hatfield calls the *X-Men* of 1963–66 "an underachieving series" compared to Lee and artist Jack Kirby's other work (2012: 131); in terms both of quality and sales, it certainly was.

3. See Wright: 263–65 for a brief history of the Claremont run.

4. The team's original ranks consisted of Cyclops/Slim (later Scott) Summers; Marvel Girl/ Jean Grey; Beast/Hank McCoy; Angel/Warren Worthington III; and Iceman/Bobby Drake.

5. The "X-Men as racial allegory" reading has become sufficiently established to inspire a backlash; see Darius and Shyminsky.

6. The series also spawned a highly successful movie franchise starting with *X-Men* (d. Bryan Singer, 2000).

7. The team/title's relaunchings include those of writer Paul Kupperberg and artist Joe Staton, starting with *Showcase*, vol. 1, #94 (Aug.–Sept. 1977) and Kupperberg and artist Steve Lightle with *Doom Patrol*, vol. 2, #1 (Oct. 1987). Morrison's celebrated run on that title unfolded over issues 19–63.

8. As Farr rather bluntly puts it late in the series: "We didn't set out to fight baddies! We also wanted to prove that 'freaks' like we [*sic*] can be valuable to the world! And, by example, to help every other outcast! Well, we made it! We gave some hope to every gimp, hare-lipped, fat, four-eyed kid in the world!" (vol. 1, #117, Feb. 1968: 7). All *X-Men* and *Doom Patrol* references in this chapter pertain to the original works, reprinted in Sedlmeier 2009/2003 and Kawasaki 2010/2009A, respectively.

9. Scholars have chiefly attributed the series' lackluster performance to Lee and Kirby's murderously overloaded work schedule in the early 1960s.

10. M.O.D.O.K., a product of AIM (Advanced Idea Mechanics) genetic engineering on the hapless George Tarleton, first appeared in *Tales of Suspense*, vol. 1, #93 (Sept. 1967, Lee/Kirby).

11. Hammond's origin unfolds in *Green Lantern*, vol. 2, #5 (Apr. 1961, Broome/Kane), *Justice League of America*, vol. 1, #14 (Sept. 1962, Fox/Sekowsky), and *Green Lantern*, vol. 2, #157 (1982, Kupperberg/Novick).

12. As Hatfield notes, "Kirby often used the combination of overgrown head and small or atrophied body to render an implicit critique of an emotionless scientism" (2012: 268fn); he cites the Fourth World figure Metron (who traverses time and space on his Mobius Chair), Modok, and other "hypercephalic" Kirby characters.

13. His charges often insist on rescuing him in battle, even when he explicitly commands them to fend for themselves: during their encounter with the Sentinels, when the ground gives out beneath them, Angel moves to save the professor, though the latter objects, "I *told* you—do not let *me* hamper your battle strategy! I'm not as helpless as you *think*!" (vol. 1, #15, Dec. 1965: 2, emphasis in original).

14. As it happens, Xavier later reveals he had been *faking* the loss of his powers as part of a "graduation test" for his students, banking on the stereotypical view of the disabled as weak and pitiful to effect his subterfuge. See chapter 3 for a detailed discussion of disability and passing.

15. I touch on this issue elsewhere in my discussion of the lame Donald Blake, the blind Matt Murdock, and, below, the radioactive Larry Trainor, all lovelorn men who experience their disabilities as a barrier to romance. As noted in chapter 4, the "deformed" Ben Grimm/Thing seems the most well-adjusted in this regard, given that he successfully maintains a relationship with Alicia Masters. However, Masters herself is blind, maintaining the unspoken prohibition against able-bodied/disabled dating.

16. Drake told an interviewer he based Caulder on a cousin who had polio and worked as a scientist: "The reason I wanted a man in a wheelchair is that I had been aware from almost the outset of comics that all the kids wanted to emulate the superheroes. They wanted to be the fastest or the strongest but there wasn't anybody who wanted to be the smartest. I decided I want a superhero for the nerds of the world" (Epstein).

17. The page number cited refers to the second story in this issue. The relatively disability-friendly depiction of a wheelchair-user in *Doom Patrol* as something other than a "defenseless cripple" recalls Irv Zola's comment upon surveying popular detective fiction, as reported by Mitchell and Snyder: "Out of hundreds of novels that forward disabled detective 'heroes,' never

once did Zola find a wheelchair user commenting, 'God dammit, how I hate stairs'" (2000: 21). Caulder, however, several times comes close to such grousing.

18. Only occasionally (again, much more rarely than is the case with Xavier) do we witness Caulder carried by other team-members, e.g., Robotman bearing him down some stairs as they depart Farr's aborted wedding (vol. 1, #104, Jun. 1966: 13).

19. Such bravado, as we have seen, is belied by the Chief's more complicated inner feelings about his paraplegia. Just before confronting Claw, he quails, "Can I defend myself while I'm a prisoner of these withered legs?" (#94: 9).

20. At various points, Dr. Death disguises himself to trick Trainor into doing his bidding. One of his aliases, interestingly, is a "Mr. Harkness," who talks Trainor into a job in part by showing off his prosthetic hook, saying, "I know what it is to be—*different!* I lost this hand ten years ago to a Bengal tiger!" (#109: 2, emphasis in original).

21. See Steele's origin story, "Robotman—Wanted Dead or Alive," aka "Robotman Unchained" (vol. 1, #100–101, 103, 105, 1965–66). Due to an "error" committed by Caulder during the brain transfer, Steele flies into an insane murderous rage, determined to exact vengeance on the unknown "mad medic" who turned him into a monster, and wreaks destruction on the city. Steele's villainous soliloquies, *mutatis mutandis*, would not seem out of place coming from the "freakish" Ben Grimm/Thing's lips during one of his revolts against the Fantastic Four: "Friends! That's a hot one! A robot's got no friends! No home—no kin no nothin'! But I've got one thing that keeps me goin'! The dream of catching up with the guy who did this to me – and *killing* him!" (#101: 8, emphasis in original).

The Lee/Kirby run of *X-Men* merely flirts with such genre-straining notions as the "borderline case," explored more fully in *Fantastic Four* and *Doom Patrol*. In "The Uncanny Threat of . . . Unus the Untouchable!" (#8), McCoy/Beast angrily resigns from the group after being attacked by an anti-mutant mob, railing, "I'm *through* risking my life for humans . . . for the *same* humans who fear us, hate us, want to *destroy* us! I think Magneto and his evil mutants are *right* . . . homo sapiens just aren't *worth* it!" (6, emphasis and ellipses in original). Rather than join Magneto or turn to crime, however, McCoy . . . launches a career as a professional wrestler.

22. As Mattozzi demonstrates in his semiotic analysis of the series, the team fought more amongst themselves when subjected to outside pressure; most deaths and accidents happened away from home; and by and large the villains were not American—suggesting a strong "us/them" structure at the heart of the stories.

23. The stability does not last; at the start of the very next issue, Madame Rouge continues to disrupt the team's familial bond, and as we know she eventually plays a hand in their deaths at series' end.

24. Mitchell and Snyder mince no words in their treatment of "mutant" superheroes as well, in ways that resonate with the present study's approach to the genre; see the epigraph to chapter 6.

25. The X-Men's arch-foes, Magneto and his Brotherhood of Evil Mutants, do not represent so complex and multilayered a community as their DC counterparts. Only the Morlocks (a subterranean group of mutants introduced in the 1980s) present as compelling a picture of alternative community predicated on physical otherness. In other early Silver Age series, Lee and Kirby did explore "dismodern" family groupings: the Mole Man's underground kingdom and the Inhumans, to name but two examples.

CHAPTER 6

1. The series also reflected Marvel's Jim Shooter-encouraged drive to produce adaptations of licensed properties in this era, e.g., *Star Wars, Battlestar Galactica, The Micronauts, Godzilla,* and *Rom: Spaceknight*—all based on films, television series, or toys. See Howe: 193.

2. Some sources claimed twenty-seven. On the Montreal stunt, including a description by the engineer who designed the rocket bike, see Michaelson. The comics series depicted a heavily fictionalized account of the Montreal accident in "Silver Charity, Sudden Death!" (*Human Fly*, vol. 1, #11, Jul. 1978, Mantlo/Elias).

3. Rojatt told *People* magazine in 1976 that he "conditions himself by rising at 3 a.m., running six miles and then plunging into a bathtub full of ice cubes" (Werner). That article listed Rojatt's age as twenty-nine.

4. In a May 17, 1977, interview with the *Ludington Daily News*, Rojatt explained that his body was not comprised of 60 percent metal, but he did have a "ball and pin" in one hip and a metal plate in his head.

5. The plane made two passes and attained a height of 5,000 feet. The impact of rain drops on Rojatt's body caused him to black out, and led to a six-week hospitalization (Silodrome). See Freeze for an account of the Mojave Desert stunt by the pilot, Clay Lacy. To access online footage of the stunt, see Silodrome.

6. As the Fly explains to reporters: "After *expenses,* any money I make goes to *charity . . .* to help the *disabled!*" (#1: 2, ellipsis and emphasis in original).

7. According to Yurkovich and Mantlo, rumors surfaced of the Ramacieri brothers' "tie-in with the Canadian underworld" and a life insurance fraud scheme (20), while other sources claimed charity fund mismanagement. A more mundane explanation: the low-selling series proved a victim of Marvel's increasing moves towards the direct market in this period. "The Human Fly was Marvel's first and so far only costumed hero based on a real person," noted *The Marvel Comics Index,* deeming it "an interesting and unusual experiment that did not quite sustain itself" (95).

8. In flashback, an MD tells the unnamed victim (wrapped in bandages), "You are in a *hospital*—in *critical* condition! We *may* be able to save your *life*—but you will be a *cripple* the rest of your *days!*" (17, emphasis in original).

9. This "montage" training scene, in particular the Fly's "self-improvement" monologue, bears some similarities to the title sequence of the ABC television series *The Six Million Dollar Man,* which ran from 1974–78.

10. In fact, the phrase "he's real" does not appear on the first issue's title page. It did subsequently, starting with #7.

11. As Reynolds further writes, such a state of affairs makes the superhero essentially reactive—"he is not called upon to act unless the status quo is threatened by the villain's plans" (51)—which, as noted in chapter 1, has in the modern era made the superhero the *sine qua non* defender of capitalist property rights, according to some. See Hughes.

12. Elsewhere he tries to "fake" his way out of a fight, telling Copperhead: "*Hold it,* mister! Squeeze that *trigger* and you'll *answer* to the *Human Fly!*", then thinks: "I hope I said that dramatically enough to *scare* him!" (#9: 23, emphasis in original).

13. We can read this curious error as a "hiccup," symptomatic of something "amiss" in the genre's usual flow. See chapters 7 and 8's discussion of other such "Freudian slips" in the so-called Silver and Bronze ages.

14. In "Fear in Funland!" (*Human Fly,* #6, Feb. 1978, Mantlo/Robbins), the Fly thinks to himself, rather than confront some crooks: "I'm no *crimefighter!* I've got to get *back* through the *tunnel* and notify the *police!*" (16, emphasis in original).

15. In "Rocky Mountain Nightmare!" (*Human Fly,* #4, Dec. 1977, Mantlo/Elias), the Fly regrets killing a panther in self-defense, thinking "I-I'm . . . *sorry!*" as it plunges to its death (16, ellipsis and emphasis in original).

16. Compare the Fly's non-violent ethos to that of Jim Starlin's enlightened "cosmically-aware" Captain Marvel, discussed in the next chapter.

17. One letter, written by Paul Chiasson of Cape Breton, Nova Scotia, stands out:

> I am pleased to see a mag on the stands that will give some hope to the millions of handicapped people in the world. I would like to make a suggestion, but I know it is probably economically impossible—why don't you try putting *The Human Fly* in braille, for the blind?
>
> I know from experience what it is like to be handicapped. I myself have a mild form of Cerebral Palsy that causes me to limp, as well as a grand mal Epilepsya and a mild asthma. My girlfriend is confined to a wheelchair because of Cerebral Palsy. Although a cripple from birth, she has remarkable self-confidence and courage. (#4, Dec. 1977: 19)

18. The story strongly hints that Larry's vindictive anger at the VA is in part caused by shrapnel in his skull from a war wound (15).

19. For an account of the San Francisco occupation, see Shapiro: 66–69.

20. For a view of disability and infantilization going back to Victorian literature, see Fiedler 1996: 43–47.

21. A kid knocks the gun out of a villain's hand with his crutch (#5: 23); a blind boy wards off a bear with a flare (#7: 30-31).

22. We can compare these innocuous child characters to, among others, Billy Anders, a boy who uses crutches, introduced in *Superman*, vol. 1, #253 (Jun. 1972, O'Neil/Swan).

23. In this respect, *The Human Fly* resembled another licensed Marvel series with which it is sometimes compared: the motorcycle-themed *Team America* (1982).

24. The Fly recruits the nebbish Berman after the latter fearlessly rescues him from a parachute jump gone awry (*Human Fly*, #12).

25. As one mid-melee caption puts it: "But the mercenary is *wrong!* The Fly is the embodiment of the *hopes* of *many* men! He will *not* be stopped lest he let those *others* down!" (*Human Fly*, #1: 26, emphasis in original).

26. The extra-diegetic reason for the non-reveal, of course, had to do with Rojatt never appearing in public unmasked. In the inaugural essay, Mantlo opines the Fly "kept his identity secret because he wanted to be identified as 'everyman' . . . not as a lone, glory-seeking, self-serving individual."

27. These words carry an even more poignant ring, given that the man who wrote them would later suffer a severe head trauma that rendered him paralyzed, brain-damaged, and bankrupt. See Yurkovich and Mantlo: 68 and Coffin.

28. The bandaged crash survivor also superficially resembles Larry Trainor/Negative Man of *Doom Patrol*—though as argued in a previous chapter, Trainor is the much more complex figure.

29. Interestingly, the technically adept Locke functions as a working-class version of Stark; the former only lacks the resources of the latter (the wealthy, politically connected head of Stark Industries and alter ego of Iron Man)—cementing the notion of disability's social construction.

30. Again, note the similarity to the origin story of *Doom Patrol*, wherein the Chief (Niles Caulder) recruits "broken" and disenchanted individuals for his team of misfits, appearing in silhouette until his dramatic reveal.

31. We can in this regard compare Locke to other "comfortable in their skin" disabled supporting characters of the Late Silver and Bronze ages, such as the blind I-Ching, introduced in *Woman Wonder*, vol. 1, #179 (Nov. 1968, O'Neil/Sekowsky); Clark Kent's landlady Mrs. Goldstein, who uses a wheelchair, in *Superman*, vol. 1, #246 (Dec. 1971, Wein/Swan); and Becky Blake, the Nelson & Murdock secretary, also in a wheelchair, in *Daredevil*, vol. 1, #155 (Nov. 1978, McKenzie/Robbins).

32. Incidentally, Locke appears as the first figure we see (reading top left to bottom right) in the series' very first panel, bracing the Fly's tether from the team helicopter (*Human Fly*, #1: 1). What a series that might have been!

33. Disability Studies scholars and activists have long echoed such a stance. Rosemarie Garland-Thomson, for example, has written: "The emphasis on cure reduces the cultural tolerance for human variation and vulnerability by locating disability in bodies imagined as flawed rather than social systems in need of fixing" (2004A: 87). Overcoming, a species of cure which she deems "the overdetermined cultural response to disability" (ibid.: 85), is grounded in a "cultural fantasy of the body as a neutral, compliant instrument of some transcendent will" (ibid.: 77).

34. He notes that

> the ideology of ability is at its simplest the preference for able-bodiedness. At its most radical, it defines the baseline by which humanness is determined, setting the measure of body and mind that gives or denies human status to individual persons. It affects nearly all our judgments, definitions and values about human beings ... It describes disability as what we flee in the past and hope to defeat in the future. Disability identity stands in uneasy relationship to the ideology of ability, presenting a critical framework that disturbs and critiques it. (2008: 8–9)

35. In second-person narration reminiscent of 1950s EC horror comics, a caption laments: "Too bad Hal was a *cripple!* He was always aware that, though your parents *loved* him, it was his *older brother* they doted on. It was only *natural*, after all ... Weren't you already considered the *best test pilot* in the country ... except for the fabled *Ben Grimm?*" (MP, #35: 7, emphasis and ellipsis in original). Only in a subsequent story, "Whatever Happened to 3D Man?" (*Incredible Hulk*, vol. 1, #251, Sept. 1980)—set in the present—would writer Bill Mantlo and artist Sal Buscema explore those fraught sibling psychodynamics: Hal has kept Chuck imprisoned in his glasses for over two decades, and started a family with Chuck's sweetheart, Peggy. Once more, the "embittered" disabled person resents the able-bodied and takes revenge.

36. A later story, "Darkness, Darkness ...", even flirts with the "pity" model when the Shroud reveals his scarred face to Peter Parker (aka Spider-Man), to reassure him that he is incapable of revealing the latter's secret identity. Though he has learned of it through his mystic senses, "... I certainly can't tell anyone what you *look* like!" (*Marvel Team-Up*, vol. 1, #94, Jun. 1980, Grant/Zeck: 30, emphasis in original).

37. Cloak and Dagger debuted in *Peter Parker, The Spectacular Spider-Man*, vol. 1, #64, Mar. 1982. Created by writer Bill Mantlo and artist Ed Hannigan, the duo waged merciless war on drug dealers who preyed on homeless youth in New York's seedier districts. Their origin was revealed in a later miniseries.

38. As his high-school teacher sheepishly tells Johnson's parents: "Tyrone has a ... disability ... that makes academic achievement difficult for him" (*Cloak and Dagger*, #4: n.p.).

39. Bochs/Box debuted in *Alpha Flight*, vol. 1, #11 (Jun. 1984, Byrne); Wilson/Jericho in *Teen Titans*, vol. 1, #44 (Jul. 1984, Wolfman/Pérez). Previously alluded to: the Morlocks, a subterranean group of mutants too physically different to integrate with "normals," introduced in *Uncanny X-Men*, vol. 1, #169 (May 1983, Claremont/Smith).

CHAPTER 7

1. Quoted on the back cover of Starlin and Aparo 1988, the trade paperback collection of the "Death in the Family" storyline. In a later interview, after Jason Todd was revived, O'Neil said, "The promise I made to the comics community was that on my watch, he won't be back. We

wanted some deaths to be permanent. I mean, it's the biggest cliché in comic books: nobody ever stays dead. I kinda expected our editors down the line would not be bound by that, nor should they have" (O'Neil 2010).

2. Though, as noted in chapter 1, "mythological" readings of superheroes have been strongly critiqued by, among others, Ben Saunders (16–17) and Rogers.

3. Gustines refers the reader to a blog detailing Jean Grey/Phoenix's numerous deaths by that time (numbering fourteen) and resurrections. See http://www.alternatecover.com/features/how-many-times-has-jean-grey-died/.

4. Some important works that address death as a cultural phenomenon, published in the last thirty-five years, include Philippe Ariès's *The Hour of Our Death* (1981), Irina Paperno's *Suicide as a Cultural Institution in Dostoyevsky's Russia* (1997), and Sandra Gilbert's *Death's Door: Modern Dying and the Ways We Grieve* (2006).

5. The British sociologist Geoffrey Gorer's important 1955 essay, "The Pornography of Death," argued that most moderns considered death's natural processes "morbid and unhealthy" (196) to ponder, much less bring up in conversation. His thesis has been challenged by, among others, Tony Walter (1998 and 1994).

6. For a discussion of the brain death concepts and the debates they launched, see Gary Greenberg; Zucker: 397; and Peter Singer: 171–76.

7. The first American hospice opened in 1974, in New Haven, Connecticut, applying and adapting the methods of Dame Cicely Saunders, who had started the modern hospice movement in England in the previous decade. The model soon spread to other cities. By the 1990s, hospices could be reimbursed by Medicare and over 200,000 people a year were utilizing their services (Filene: 216).

8. For a useful summary of these cases and laws, see Webb, chapter 6.

9. In *Symbolic Exchange and Death*, Jean Baudrillard affirms that in a "semiurgic" postmodernity, the body has vanished, swallowed up in sea of exchangeable signs (114). Death does remain—as a sign which culture opposes to life, endowing the latter with all the power it denies to the former, and disrupting/prohibiting any exchange between the two. This primary oppositional relationship structures all other economies: monetary, libidinal, and aesthetic.

10. They further elaborate:

> Perhaps paramount is death's double position as anomalous, marginal, repressed, and the same time masterful, central, everywhere manifest. Both the collective and the individual body locate their meanings within this doubled given, in a kind of perpetual vacillation. The gesture of repression, which is also a gesture to obtain (the fiction of) mastery, is so multiply encoded, so infinitely various, that we might call it pied beauty. But uncanny beauty. Every representation of death necessarily represses what it purports to reveal. (Goodwin/Bronfen, 19)

11. Note, for example, the controversy over whether the media would/should be allowed to publish photographs of coffins of American war dead returning from the 2000s Iraq and Afghanistan theaters. See John Taylor, especially chapter 9.

12. For a critique of Becker's pessimism, see Carveth.

13. The sociologist Clive Seale, locating the process of "transference heroics" in everyday life, notes that it "helps the worshipper deny his or her own creaturely nature, and aspire to greater things" (1998: 57). On the inadequately "fictional" nature of hero-systems see Becker 1971, chapter 10.

14. Similarly, Freud notes overcoming the fear of death "may even be the secret of heroism" (1915A: 292).

15. While similar material had appeared since the 1940s, the Silver Age "Imaginary Stories" were pioneered by the writer Otto Binder at DC, and promoted by Weisinger as part of his drive to reinvigorate the Superman family of titles. The first such story, "Mr. and Mrs. Clark (Superman) Kent!" (*Superman's Girlfriend, Lois Lane*, vol. 1, #19, Aug. 1960, Seigel/Schaffenberger), featured Lois Lane marrying Superman. See Jacobs/Jones: 26 and 81.

16. Obviously, this is a highly specialized usage of the term; we are discussing entirely fictional works, whether "imaginary," part of "official" continuity, or not. As Alan Moore winkingly wrote in the prologue to "Whatever Happened to the Man of Tomorrow?": "This is an *imaginary story* . . . Aren't they all?"

17. As we will see in chapter 9, many of the details in this "imaginary story" prefigure the "Death of Superman" storyline of three decades later.

18. Moore had already explored this aspect of superheroes earlier in the decade, and in much more graphic ways, in his revisionist British series *Marvelman/Miracleman*.

19. On the paradoxes and entanglements evoked by retcons, see Niederhausen.

20. For an account of the story's origin and production, see Kupperberg, from which I took the Schwartz and Helfer quotes.

21. Moreover, Frenz had a reputation as an unusually slavish epigone of the Kirby/Buscema Marvel house style. There is, curiously, a not-inconsiderable overlap between "real-looking" "imaginary stories" and conceptualist parody of the sort produced by R. K. Sikoryak in his *Masterpiece Comics*, in which the look of the work is paramount.

22. Contrast this with the pre-Death with Dignity reality of patients in American hospitals described by Kübler-Ross: "Slowly but surely he is being treated like a thing. He is no longer a person. Decisions are made often without taking his opinion" (7).

23. The location of the gathering remains ambiguous: we see only pews and a podium. Also, curiously, we never witness Susan's coffin, her body, nor her place of burial or disposal.

24. Freud's description of psychogenic melancholia seems tailor-made for Richards's condition: "a profoundly painful dejection, cessation of interest in the outside world, loss of the capacity to love, inhibition of all activity, and a lowering of the self-regarding feelings to a degree that finds utterance in self-reproaches and self-revilings" (244), whose violence, as he would write subsequently in *Beyond the Pleasure Principle* (1920) could be turned outward by the ego through the mechanisms of the death drive. See the discussion of Marathon in chapter 8.

25. In another odd oversight, we are told that Sue and Reed's child survived, but we never see it. Why does no one show any interest in its welfare?

26. We can usefully compare Richards's downfall with that of Scottie, played by James Stewart, in Alfred Hitchcock's *Vertigo* (1958), another lurid tale of obsessive love and death.

27. A reading of "What If The Invisible Girl Had Died?" may also be illuminated by Renato Rosaldo's "Grief and a Headhunter's Rage," the introduction to his 1989 book *Culture and Truth: The Remaking of Social Analysis*, the writing of which, he acknowledges, served in part as a therapeutic response to the rage he experienced in the wake of his own wife's untimely death.

28. For more on the multiverse concept in the early Silver Age, see Kukkonen: 49 and Jacobs/Jones: 45.

29. On the "duplicative" and "proliferative" aspects of postmodernism, see Kawa (2006). On the links between alternate universes in literature and modern physics, see Ryan 2006.

30. The landmark series *Watchmen* (Moore/Gibbons, 1986) and *The Dark Knight Returns* (Miller, 1986) properly belong in the "non-continuity" universe and alternate future categories, respectively, hence their freedom to explore the ramifications of many real deaths.

31. Though it goes beyond the purview of this study, see Derek Johnson on the transmedial impact of the *X-Men* films on the comics image of Wolverine.

32. One of these bears mention: the DC Elseworlds titles, a variation on the multiverse model, which debuted in the late 1980s. These stories reset familiar characters in different historical

eras and/or circumstances, at times departing from the superhero genre itself. The gatekeeping function of declaring their "unofficial" status was taken on by the Elseworlds imprint affixed to these titles starting in 1991. The first such story, *Gotham by Gaslight* (Augustyn/Mignola, 1989) featured Batman in the Victorian era.

33. This forms part of Douglas Wolk's "superreaders" thesis, applicable since the Silver Age's turn to continuity. The multiverse model is, in effect, the uncontained eruption of continuity in all directions. As Wolk writes, "Picking up a superhero comic book right now, if you're not already immersed in that world, is likely to make you feel simultaneously talked down to and baffled by the endless references to stuff you're already supposed to know" (90).

34. Among Quarter Bin's "Rules of Death" in superhero comics is cited "never show the body" for supervillains, which allows them to return relatively plausibly over and over (*Revolving Door of Death*, #15, Oct. 4, 2001). Similarly, the DC and Marvel writer/editor Len Wein told me: "In comic books, nobody's ever dead unless you can see the body. And usually not even then" (2011). See also this useful reference of supervillain deaths and resurrections: http://sacomics.blogspot.com/2012/01/and-on-third-issue-he-arose-again.html .

35. A notable example: after his Silver Age "reawakening" in *The Avengers*, Captain America's ongoing trauma and survivor guilt over the loss of his sidekick Bucky in World War II (as discussed in chapter 1).

36. The case of Lightning Lad has an additional wrinkle: in a previous issue a glimpse into the future had revealed Lightning Lad and Saturn Girl would marry, making his return from the dead a plot "necessity."

37. The issue's cover uses superhero death as a selling point, announcing: "*One of the legion-naires* on this cover will *die!* You'll be *shocked* by the identity of '*The Doomed Legionnaire!*'" (emphasis in original). Such attention-grabbing approaches became common.

38. He told me, "They just couldn't live with [Lightning Lad dead]. I, as a reader, was offended. I found that more troubling than if they'd just left him dead" (2012).

39. Freud returned more than once to the theme of guilt as the origin of spirits in his later, more "philosophical" and speculative works, such as the 1913 essay "Animism, Magic and the Omnipotence of Thoughts": "[The neurotic's] sense of guilt has a justification: it is founded on the intense and frequent death-wishes against his fellows which are unconsciously at work in him" (87). In his fear of death, Freud argued, modern man was at his most primeval and superstitious; in "The Uncanny" (1919) he writes, "Most likely our fear still implies the old belief that the dead man becomes the enemy of his survivor and seeks to carry him off to share the new life with him" (242).

40. This scene bears some striking similarities to Ben Saunders's reading of Peter Parker/Spider-Man's repeated encounters with death—which threaten to strip the "self-protective fiction" which "keep[s] at bay the awareness that we live in an unpredictable universe where Bad Things happen that *no one* can prevent" (85, emphasis in original), a notion anathema to the superhero's very identity. I take up the theme in the conclusion to the present study.

41. This despite Shooter's claim: "My plan always was, the guy's dead, that's it, he's not coming back" (2012).

42. The decision to kill Jean Grey—a founding member of the X-Men, in continuity since 1963—did not come about without controversy. Marvel editor in chief Jim Shooter (moved on from DC) insisted Phoenix's crimes called for more than her originally planned punishment: "demotion" to normal human status. The at-times rancorous back-and-forth between Shooter and the X-Men creative team eventually led to the final result. See Broertjes: 10, Claremont/Byrne 1984, and Shooter 2011. Shooter confirmed this version to me in 2012.

43. Despite such statements by Shooter as "if we kill a [non-supervillain] character and do it in a convincing way, I want that character to stay dead. I want to preserve our credibility" (Broertjes: 10–11), Grey returned from the dead under Shooter's watch, in 1986. Some in the fan

community felt the resurrection/retcon betrayed the grandeur of the original classic saga, and saw the move as crassly commercial, since the original X-Men was then being regrouped in a new title, *X-Factor*. Grey was revived, according to Quarter Bin, because "project trumps death" (Oct. 4, 2001).

44. As in chapter 5, all *Doom Patrol* page number references pertain to the original published issue, reprinted in Kawasaki 2010.

45. Writer Arnold Drake, at the time embroiled in a contract dispute over the ending of the series, removed himself from the framing story; Boltinoff replaced him.

46. The editorial comment on the letters page of *Doom Patrol* #121 put it even more explicitly: "You, and only you and your pals, have the only answer, and that answer is in a sudden spurt in sales! So tell your friends! Tell your enemies, even . . . to buy, BUY this issue—or it's bye-bye DOOM PATROL!" (emphasis and ellipses in original).

47. O'Neil expounded on the poll, and his regrets about the decision, in the documentary *Robin's Requiem: The Tale of Jason Todd* (2010). For his part, the writer Jim Starlin, burnishing his reputation as "undertaker" to the genre (which we examine in the discussion of his *Death of Captain Marvel*) wanted to kill Jason Todd: "Yes, everyone hated Jason Todd. I wanted to kill off Robin as soon as I started writing Batman. The idea of taking a kid along to fight crime is ludicrous" (UHQ Team).

48. Page numbers refer to the original work, reprinted in Starlin and Aparo.

49. The storyline unfolded in *Web of Spider-Man*, vol. 1, #31–32, *The Amazing Spider-Man*, vol. 1, #293–94, and *Spectacular Spider-Man*, vol. 1, #131–32.

50. Essentially, the *causa sui* refers to embracing absolute responsibility for oneself. See the discussion of *The Death of Captain Marvel* later in the chapter for an examination of this Beckerian concept.

51. Although Superman's parents were added to the mythos subsequently, Superman's "origin" story does begin with the destruction of his home planet (later called Krypton).

52. Admittedly, most of these "dead" characters were "revived" through flashback sequences, "Untold Tales" and other tactics, while in more recent years some have indeed returned from the dead into standard continuity. Peter Parker's Aunt May here represents the most extreme case, having "died," nearly died, and returned innumerable times.

53. Reynolds (chapter 3) sees the theme of absent or deceased parents as a common motif in the genre.

54. In a less generous reading of material such as the Jarella and Gwen Stacy episodes (the latter examined in the next section), Quarter Bin considers the frequent deaths of superheroes' "normal" girlfriends a convenient (and misogynistic) plot device for resolving relationships that have served their narratival purpose (2002). It has certainly become so since the 1960s/70s examples cited above. See the "Women in Refrigerators" website (1999), at http://www.unheard taunts.com/wir/.

55. The story's writer, Len Wein, told me he had never intended for Jarella's death to be permanent (her non-human status would have made a resurrection more plausible), but he left the series before he could carry out the plan. When asked if such a return would have somehow invalidated the Hulk's "grief work," as described, he replied it would not have, as she would not have come back for several months and the Hulk would still have gone through his stages of grief. "Death is a stalling tactic" in superhero comics, he insisted (2011).

As revealed two years later, in "The Monster's Analyst" (*Incredible Hulk*, vol. 1, #227, Sept. 1978, Stern/Buscema), the Hulk remained deeply traumatized by the deaths of Jarella and others in his past. Under a form of dream therapy, he sees his many dead friends and pleads with them, "Hulk does not want you to die. Hulk *needs* you!" (27, emphasis in original).

56. The story even holds back from revealing its title until the very last page, once the shocking death has taken place.

57. Some dispute persists as to whether the Green Goblin (aka Norman Osborn) had already disposed of Gwen Stacy atop the George Washington Bridge by the time of Spider-Man/Parker's arrival, or, as Ralph Macchio points out, "did Spider-Man unknowingly break her neck when he shot out his web to halt her fatal fall? No one seemed to know who added the telltale 'snap' sound effect in that critical panel which pointed an inadvertent finger of blame at her would-be rescuer" (Youngquist 2004A: 2). The panel appears on page seventy-eight of the story. Blumberg "clears up" this "mystery" in his essay; Kakalios (chapter 3) also addresses Stacy's death.

58. As Blumberg notes in advancing this argument: "Here was the quip-happy hero, always so light-hearted in the face of evil, vowing bloody revenge to the heavens as he cradled the lifeless form of Gwen Stacy. Here was the girlfriend of the hero, dead and gone, never to return. Every expected motif in superhero stories was turned on its ear in a few simple panels, irrevocably transforming the world of comics and its readers" (200).

59. All the same, Gwen's passing is an exception for the genre, occurring in a comics series that had long featured the most death-scarred of superheroes, Spider-Man. See Sims for an exploration of death as a motivating factor for the character. To the end of the period covered in this book (the early 1990s), the "heroic model" of death for loved ones remained the genre standard. On Marvel's controversial efforts to bring Gwen Stacy back from the dead through cloning, see Kawa and Saunders (chapter 3).

60. The child is later shown to have been miraculously saved by Franklin Richards, and is eventually born as Valeria.

61. The Hulk also had another African-American friend in the 1970s, Crackerjack Jackson, a hobo. He also died, in the same issue as his first appearance, *The Incredible Hulk*, vol. 1, #182 (1974, Wein/Trimpe).

62. Wilson first revealed his HIV status in "Thicker Than Water!" (*Incredible Hulk*, vol. 1, #388, Dec. 1991, David/Keown). It may be safely conjectured that the political ramifications of AIDS make for an additional factor in Wilson staying dead.

63. Left out of this discussion of existential death is the inadvertent or intentional killing of unnamed civilians caught in the crossfire of superhero battles, a taboo increasingly violated after Alan Moore's incorporation of such violence in the UK *Marvelman/Miracleman* series of the early 1980s. I take up the theme in the conclusion to chapter 9.

64. Compare this cover to that of the *Amazing Spider-Man* issue in which Gwen Stacy dies, which similarly shows the hero guessing which of his close acquaintances would perish.

65. The later retconning of the event to show Hudson not killed in the blast but transported to another planet takes nothing away from the survivors' reactions, "pre-selling" of the death.

66. That said, by the mid-1980s Marvel had taken steps to "officially" incorporate superhero death into its universe-building; witness the two issues of *The Official Handbook of the Marvel Universe* (vol. 1, #13–14, Feb./Mar. 1984) devoted to the "dead and inactive."

67. As Starlin told an interviewer, "It was a cheap form of therapy" (UHQ Team). He confirmed to me that by working on *The Death of Captain Marvel* he was "saving myself psych fees, talking about my dad" (2011).

68. Quarter Bin calls him "Starlin the Undertaker" (1991).

69. Wolk writes: "[Starlin] belonged to the first generation of cartoonists who'd grown up as much on single-cartoonist underground comix as on assembly-line superhero comics, and he'd effectively been given license to cut loose" (2006: 122). See Wolk 2006 for a thorough treatment of Starlin's mid-1970s Warlock saga and its place in the canon.

70. See Howe: 86–87 and Jon Morris.

71. Shooter and Starlin confirmed this version to me in their interviews. Starlin added that the manner of Marvel's death was left to him; after mulling several "heroic death" variants, Starlin opted for the death by cancer plotline. As Starlin told me, "They were all him dying heroically at the end in some explosion or something, in ways that had already been done. The Doom

Patrol, for example, had already died in a similar spectacular fashion. My father had, about six months earlier, died of cancer. So that came to mind" (2011). Shooter, then Marvel's editor in chief, enthusiastically approved.

72. Most pre-*Death of Captain Marvel* page number references for Captain Marvel stories pertain to the original works. See Fingeroth 1990 for reprints of series issues 25–34.

73. Oncological references appear with odd regularity in Starlin's *Captain Marvel* run: in #29 Eon refers to Mar-Vell's id-like shadow version as "your *cancerous other self*. He is your *hostility*, your *battle lust*, the side of you which *loves destruction*, perpetuates *hate* and seeks *death!*" (emphasis in original), while in #30, Mar-Vell mentions his mission, to "*stop* the spreading cancer known as . . . *Thanos!*" (emphasis and ellipses in original).

74. *The Death of Captain Marvel* is unpaginated.

75. Apart from Kübler-Ross's already-noted *On Death and Dying* (1969), which features many such life/death stories and spawned several sequels, *The Death of Captain Marvel* shares much with foundational thanatographic and "mourning" texts such as C. S. Lewis's *A Grief Observed* (1961); Simone De Beauvoir's memoir on her mother's succumbing to illness, *A Very Easy Death* (1964); and the modern thanatographic urtext, John Gunther's *Death Be Not Proud* (1949), which recounts the death from brain cancer of the author's teenage son. More recent iterations include Mitch Albom's *Tuesdays With Morrie* (1995), Anatole Broyard's *Intoxicated by My Illness* (1992), Geneviève Jurgensen's *The Disappearance* (1994), various books by the pathologist F. González-Crussi, the poet and undertaker Thomas Lynch, the surgeon Sherwin Nuland, and the surgeon Atul Gawande (*Complications*, 2003).

76. Starlin told me he knew of these discourses, and noted that Dr. Jack Kervorkian, the notorious 1990s assisted suicide activist, lived in a nearby small town outside Detroit. "I was aware of all that stuff," he said (2011).

77. A word on Starlin's art in the novel, which differs stylistically from that of his previous work. Soon after starting to ink the material, Starlin seriously dislocated a finger on his drawing hand while playing volleyball. With no budget to hire an inker, he taped a pen to his hand and kept on. He could produce no flowing lines, only short feathery ones; Starlin himself called it "Moebius-type inking," referring to the French fantasy comics artist Jean Giraud (2011). Though unintended, the change in effect creates a different, "special" version of Starlin's art, to match the special presentation, format and marketing of the first Marvel Graphic Novel. This further contributes to the mature, "serious" treatment of the death theme.

78. The similarities with European graphic albums were no coincidence; Shooter was then seeking to inaugurate the format in America; he decided *The Death of Captain Marvel* would make a suitable storyline for such an auspicious launch. This was happening at a time when, at Shooter's initiative, Marvel was experimenting with different publishing formats (such as *Epic* magazine) and the move to the direct market (Shooter 2012). Furthermore, the new format came with an innovative contract for Starlin, who negotiated an advance and royalties rather than a per-page rate (which was then industry practice). The book's great success meant Starlin managed to pay off his home mortgage ahead of schedule (2011). For a critique of the novel's production values, including its "disgracefully ugly" typesetting and design (52), see Kim Thompson.

79. Other book formats previously published, such as Stan Lee's *Origins of Marvel Comics* (1974) and its sequels, contained reprints (as did the Treasury Editions), while Lee and Kirby's *The Silver Surfer* graphic novel (1978) featured an alternate, non-continuity version of the character.

80. Given such top-quality, premium treatment, one would have thought one was reading of the death of a Superman or Spider-Man, not of the second-tier corporate disappointment Captain Marvel. If nothing else, Shooter and Marvel certainly excelled at the art of packaging!

81. Significantly, in another move to "Europeanize" the superhero comic, this recap contains no editorial captions directing the reader to past issues ("See ish #25!"). Marvel under Lee had

pioneered the "smart-alecky" editorial meta-commentary caption in the 1960s; here, it apparently was deemed out of keeping with the somber mood and "quality" production values.

82. Reprinted in Lee 1974: 150.

83. Dylan Thomas, "Do Not Go Gentle Into That Good Night" (1951).

84. Levin L. Schücking traces Shakespeare's Alexander reference to earlier than St. Bernard, to the *Meditations* (ca. 170 CE) of Marcus Aurelius (136).

85. Shakespeare was almost certainly influenced by his contemporary Michel de Montaigne, whose essay "To Philosophize Is To Learn to Die" (1580) notes: "It is completely reasonable and pious to take our example from the humanity of Jesus Christ himself; now he finished his life at thirty-three. The greatest man that was simply a man, Alexander, also died at that age. How many ways has death to surprise us!" (18).

86. Tolstoy's *The Death of Ivan Ilyich* continues to be used as a case study by doctors, hospice staff and psychologists. See Dayananda, Rancour-Lafferie, Mico, et al. It is even dispensed in some palliative care units, as reported in the series *Moyers on Dying* (2000). This despite the novel's intensely symbolist and expressionist approach to its subject matter, as demonstrated by figures like Vladimir Nabokov and critics.

87. This passage also recalls Freud's argument on the modern disavowal of death's inevitability; in ways large and small, we think ways around it: "Our habit is to lay stress on the fortuitous causation of the death—accident, disease, infection, advanced age: in this way we betray an effort to reduce death from a necessity to a chance event" (1915A: 290).

88. The non-superpowered Jones's tirade echoes the anonymous African-American man's pointed questioning of the heroes' misplaced priorities in "No Evil Shall Escape My Sight!" (*Green Lantern/Green Arrow*, vol. 1, #76, Apr. 1970, O'Neil/Adams: 6), a high water mark in the genre's 1970s "social relevance" phase. See Hill for a reprint.

89. Starlin had established the link between Jesus and his "spandex-suited saint" before, in a parody of Leonardo's *Last Supper* (ca. 1490), with Mar-Vell assuming the Savior's pose (*Captain Marvel*, vol. 1, #31, Mar. 1974: 10). For more on the superhero as Jesus figure (and vice versa), see chapter 9 of the present study, as well as Koosed and Schumm. Incidentally, another Biblical art reference in *The Death of Captain Marvel* occurs when the repentant Rick Jones collapses in guilt at Mar-Vell's bedside, in a composition that somewhat recalls Rembrandt's *Return of The Prodigal Son* (ca. 1665).

90. As in our discussion of "The Ghost of Ferro Lad," Bronfen goes on to argue that male-driven representational systems, in effect, use the image of woman-as-death to mask the even more terrifying, intolerable specter of capital-D death itself (433). I take up this point in the book's conclusion.

91. Examples of death-as-woman with which Starlin was conversant in 1982 include Hela, the Norse goddess of death and recurring character in *The Mighty Thor*, and the "Woman in White" from Bob Fosse's *All That Jazz* (1979). For a salient reading of the overdetermined death and femininity trope, see Bronfen's treatment of Gabriel Von Max's painting *The Anatomist* (1869) in her chapter 1. On the other hand, a queer reading would emphasize the death figure's gender instability—it shifts from female to skeleton and back again (the robe prevents us from seeing if it is a male or female skeleton).

92. On the "*pièta*" cover, see Duncan and Smith: 235, as well as, for a survey, http://goodcomics.comicbookresources.com/2008/06/22/cool-comic-cover-gallery-the-best-pieta-covers/.

93. The term refers to male terror at unconstrained maternality/femininity, a common trope in horror movies such as Ridley Scott's *Alien* (1979); see Creed.

94. Simon provides a useful genealogy of the development of the concept of kitsch in, among others, the writings of Greenberg, Dwight MacDonald ("A Theory of Popular Culture," 1944) and Fredric Jameson ("Reification and Utopia in Mass Culture," 1979); the latter emphasized the "profound structural interrelatedness of modernism and mass culture" (quoted in Simon: 347).

See also Jachec on Greenberg's place in modernist intellectual thought. The foregoing, of course, owe a debt to the Frankfurt School's "culture industry" critiques and Walter Benjamin's seminal essay "The Work of Art in the Age of Mechanical Reproduction" (1936). They form an illuminating contrast to other critics of comics and popular culture, such as Gilbert Seldes, Robert Warshow, and M. Thomas Inge.

95. On this sort of borrowing, the unsparing Morreal and Joy refer to Gillo Dorfles's concept of transposition, which they define as "*recklessly* translating works of art from one medium to another. It offers itself as instant art" (68, my emphasis). The high/low split expressed in this rhetoric until fairly recently formed an impediment to the study of comics for many art historians. For an eminently balanced treatment of the often-fraught history between Pop Art, modernism, and comics, see Beaty: chapter 3.

96. When asked what inspired him to produce the image, Starlin told me only that the original sculpture was probably on his mind then because he recalled it had been damaged by a deranged man (in 1972). Interestingly, the maniac László Toth hammered off Mary's nose and gouged out an eye, so that she indeed more closely resembled a skeleton. On the incident and related vandalism of artwork seen from a Disability Studies perspective, see Siebers 2010: chapter 4.

97. It bears repeating that, as indicated by the reading of Gilles Barbier's installation *Nursing Home* (2002) which opens this book, the borrowing extends in both directions: superheroes also inspire fine art—increasingly so. The high/low hierarchy also leads to blind spots and omissions. A recent case in point: the Flemish Jan Fabre's *Merciful Dream (Pietà V)* (2011) reinterprets Michelangelo's original with a self-portrait of the artist as Jesus and Mary as a skeletal figure. Oddly, Fabre's website calls this "an unprecedented reinterpretation of Michelangelo's *Pietà*" (http://www.janfabre.be/Pages/Press_release.php). Not for readers of *The Death of Captain Marvel.*

98. Adding as well to the "three-dimensionality" of the image: the "Captain Marvel" of the title, which encroaches from above into the space of the art, as Thor's hammer reaches out of the frame toward the text—comics' hybrid text/image strategies "infiltrating" the presumed "purity" of the fine-art image.

99. This is not to suggest the figures are scattered randomly through the space. On the contrary, their order of battle follows a specific chronology, with early Marvel Silver Age characters (Hulk, Spider-Man, the Thing) to the "front," more recent characters (Wolverine, Colossus) "behind."

100. An early scene in Leo Tolstoy's *The Death of Ivan Ilyich* underscores the presence-absence ambiguity of the corpse:

> The body lay, as the dead invariably do, in a peculiarly heavy manner, with its rigid limbs sunk into the bedding of the coffin and its head eternally bowed on the pillow . . . as with all dead men, his face had acquired an expression of greater beauty—above all, of greater significance—than it had in life. Its expression implied that what needed to be done had been done and done properly. Moreover, there was in this expression a reproach or a reminder to the living. (39–40)

101. Interestingly, the Watcher neither comments on nor serves as a narrative guide to the events surrounding Mar-Vell's death, as he so often does at momentous turns in Marvel history. Starlin depicts him only once, as a distant figure presumably on Earth's moon, gazing dispassionately.

102. Unlike most previous examples, such as "The Death of Superman" (1961), Starlin's novel does not depict the hero's funeral, only comrades mourning at his grave.

103. This "wider continuity" even transcends the Marvel universe, thanks to a Starlin in-joke. The novel's back cover, depicting a similar gathering of heroes presiding over the late Mar-Vell's monument, features a slyly inserted Superman (on the right, just behind Wolverine).

104. Compare this scene to episodes of such "ensemble action" in *The Human Fly*, discussed in chapter 7.

105. As discussed, the possibility of superpowers that also kill their bearers had been explored before, notably in the case of Wonder Man, but never to this extent (at least for heroes). We return to the theme in chapter 8, on *Strikeforce: Morituri*, an unusual series which made this a central trope.

106. Russian-speaking scholars have pointed that *ona* (feminine third person pronoun, "she"), rendered into English as "it," has numerous ambiguities and blurrings with other uses of *ona* in Tolstoy's text. *Bol'* (pain), *smert'* (death), and *zhizn'* (life) are all feminine nouns. On this suggestive, expressionist peculiarity of Tolstoy's language see Jahn: 58. Intriguingly, in their interviews with cancer patients Dennis Waskul and Pamela van der Riet encountered a similarly vague use of the word "it". As they note, "One wonders what this 'It' might be. Her body? Cancer? Treatment side effects?" (495).

107. Such a message further links *The Death of Captain Marvel* with past thanatopic literature, in which insights of this sort are common, along with the impossibility of staving off disease and death, and the futile efforts of doctors and caregivers, as seen in works as different as Tolstoy's *The Death of Ivan Ilyich*, Gunther's *Death Be Not Proud*, and Franz Kafka's *The Metamorphosis* (1915). Ultimately, the cause of death matters less than the protagonist's ability to accept his/her fate with some sort of dignity.

108. According to Hope Nash Wolff, "Enkidu serves . . . as an example of the hero who wins fame but dies early and miserably; what is the use, the poet seems to ask, in such a life?" (392).

109. The typical hero in *The Iliad*, notes Seth L. Schein, "lives and dies in pursuit of honor and glory" in war (69), and is often cut down young. On Homeric death see Schein: chapter 2.

110. Clive Seale refers to this more "feminine" expressive mode of confronting death as "aware dying"; see chapter 8.

111. Interdependence forms a central pillar of Lennard Davis's concept of dismodernism; see chapter 5.

112. For Daniel Rancour-Laferriere, the message is more mixed, with Ivan engaged in a delirious form of death denial: "Even as he is dying Tolstoy's hero denies death and affirms light, experiences it, *becomes* it even in his intense joy" (128, emphasis in original).

113. In fact, Mar-Vell's final showdown—in its setting and action—closely mirrors his confrontation with his "shadow-self" through which he earned Cosmic Awareness from Eon in *Captain Marvel*, #29.

114. Compare this cliché-ridden dialogue to that of Dr. Manhattan at the climax of the more overtly self-conscious *Watchmen*, delivered in stentorian tones: "*I am disappointed, Veidt. Very disappointed. Restructuring* myself after the subtraction of my *intrinsic field* was the first trick I *learned*. It didn't kill *Osterman*. Did you think it would kill me? . . . What's that in your hand, Veidt? Another ultimate weapon?" (*Watchmen*, vol. 1, #12, Moore/Gibbons: 18, emphasis in original).

115. A disembodied head of himself, which Thanos holds like Yorick's skull, continues muttering over and over, "Illusion . . ." (ellipsis in original).

116. We may usefully compare the sequence's metafictive dialectic between text and image to that of Chris Ware's far more deconstructive *I Guess* (1991), a superhero "tale" in which words and visuals have a much more tenuous, ironic link.

117. Kristeva based her concept in part on the work of anthropologist Mary Douglas. In her *Purity and Danger* (1966), Douglas emphasizes the cultural role played by "disorder" and its containment, the anxious defense of boundaries against contamination. Cancer, as discussed, blurs such simple distinctions between the "I"/"not I" which exemplify abjection. I return to the concept of abjection in chapter 8.

118. As Stacey further puts it: "The malignant cell of the cancer tumor is not an invader, an outsider, like a virus or a bacterium, it is produced by the body, it is of the body, and yet it is a threat to the body. Neither self nor other, it is both the same as and different from its host" (77).

119. It goes without saying that the resistance is entirely contextual. Compare this imagery of Mar-Vell with that at the climax of the first Thanos story, when an elderly, cadaverous Captain Marvel drained of his life force smashes the Cosmic Cube, source of Thanos's power (*Captain Marvel*, vol. 1, #33). The difference, of course, is that in this portrayal the hero is acting heroically to vanquish the villain, pulling victory from the jaws of defeat—and in the very next page, is fully restored to vigor.

120. We observe a similar shying-away from "disheartening," "too-real" depictions of illness in Hollywood films, even in such landmark representations of death from AIDS as Jonathan Demme's *Philadelphia* (1993).

121. Tolstoy, too, had condemned the inhumanity of doctors a century before, in *The Death of Ivan Ilyich*; see chapter 4.

122. For a discussion of the medical gaze model and comics, see Alaniz 2003.

123. One questionable double-portrait in the lab scene shows Mar-Vell in an angled three-quarter view with the older man behind him; the two look in each other's general direction.

124. In perhaps an extension of the death-femininity theme, the "tombstone panels'" black parallels Elysius's lusterless black hair.

125. As an aside, *The Death of Captain Marvel* contains a number of printing and production errors, sometimes appearing at oddly "appropriate" moments of superheroic anxiety—which means we can relate them to the abjection theme. For example, at one point Mar-Vell explains, "Because of this, is ac [*sic*] only gives me a .09 percent chance for recovery." (he means Isaac). Elsewhere, he says, "I've not asked for your help before because I've I've [*sic*] been unable to voice my fear." These generic "hiccups" suggest a link to the film theorist Kristin Thompson's concept of cinematic excess; see Alaniz 2008 and chapter 8 for further discussion.

126. In just such a "less than generous" tone, Kim Thompson writes that Starlin's "control of facial expression is strained by the challenge of distinguishing a smile from a frown" (51). Ouch.

127. Several death narratives or stories ending in death conclude in just this way, with a "split" between body and spirit. Tolstoy's *The Death of Ivan Ilyich*, after the hero's subjective "victory" over death, ends more "objectively": "He drew in a breath, broke off in the middle of it, stretched himself out, and died" (134). To cite three other disparate examples: Vladimir Nabokov's *Invitation to a Beheading* (1936), in which the hero "separates" from his mortal coil as the blade falls; the Bette Davis weepie *Dark Victory* (1938), whose final image goes out of focus as the heroine dies; and the aforementioned *All That Jazz*, in which the doomed choreographer Joe Gideon's uproarious (imagined) "farewell concert," crowned by his "consummation" with The Lady in White (i.e., Death), ultimately cuts away to show his real-life corpse being zipped up into a body bag. Starlin confirmed to me that he saw the latter upon release, and that it might have subconsciously influenced his own ending for the novel (2011).

128. Or, as Philippians 2: 5–8, puts it: "Let this mind be in you, which was also in Christ Jesus: Who, being in the form of God, thought it not robbery to be equal with God: But made himself of no reputation, and took upon him the form of a servant, and was made in the likeness of men: And being found in fashion as a man, he humbled himself, and became obedient unto death, even the death of the cross."

129. The "caveats" include the fact that since 1982 Mar-Vell has been "brought back" under various pretenses (Legion of the Unliving; Skrull impersonation; flashbacks), though never "officially" revived.

130. Freud's editor, James Strachey, points out, on the same page, the misquotation of Shakespeare's *Henry IV, Part I*, Act V, Scene I: "Thou owest God a Death."

CHAPTER 8

1. Gene Day (1951–82) worked as an artist and inker at Marvel.

2. *Strikeforce: Morituri*, vol. 1, #13, Dec. 1987: 26, unconventional punctuation in original. Wildcard/John Crenella, a second generation Morituri, dies only weeks after undergoing the Morituri process, apparently because during the aforementioned battle he inadvertently absorbs the powers of his first-generation teammate Blackthorn/Aline Pagrovna, who was due to expire.

3. Elsewhere, Becker describes man's "creaturely" nature as overwhelmed not only by death's reality but by "the face of creation" itself, what he calls "the *mysterium tremendum et fascinosum* of each single thing, of the fact that there are things at all" (1973: 49).

4. As already noted, Freud too thought death the seed of heroism; see chapter 7.

5. Throughout *Denial of Death*, Becker speaks in deeply gendered terms of who is and is not competent to stare down "real" death; "manliness" comes across as the key quality. To cite one of several such instances, he argues that it "takes men of granite, men who are automatically powerful, secure in their drivenness, we might say" to be truly reborn with an acceptance of death (58).

6. We may compare this traumatic point of *touch* by the image to Roland Barthes's *punctum*, the uncontrollable X-factor of the photograph, the real that we "add but is nonetheless already there," which "shoots out of it like an arrow, and pierces me" (55) through the eye.

7. Foster here invokes Jacques Lacan's seminar on the gaze, a milestone of structuralist psychoanalysis, in which the subject perceives the "gaze of the world"—of the object—as a threat. Rewriting the familiar Renaissance understanding of perspective, in which the subject looks upon the object from a privileged and unified geometrical point (as from the apex of a cone that takes in the object), Lacan fixes the subject in a double position (the object emanates its own cone which swallows up the subject); this doubled, two-way gaze meets at the level of the screen—an intermediary space or shield much like Warhol's repetitions. Lacan's treatment has proven deeply influential to Trauma Studies. See Felman. For an application of Trauma Studies to comics, see Chute: 2007.

8. When the Real "enters us, violates us through the eye," Foster claims, it does so through a negation of borders, a blinding rupture of the screen; the image "refuses to unite the imaginary and the symbolic against the real":

> It is as if this art wanted the gaze to shine, the object to stand, the real to exist, in all the glory (or the horror) of its pulsatile desire, or at least to evoke this sublime condition. To this end it moves not only to attack the image but to tear at the screen, or to suggest that it is already torn. (140, emphasis in original)

9. Recall passages such as this, of the eponymous protagonist's deterioration in Leo Tolstoy's 1886 novella, *The Death of Ivan Ilyich* (discussed in chapter 7), which bear some striking resemblances to Becker and Foster's metaphors:

> And suddenly *It* flashed through the screen and he saw *It*. *It* had only appeared as a flash, so he hoped *It* would disappear, but involuntarily he became aware of his side: the pain was still gnawing away at him and he could no longer forget—*It* was staring at him distinctly from behind the plants. What was the point of it all? (96–97)

10. Latin for "Hail, Emperor, we who are about to die salute you," the legendary greeting of Roman gladiators to the sovereign as they prepared to engage their deadly games. See Plass: 201fn.

11. As noted in chapter 7, a similar premise had been explored through the early Silver Age villain-turned-hero Wonder Man/Simon Williams, in the pages of *The Avengers*, vol. 1, #9. A Tower Comics hero, Dynamo/Leonard Brown of the T.H.U.N.D.E.R Agents, could make use of his super-strength only for short periods, as it drained his life energies with every activation. Dynamo debuted in *T.H.U.N.D.E.R Agents*, vol. 1, #1 (Nov. 1965, Brown/Wood).

12. Ibid.: 5, emphasis in original.

13. The parodic *Black Watch* comic book's idealized denouement very much fits the pattern for heroic death discussed in the previous chapter. In fact, the staging and dialogue make it practically a retelling of the Doom Patrol's demise.

14. Gillis and Anderson do make Everson (despite his name, "eternal son," which tells us he has yet to grow up) a bit more complicated than this. At one point he wonders, "But I'm not going to sacrifice my life because of a comic book. I've got no illusions there—or do I?" (11). The motif of young men inspired to go off to war by idealized notions of battlefield glory has a long literary pedigree; the schoolmaster Kantorek urging his students to enlist in Erich Mariah Remarque's *All Quiet in the Western Front* (1928) represents its modern incarnation. But Everson, interestingly, self-deludes; it's his commanders-to-be who cruelly rip the veil from his childish illusions.

15. See for example David Stannard's discussion of the 1544 tomb of René of Chalons (22, 25).

16. The first three lines appear on the previous page (21), as Everson retrieves, tries to reread, then lets drop his old copy of *The Blackwatch*. I include them here because they clearly initiate the line of thought in the splash.

17. A number of characters in the series go through similar death-panics, e.g., Greg Mattingly/Backhand (a former actor who played Vyking in a television series, now part of the team itself) runs off hysterically upon seeing Wildcard's demise, screaming, "*I don't want to be a Morituri! I don't I don't I don't!*" (*Strikeforce: Morituri*, #13: 27, emphasis in original).

18. Unlike mainstream titles, which had come to utilize their covers to "tease" a death ("In this issue: *Someone Dies!*"), *Strikeforce: Morituri* never resorted to such cheap buyer-bait. The series seemed to delight in foiling readerly expectations about who would fall next, providing no definite clues along the way.

19. Humorously, Anderson's bookshelf in this splash holds some decidedly non-Christian fare, including *Lake Woebegone Days* and the *I Ching*.

20. Anderson's religious behavior runs the gamut from silly—the Garden, a tropical training center, strikes her as "like Genesis—it's so lovely" (*Strikeforce: Morituri*, #2: 11)—to poignant, as when she recites the Lord's Prayer over a human victim of the Horde in the middle of a battle (*Strikeforce: Morituri*, #3: 18). Gillis is not, however, above the occasional gentle parody of her faith; in *Strikeforce: Morituri* #5, she produces healing tears, recalling John 11:35: "Jesus wept" (22).

21. Significantly, given my discussion of editorial errors in chapters 6 and 7, Anderson's word balloon here has her refer to Aline Pagrovna as "Jelene." I take such representational slips—particularly when they occur at generically atypical moments—as neurotic symptoms, traces of the genre's unconscious (?) awareness of violating some taboo. Saunders, discussing similar "mistakes" in the portrayal of Gwen Stacy's death, relates them to the "traumatic disruption of memory" (88). Production errors in comics remain an understudied area.

22. Kierkegaard's "knight of faith" and "knight of resignation" concepts from *Fear and Trembling* (1843) influenced Becker's notions of heroism; he admires the knight, who like Anderson "accepts his life in this visible dimension without complaint, lives his life as a duty, faces his death without a qualm" (1973: 257–58). See also Saunders's comparison of the death-haunted Spider-Man to the "knight of faith" (94).

23. These words echo the lyrics of *I Look to Thee in Every Need*, an 1864 Christian hymn with lyrics by Samuel Longfellow.

24. Gillis explained to me that a great deal of thought went into this sequence precisely to keep it suggestive but open-ended: "[I] was impressed that Brent got it right the first time: Aline's [sic] astral form-hand clasping something that might be a hand formed out of the fabric of space—or might not" (2013).

25. Marathon's "rebirth" as a near-psychotic is also evoked through his miraculously surviving an initial brush with death. Thought killed after an assault on an exploding Horde ship (*Strikeforce: Morituri*, #8: 6), he returns soon after, altered mentally and physically (*Strikeforce: Morituri*, #9: 7). Unnerved by him, new team member Toxyn/Ruth Mastorakis thinks Marathon "an elemental force—!" (ibid.: 10).

26. The Freud of *Beyond the Pleasure Principle* (1920) characterizes such behavior—whereby an overwhelmed psychological "stimulus shield" treats "internal stimulations" in the wake of trauma "as though they were acting, not from the inside, but from the outside" as the origin of projection, a fundamentally pathological process (33).

27. While Marathon (partly, one suspects, due to his unwieldy height) had appeared in "abject" imagery before the personality shift, such portrayals increased sharply after it. Another figure that does much to challenge the superhero status quo, Blackthorn, also appears in a disproportionate number of "abjected" portraits throughout the series.

28. This mode was revived in the modern era by Tolstoy in *The Death of Ivan Ilyich*.

29. On the impact of page design on the reading experience, see also Peters.

30. Which makes all the more delicious the irony that, in *Strikeforce: Morituri* #12, Marvel chose to run, opposite the climactic "mandala-page," an ad for the "Kraven's Last Hunt" crossover series (discussed in chapter 7). It features a hyper-masculine, gun-toting, bare-chested Kraven.

31. The Marathon/Nion death sequence substantiates Alisia Chase's concept of "matrixial graphics" (adapted from Bracha L. Ettinger's "matrixial gaze" film theory), as compared to the feminist film scholar Barbara Creed's more male-centered concept of the "Monstrous Maternal." For an application of the latter to comics, see Walton.

32. A brief scene shows Lisieux meditating on her "spirit guide" before a candle on a rug with a pentagram—quite a mix of "religio-emes." Smugly, she muses, "I do hope Jelene won't be too upset when she finds that side isn't like her church told her it would be – but she'll flourish there anyway! She thinks it's *my* view of spiritual things that is the subjective delusion!" (*Strikeforce: Morituri*, #19: n.p., emphasis in original).

33. For another near-contemporary example of the "white background" afterlife trope, see the ending of *Somewhere in Time* (d. Jeannot Szwarc, 1980).

34. See Nuland, chapter 6 for a scientific discussion of near-death experience along the lines Gillis maintains.

35. Gillis and Anderson vigorously resisted this reading when I broached it to them: "Not only was it not someone we knew (and not Carl), it's not someone Scaredycat knew: and instead of a fulfillment of expectations, there's the 'it's completely different'—and the smile" (Gillis: 2013); "[I] had no one particular in mind for the 'mystery man.' I believe Peter described in the script a nice-looking young man Pilar would perceive of as her ideal life-mate, or something like that; a very attractive engaging welcoming person, a guide and counselor (someone akin to Jesus, maybe)" (Anderson: 2013).

36. For a more blatantly parodic example of such "thrift" in superhero comics, see John Byrne's depiction of Snowbird's battle with Kolomaq in a blizzard (rendered mostly as white panels with word balloons and sound effects) in *Alpha Flight*, vol. 1, #6 (Jan. 1984).

37. A standard "imaginary story" closing, this one from "The Death of Superman" (Gold/Greenberger: 206, emphasis and ellipsis in original), discussed in chapter 7.

38. In this feminist light, Blackthorn/Aline Pagrovna, one of the longest-lived characters, takes on particular significance. A tortured soul, especially after discovering her

post-Morituri-process pregnancy, Pagrovna appears in a recurring "pietà" portrait, weeping. She shares to some extent Marathon's "abject" depiction, and as with Everson, she is haunted by Green's "transi" image. Rarely have depression and death-fear been rendered in superhero comics with such nuance.

39. These include the transi; the Morituri as modern-day moriens (see chapter 7); Morituri central headquarters described as "so much like a cemetery" (*Strikeforce: Morituri*, #1: 7); and a parody of *Laocoön and His Sons* (ca. 100 BC) on the cover of *Strikeforce: Morituri* #15.

40. No other series programmed death so routinely into its premise. Not until Peter Milligan and Mike Allred's late-1990s satirical *X-Force/X-Statix* would an ongoing mainstream supergroup again experience such a frequent turnover body count.

CHAPTER 9

1. Mike Carlin served as an editor on the *Superman* titles at the time of the "Death of Superman" story arc.

2. The US media had reported on comic book superheroes before; in 1988, it covered the death of Batman's second Robin, Jason Todd, at the hands of the Joker, and even devoted space to Marvel's Canadian hero Northstar, who came out as gay in *Alpha Flight*, vol. 1, #106 (Mar. 1992).

3. As Quarter Bin pointed out, none but the most unschooled expected Superman to remain dead; the character appeared in four titles, comprising a significant portion of DC's market share (Oct. 2001); Duffy succinctly put it: "The same economic and narratological factors that forced [Superman] to be killed also mandated that he be revived" (260).

4. See De Haven: 11. Similar images adorned a number of variant covers. For more on the "Death of Superman and the 1990s collectibles craze, see Beaty, chapter 7.

5. The essay was translated into English and revised in 1972.

6. Eco wrote at a time before continuity had become a standard element of American superhero comics.

7. For more on Superman as a Jesus figure, see Koosed and Schumm, and Kozlovic. For a critique of the "mythological" approach to superheroes, see Saunders 16–17.

8. Rozanski chastises DC's deceptive marketing for making the "death" seem real: "I continue to hear from at least one non-comics fan a month about how they felt ripped off when they were 'tricked' into believing that Superman was really going to die."

9. "Funeral for a Friend" unfolded in *Superman*, vol. 2, #76 (Feb. 1993) and #77 (Mar. 1993); *Superman: The Man of Steel*, vol. 1, #20 (Feb. 1993) and #21 (Mar. 1993); *Action Comics*, vol. 1, #685 (Jan. 1993) and #686 (Feb. 1993); *Adventures of Superman*, vol. 1, #488 (Jan. 1993) and #489 (Feb. 1993). The covers of this eight-issue "mini-arc" within the "Death of Superman" storyline appeared with funereal thick black borders. All references to "Funeral for a Friend" pertain to Kahan 1993A.

10. In some sly meta-commentary, the hawker sells much the same merchandise as in the commemorative "Death of Superman" edition: T-shirt with dripping "S," black armband, and *Daily Planet* obituary.

11. This episode recalls the opening of Leo Tolstoy's novella *The Death of Ivan Ilyich* (1886), the first modern depiction of death, in which the eponymous character (now dead) is mentioned to his office coworkers, prompting them each to think of how the new vacancy will advance their careers.

12. A major theme of Brooke Gladstone and Josh Neufeld's comics manifesto on the media, *The Influencing Machine* (2011).

13. Lois calls these people "morbid leeches" (83).

14. An emotionally fraught fan letter reacting to Superman's death also focuses on the profit motive: "After all, DC *is* a corporation, no matter what comic-book readers like to think—you

are a group of people who raise money any way you can. . . . To sum all of this up, you are good at what you do, but it shouldn't be done" (*Superman*, vol. 2, #79, Jul. 1993, emphasis in original).

15. They received still more prominent media attention in the wake of the 1995 Oklahoma City bombing and the 1999 Columbine school shootings. As Doss notes, "The images, artefacts and rituals of these visibly public death-shrines . . . framed issues of memory, tribute and collectivity in contemporary America; their visual and performative dimensions clearly embodied a vast collaboration of mourners and media" (69). It is intriguing to speculate that at least some of the objects left at Superman's monument honor not the hero but the human victims of Doomsday's onslaught, a topic I address in the conclusion.

16. The Uniform Determination of Death Act (UDDA), based on the findings of a Carter Administration Presidential Commission that advocated "whole brain death" as the new standard, was implemented in 1981. See Peter Singer: 171–76 and Gary Greenberg.

17. Interestingly, this happens despite the fact that Superman, along with the entire DC line, had been assiduously retconned after the 1985–86 *Crisis on Infinite Earths* mega-series, so that much of that history no longer officially "existed"; see chapter 7.

18. Kitch discusses the "nostalgia effect" produced by black-and-white photography (299) in news reports of public deaths.

19. Though Bibbo does deliver an impassioned prayer for Superman's soul to the Virgin Mary—in private.

20. On the decision to keep the casket closed due to Kennedy's disfigured corpse and other reasons, see Laderman: xxxi and Mitford: 137.

21. Strictly speaking, Superman had not earned a flag on his coffin, having served neither in government nor the military. In this, his funeral anticipated that of John F. Kennedy, Jr., in 1999, who received similar honors despite his lack of "qualifications." Kitch sees the incident as indicative of the Kennedy family's high esteem in American life (303).

22. The scene before the Children's Aid Society (66) recalls the famous photograph of "John-John" (the three-year-old John F. Kennedy, Jr.), though none of the kids salute the passing coffin.

23. To cite another connection between these two national heroes, in 1964 DC published the story "Superman's Mission for President Kennedy" (*Superman*, vol. 1, #170, Jul. 1964), which had previously been slated for publication but withdrawn due to the assassination. The story appeared at the personal request of President Lyndon B. Johnson (Gold/Greenberger: 180).

24. As exemplified by this piece of reportage on the aftermath of Kennedy's death:

> A great shadow fell on the land and in the perspective of death there was a great slowing down and a great stopping. The farmer summoned to the house did not find the will to return to the field, nor the secretary to the typewriter, nor the machinist to the lathe, nor the wife to the dishes, nor the judge to the bench, nor the carpenter to the saw. There was a great slowing down and a great stopping and the big bronze gong sounded and a man shouted the market is closed and the New York Stock Exchange stopped, just stopped. The Boston Symphony Orchestra stopped a Handel concerto and started a Beethoven funeral march and the Canadian House of Commons stopped and a dramatic play in Berlin stopped and the United Nations in New York stopped and courts and schools and a race track in Rhode Island and a race track in Maryland and race track in New York stopped, just stopped. (Associated Press, 1963; the author of these lines is Saul Pett)

25. For more on monuments and postwar memory, see Tatum, chapter 1.

26. Compare such complacency to the "geek rage" that erupted in the wake of the June 2013 release of Zack Snyder's *Man of Steel*. Several commentators faulted the film not only for getting Superman "wrong," but also for its callous portrayal of ultra-violence: the cities of Smallville

and Metropolis are all but leveled, with thousands of presumed casualties, yet no one (least of all Superman himself) remarks on the carnage or its consequences. See Waid, Singer 2013 and Hatfield 2013 for, ahem, post-mortems.

27. In fact, DC did eventually address the subject of Doomsday's direct and indirect victims in the 2003 miniseries *Superman: Day of Doom*, written by "Death of Superman" writer Dan Jurgens.

CHAPTER 10

1. Dalton's description of Bizarro, from "The Boy of Steel Versus The Thing of Steel," discussed below.

2. On the foregoing, see Howe, part IV and Raviv.

3. On industry mistreatment of the inventors of the genre, Siegel and Shuster, see Jones's prologue and Ricca. Also see Hatfield 2012: 78–80 for Jack Kirby's creative ownership struggle with Marvel.

4. The Legion of the Unliving (along with zombie movies) inspired the twenty-first-century "undead" superhero concept, seen in DC's *Blackest Night* (2009–10) and various manifestations of the Marvel Zombies (debuted in *Ultimate Fantastic Four*, vol. 1, #21, Sept. 2005, Millar/Land).

5. See Greil Marcus for a further treatment of public fascination with death through popular culture, with the posthumous Elvis Presley as his example.

6. It bears mention that not everyone saw Marvel's introduction of physical difference as a consistent element of the genre in positive terms. As the writer Alan Moore told an interviewer: "That's characterization the Marvel way. They're neurotic. They worry a lot. If they haven't got anything mentally wrong with them like that, something physically wrong with them will do—perhaps a bad leg, or dodgy kidneys, or something like that. To Marvel, that's characterization" (Berlatsky: 14).

7. Misunderstood but also mocked, Bizarro seems to be a superhero representation of autism as comic relief. Superboy uses a life-size marionette of Bizarro's friend Melissa to dupe him (he's too "dim-witted" to tell the difference [130]), saying, "Good grief! How dumb can you be, *Bizarro*? Stop blubbering! That's only a *dummy* I used to lure you here!" (134, emphasis in original).

8. "How was I terrified when I viewed myself in a transparent pool! At first I started back, unable to believe that it was indeed I who was reflected in the mirror; and when I became fully convinced that I was in reality the monster that I am, I was filled with the bitterest sensations of despondence and mortification" (Shelley: 159).

9. In both instances the creature's mere appearance sets off revulsion and horror. Bizarro very much lives up to his precursor's effect on the eyewitness: "[I] beheld the wretch—the miserable monster whom I had created. . . . No mortal could support the horror of that countenance. A mummy endued with animation could not be so hideous as that wretch" (Shelley: 106). As noted previously, the early incarnation of Ben Grimm/the Thing also followed this model.

10. Schwartz (who wrote for the *Superman* comic strip) was influenced by Carl Jung's archetype of the shadow in his creation of Bizarro, while Mort Weisinger (then-editor of the Superman family titles) more simplistically saw the figure as a variation on the Frankenstein monster: a "grotesque, stupid, imperfect duplicate of the Boy of Steel" (Conroy: 244). The better-known, adult version of the character debuted in "The Battle With Bizarro!" (*Action Comics*, vol. 1, #254, Jul. 1959, Binder/Plastino).

11. One gets the impression the sequence could indulge in such grisly imagery in part due to the storyline's publication minus the Comics Code Authority seal (the storyline dealt in frank terms with drug addiction). See Rogers: 84 for a discussion of how that came about.

12. I'm hardly the first to speak of her in these terms. See Saunders, chapter 3, and Blumberg, who calls the storyline "a mind-numbing tragedy that would symbolize the shifting tide of

history and usher in a new age of comics. Gwen Stacy . . . was to be the sacrificial lamb in this tragic ritual" (199).

13. In this regard, Osborn/Green Goblin's death is comparable to the death of Dark Phoenix/Jean Grey, whose lust for power (rendered as a form of cosmic drug addiction) leads to mass murder, necessitating her own self-execution. See chapter 7 for more on this controversial decision.

14. And not just any woman; that Barbara Gordon, aka Batgirl, had existed in Batman continuity since 1967, made the event all the more shocking. I remind the reader that Barbara is not only shot, but stripped naked and photographed in agony so as to drive Commissioner Gordon insane.

15. He goes on, "The revisionary superhero narrative may organize history, but the Joker knows that the imposition of order is just a trick of the light, that for convoluted fictional overdetermination to step into some final rationalization will only result in death" (61).

16. "Possible" because of the Joker's supreme unreliability as a witness. As he says elsewhere in the novel: "Sometimes I remember it *one* way, sometimes *another* . . . If I'm going to have a past, I prefer it be *multiple choice! Ha ha ha!*" (ellipsis and emphasis in original).

17. As the Joker raves, thinking he has succeeded in "getting to" Gordon: "I've proved my point. I've demonstrated there's *no difference* between *me* and everyone *else!* All it takes is *one bad day* to reduce the *sanest man alive* to *lunacy. That's* how far the *world* is from where *I* am. Just *one bad day*" (emphasis in original).

18. In Frank Miller's seminal *The Dark Knight Returns* (1986), Joker and Batman do indeed fight to the death.

19. For more on media linkages between Lanza's cognitive status and the violence, see Brainard. For the rates of autistic victimization—including murder by their parents—see Solomon, chapter 5, and Joel Smith. Given these trends, Ma Kent's cold rebuffing of Bizarro takes on a more disturbing tinge.

20. Autism, an umbrella term coined in 1912 by Swiss psychiatrist Eugen Bleuler, refers to a range of early-onset behaviors, including poor nonverbal communication; repetitive movement; compromised empathy and emotional involvement; and extremely concrete thinking. For part of the twentieth century, autism was considered a subset of "childhood schizophrenia." See Solomon, chapter 5.

21. For a particularly salient treatment of disability's "latent notion of threat" through the lens of popular culture, see Sarah Hoedlmoser's presentation "They Came from Beyond the Grave: Examining Interactions of Zombies, Pop Culture, and Disabilities Studies," presented at the "Fantastic! Heroic! Disabled?: 'Cripping' the Con" conference (Syracuse University, Apr. 11, 2013).

22. Squier arrives at these insights through a reading of Paul and Judy Karasik's *The Ride Together*, a 2003 part-comics memoir of growing up with an autistic brother, and David B.'s *Epileptic* (2003).

23. He also appears this way—his gaze almost vacuous—in a series of head portraits of him Newley made that same year. See the gallery at http://www.sachanewley.com/.

24. As noted in chapter 2, some in the disabled community leveled strong critiques of Reeve (1952–2004) for what they saw as the harm done by his insistent focus on curing his paralysis. In fairness, the Christopher and Dana Reeve Foundation's mission involves not only spinal cord injury research but also quality-of-life issues.

25. Jerry Siegel and Joe Shuster debuted the Ultra-Humanite in *Action Comics*, vol. 1, #13 (Jun. 1939).

26. Other contemporary artists, such as Philip Knoll with his *Real and Imagined* (2000), Nadín Ospina with *El Pensador* (2009), and the aforementioned René Garcia and Gilles Barbier have pursued subjects related to superheroes. It bears mentioning that several disabled artists arrived at their own critique of the superhero body, have appropriated its iconography largely

to ridicule, and lambast the supercrip ethic. Among these I would include Bob Flanagan, Super Masochist, the late performance artist who suffered from cystic fibrosis and resorted to public sadomasochism to explore and even revel in his body's diseased state; and Bridget Powers, Super Midget, a porn actress who, like Flanagan, violates the taboo against the disabled expressing, or even having a right to, their sexuality. Unlike the supercrip's overcompensatory fixation predicated on the perceived need to comply with and exceed societal expectations, these artists embrace their physical difference as a badge of empowerment and self-worth in itself. Rather than applaud this as some sort of (super)heroic gesture, therefore, it would seem a better move for those of us outside the disabled community looking in to merely acknowledge and support it with a hearty "Vive la Différence!"

27. See Garland-Thomson's discussion of Assistant Secretary of Education Judith E. Heumann's photographic portrait: "The photo suggests neither that her accomplishments are superhuman nor that she has triumphantly overcome anything. She thus becomes more familiar than strange" (2001: 370).

BIBLIOGRAPHY

Abernathy, Ben. *Essential Fantastic Four*. Vol. 1. New York: Marvel Comics, 2001.

Alaniz, José. "Chris Ware and Autistic Realism." *International Journal of Comic Art* 13, no. 1 (Spring 2011): 514–29.

——. *Komiks: Comic Art in Russia*. Jackson: University Press of Misssissippi, 2010.

——. "Masculinity and the Superhero in Post-Soviet Russian Comics." *International Journal of Comic Art* 11, no. 1 (Spring 2009): 396–425.

——. "'Nature,' Illusion and Excess in Sokurov's *Mother and Son*." *Studies in Russian and Soviet Cinema* 2, no. 2 (2008): 183–204.

——. "Into Her Dead Body: Moore and Campbell's *From Hell*." In *Alan Moore: Portrait of an Extraordinary Gentleman*, ed. smoky man and Gary Spencer Millidge, 145–49. Leigh-on-Sea, England: Abiogenesis Press, 2003.

Alexander, Mark, Jack Kirby, and Stan Lee. *Lee & Kirby: The Wonder Years*. Raleigh, NC: Two-Morrows, 2011.

Anderson, Brent. E-mail correspondence. Apr. 2013.

Aquilone, James. "Lame Superhero of the Week: She-Thing." *Blogzarro*, Jun. 11, 2007. http://blog zarro.com/2007/06/lame-superhero-of-the-week-she-thing/#more-268.

Ariès, Philippe. *The Hour of Our Death*. Translated by Helen Weaver. New York: Random House, 1980.

Armstrong, David. *Political Anatomy of the Body: Medical Knowledge in Britain in the Twentieth Century*. Cambridge: Cambridge University Press, 1983.

ASAN. "ASAN Statement on Media Reports Regarding Newtown, CT Shooting." Dec. 14, 2012. http://autisticadvocacy.org/2012/12/asan-statement-on-media-reports-regarding -newtown-ct-shooting/.

Asch, Adrienne. "Disability, Bioethics and Human Rights." In *Handbook of Disability Studies*, ed. Gary L. Albrecht, Katherine D. Seelman, and Michael Bury, 297–326. Thousand Oaks, CA: Sage Publications, 2001.

Associated Press. *The Torch Is Passed: The Associated Press Story of the Death of a President*. Cleveland: Plain Dealer, 1963.

Bachman, Randall W. "Would a Mental Health Registry Have Prevented Sandy Hook?" *Minn-Post*, Jan. 10, 2013. http://www.minnpost.com/community-voices/2013/01/would-national -mental-health-registry-have-prevented-sandy-hook.

Bacon, Francis. *The Works of Lord Bacon*. Vol. 1. London: Henry G. Bohn, 1850.

Badinter, Elisabeth. *Xy, on Masculine Identity*. New York: Columbia University Press, 1995.

Bainbridge, Jason. "'Worlds Within Worlds': The Role of Superheroes in the Marvel and DC Universes." In *The Contemporary Comic Book Superhero*, ed. Angela Ndalianis, 64–85. New York: Routledge, 2009.

Barthes, Roland. *Camera Lucida*. Translated by Richard Howard. New York: Farrar, Straus & Giroux, 1980.

Baudrillard, Jean. *Symbolic Exchange and Death*. Translated by Iain Hamilton Grant. London: Sage Publications, 1993.

Baynton, Douglas C. "Disability and the Justification of Inequality in American History." In *The New Disability History: American Perspectives*, ed. Paul Longmore and Lauri Umansky, 33–57. New York: New York University Press, 2001.

Beaty, Bart. *Comics Versus Art*. Toronto: University of Toronto Press, 2012.

Becker, Ernest. *The Denial of Death*. New York: The Free Press, 1973.

————. *The Birth and Death of Meaning*. 2nd ed. New York: The Free Press, 1971.

Berenstein, Rhonda. "Spectatorship as Drag: The Act of Viewing Classic Horror Cinema." In *Defining Cinema*, ed. Linda Williams. New Brunswick: Rutgers University Press, 1995: 231–69.

Berger, Arthur A. *The Comic-Stripped American: What Dick Tracy, Blondie, Daddy Warbucks and Charlie Brown Tell Us About Ourselves*. New York: Walker, 1973.

Berlatsky, Eric L., ed. *Alan Moore: Conversations*. Jackson: University Press of Mississippi, 2012.

Berman, Margaret Fink. "Imagining an Idiosyncratic Belonging: Representing Disability in Chris Ware's *Building Stories*." In *The Comics of Chris Ware: Drawing Is a Way of Thinking*, ed. David M. Ball and Martha B. Kuhlman, 191–205. Jackson: University Press of Mississippi, 2010.

Best, Mark. "Domesticity, Homosociality and Male Power in Superhero Comics of the 1950s." *Iowa Journal of Cultural Studies*, Spring 2005, 80–99.

Birge, Sarah. "Comics, Autism, and Empathetic Scholarship." *Disability Studies Quarterly* 30, no. 1 (2010). http://dsq-sds.org/article/view/1067/1255.

Blazina, Chris. *The Cultural Myth of Masculinity*. Westport, CT: Praeger, 2003.

Blumberg, Arnold T. "The Night Gwen Stacy Died: The End of Innocence and the 'Last Gasp of the Silver Age.'" *International Journal of Comic Art* 8, no. 1 (Spring/Summer 2006): 197–211.

Blume, Stuart S. *The Artificial Ear: Cochlear Implants and the Culture of Deafness*. New Brunswick, NJ: Rutgers University Press, 2010.

Bogdan, Robert. "The Social Construction of Freaks." In *Freakery: Cultural Spectacles of the Extraordinary Body*, ed. Rosemarie Garland-Thomson, 23–37. New York: New York University Press, 1996.

Bourdieu, Pierre. *Outline of a Theory of Practice*. Cambridge: Cambridge University Press, 1977.

Bower, Kathrin M. "Holocaust Avengers: From 'The Master Race' to Magneto." *International Journal of Comic Art* 6, no. 2 (Fall 2004): 182–94.

Brainard, Curtis. "Lanza, Autism and Violence." *Columbia Journalism Review*, Dec. 17, 2012. http://www.cjr.org/the_observatory/lanza_autism_speculation_newto.php?page=all.

Braswell, Harold. "Can There Be a Disability Studies Theory of 'End-of-Life Autonomy'?" *Disability Studies Quarterly* 31, no. 4 (2011). http://dsq-sds.org/article/view/1704/1754.

Broertjes, Harry. "Jim Shooter Interview." *The X-Men Chronicles* 1, no. 1 (1981): 9–11.

Bronfen, Elisabeth. *Over Her Dead Body: Death, Femininity, and the Aesthetic*. New York: Routledge, 1992.

Brown, Jeffrey A. *Black Superheroes, Milestone Comics, and Their Fans*. Jackson: University Press of Mississippi, 2001.

Brueggemann, Brenda J., Linda F. White, Patricia A. Dunn, Barbara A. Heifferon, and Johnson Cheu. "Becoming Visible: Lessons in Disability." *College Composition and Communication* 52, no. 3 (2001): 368–98.

Brune, Jeffrey A. "Blind Like Me: John Howard Griffin, Disability, and the Fluidity of Identity in Modern America." Unpublished manuscript, 2009.

Brune, Jeffrey A., and Daniel J. Wilson. *Disability and Passing: Blurring the Lines of Identity*. Philadelphia: Temple University Press, 2013.

Bukatman, Scott. "Secret Identity Politics." In *The Contemporary Comic Book Superhero*, ed. Angela Ndalianis, 109–25. New York: Routledge, 2009.

————. *Matters of Gravity: Special Effects and Supermen in the 20th Century*. Durham: Duke University Press, 2003.

Butler, Judith. *Precarious Life: The Powers of Mourning and Violence*. London: Verso, 2003.

————. *Gender Trouble: Feminism and the Subversion of Identity*. New York: Routledge, 1990.

Byrne, John. "Lost Love." *Superman*, vol. 2, no. 12 (Dec. 1987).

——. ". . . And One Shall Surely Die!" *Alpha Flight*, vol. 1, no. 12 (Jul. 1984).

——. "This Land is Mine!" *Fantastic Four*, vol. 1, no. 247 (Oct. 1982).

——. "Too Many Dooms!" *Fantastic Four*, vol. 1, no. 246 (Sept. 1982).

——. "Terror in a Tiny Town." *Fantastic Four*, vol. 1, no. 236 (Nov. 1981).

Carlin, John, and Wagstaff, Sheena. *The Comic Art Show: Cartoons in Painting and Popular Culture*. New York: Whitney Museum of American Art, 1983.

Carrier, David. *The Aesthetics of Comics*. University Park: Pennsylvania State University Press, 2000.

Carroll, Noël. *The Philosophy of Horror, Or, Paradoxes of the Heart*. New York: Routledge, 1990.

Carveth, Donald L. "The Melancholic Existentialism of Ernest Becker." *Free Associations* 11, part 3, no. 59 (2004): 422–29.

Chabon, Michael. "Secret Skin: An Essay in Unitard Theory." *Superheroes: Fashion and Fantasy*, ed. Andrew Bolton and Harold Koda, 12–23 New Haven: Yale University Press, 2008.

——. *The Amazing Adventures of Kavalier and Clay: A Novel*. New York: Random House, 2000.

Charlton, James I. *Nothing About Us Without Us: Disability Oppression and Empowerment*. Berkeley: University of California Press, 1998.

Chase, Alisia. "Matrixial Graphics: Motherhood and Politics in Megan Kelso's *Watergate Sue*." Presentation, International Comic Arts Forum 2013, Portland, OR, May 24, 2013.

Chute, Hillary L. *Graphic Women: Life Narrative and Contemporary Comics*. New York: Columbia University Press, 2010.

——. "'The Shadow of a Past Time': History and Graphic Representation in *Maus*." In *A Comics Studies Reader*, ed. Jeet Heer and Kent Worcester, 340–362. Jackson: University Press of Mississippi, 2009.

Clare, Eli. *Exile and Pride: Disability, Queerness and Liberation*. Cambridge, MA: South End Press, 2009 [1999].

Claremont, Chris, and John Byrne. *Phoenix: The Untold Story*. New York: Marvel Comics, 1984.

Clogston, John. *Disability Coverage in 16 Newspapers*. Louisville: Advocado Press, 1990.

Coates, Ta-Nehisi. "The Worst Thing About Marvel Comics." *The Atlantic Monthly* blog, Jun. 16, 2009. http://www.theatlantic.com/entertainment/archive/2009/06/the-worst-thing-about -marvel-comics/19466/.

Coffin, Bill. "Tragic Tale." *National Underwriter Life & Health*, Nov. 7, 2011. http://www.lifehealth pro.com/2011/11/07/tragic-tale.

Conroy, Mike. *500 Comic Book Villains*. Hauppauge, NY: Barrons Educational Series, Inc, 2004.

Coogan, Peter. *Superhero: The Secret Origin of a Genre*. Austin, TX: MonkeyBrain Books, 2006.

Corker, Mairian. "Sensing Disability." *Hypatia* 16, no. 4 (2001): 34–52.

Costello, Matthew J. *Secret Identity Crisis: Comic Books and the Unmasking of Cold War America*. New York: Continuum, 2009.

Creed, Barbara. "Horror and the Monstrous Feminine: An Imaginary Abjection." In *The Dread of Difference: Gender and the Horror Film*, ed. Barry Keith Grant, 66–115. Austin: University of Texas Press, 1996.

Curley, Pat. "The Blinded Daredevil." *Silver Age Comics*, Feb. 18, 2008. http://sacomics.blogspot .com/2008/02/blinded-daredevil.html

Daniels, Les. *Superman: The Complete History, the Life and Times of the Man of Steel*. San Francisco: Chronicle Books, 1998.

Darius, Julian. "X-Men Is Not An Allegory of Racial Tolerance." *Seqart.org*, Sept. 25, 2002. http:// sequart.org/magazine/3201/x-men-is-not-an-allegory-of-racial-tolerance/.

Darling, Michael. "Plumbing the Depths of Superflatness." *Art Journal* 60, no. 3 (Autumn 2001): 76–89.

David, Peter, and Gary Frank. "Let Darkness Come." *The Incredible Hulk*, vol. 1, no. 420 (Aug. 1994).

Davis, Lennard J. *Bending Over Backwards: Disability, Dismodernism, and Other Difficult Positions.* New York: New York University Press, 2002.

———. "Introduction." In *The Disability Studies Reader.* 1st ed., ed. Lennard Davis, 1–6. New York: Routledge, 1997.

———. "Nude Venuses, Medusa's Body and Phantom Limbs: Disability and Visuality." In *The Body and Physical Difference,* ed. David T. Mitchell and Sharon L. Snyder, 51–70. Ann Arbor: University of Michigan Press, 1997B.

Davies, Douglas J. *Death, Ritual, and Belief: The Rhetoric of Funerary Rites.* London: Cassell, 1997.

Dayananda, Y. J. "*The Death of Ivan Ilyich:* A Psychological Study on Death and Dying." *Literature and Psychology,* no. 22 (1972): 191–98.

Defalco, Tom, and Paul Ryan. "Only Death Be My Salvation!" *Fantastic Four,* vol. 1, No. 379 (Aug. 1993).

De Haven, Tom. *Our Hero: Superman on Earth.* New Haven, CT: Yale University Press, 2010.

de Man, Paul. *The Rhetoric of Romanticism.* New York: Columbia University Press, 1984.

de Montaigne, Michel. "To Philosophize is To Learn to Die." 1580. In *The Grim Reader,* ed. Maura Spiegel and Richard Tristman, 16–32. New York: Anchor Books, 1997.

Dinsmore, Alan M. "The Decline in Employment of People with Disabilities—A Policy Puzzle." *Disability Studies Quarterly* 24, no. 3 (Summer 2004). http://dsq-sds.org/article/view/514/691.

Dony, Christophe, and Caroline Van Linthout. "Comics, Trauma, and Cultural Memory(ies) of 9/11." In *The Rise and Reason of Comics and Graphic Literature: Critical Essays on the Form,* ed. Joyce Goggin and Dan Hassler-Forest, 178–88. Jefferson, NC: McFarland & Co, 2010.

Doss, Erika. "Death, Art and Memory in the Public Sphere: the Visual and Material Culture of Grief in Contemporary America." *Mortality* 7, no. 1 (2002): 63–82.

Dougherty, Margot, and Sandra Rubin Tessler. "Tiring of Life Without Freedom, Quadriplegic David Rivlin Chooses to Die Among Friends." *People,* Aug. 7, 1989. http://www.people.com/people/archive/article/0,,20120912,00.html.

Douglas, Mary. *Purity and Danger.* New York: Routledge, 1966.

Duffy, William. "Sing, Muse, of the Immortal Hero: Using Epic to Understand Comic Books." *International Journal of Comic Art* 8, no. 1 (Spring/Summer 2006): 258–70.

Duncan, Randy, and Matthew J. Smith. *The Power of Comics: History, Form and Culture.* New York: Continuum, 2009.

Eco, Umberto. "The Myth of Superman." Translated by Natalie Chilton. In *Arguing Comics: Literary Masters on a Popular Medium,* ed. Jeet Heer and Ken Worchester, 146–64. Jacksonville: University Press of Mississippi, 2004.

Engel, David M., and Frank W. Munger. *Rights of Inclusion: Law and Identity in the Life Stories of Americans with Disabilities.* Chicago: University of Chicago Press, 2003.

Englehart, Steve. Personal interview, Skype. Jan. 2012.

Englehart, Steve, and Sal Buscema. "The Tunnels of the Mole Man!" *Fantastic Four,* vol. 1, no. 313 (Apr. 1988).

Englehart, Steve, and Ron Lim. "After the Fall." *Fantastic Four,* vol. 1, no. 321 (Dec. 1988).

Englehart, Steve, and Keith Pollard. "Last Kiss." *Fantastic Four,* vol. 1, no. 317 (Aug. 1988).

———. "I Want to Die!" *Fantastic Four,* vol. 1, no. 311 (Feb. 1988).

———. "Things to Come!" *Fantastic Four,* vol. 1, no. 310 (Jan. 1988).

Englehart, Steve, and Herb Trimpe. "Who Is . . . The Shroud?" *Supervillain Team-Up,* vol. 1, no. 7 (Aug. 1976).

Epstein, Daniel Robert. "Talking to Arnold Drake." *Newsarama.com,* Oct. 11, 2007. http://web.archive.org/web/20071011174524/http://newsarama.com/general/ArnoldDrake/DrakeInterview.htm.

Estes, Adam Clarke. "Revelations About Adam Lanza's Mental Health Still Don't Explain the Violence." *The Atlantic Wire,* Feb. 19, 2013. http://www.theatlanticwire.com/national/2013/02/revelations-about-adam-lanzas-mental-health-still-dont-explain-violence/62317/.

Fadem, P., et al. "Attitudes of People with Disabilities Toward Physician-Assisted Suicide Legislation: Broadening the Dialogue." *Journal of Health Politics, Policy and Law* 28, no. 6 (2003): 977–1001.

Faludi, Susan. *Stiffed: The Betrayal of the American Man.* New York: William Morrow and Co., 1999.

Farnell, B. "Moving Bodies, Acting Selves." *Annual Review of Anthropology* 28, no. 1 (1999): 341–73.

Feiffer, Jules. *The Great Comic Book Heroes.* New York: Dial Press, 1965.

Feinstein, Sharon. "Portrait of a Superhero." *Sunday Express*, Jun. 13, 2004. http://issuu.com/sachanewley/docs/press_article_sunex_01.

Felman, Shoshana. *The Juridical Unconscious: Trials and Traumas in the Twentieth Century.* Cambridge: Harvard University Press, 2002.

Fiedler, Leslie. *Tyranny of the Normal.* Boston: David R. Godine, 1996.

——. *Freaks: Myths and Images of the Secret Self.* New York: Simon & Schuster, 1978.

Filene, Peter. *In the Arms of Others: A Cultural History of the Right-to-Die in America.* Chicago: Ivan R. Dee, 1998.

Fingeroth, Danny. Personal interview, New York City. Jun. 2008.

——. *Disguised As Clark Kent: Jews, Comics, and the Creation of the Superhero.* New York: Continuum, 2007.

——. *Superman on the Couch: What Superheroes Really Tell Us About Ourselves and Our Society.* New York: Continuum, 2004.

——, ed. *The Life of Captain Marvel.* New York: Marvel Comics, 1990.

Fischer, Craig. "Fantastic Fascism? Jack Kirby, Nazi Aesthetics, and Klaus Theweleit's *Male Fantasies.*" *International Journal of Comic Art* 5, no. 1 (Spring 2003): 334–54.

Foster, Hal. *The Return of the Real: The Avant Garde at the End of the Century.* Cambridge: MIT Press, 1996.

Foucault, Michel. *Madness and Civilization: A History of Insanity in the Age of Reason.* 1961. New York: Vintage, 1988.

Freeman, Gillian. *The Undergrowth of Literature.* London: Nelson, 1967.

Freeze, Di. "Clay Lacy: the Planes I've Flown and the People I've Known: Part 2." *Airport Journals*, Sept. 2003. http://www.airportjournals.com/Display.cfm?varID=0309001.

Freud, Sigmund. *Beyond the Pleasure Principle.* 1920. Translated and edited by James Strachey. New York: W. W. Norton, 1961.

——. "The Uncanny." 1919. *Standard Edition of the Complete Psychological Works of Sigmund Freud.* Vol. 17. Edited by James Strachey. London: Hogarth Press, 1957: 217–52.

——. "Mourning and Melancholia." 1917. *Standard Edition.* Vol. 14: 243–58.

——. "Thoughts for the Times on War and Death." 1915A. *Standard Edition.* Vol. 14: 275–300.

——. "On Transience." 1915B. *Standard Edition.* Vol. 14: 305–308.

——. "Animism, Magic and the Omnipotence of Thoughts." 1913. *Totem and Taboo.* Translated by James Strachey. New York: W. W. Norton, 1950.

Gabilliet, Jean-Paul. *Of Comics and Men: A Cultural History of American Comic Books.* Translated by Bart Beaty and Nick Nguyen. Jackson: University Press of Mississippi, 2010.

Garber, Marjorie B. *Vested Interests: Cross-dressing and Cultural Anxiety.* New York: Routledge, 1992.

Garland-Thomson, Rosemarie. *Staring: How We Look.* Oxford: Oxford University Press, 2009.

——. "Feminist Disability Studies." *Signs* 30, no. 2 (Winter 2005): 1557–87.

——. "Integrating Disability, Transforming Feminist Theory." In *Gendering Disability*, ed. Bonnie G. Smith and Beth Hutchison, 73–103. New Brunswick, NJ: Rutgers University Press, 2004A.

——. "The Cultural Logic of Euthanasia: 'Sad Fancyings' in Herman Melville's *Bartleby.*" *American Literature* 76, no. 4 (Dec. 2004B): 777–806.

——. "Seeing the Disabled: Visual Rhetorics of Disability in Popular Photography." In *The New Disability History: American Perspectives*, ed. Paul Longmore and Lauri Umansky, 335–74. New York: New York University Press, 2001.

——. *Extraordinary Bodies: Figuring Physical Disability in American Culture and Literature.* New York: Columbia University Press, 1997.

Gilbert, Sandra M. *Death's Door: Modern Dying and the Ways We Grieve.* New York: W. W. Norton, 2006.

Gillis, Peter. E-mail correspondence. Apr. 2013.

Gillis, Peter, and Brent Anderson. "The Sun is But a Morning Star." *Strikeforce: Morituri*, vol. 1, no. 19 (Jun. 1988).

——. "Johnny, We Hardly Knew Ye . . ." *Strikeforce: Morituri*, vol. 1, no. 13 (Dec. 1987).

——. "The Birthgrave." *Strikeforce: Morituri*, vol. 1, no. 12 (Nov. 1987).

——. "The Undiscovered Country." *Strikeforce: Morituri*, vol. 1, no. 9 (Aug. 1987).

——. "Foray for Holowood." *Strikeforce: Morituri*, vol. 1, no. 6 (May 1987).

——. "Healing." *Strikeforce: Morituri*, vol. 1, no. 5 (Apr. 1987).

——. "Strikeforce: Morituri." *Strikeforce: Morituri*, vol. 1, no. 1 (Dec. 1986).

Gillis, Peter, and Ron Frenz. "What If The Invisible Girl Had Died?" *What If?*, vol. 1, no. 42 (Dec. 1983).

Gilman, Sander L. *Making the Body Beautiful: A Cultural History of Aesthetic Surgery.* Princeton: Princeton University Press, 1999.

Gladstone, Brooke, Josh Neufeld, Randy Jones, and Susann Jones. *The Influencing Machine: Brooke Gladstone on the Media.* New York: W. W. Norton, 2011.

Glaser, J. "An Imaginary Ararat: Jewish Bodies and Jewish Homelands in Ben Katchor's *The Jew of New York.*" *Melus Amherst* 32, no. 3 (2007): 153–74.

Goffman, Erving. *Stigma: Notes on the Management of Spoiled Identity.* New York: Simon & Schuster, 1963.

——. *The Presentation of Self in Everyday Life.* Garden City, NY: Doubleday, 1959.

Gold, Mike, and Robert Greenberger. *The Greatest Superman Stories Ever Told.* New York: DC Comics, 1986.

Gordon, Deborah. "Tenacious Assumptions in Western Medicine." In *Biomedicine Examined*, ed. Margaret M. Lock and Deborah Gordon, 19–56. Dordrecht: Kluwer Academic Publishers, 1988.

Gordon, Ian. "Nostalgia, Myth and Ideology: Visions of Superman at the End of the 'American Century.'" In *Comics and Ideology*, ed. Matthew P. McAllister, Edward H. Sewell, and Gordon, 177–93. New York: Peter Lang, 2001.

Gorer, Geoffrey. *Death, Grief and Mourning.* Garden City, NY: Doubleday, 1965.

Gouveia, Georgette. "Art's Country." *The Journal News*, Jul. 4, 2003. http://www.nynews.com/newsroom/070403/e0104whitney.html.

Green, Avi. "When Superman 'Died' in 1992, Some Bought It for Profit, Not Because They Cared About the Story." *The Four-Color Media Monitor*, Jan. 27, 2011. http://fourcolormedmon.blogspot.com/2011/01/when-superman-died-in-1992-some-bought.html.

Greenberg, Clement. *The Collected Essays and Criticism: Perceptions and Judgments, 1939–1944.* Chicago: University of Chicago Press, 1988.

Greenberg, Gary. "As Good as Dead." *The New Yorker*, Aug. 13, 2001, 36–41.

Greenberger, Robert, ed. *Showcase Presents: Metamorpho the Element Man.* Vol. 1. New York: DC Comics, 2005.

Groensteen, Thierry. *The System of Comics.* Translated Bart Beaty and Nick Nguyen. Jackson: University Press of Mississippi, 2007.

Grosz, Elizabeth. "Intolerable Ambiguity: Freaks as/at the Limit." In *Freakery: Cultural Spectacles of the Extraordinary Body*, ed. Rosemarie Garland-Thomson, 55–66. New York: New York University Press, 1996.

———. *Volatile Bodies: Toward a Corporeal Feminism*. Bloomington: Indiana University Press, 1994.

Gunther, John. *Death Be Not Proud*. 1949. New York: Harper Perennial, 1998.

Gustines, George Gene. "The Life, Death and Life of Superheroes." *The New York Times: Arts Beat*, Jan. 25, 2011. http://artsbeat.blogs.nytimes.com/2011/01/25/the-life-death-and-life-of -superheroes/.

Hahn, Harlan. "Can Disability Be Beautiful?" *Social Policy*, Fall 1988, 26–31.

Haller, Beth. "False Positive." *Ragged Edge Online*, Jan./Feb. 2000. http://www.ragged-edge-mag .com/0100/c0100media.htm.

Hart, David M. "Batman's Confrontation With Death, Angst and Freedom." In *Batman and Philosophy: The Dark Knight of the Soul*, ed. Mark D. White and Robert Arp, 212–24. Hoboken, NJ: John Wiley & Sons, 2008.

Harvey, Robert C. *The Art of the Comic Book: An Aesthetic History*. Jackson: University Press of Mississippi, 1996.

Hatfield, Charles. "Hollow Man." *See Hatfield*, Jun. 30, 2013. http://seehatfield.wordpress .com/2013/06/30/hollow-man/.

———. *Hand of Fire: The Comics Art of Jack Kirby*. Jackson: University Press of Mississippi, 2012.

———. "Superheroes and the Silver Age." In *Faster Than a Speeding Bullet: The Art of the Superhero*, ed. Ben Saunders, 17–20. University of Oregon: Jordan Schnitzler Museum of Art, 2009.

———. *Alternative Comics: An Emerging Literature*. Jackson: University Press of Mississippi, 2005.

Hatty, Susan. *Masculinities, Violence, Culture*. London: Sage, 2000.

Hebl, Michelle R., and Kleck, Robert E. "The Social Consequences of Physical Disability." In *The Social Psychology of Stigma*, ed. Todd F. Heatherton, 419–39. New York: Guilford Press, 2000.

Heer, Jeet, and Kent Worcester. *A Comics Studies Reader*. Jackson: University Press of Mississippi, 2009.

Hesse, Hermann. *The Glass Bead Game (Magister Ludi)*. 1943. Translated by Richard and Clara Winston. New York: Holt, Rinehart and Winston, 1969.

Hill, Michael Charles, ed. *Hard-Traveling Heroes: The Green Lantern/Green Arrow Collection*. Vol. 1. New York: DC Comics, 1992.

Horrocks, Roger. *Male Myths and Icons: Masculinity in Popular Culture*. New York: St. Martin's Press, 1995.

Horrocks, Roger, and Jo Campling. *Masculinity in Crisis: Myths, Fantasies, and Realities*. New York: St. Martin's Press, 1994.

Howe, Sean. *Marvel Comics: The Untold Story*. New York: Harper, 2012.

Hughes, Jamie A. "'Who Watches the Watchmen?': Ideology and 'Real World' Superheroes." *Journal of Popular Culture* 39, no. 4 (2006): 546–57.

Humphry, Derek, and Ann Wickett. *Jean's Way*. Los Angeles: Hemlock Society, 1984.

Inge, M. T. *Comics As Culture*. Jackson: University Press of Mississippi, 1990.

Jachec, N. "Modernism, Enlightenment Values, and Clement Greenberg." *Oxford Art Journal* 21, no. 2 (1998): 121–32.

Jacobs, Will and Gerard Jones. *The Comic Book Heroes: From the Silver Age to the Present*. New York: Crown, 1985.

Jahn, Gary R. *The Death of Ivan Ilyich: An Interpretation*. New York: Twayne Publishers, 1993.

Jared M. "A Daytime Soap Opera Would Reject This Fake Twin . . ." *Blog Into Mystery*, Nov. 6, 2010. http://blogintomystery.com/2010/11/06/a-daytime-soap-opera-would-reject-this-fake -twin-for-being-too-ridiculous-daredevil-26/.

Jenkins, Henry. *The Wow Climax: Tracing the Emotional Impact of Popular Culture.* New York: New York University Press, 2007.

Jewett, Robert, and John S. Lawrence. *Captain America and the Crusade against Evil: The Dilemma of Zealous Nationalism.* Grand Rapids, MI: W. B. Eerdmans, 2003.

Johnson, Derek. "Will The Real Wolverine Please Stand Up?" In *Film and Comic Books,* ed. Ian Gordon, Mark Jancovich, and Matthew P. McAllister, 64–85. Jackson: University Press of Mississippi, 2007.

Johnson, Mary. *Make Them Go Away: Clint Eastwood, Christopher Reeve and the Case Against Disability Rights.* Louisville: Advocado Press, 2003.

———. "Right to Life, Right to Die: The Elizabeth Bouvia Saga." 1984. *Electric Edge,* Jan./Feb. 1997. http://www.raggededgemagazine.com/archive/bouvia.htm.

———. "Unanswered Questions." In *The Ragged Edge,* ed. Barret Shaw, 194–210. Louisville, KY: Advocado Press, 1994.

Jones, Gerard. *Men of Tomorrow: Geeks, Gangsters, and the Birth of the Comic Book.* New York: Basic Books, 2004.

Kafka, Franz. *The Complete Stories.* Edited by Nahum N. Glazer. New York: Schocken Books, 1971.

Kahan, Bob, ed. *Superman: Whatever Happened to the Man of Tomorrow?* New York: DC Comics, 1997.

———. *World Without a Superman.* London: Titan Books, 1993A.

———. *The Death of Superman.* New York: DC Comics, 1993B.

Kakalios, James. *The Physics of Superheroes.* New York: Gotham Books, 2005.

Karasik, Paul, and Judy Karasik. *The Ride Together: A Brother and Sister's Memoir of Autism in the Family.* New York: Washington Square Press, 2004.

Kauffman, Linda. *Bad Girls and Sick Boys: Fantasies in Contemporary Art and Culture.* Berkeley: University of California Press, 1998.

Kawa, Abraham. "The Universe She Died In." *International Journal of Comic Art* 8, no. 1 (Spring/ Summer 2006): 212–33.

Kawasaki, Anton, ed. *Showcase Presents: The Doom Patrol, Vol. 2.* New York: DC Comics, 2010.

———. *Showcase Presents: The Doom Patrol, Vol. 1.* New York: DC Comics, 2009A.

———. *The Legion of Superheroes: The Life and Death of Ferro Lad.* New York: DC Comics, 2009B.

———. *Legion of Superheroes: 1,050 Years of the Future.* New York: DC Comics, 2008.

———. *Showcase Presents: Justice League of America, Vol. 2.* New York: DC Comics, 2007.

———. *Batman: The Greatest Stories Ever Told.* New York: DC Comics, 2005.

Kierkegaard, Søren. *Fear and Trembling: Repetition.* 1843. Edited by Howard V. Hong and Edna H. Hong. Princeton: Princeton University Press, 1983.

Kimmel, Michael S. *Manhood in America: A Cultural History.* New York: Free Press, 1996.

Kitch, Carolyn. "'A Death in the American Family': Myth, Memory, and National Values in the Media Mourning of John F. Kennedy, Jr." *Communication Abstracts* 26, no. 2 (2003): 294–309.

Klock, Geoff. *How to Read Superhero Comics and Why.* New York: Continuum, 2006.

Komesaroff, Linda R., ed. *Surgical Consent: Bioethics and Cochlear Implantation.* Washington, D.C.: Gallaudet University Press, 2007.

Koosed, Jennifer L., and Darla Schumm. "From Superman to Super Jesus: Constructions of Masculinity and Disability on the Silver Screen." *Disability Studies Quarterly* 29, no. 2 (Spring 2009). http://dsq-sds.org/article/view/917/1092.

Kozlovic, Anton K. "Superman As Christ-Figure: the American Pop Culture Movie Messiah." *Journal of Religion and Film* 6, no. 1 (2002).

Kübler-Ross, Elisabeth. *Death: The Final Stage of Growth.* Englewood Cliffs, NJ: Prentice-Hall, 1975.

———. *On Death and Dying*. New York: Macmillan, 1969.

Kukkonen, Karin. "Navigating Infinite Earths: Readers, Mental Models, and the Multiverse of Superhero Comics." *Storyworlds: A Journal of Narrative Studies* 2, no. 1 (2010): 39–58.

Kundera, Milan. *The Unbearable Lightness of Being*. 1984. New York: Harper Perennial, 1999.

Laderman, Gary. *Rest in Peace: A Cultural History of Death and the Funeral Home in Twentieth-Century America*. New York: Oxford University Press, 2003.

Lang, Jeffrey S., and Patrick Trimble. "Whatever Happened to the Man of Tomorrow? An Examination of the American Monomyth and the Comic Book Superhero." *Journal of Popular Culture* 22 (Winter 1988): 157–73.

Lapitskii, Isaak. *V teni neboskrebov*. Moscow: Molodaia Gvardia, 1958.

Lee, Stan. *Son of Origins of Marvel Comics*, New York: Simon & Schuster, 1975.

———. *Origins of Marvel Comics*. New York: Simon & Schuster, 1974.

Lee, Stan, and Gene Colan. "Brother, Take My Hand!" *Daredevil*, vol. 1, no. 47 (Dec. 1968).

———. "To Fight the Impossible Fight!" *Daredevil*, vol. 1, no. 32 (Sept. 1967).

———. "Blind Man's Bluff!" *Daredevil*, vol. 1, no. 31 (Aug. 1967).

———. "—If There Should Be a Thunder God!" *Daredevil*, vol. 1, no. 30 (Jul. 1967).

———. "Unmasked!" *Daredevil*, vol. 1, no. 29 (Jun. 1967).

———. "Stilt-Man Strikes Again!" *Daredevil*, vol. 1, no. 26 (Mar. 1967).

———. "Enter: The Leap Frog!" *Daredevil*, vol. 1, no. 25 (Feb. 1967).

Lee, Stan, and Jack Kirby. "Within this Tortured Land." *Fantastic Four*, vol. 1, no. 85 (Apr. 1969).

———. "Let There Be . . . Life!" *Fantastic Four Annual*, vol. 1, no. 6 (Nov. 1968).

———. "Slave of the Skull!" *Captain America*, vol. 1, no. 104 (Aug. 1968).

———. "The Brutal Betrayal of Ben Grimm!" *Fantastic Four*, vol. 1, no. 41 (Aug. 1964).

———. "Death of a Hero!" *Fantastic Four*, vol. 1, no. 32 (Nov. 1964).

Lee, Stan, and George Mair. *Excelsior!: The Amazing Life of Stan Lee*. New York: Fireside, 2002.

Lee, Stan, and John Romita. "Unmasked at Last!" *Amazing Spider-Man*, vol. 1, no. 87 (Aug. 1970).

Leming, Michael R., and George E. Dickinson. "The American Ways of Death." In *The Unknown Country: Death in Australia, Britain, and the USA*, ed. Kathy Charmaz, Glennys Howarth, and Allan Kellehear, 169–83. New York: St. Martin's Press, 1997.

Levitz, Paul. Personal interview, San Francisco. 2011.

———, ed. *Batman's Strangest Cases*. New York: DC Comics, 1978.

Lewis, Barbara Jo. "Cyborg Might: Conceptions of Power in Comic Book Art." *International Journal of Comic Art* 2, no. 1 (Spring 2000): 144–58.

Lewis, David. E. "The Secret, Untold Relationship of Biblical Midrash and Comic Book Retcon." *International Journal of Comic Art* 4, no. 2 (Fall 2002): 261–75.

Lieber, Larry, George Tuska, and Wally Wood. "The Invaders!" *Super-Villain Team-Up* 1, no. 15 (Nov. 1978).

Lifton, Robert Jay, and Eric Olson. "Symbolic Immortality." In *Death, Mourning, and Burial: A Cross-Cultural Reader*, ed. Antonius C. G. M. Robben, 32–39. Malden, MA: Blackwell, 2004.

Linton, Simi. *Claiming Disability: Knowledge and Identity*. New York: New York University Press, 1998.

Lock, Margaret. "Cultivating the Body: Anthropology and Epistemologies of Bodily Practice and Knowledge." *Annual Review of Anthropology* 22, no. 1 (1993): 133–55.

Longmore, Paul K. *Why I Burned My Book and Other Essays on Disability*. Philadelphia: Temple University Press, 2003.

———. "The Strange Death of David Rivlin." *Western Journal of Medicine*, no. 154 (May 1991): 615–16.

Looser, Thomas. "Superflat and Layers of Image and History in 1990s Japan." In *Mechademia 1: Emerging Worlds of Anime and Manga*, ed. Frenchy Lunning, 92–110. Minneapolis: University of Minnesota Press, 2006.

Lutz, Tom. *Crying: The Natural and Cultural History of Tears.* New York: W. W. Norton, 1999.

Lynch, Thomas. *The Undertaking: Life Studies from the Dismal Trade.* New York: W. W. Norton, 1997.

Mairs, Nancy. "Carnal Acts." In *Staring Back: The Disability Experience From The Inside Out,* ed. Kenny Fries, 51–61. New York: Plume, 1997.

Mantlo, Bill, and Carmine Infantino. ". . . Race to Destruction!" *The Human Fly,* vol. 1, no. 2 (Oct. 1977).

Mantlo, Bill, and Lee Elias. "War in the Washington Monument!" *The Human Fly,* vol. 1, no. 15 (Nov. 1978).

——. "Castle in the Clouds!" *The Human Fly,* vol. 1, no. 3 (Nov. 1977).

——. "Death-Walk!" *The Human Fly,* vol. 1, no. 1 (Sept. 1977).

Mantlo, Bill, and Rick Leonardi. "True Confessions!" *Cloak and Dagger,* vol. 1, no. 4 (Jan. 1984).

Mantlo, Bill, and Frank Robbins. ". . . And Daredevil Makes Three!" *The Human Fly,* vol. 1, no. 9 (May 1978).

——. "The Tiger and the Fly!" *The Human Fly,* vol. 1, no. 8 (Apr. 1978).

Marcus, Greil. *Dead Elvis: A Chronicle of a Cultural Obsession.* New York: Doubleday, 1991.

Marcus, Laura. *Auto/biographical Discourses: Theory, Criticism, Practice.* Manchester: Manchester University Press, 1994.

Mattozzi, Alvise. "Innovating Superheroes." *Reconstruction* 3, no. 2. (Spring 2003). http://reconstruction.eserver.org/032/mottazzi.htm .

Mauss, Marcel, and Nathan Schlanger. *Techniques, Technology and Civilisation.* New York: Durkheim Press/Berghahn Books, 2006.

McKee, Gabriel. "The Many Pleasant Surprises of *Strikeforce: Morituri.*" *SF Gospel,* Sept. 8, 2009. http://sfgospel.typepad.com/sf_gospel/2009/09/the-many-pleasant-surprises-of-strikeforce-morituri.html.

McRuer, Robert. "Critical Investment: AIDS, Christopher Reeve and Queer/Disability Studies." In *Thinking the Limits of the Body,* ed. Jeffrey Jerome Cohen and Gail Weiss, 145–66. Albany, NY: SUNY Press, 2003.

Melrose, Kevin. "Wait, Did X-Men *Really* Rip Off Doom Patrol?" *ComicBookResources.com,* Apr. 30, 2009. http://robot6.comicbookresources.com/2009/04/wait-did-x-men-really-rip-off-doom-patrol/.

Michaelson, Ky. Untitled. *The Rocketman.com,* 2005. http://www.the-rocketman.com/human-fly.html.

Miner, Madonne. "'Making Up the Stories As We Go Along': Men, Women and Narratives of Disability." In *The Body and Physical Difference: Discourses of Disability,* ed. David T. Mitchell and Sharon L. Snyder, 283–95. Ann Arbor: University of Michigan Press, 1997.

Mitford, Jessica. *The American Way of Death Revisited.* New York: Vintage Books, 2000.

Mitchell, David T., and Sharon L. Snyder. "Minority Model: From Liberal to Neoliberal Futures of Disability." In *Routledge Handbook of Disability Studies,* ed. Nick Watson, Alan Roulstone, and Carol Thomas, 42–50. New York: Routledge, 2012.

——. *Narrative Prosthesis: Disability and the Dependencies of Discourse.* Ann Arbor: University of Michigan Press, 2000.

——, eds. *The Body and Physical Difference: Discourses of Disability.* Ann Arbor: University of Michigan Press, 1997.

Mitchell, Stephen. *Gilgamesh: A New English Version.* New York: Free Press, 2004.

Mitchell, W. J. T. "Seeing Disability." *Public Culture* 13, no. 3 (Fall 2001): 391–97.

——. *Iconology: Image, Text, Ideology.* Chicago: University of Chicago Press, 1986.

Montagu, Ashley, and Frederick Treves. *The Elephant Man: A Study in Human Dignity.* New York: E. P. Dutton, 1979.

Moody, Raymond A. *Life After Life: The Investigation of a Phenomenon-Survival of Bodily Death.* 1975. San Francisco: Harper San Francisco, 2001.

Moore, Alan, and Dave Gibbons. *Watchmen.* New York: DC Comics, 1986.

Moore, Alan, and Bill Willingham. "In Blackest Night." *Green Lantern Annual,* vol. 1, no. 3 (May 1987).

Morreall, John, and Jessica Loy. "Kitsch and Aesthetic Education." *Journal of Aesthetic Education* 23, no. 4 (Winter 1989): 63–73.

Morris, Harry. "*Hamlet* As a 'Memento Mori' Poem." *PMLA* 85, no. 5 (1970): 1035–40.

Morris, Jon. "The Death of Captain Marvel." *Gone and Forgotten,* Sept. 2, 2007. http://gone-and -forgotten.blogspot.com/2007/09/classic-gone-and-forgotten-death-of.html.

Murphy, Robert F. *The Body Silent.* New York: Henry Holt, 1987.

Murray, Christopher. "Superman vs. Imago: Superheroes, Lacan and Mediated Identity." *International Journal of Comic Art* 4, no. 2 (Fall 2002): 186–208.

Murray, Stuart. *Autism.* New York: Routledge, 2012.

———. *Representing Autism: Culture, Narrative, Fascination.* Liverpool: Liverpool University Press, 2008.

———. "Autism Functions/The Function of Autism." *Disability Studies Quarterly* 30, no. 1 (2010). http://www.dsq-sds.org/article/view/1048/1229.

———. "Autism and the Contemporary Sentimental: Fiction and the Narrative Fascination of the Present." *Literature and Medicine* 25, no. 1 (Spring 2006): 24–45.

Nama, Adilifu. *Super Black: American Pop Culture and Black Superheroes.* Austin: University of Texas Press, 2011.

Niederhausen, Michael. "Deconstructing Crisis on Infinite Earths: Grant Morrison's Animal Man, JLA: Earth 2, and Flex Mentallo." *International Journal of Comic Art* 8, no. 1 (Spring/ Summer 2006): 271–82.

Nuland, Sherwin B. *How We Die: Reflections on Life's Final Chapter.* New York: Alfred A. Knopf, 1994.

Olshevsky, George. "Synopsis: The Human Fly." *The Marvel Comics Index* 1, part 9B: Daredevil (Apr. 1982): 95.

O'Neil, Denny. Personal interview. *Jay Toddz For the Masses,* 2010. http://fuckyeahjasontodd .tumblr.com/post/898206718/robins-requiem-the-tale-of-jason-todd.

O'Neil, Denny, David Mazzucchelli, and Jim Shooter. "The Price." *Daredevil,* vol. 1, no. 223 (Oct. 1985).

O'Neil, Tim. "The Chronicles of the Human Fly: Chapter Two." *The Hurting,* Sept. 1, 2005. http://whenwillthehurtingstop.blogspot.com/2005_09_01_whenwillthehurtingstop_archive .html#112557910478754091.

Orwell, George. "How the Poor Die." In *The Grim Reader,* ed. Maura Spiegel and Richard Trist-man, 352–62. New York: Anchor Books, 1997.

Ouzamandias. "Revolving Door of Death 19: 'Day of Doom' and the De-Trivialization of Death." *Quarter Bin,* Feb. 2003. http://www.quarterbin.net/revolvin/rdd19.html.

———. "Revolving Door of Death 17: Starlin's Explorations of Mortality." *Quarter Bin,* Oct. 2002. http://www.quarterbin.net/revolvin/rdd17.html.

———. "Opinions 66: Alternatives to Commitment." *Quarter Bin,* May 2002. http://www.quar terbin.net/opinion/opi66.html.

———. "Revolving Door of Death 15: Superhero Comics and the Rules of Death." *Quarter Bin,* Oct. 2001. http://www.quarterbin.net/revolvin/rdd15.html.

———. "Revolving Door of Death 11: The Return of Professor X – Death Without Trivialization." *Quarter Bin,* Sept. 2000. http://www.quarterbin.net/revolvin/rdd11.html.

———. "The Talent Pool 17: Jim Starlin—Midwife and Layer-Out." *Quarter Bin,* Oct. 1999. http:// www.fortunecity.com/tatooine/niven/142/talentpo/tp17.html.

Packer, Sharon. *Superheroes and Superegos: Analyzing the Minds Behind the Masks*. Santa Barbara: Praeger/ABC-CLIO, 2010.

Paperno, Irina. *Suicide As a Cultural Institution in Dostoevsky's Russia*. Ithaca: Cornell University Press, 1997

Parille, Ken. "'This Man, This Monster': Super-Heroes and Super-Sexism." *The Comics Journal Online*, Mar. 7, 2012. http://www.tcj.com/%E2%80%9Cthis-man-this-monster%E2%80%9D -super-heroes-and-super-sexism/.

Peeters, Benoit. "'Four Conceptions of the Page' From *Case, planche, recit: lire la bande dessinee.*" Translated by Jesse Cohn. *ImageTexT: Interdisciplinary Comics Studies* 3, no. 3 (2007). http:// www.english.ufl.edu/imagetext/archives/v3_3/peeters/.

Plass, Paul. *The Game of Death in Ancient Rome: Arena Sport and Political Suicide*. Madison: University of Wisconsin Press, 1995.

Potts, Carl. E-mail correspondence. Apr. 2013.

Quayson, Ato. *Aesthetic Nervousness: Disability and the Crisis of Representation*. New York: Columbia University Press, 2007.

Rancour-Laferriere, Daniel. "Narcissism, Masochism and Denial in *Death in Ivan Ilyich*." In *Tolstoy's The Death of Ivan Il'ich: A Critical Companion*, ed. Gary R. Jahn, 117–33. Evanston: Northwestern University Press, 1999.

Raphael, Rebecca. "The Doomsday Body, or Dr. Strangelove as Disabled Cyborg." *Golem: Journal of Religion and Monsters* 1, no. 1 (Spring 2006). http://golemjournal.org/Spinrg_2006_Issue/Raphael_Strangelove_S06.pdf.

Raviv, Dan. *Comic Wars: How Two Tycoons Battled Over the Marvel Comics Empire-and Both Lost*. New York: Broadway Books, 2002.

Regalado, Aldo. "Modernity, Race, and the American Superhero." In *Comics as Philosophy*, ed. Jeff McLaughlin, 84–99. Jackson: University Press of Mississippi, 2005.

Remson Mitchell, Laura. "Why I Hate Supercrip Stories!" *LRM's Place*, 1996. http://webspace webring.com/people/rl/lrmidi/articles.htm#supcrip.

Renfrow, Daniel G. "A Cartography of Passing in Everyday Life." *Symbolic Interaction* 27, no. 4 (2004): 485–506.

Reynolds, Richard. *Super Heroes: A Modern Mythology*. Jackson: Mississippi University Press, 1992.

Ricca, Brad. *Super Boys: The Amazing Adventures of Jerry Siegel and Joe Shuster, the Creators of Superman*. New York: St. Martin's Press, 2013.

Riley, Charles A. *Disability and the Media: Prescriptions for Change*. Hanover, NH: University Press of New England, 2005.

Robert. Untitled. *The Matt Murdock Chronicles*, Feb. 15, 2009. http://themattmurdockchronicles .blogspot.com/search?updated-min=2008-12-31T16:00:00-08:00&updated-max=2009-02 -22T20:46:00Z&max-results=50&start=114&by-date=false.

———. Untitled. *The Matt Murdock Chronicles*, Jan. 8, 2009. http://themattmurdockchronicles. blogspot.com/search?updated-min=2008-12-31T16:00:00-08:00&updated-max=2009-01 -18T20:36:00Z&max-results=50&start=124&by-date=false.

Roeder, Katherine. "Looking High and Low at Comic Art." *American Art* 22, no. 1 (Spring 2008): 2–9.

Rogers, Brett M. "Heroes Unlimitied: The Theory of the Hero's Journey and the Limitation of the Superhero Myth." In *Classics and Comics*, ed. George Kovacs and C. W. Marshall, 73–86. Oxford: Oxford University Press, 2011.

Rosaldo, Renato. *Culture and Truth: The Remaking of Social Analysis*. Boston: Beacon Press, 1989.

Rozanski, Chuck. "*Death of Superman* Promotion of 1992." *Tales of the Database*, Jul. 2004. http://www.milehighcomics.com/tales/cbg127.html.

Russell, Marta. "Malcolm Teaches Us, Too." In *The Ragged Edge: The Disability Experience from the Pages of the First Fifteen Years of the Disability Rag*, ed. Barrett Shaw, 11–14. Louisville, KY: Advocado Press, 1994.

Ryan, Marie-Laure. *Possible Worlds, Artificial Intelligence and Narrative Theory*. Bloomington: Indiana University Press, 1991.

Sandars, N. K., trans. *The Epic of Gilgamesh*. Harmondsworth: Penguin, 1977.

Sanderson, Peter. Personal interview, New York City. Jun. 2008.

Saunders, Ben. *Do the Gods Wear Capes?: Spirituality, Fantasy, and Superheroes*. London: Continuum, 2011.

Savage, William W. *Comic Books and America, 1945–1954*. Norman: University of Oklahoma Press, 1990.

Saverese, Emily Thornton, and Ralph James Saverese. "'The Superior Half of Speaking': An Introduction." *Disability Studies Quarterly* 30, no. 1 (2010). http://www.dsq-sds.org/article/view/1062/1230.

Scarry, Elaine. *The Body in Pain: The Making and Unmaking of the World*. New York: Oxford University Press, 1985.

Schein, Seth L. *The Mortal Hero: An Introduction to Homer's Iliad*. Berkeley: University of California Press, 1984.

Scheper-Hughes, Nancy. *Death Without Weeping: The Violence of Everyday Life in Brazil*. Berekley: University of California Press, 1992.

Scheper-Hughes, Nancy, and Loic J. D. Wacquant, eds. *Commodifying Bodies*. London: Sage Publications, 2002.

Schjeldahl, Peter. "Target America." *The New Yorker*, Aug. 4, 2003, 82–83.

Schücking, Levin L. "The Churchyard-Scene in Shakespeare's Hamlet, V. i.: An Afterthought?" *The Review of English Studies* 11, no. 42 (Apr. 1935): 129–38.

Schweik, Susan M. *The Ugly Laws: Disability in Public*. New York: New York University Press, 2009.

Seale, Clive. *Constructing Death: The Sociology of Death and Bereavement*. Cambridge: Cambridge University Press, 1998.

——. "Heroic Death." *Sociology* 29, no. 4 (1995): 597–613.

Sedgwick, Eve K. *Epistemology of the Closet*. Berkeley: University of California Press, 1990.

Sedlmeier, Cory, ed. *Marvel Masterworks: The Fantastic Four, Vol. 1*. New York: Marvel Comics, 2011.

——. *Marvel Masterworks: The X-Men, Vol. 2*. New York: Marvel Comics, 2009.

——. *Marvel Masterworks: The X-Men, Vol. 1*. New York: Marvel Comics, 2003

Shakespeare, William. *Hamlet*. Edited by Harold Jenkins. New York: Methuen, 1982.

Shapiro, Joseph P. *No Pity: People with Disabilities Forging a New Civil Rights Movement*. New York: Times Books, 1993.

Shelley, Mary. *Frankenstein or, The Modern Prometheus*. 1818. Edited by Maurice Hindle. New York: Penguin, 1985.

Shooter, Jim. Personal interview, Skype. Jan. 2012.

——. "The Origin of the Phoenix Saga." *Jim Shooter Blog*, Jun. 12, 2011. http://www.jimshooter.com/2011/06/origin-of-phoenix-saga.html.

Shyminsky, Neil. "Mutant Readers, Reading Mutants: Appropriation, Assimilation, and the X-Men." *International Journal of Comic Art* 8, no. 2 (Fall 2006): 387–405.

Siebers, Tobin. *Disability Aesthetics*. Ann Arbor: University of Michigan Press, 2010.

——. *Disability Theory*. Ann Arbor: University of Michigan Press, 2008.

Sikoryak, R. K. *Masterpiece Comics*. Montreal: Drawn and Quarterly, 2009.

Silodrome. "Rick Rojatt—The Human Fly." *Silodrome: Gasoline Culture*. silodrome.com/rick-rojatt-the-human-fly/.

Silverman, Kaja. "Historical Trauma and Male Subjectivity." In *Psychoanalysis and Cinema*, ed. Ann Kaplan, 110–27. New York: Routledge, 1990.

Simon, Richard Keller. "Modernism and Mass Culture." *American Literary History* 13, no. 2 (Summer 2001): 343–53.

Sims, Chris. "Ask Chris #96: Why Spider-Man Is The Best Character Ever (Yes, Even Better Than Batman)." *Comics Alliance*, Mar. 9, 2012. http://www.comicsalliance.com/2012/03/09/ask-chris-96-why-spider-man-is-the-best-character-ever-yes/#ixzz1oeTtqKwG.

Singer, Marc. "Men of Steel." *I Am NOT the Beastmaster*, Jun. 17, 2013. http://notthebeastmaster.typepad.com/weblog/2013/06/men-of-steel.html.

———. *Grant Morrison: Combining the Worlds of Contemporary Comics*. Jackson: University Press of Mississippi, 2012.

———. "'Black Skins' and White Masks: Comic Books and the Secret of Race." *African American Review*, no. 36 (2002): 107–20.

Singer, Peter. *Writings on an Ethical Life*. New York: Ecco Press, 2000.

Smith, Joel. "Murder of Autistics." *This Way of Life*, 2006. http://www.geocities.com/growingjoel/murder.html.

Smyrniw, W. "Tolstoy's Depiction of Death in the Context of Recent Studies of the 'Experience of Dying.'" *Canadian Slavonic Papers* 21, no. 3 (1979): 367–79.

Snyder, Sharon L., Brenda J. Brueggemann, and Rosemarie Garland-Thomson. *Disability Studies: Enabling the Humanities*. New York: Modern Language Association of America, 2002.

Solomon, Andrew. *Far From The Tree: Parents, Children and The Search for Identity*. New York: Scribner, 2012.

Sontag, Susan. *Illness as Metaphor and AIDS and Its Metaphors*. New York: Doubleday, 1989.

———. "Fascinating Fascism." In *A Susan Sontag Reader*, ed. Elizabeth Hardwick, 305–25. New York: Vintage, 1983.

Spurgeon, Tom. "The Worst Thing About Marvel Comics." *The Comics Reporter*, Jun. 18, 2009. http://www.comicsreporter.com/index.php/the_worst_thing_about_marvel_comics/.

Squier, Susan. "So Long As They Grow Out of It: Comics, the Discourse of Developmental Normalcy and Disability." *Journal of Medical Humanities* 29, no. 2 (2008): 71–88.

Stacey, Jackie. *Teratologies: A Cultural Study of Cancer*. London: Routledge, 1997.

Stannard, David E. *The Puritan Way of Death: A Study in Religion, Culture, and Social Change*. New York: Oxford University Press, 1977.

Stapleton, David C., and Richard V. Burkhauser, eds. *The Decline in Employment of People with Disabilities—A Policy Puzzle*. Kalamazoo, MI: W. E. Upjohn Institute for Employment, 2003.

Starlin, Jim. Personal interview, Skype. Dec. 2011.

———. *The Death of Captain Marvel*. New York: Marvel Comics, 1982.

Starlin, Jim, and Jim Aparo. *Batman: A Death in the Family*. New York: DC Comics, 1988.

Stars, Gringo. "The Slope Has Slipped." *Portland Independent Media Center*, Jul. 28, 2003. http://portland.indymedia.org/en/2003/07/268785.shtml.

Stern, Roger, and Sal Buscema. "The Monster's Analyst." *Incredible Hulk*, vol. 1, no. 227 (Sept. 1978).

Stevens, Mark. "New York Cheese." *New York*, Jul. 21, 2003. http://newyorkmetro.com/nymetro/arts/art/reviews/n_8958/.

Tatum, James. *The Mourner's Song: War and Remembrance From the Iliad to Vietnam*. Chicago: University of Chicago Press, 2003.

Taylor, Diana. *Disappearing Acts: Spectacles of Gender and Nationalism in Argentina's "Dirty War."* Durham: Duke University Press, 1997.

Taylor, John. *Body Horror: Photojournalism, Catastrophe and War*. Manchester: Manchester University Press, 1998.

Taussig, Michael. *The Nervous System*. New York: Routledge, 1992.

Thomas, Roy, and Jim Craig. "The Devil's Music!" *Marvel Premiere* 1, no. 36 (Jun. 1977).

———. "The Origin of 3D Man." *Marvel Premiere* 1, no. 35 (Apr. 1977).

Thompson, Kelly. "She Has No Head!: No It's Not Equal." *ComicBookResources.com*, Feb. 21, 2012. http://goodcomics.comicbookresources.com/2012/02/21/she-has-no-head-no-its-not -equal/.

Thompson, Kim. "Death Warmed Over." *The Comics Journal*, no. 73 (Jul. 1982): 50–52.

Titchkosky, Tanya. *Disability, Self, and Society*. Toronto: University of Toronto Press, 2003.

Tolstoy, Leo. *The Death of Ivan Ilyich*. 1886. Translated by Lynn Solotaroff. New York: Bantam, 1981.

Turner, Bryan S. *The Body and Society: Explorations in Social Theory*. Oxford: B. Blackwell, 1984.

UHQ Team. "UHQ Interview: Jim Starlin—A Success Written in the Stars." *Universo HQ*, Mar. 3, 2003. http://www.universohq.com/quadrinhos/entrevista_starlin_engo1.cfm.

Ulrich, George. "Masks." *LORE* 39, no. 3 (Fall 1989): 2–9. http://www.bsu.edu/classes/ magrath/305s02/masks/MuseumMask.html.

UPI. "Human Fly Says He's 'Greatest' Daredevil of All." *Ludington Daily News*, May 20, 1977, 8.

Van Dyk, Michael. "What's Going On? Black Identity in the Marvel Age." *International Journal of Comic Art* 8, no. 1 (Spring/Summer 2006): 466–90.

Van Gennep, Arnold. "The Rites of Passage." In *Death, Mourning, and Burial: A Cross-Cultural Reader*, ed. Antonius C. G. M. Robben, 213–23. Malden, MA: Blackwell, 2004.

Varnum, Robin, and Christina T. Gibbons. *The Language of Comics: Word and Image*. Jackson: University Press of Mississippi, 2001.

Vaughn, Owen. "Jacko Tried to Buy Spider-Man: 70 Facts You Didn't Know About Marvel." *Times of London*, Oct. 30, 2009. http://www.thetimes.co.uk/tto/arts/film/article2432208.ece.

Versaci, Rocco. *This Book Contains Graphic Language: Comics As Literature*. New York: Continuum, 2007.

Wade, Cheryl Marie. "I Am Not One of The." *The Disability Studies Reader*. 1st ed. Edited by Lennard Davis. New York: Routledge, 1997: 408.

Waid, Mark. "Man of Steel, Since You Asked." *Thrillbent*, Jun. 14, 2013. http://thrillbent.com/blog/ man-of-steel-since-you-asked/.

Walker, Karen, and Doug Walker. "The Death of Captain Marvel." *Bronze Age Babies*, Nov. 16, 2011. http://bronzeagebabies.blogspot.com/2011/11/death-of-captain-marvel.html.

Walter, Tony. *On Bereavement: The Culture of Grief*. Buckingham: Open University Press, 1999.

———. "Classics Revisited: *A Sociology of Grief*." *Mortality* 3, no. 1 (1998): 83–87.

———. *The Revival of Death*. London: Routledge, 1994.

Walter, Tony, Jane Littlewood, and Michael Pickering. "Death in the News: The Public Invigilation of Private Emotion." *Sociology* 29, no. 4 (1995): 579–96.

Walton, Peter. "The 'Archaic Mother' in Charles Burns' *Black Hole*: A Psychoanalytic Reading." *International Journal of Comic Art* 10, no. 1 (2008): 522–34.

Wanzo, Rebecca. "Infinite Representational Crisis: Race, Gender, the Superhero." In *Faster than a Speeding Bullet: The Art of the Superhero*, ed. Ben Saunders, 21–23. Eugene, OR: Jordan Schnitzer Museum, 2009.

Waskul, Dennis D., and Pamela van der Riet. "The Abject Embodiment of Cancer Patients: Dignity, Selfhood and the Grotesque Body." *Symbolic Interaction* 25, no. 4 (2002): 487–513.

Watson, Polly, ed. *The Villainy of Doctor Doom*. New York: Marvel Comics, 1999.

Webb, Marilyn. *The Good Death: The New American Search to Reshape the End of Life*. New York: Bantam, 1997.

Wein, Len, and Sal Buscema. "Alone Against the Defenders." *The Incredible Hulk*, vol. 1, no. 207 (Jan. 1977).

———. "Do Not Forsake Me!" *The Incredible Hulk*, vol. 1, no. 205 (Nov. 1976).

Weinberg, Nancy, and Rosina Santana. "Comic Books: Champions of the Disabled Stereotype." *Rehabilitation Literature* 39, no. 11–12 (Nov.–Dec. 1978): 327–31.

Weiss, Gail. *Refiguring the Ordinary*. Bloomington: Indiana University Press, 2008.

Wells, Earl. "Once and For All, Who Was the Author of Marvel?" In *The Comics Journal Library, Vol. 1. Jack Kirby*, ed. Milo George, 74–87 Seattle: Fantagraphics Books, 2002.

Weltzien, Friedrich. "Masque-ulinities: Changing Dress As a Display of Masculinity in the Superhero Genre." *Fashion Theory: The Journal of Dress, Body & Culture* 9, no. 2 (2005): 229–50.

Wendell, Susan. *The Rejected Body: Feminist Philosophical Reflections on Disability*. New York: Routledge, 1996.

Werner, Jeffery R. "What Can a Passenger Do If the Flight Is Booked Solid? The Human Fly Has One Solution." *People*, Jul. 19, 1976. http://www.people.com/people/archive/article/0,,20066688,00.html.

West, Cornel. "The New Cultural Politics of Difference." In *The Cultural Studies Reader*, ed. Simon During, 203–17. London: Routledge, 1993.

Williams, Simon J. *Medicine and the Body*. London: Sage Publications, 2003.

Witek, Joseph. "The Arrow and the Grid." In *A Comics Studies Reader*, ed. Jeet Heer and Kent Worchester, 149–56. Jackson: University Press of Mississippi, 2008.

Wolfman, Marv, and George Pérez. "Cyborg." *Tales of the New Teen Titans*, vol. 1, no. 1 (Jun. 1982).

Wolfman, Marv, and Keith Pollard. "When Titans Clash!" *Fantastic Four*, vol.1, no. 200 (Nov. 1978).

———. "The Son of Doctor Doom!" *Fantastic Four*, vol. 1, no. 199 (Oct. 1978).

———. "Invasion!" *Fantastic Four*, vol. 1, no. 198 (Sept. 1978).

Wolff, Hope Nash. "Gilgamesh, Enkidu, and the Heroic Life." *Journal of the American Oriental Society* 89, no. 2 (Apr.–Jun. 1969): 392–98.

Wolk, Douglas. *Reading Comics: How Graphic Novels Work and What They Mean*. Cambridge: Da Capo Press, 2007.

———. "The Dark Mirrors of Jim Starlin's Warlock." *Comic Art*, no. 8 (Summer 2006): 114–24.

Woo, Benjamin. "An Age-Old Problem: Problematics of Comic-Book Historiography." *International Journal of Comic Art* 10, no. 1 (Spring 2008): 268–79.

Wright, Bradford W. *Comic Book Nation: The Transformation of Youth Culture in America*. Baltimore: Johns Hopkins University Press, 2001.

Youngquist, Jeff, ed. *Spider-Man: The Death of Gwen Stacy*. New York: Marvel Comics, 2004A.

———. *Spider-Man: The Death of Captain Stacy*. New York: Marvel Comics, 2004B.

Yurkovich, David, and Michael Mantlo. *Bill Mantlo: A Life in Comics*. Los Angeles: Sleeping Giant, 2007.

Zeichmann, Christopher B. "Black Like Lois: Confronting Racism, Configuring African American Presence." In *The Ages of Superman: Essays on the Man of Steel in Changing Times*, ed. Joseph J. Darowski, 78–90. Jefferson, NC: McFarland & Co, 2012.

Zelizer, Barbie. *Covering the Body: The Kennedy Assassination, the Media, and the Shaping of Collective Memory*. Chicago: University of Chicago Press, 1992.

Zucker, Arthur. "Rights and the Dying." In *Dying: Facing the Facts*, ed. Hannelore Wass, Felix M. Berardo, and Robert A. Neimeyer, 385–403. Washington: Hemisphere Pub. Corp., 1988.

INDEX

CPSIA information can be obtained
at www.ICGtesting.com
Printed in the USA
FFOW03n1716031215
19201FF